KOREA

JAPAN

PACIFIC

OCEAN

FORMOSA

HONG KONG

Hanoi

V I E T N A M

D

MBODIA

nh
⊙ Saigon

S O U T H   C H I N A   S E A

PHILIPPINE   ISLANDS

AYA

Lumpur

Singapore

NORTH BORNEO

BRUNEI

SARAWAK

BORNEO
(KALIMANTAN)

N D O N

HALMAHERA

NEW
GUINEA

(WEST
IRIAN)

CELEBES

D1211803

Djakarta

JAVA

TRALIA

From S. Rose: *Socialism in Southern Asia* by kind permission of Oxford University Press

POLITICS IN SOUTHERN ASIA

POLITICS IN
SOUTHERN ASIA

EDITED BY

SAUL ROSE
FELLOW OF ST ANTONY'S COLLEGE, OXFORD

LONDON
MACMILLAN & CO LTD
NEW YORK · ST MARTIN'S PRESS
1963

MACMILLAN AND COMPANY LIMITED
St Martin's Street London WC2
also Bombay Calcutta Madras Melbourne

THE MACMILLAN COMPANY OF CANADA LIMITED
Toronto

ST MARTIN'S PRESS INC
New York

PRINTED IN GREAT BRITAIN

PREFACE

THROUGH the generosity of the Ford Foundation a symposium was held at St Antony's College, Oxford, at the end of 1961 on the subject of 'The Political Evolution of South and South-East Asia since Independence'. The intention was to review the development that had taken place in the region of South and South-East Asia during recent years and to see whether any trends could be distinguished. It would have been possible to approach this task with a preconceived notion of what was wanted, to which contributors might have been asked to conform. This line of approach was deliberately not adopted: partly because the participants in the gathering, although specialists in the area of study, were drawn from different disciplines — history, political science, geography, journalism, commerce — and partly because the aim was to see whether from these different lines of approach a common viewpoint or consensus would emerge. The results of this experiment are embodied in this volume.

It begins with a basic question posed by Professor Rupert Emerson of Harvard — whether South and South-East Asia properly constitute an area suitable for academic inquiry — a point on which some doubts were expressed. It continues with a series of papers on the evolution of each country in the region; and concludes with three papers which attempt a general analysis of political theory, institutions and operative forces or motivations. Some extracts from the proceedings have been included; much more has had to be omitted through limitations of space. The results are here presented to a wider audience in the hope that they may contribute something to the dissemination of knowledge about South and South-East Asia, and perhaps also afford material for comparison with development in other areas. The region is one which may be described as underdeveloped not only economically but also in terms of academic study, and this volume will have served a purpose if it merely provokes further interest in the political evolution of an extensive and important area of the globe.

In accepting sole responsibility for the editing of the volume I should like to express my gratitude to the participants for their ready co-operation and to Mrs Anne Liley for her secretarial assistance.

SAUL ROSE

Oxford
February 1962

CONTENTS

LIST OF PARTICIPANTS

Mr W. A. C. Adie   *St Antony's College*
Professor R. Butwell   *University of Illinois*
Mr F. Carnell   *Institute of Commonwealth Studies, Oxford*
Dr O. D. Corpuz   *School of Oriental and African Studies, London*
Professor C. D. Cowan   *School of Oriental and African Studies, London*
Mr P. Devillers   *Fondation nationale des Sciences politiques, Paris*
Mr J. Driver   *St Antony's College*
Professor Rupert Emerson   *Harvard University*
Mr B. H. Farmer   *St John's College, Cambridge*
Mr G. Fischer   *Centre national de la Recherche scientifique, Paris*
Mr P. J. Honey   *School of Oriental and African Studies, London*
Mr S. S. Hsueh   *St Antony's College*
Mr G. F. Hudson   *St Antony's College*
Mr R. N. Iyer   *St Antony's College*
Professor G. McT. Kahin   *Cornell University*
Professor W. H. Morris-Jones   *University of Durham*
Mr A. S. B. Olver   *Royal Institute of International Affairs*
Mr E. Paget   *Jesus College, Oxford*
Mr I. B. Powell   *University College of South Wales*
Dr V. Purcell   *University of Cambridge*
Professor K. Robinson   *Director, Institute of Commonwealth Studies, London*
Dr S. Rose   *St Antony's College*
Mr Stuart Simmonds   *School of Oriental and African Studies, London*
Mr T. E. Smith   *Institute of Commonwealth Studies, London*
Professor H. Somjee   *University of Baroda*
Dr P. Spear   *Selwyn College, Cambridge*
Dr H. Tinker   *School of Oriental and African Studies, London*
Dr Wang Gung-wu   *University of Malaya*
Mr G. Wint   *St Antony's College*
Mr M. Zinkin   *Lever Brothers and Associates Ltd.*
Mrs Taya Zinkin   *The Guardian*

Chapter one

SOUTH AND SOUTH-EAST ASIA AS A POLITICAL REGION

by Rupert Emerson

MY FIRST question, to put it in the largest terms, is what are we to make of democracy in South and South-East Asia? I take it that when we speak about democracy our concern is not with the adoption of any particular political forms but rather to try to ensure that the people's will is done and that the people have a chance to formulate that will in some measure of freedom. But there is the question whether these are relevant ideas and ideals for South Asia. Are we perhaps being parochially limited in the assumption that democracy, defined in those very general terms, is something appropriately to be seen as a goal for Asians? For myself, reflecting on democracy in recent years, particularly since the democracies that were set up after the war started drifting down the drain, I have increasingly tended to identify it as a working political system characterized by the existence of an opposition — an opposition endowed with the freedom necessary to seek to persuade the people that it should form the next government and of course, if it succeeds in persuading them, the freedom in fact to form the government. But precisely the opposition and the freedoms necessary for an opposition are under a ban in a growing number of the new countries, and the mere idea of an opposition as a desirable thing is itself under very heavy attack.

The question must also be asked whether it is necessary or sensible to distinguish between an Eastern and Western, or perhaps between a Northern and a Southern, kind of democracy? Is there only a single kind of democracy, and, if so, what are the ingredients of it that one must regard as essential? Furthermore, we cannot wholly evade the question as to whether, if we look at the matter through Asian eyes, so much attention should be paid to the problem of democracy. The term democracy certainly has to be used; it is a good word and has to be kept on the records. The substance of it, it seems to me, may not necessarily be desired. If I can give an illustration: anything in Moscow has to be done under the label of 'Socialism' or 'Communism', whereas in Washington nothing can be done under the label of 'Socialism'. Identical programmes may be put forward but if they are labelled wrongly they cannot be accepted. I assume that the democratic label has to be accepted in Asia, but I wonder if the substance is really desired. Some of the remarks which have been made, for example, about political parties as essentially transmission belts for the establishing of power, for lining up the people, for getting people organized, and for the execution of government programmes, do not have a very solidly democratic ring to them.

From another angle, if one looks at it from outside, is it really desirable where there are predominantly illiterate populations with very little acquaintance with the world at large, and particularly with the modern world into which one assumes they want to move, that government should operate on the basis of consultation with the people? Or is it reasonable to assume that decisions should be taken by the relatively few on top who know better where they want to go and how to get there? And perhaps a more fundamental question: is there reason to assume that the mass of the population in these countries really cares about the exercise of democratic rights? Are they concerned to be consulted or are they prepared, from the experience of both their traditional past and the colonial days, to assume that the people on high are the ones who make the decisions; that once in a while, if things get bad enough, a revolution breaks out and somebody's throat gets cut, but for the rest that it is properly the role of the people on top of the heap to make the decisions, and to see that they stick and are carried through? It seems to me wide open to question whether democracy, in the kind of Western substance that we attribute to it, is either the desirable form or, for the mass of people, the desired form.

Another question that seems to me intensely absorbing: to

what extent are distinctively native forms breaking through in the Asian context? The political institutions, at least at the central level and a good deal below that as I understand it, set off from Western models, and the top management of the new countries is on the whole familiar rather with the West than with the traditional systems of these countries. Now to my mind it is inevitable that more authentically local forms of political life will take over, perhaps coming up gradually within the Western framework and transforming it; that is, no revolutionary overturn with the appearance of completely new systems but rather working within a Western-borrowed system in such a fashion as to turn it into something other than what it set out to be.

But what direction will the change take? And from what sources is it likely to draw? Or to what extent can one already, in these few years of independence, see that these countries have begun to move away from the Western forms and to develop something which can be called peculiarly Asian, or peculiarly Indian, or Indonesian, or Filipino? What new forces are coming into play? I do not find one-man authoritarianism, which has come up so frequently, or military rule, distinctively Asian — but perhaps here one should not look so much at these outward or institutional forms as to some subtler elements of political style. Maybe any kind of political form that one can think of is already embraced within the Western ideology, in our Western concepts, and one should look rather to the style of political life.

A further question that I suppose one has at least to pose is whether South and South-East Asia constitute a region, a political region, in some fashion; whether it is sensible to deal with them in regional terms. More frequently probably South Asia is spoken of as one region, South-East Asia as another. I believe that this is a query that can be answered in the affirmative better from outside than from inside: that is, many people looking at these areas find it convenient — and I incline to think convenient rather than necessary — to bring them together within a common framework of analysis.

The two major approaches perhaps could be, first, the academic where there is unquestionably a convenience in lumping the very different countries in this region together, and the second would be that of the statesman.

There is no question that in the United States there has been a very strong inclination to treat South-East Asia as a region which is susceptible of academic inquiry, and a substantial array of literature on South-East Asia has been built up. In the same fashion some work has been done on South Asia but it seems to me that that has been treated less as a region to be dealt with by institutes and programmes specifically focused on it.

I require no persuasion that at least South-East Asia is a sensible and intelligible unit to study, in part on the assumption that precisely the contrasts and differences among the countries are illuminating. When India and Pakistan are added in to what is already a big and complex area, I grow more dubious, however, as to whether it is possible to make so vast a segment of the world a comprehensible and intelligible unit. India is so much a world in itself that one must be sceptical of lumping it in with a number of other countries. But for the rest of the area I have no doubt that, so long as one sets off from the recognition of diversity, attempting to deal with it within a single framework is both feasible and useful.

As for the statesman, I suppose that his major concern would be to seek to line up all these adjoining territories in one block and preferably, of course, all within his own orbit. The one serious effort which has been made in that direction, and which has seemed to me a misguided one from the outset, is SEATO. With a regional membership that consists only of the Philippines and Thailand within South-East Asia plus Pakistan outside South-East Asia quite obviously it is a regional organization dominated by outsiders and in no sensible terms in fact can it be regarded as a regional agency. I take it that since the beginning, and presumably now, SEATO has been regarded by some of its potential members as a more dangerous enemy than the enemy it is supposed to guard against.

No other regional organization has come into being unless one wants to regard the Colombo Plan which, of course, is more widely embracing, as a regional agency.

Within the area itself I would incline to say that even less of a sense of regional unity exists than is found outside. I would be surprised if South-East Asia felt itself in any sense as a unity to the degree that, say, American academics concerned with such matters, regard it as such. Certainly the degree of diversity within the area is very amply demonstrated by the papers that have been laid before us. One particular remark struck me in the paper by Mr Zinkin: he mentions one sort of modernity in South and South-East Asia on which everybody is agreed, that is, the creation of nation states. Nobody in South Asia suggests that the area should be organized on any other basis. In South and South-East Asia he maintains that devotion to the Austinian sovereign state is still general.

This indicates a very striking difference between the repeated insistence of virtually all the African leaders on Pan-Africanism, on their asserted readiness to sacrifice sovereignty for Pan-African purposes, and the apparent acceptance by the South and South-East Asians of the sovereign states as the final compartments within which they live. It may be that this is merely a time difference. In a slightly earlier phase Asia had its Asian Relations Conference at New Delhi in 1947, the Conference on Indonesian problems at Delhi in 1949, the Baguio Conference in 1950, then the Colombo Group, which I take it has vanished from this earth—India, Pakistan, Indonesia, Burma and Ceylon —leading to the most spectacular of the meetings, the Bandung Conference of April 1955, reaching out for a very considerably broader grouping than South and South-East Asia. The Bandung Conference has been succeeded by some other Afro-Asian meetings, but by nothing within the region.

African independence is certainly still at a very early stage, but the vehemence and universality of the Pan-African cry exceeds anything that I can remember in South Asia at a comparable time, or any other time. There does appear to be a real sense of solidarity, at least an asserted sense of solidarity, among Africans who spend a great part of their time in meetings with each other, in starting organizations, holding conferences. It may be that their efforts will prove abortive, but over and over again it has been asserted that if any part of Africa remains unfree no part is really free. Nkrumah in Ghana, for instance, has said time and again that so long as colonialism lingers in any part of Africa Ghana really has not achieved its own freedom.

I do not remember, except in very casual remarks, that that kind of thing was said at a comparable time in South and South-East Asia. It seems to me that there each country proceeded to secure its own independence, with no great sense that the unfreedom of one part significantly affected the rest. Various of the African constitutions contain provisions, which may, of course, never be called into play, to the effect that sovereignty can be abandoned on behalf of a larger African organization — again, an assertion that as far as I know finds no place in the Asian setting.

Unquestionably in Africa as in Asia there is also a real trend toward consolidation within the former colonial boundaries, and it may be that Austinian sovereignty will become effective for the Africans too. But I would suggest that the sense of solidarity among the Africans seems to go far beyond what has been apparent for the Asians. Perhaps one of the key reasons is that Black Africa has no national solidity in depth in any of its states although the national sense has unquestionably grown. That lack of a sense of national community is something that certainly is not true for many of the Asian countries. Asia possessed the foundations on which national states could easily be built. The African nationalists still have their nations to create; the Asian nationalists could very often build upon an ancient past. I am by no means saying that all the countries we are concerned with here are solid monolithic nations, for obviously they are not: each has its cleavages, its minorities, its regional groupings, and its linguistic divisions. But when that has been said there still remains for many of them a sense of a community which reaches far back into the past, a community of a sort which the African states almost completely lack.

One of the points of difference between the African and the Asian countries in general is that the former achieved their independence with very little in the way of struggle. It is reasonable to assume that this has a real bearing on their lack of national solidarity. They did not go through the kind of experience that India and Indonesia went through with a relatively long period of nationalist organization and agitation which in the Indonesian case involved actual warfare. Independence, in a way, has come to most of Africa on a silver platter, which perhaps leaves a revolution still to be made and which removes from the scene the sense of national solidarity fostered by joining in battle against the imperialists. Conceivably, this difference works to the disadvantage of the potential African nations, although it may contribute to making easier a transition to Pan-

Africanism precisely because of the lack of profound national attachments.

I find in South and South-East Asia almost no movement to build common institutions. Quezon and a few Filipinos looked to a Malayan race unity of some sort; there was some earlier talk of joining Malaya and Indonesia; now it is proposed to create a new and limited Malaysia made up of Malaya, Singapore, and the North Borneo territories; and there has recently been set in motion the Association of South-East Asia — Malaya, Philippines and Thailand joining for economic, social and cultural purposes. I see no evidence of the existence of a general sense that the peoples in the huge area reaching from West Pakistan across to the Philippines constitute a common entity and must join to pursue a common destiny.

One of the things that are most significant in producing some degree of identity among the South and South-East Asians is the fact that all of them underwent the colonial experience — all, that is, except Thailand — and that colonial experience is still a vital element in their mentality. Panikkar's Vasco da Gama era is going to have consequences reaching far beyond itself. The colonial régimes shaped some of the major Asian areas and certainly shaped the present political systems. Everywhere they brought into being the élites that are now dominating their countries. The happy sense of escape from the bitter fact of colonialism is a thing that is of dominant consequence in people's minds. The people of Asia like the people of Africa in large part had their consciousness shaped by the sense of the colonial experience. If we drop that out, we drop, it seems to me, something that has been a major element in bringing them into the position they hold in the modern world.

Maurice Zinkin

I think perhaps one ought to ask the question the other way round: Is there any reason why an Asian should be Pan-Asian at all? In Africa a lot of the states are too small. Secondly, they have no particular reason to be as they are — their boundaries are often rather arbitrary. Thirdly, a lot of them were in fact quite recently united: several of the West African states were once part of a French

West Africa; Kenya, Uganda and Tanganyika have been part of an East African semi-federation. The African states have perfectly valid reasons for wishing to belong to larger units. In South and South-East Asia there are no such valid reasons. If you are an Indian or a Ceylonese it seems to me the sensible thing to wish to continue to be is an Indian or a Ceylonese. You will get no advantage from pooling sovereignty. It would be more than outweighed by the great dis-advantage of having within a common government people of differ-ent national traditions and different ambitions.

I think that the sense in which South and South-East Asia are one is rather a cultural and historical sense. There is the fact that over large areas there is a common Hindu-Buddhist religious tradition, sometimes on top, sometimes, as in Indonesia or East Bengal, under-neath, but nevertheless still to some extent there. And then there is the fact that these are the original areas of colonialism. This is the area that colonialism was about. It was to this area people went for spices, etc.

These Asian countries have therefore had 300 years of an almost exactly common historical tradition. The colonial powers were the same Western Europeans basically in many ways. We and the French and the Dutch are different people in our own eyes but not so different in the eyes of anybody else. The way we ran Asia, the fact that they were being run from a long way away, the sort of govern-ment we instituted — these are the same, and so also was the way in which we used local society.

I am not clear who the new African élites are, but the new Asian élites, if I understand the position correctly, are the old Asian élites, and this, I think, is important. The people who came on top in Java were the old aristocracy, the people who led the independence move-ment in India were the old upper castes; the people who led in Vietnam were of old mandarin families. In Cambodia you still have the king; in Thailand you still have the king and the old noble families. You had a process of Westernization part of the purpose of which was to enable the old governing classes to be also the new governing classes. And this runs right through Asia. So you began with a cultural tradition that was in many ways common. You put on top of that a process of adaptation which was again common. Inevitably, you then get many common attitudes and it is these attitudes that make South and South-East Asia look to us so very much the same. This does not, I think, mean in any way that they therefore feel any need for political unification, of which the advantages to them are not obvious.

Chapter two

STABILITY AND CHANGE
IN INDIAN POLITICS

by W. H. Morris-Jones

I

FOR various reasons the subject of Indian politics has become an arena for battle between sceptics and optimists. India's very size and prominence in international affairs attract attention which a Malaya or Ceylon can for long periods easily escape. Her supposed importance as the largest member of the Afro-Asians and the most influential of the non-aligned countries excites among commentators a concern about her political prospects and an eagerness to get their assessments correct. It might be also that the actual record of India's foreign policy has given an impression of ambivalence — the Gandhian preaching of peaceful settlement of disputes and the practice of a degree of intransigence on certain matters — which has in turn provoked a mixed attitude of approval and distrust in regard to the state of her internal politics. But above all it is India's very stability in an Asia of challenged and upset régimes which stands out as an invitation to both praise and suspicion. If to some it seems both true and fine, to others it appears in the light of Asian experience as a whole to be too good to be wholly true; if the present writer endorsed the *Guardian*'s view that Delhi had become 'the school of Asia', Selig Harrison on the other hand peered into 'the most dangerous decades'.

There are further special reasons of some interest which might explain the prevalence of scepticism. One of these could be that lingering echoes of certain pessimistic pronouncements of the past can still be heard and that these provoke doubts. It is not difficult to find such statements, for every step towards responsible government and parliamentary democracy conceded and sponsored for India by British governments was accompanied by loud disclaimers and muted hopes from the official side and by prophecies of deepest gloom from the opponents of the reforms. It is surely not improbable that some of the fearful caution and profound doubt should have stuck. The more dominant themes voiced during the forty years before independence were after all not such as could conceivably be set at rest by a mere fifteen years of successful survival. They were: (a) the fragility of Indian unity and (b) the delicateness of Indian democracy.[1] The arguments of the twenties and thirties on these points have almost passed from British political memory; they were perhaps never quite at the centre of Westminster's preoccupations, even in the early 1930's. But it seems at least quite likely that Indian political memories may on these points be more retentive; the fact that all good nationalists of the time robustly denied the grounds of doubt does not mean that they were unaffected in their minds by these judgments of the men whom they regarded as opponents. Since so much of the scepticism regarding India's political achievement comes from Indians, this point has obvious relevance.

A second possible source of scepticism is to an even greater degree a purely Indian matter. Much current Indian scepticism, not to say defeatism, is an outcome of what may be called perfectionist political beliefs. The exaggeration of hopes and expectations can be a fertile soil for despondency and has proved so in independent India. Although this is especially important in relation to the 'democracy' theme, it is not without point on the matter of unity. The nationalist movement had high ambitions in terms of the integration within its ranks of all communities, classes and castes. Its members hoped and believed — against what others said and often against the evidence too — that they were succeeding; these sentiments were vital to them. (I do not have to argue that such a mood is as important

[1] A sketch of the subject is given in my *Parliament in India* (1957), Ch. II. One of the best expressions of these themes in the pre-independence period — and one by no means outstanding for its pessimism — was Schuster and Wint, *India and Democracy* (1941).

to any nationalist movement. For what other movement meant so much for so long to so many?) Partition was a shattering blow from which confidence in respect of unity could not easily recover. If sentiments extending from uneasiness to terror are readily excited by any tendency which seems fissiparous, it may be in part because experience has contained both the aspiration to perfect unity and the fact of complete severance.

Perfectionism in thinking about democracy is rather more notable. It contains three strands which may be labelled according to the features they stress: 'participation', 'consensus' and 'purity'. The participation emphasis in democratic theory is not an Indian invention but it plays a great part in Indian thinking. Democracy is seen as achieved according to the measure of popular participation in the political process. The importance attached to this comes in part from recollections — often, one suspects, far from accurate — of the 'freedom struggle' in which 'everyone' is thought of as having had a role to play. The unusual nature of such politics is not recognized and it is readily forgotten how many lives were untouched by the campaigns which enlisted the complete absorption of some. In part, the participation emphasis comes from a misunderstanding about 'Western' and in particular British politics. In some way or other — was it text-books on politics or word of mouth? — the Indian impression of the ordinary Englishman has tended to insist on his being an eager and well-informed citizen, creating and grasping opportunities to take part in the political process. Perhaps India is inclined to make too close an identification of public-spiritedness and political activity. In any case, post-independence India is often thought of as falling below an adequate standard of participation.[1] It may also be noted in passing that the need for a 'participating democracy' is often supported by a curiously unquestioning belief in its being a necessary condition for economic development.[2]

The most obvious expression of the 'consensus' theme is the

[1] On this point, as on so many, Jayaprakash Narayan speaks for many Indians. The novel twist to his presentation of the case for a 'participating democracy' (e.g., most recently, in his *Swaraj for the People* (Delhi, 1961)) is that he does not think India is behind the West in this but rather believes that she can show the way forward from the West's inadequate view of democracy as government by consent.

[2] One of the Swatantra Party's contributions to Indian political debate has been its challenge to this view.

widespread distrust of party conflict. Asok Mehta in sophisticated style described as one of the 'political compulsions of a
backward economy' the need to suspend or at least substantially
to modify the whole idea of 'opposition' to government.[1]
Jayaprakash Narayan, more radically, has preached the virtues
of a party-less democracy.[2] In very many quarters, regret is felt
that a combined effort to implement a general will for the common good is frustrated by party warfare. One of the attractions
of schemes for local small-scale democratic units and a pyramid
of indirectly elected bodies is precisely that elections may be
avoided and representatives be chosen by the sense of the community without the need for contests. This too is a form of perfectionism (albeit of a sadly mistaken kind). It owes something
to pictures, real and imagined, of the national movement seen
as containing every interest and opinion and at the same time
expressing a single purpose and policy. It regards divisions of
any kind as at best wasteful and unseemly and at worst fatal.
Moreover, since it usually implies that only goodwill is required
in order to discern and desire the common good, the condemnation of the party politician is moral as well as political.

That the last point leads on at once to the 'purity' theme is
clear; indeed, this can be regarded as one reason for the
appropriateness of Jayaprakash's association with Bhave and
bhoodan. Here we have another legacy from the national
movement, this time rather from its Gandhian side. No doubt
all nationalist movements call forth exceptional devotion and
Congress may have done better than any. But more remarkable
than the degree of devotion was its self-conscious character. It
was not necessary for all Congressmen to be able to follow
Gandhi completely in connecting self-government with self-
discipline and self-sacrifice, politics with morals; the point got
across with at least the force needed to deposit in men's minds a

[1] Of several possible sources it is sufficient to mention Mehta's paper 'The
Opposition in the New States' in *Democracy in the New States* (C.C.F. Rhodes
Seminar Papers, Delhi, 1959).

[2] It seems fair to say that in his latest *Swaraj for the People* (1961) there is less dogmatic insistence on this point than in the *Reconstruction of Indian Polity* (1959). I note
an enthusiastic endorsement of his earlier standpoint by N. Prasad, a Professor of
Sociology, who pleads for 'the voluntary dissolution of the different political parties'
and a 'National Cabinet . . . of talents [representing] all sections of public opinion'
('Democracy in Crisis' in R. N. Saksena (ed.), *Sociology, Social Research and Social
Problems in India* (1961)).

new and high standard of public duty. This standard enjoined much more than probity and rectitude, it demanded that all desires except the desire to serve be firmly suppressed. How far lives were actually changed matters less (in the present context) than the undoubted fact that the standard, as a measure to be used in judging politicians, has strongly survived. It is scarcely surprising that those Indians who employ this standard find in Indian politics cause for gloom. That they would fail to find a success story in any other country's politics does not help matters.

To suggest some of the particular sources of scepticism and pessimism is one thing; it permits us to see that gloom and despair may sometimes be in the predispositions of observers. But it does not do away with the need to examine the declared reasons given by the doubters. The two main themes around which arguments are grouped have already been mentioned: the weakness of India's unity and the shallowness of her democracy. In the discussion of both there are difficulties, some of which arise out of the assessment of complex facts and others out of the uncertainty of the standards to be applied.

II

India purports to be a federal union. This is obvious but often forgotten; yet it must be the starting-point of any discussion of unity. It at once eliminates as irrelevant so many of the (normally tacit) comparisons which are made with unitary states. It must also remove as unreasonable the comparisons made with the British period. What degree of unity is it reasonable to expect in India? British rule imposed — not without difficulty — a strong central government, and it caused to arise a strong nation-wide movement for independence led by men with an all-India standing. But that central government had found it necessary — and not only as a concession to the nationalists — to distribute some of its functions to provinces from at least 1919, and the Congress during the pre-war years was made aware of its own regional power centres. That is, India was moving steadily towards a federal structure already before independence and this trend was quite independent of the communal question and the claims of the Muslims.

It is interesting to note that there seems to have been a change of fashion in the nature of comments on this aspect of the Indian constitution. In the first years, it was usual to stress the unitary features, even to the point of wondering whether in view of the extraordinary powers of the central government, the political domination of the all-India parties and of the Congress in particular, and the administrative hegemony of the ICS/IAS, the designation 'federal' was warranted or whether 'quasi-federal' might not be less misleading. Within a decade the emphasis seems altogether to have changed: the central government is at the mercy of powerful states, the all-India parties and especially Congress are no more than loose federations of regional parties and the unifying influence of the all-India services is in decline. At the same time there have certainly been some notable swimmers against these tides — such as Paul Appleby in the early period and K. Santhanam recently — but in these cases the standards of judgment were somewhat special.[1]

This change of opinion may, however, be not a matter of fashion, not even a change of standards, rather a reflection of a movement in the real situation. Is it possible to draw up a balance sheet of unity's gains and losses since 1947? In a very rough way it can be done, and the conclusion suggested in my view is that a shift away from what must be regarded (from the point of view of a federal standard) as excessive centralism has indeed taken place. This answer is, however, less simple than at first appears because the shift is made up of several factors, not all of which have individually operated in the same direction.

The position in the half-dozen years after independence was such that factors inherited from the British period were of paramount importance. First, the administrative machine was taken over almost intact. In terms both of personnel and procedures it was an all-India machine, not unaccustomed — despite provincial autonomy — to looking to Delhi for guidance and direction. This unifying character had been especially marked by the war period, by the preparation for partition and inde-

---

[1] P. Appleby, *Report on Public Administration in India* (1953); K. Santhanam, *Union-State Relations in India* (1960). Appleby found the centre from the start deplorably dependent on the states; Santhanam claims that state dependence on the centre has so increased that the original federal constitution has been transformed in practice. The former sees mainly what smooth planning demands; the latter has his eyes on the rights of the states.

pendence and by the challenge to order encountered in the first years of the new régime. Secondly, there was taken over the set of political institutions which had served to 'mediate' between *Raj* and Movement during the inter-war period: primarily the legislative and judicial bodies. These were perhaps more genuinely federal in character than the administrative system, but they had hardly recovered from their war-time limitations of role and had been somewhat overtaken by the scale and nature of the political operations leading up to independence. Already before 1947 interest had moved rather to the new Constituent Assembly in Delhi; this central body was in a good position, when it assumed the role of national legislature, to overshadow the provincial assemblies. (It of course contained during 1946–8 a very large number of the important provincial political leaders. To some extent they represented and some-times pressed provincial points of view, but it is also true that their presence enhanced the standing of the central body itself and somewhat weakened their provincial links.) Third, and perhaps most important, there was inherited from the British period the all-India political leadership, almost wholly con-tained within the Congress Party. Like their Indian Civil Service counterparts on the official side, these men were accustomed to thinking in terms of India as a whole even if their habitual spheres of operations were provincial. There may have been moments during 1937–40 when their orientation had changed and tasks within the province absorbed their minds and visions. But already then the High Command was liable to recall them to a sense of the whole. Certainly, from 1940 on-wards the national scene — Cripps, 'Quit India', Simla, Cabinet Mission and the moves that led to the transfer of power — had predominated. They were Congressmen first and men of their regions second. Many of them had been drawn into Delhi and had stayed there through the times of trouble; when conditions eased and fortress India was politically safe, they moved (or were moved) back to the regional capitals. But in doing so they brought about no immediate change in the balance between centre and regions. To use military terms (and it was Gandhi who said Congress had to be like an army), they did not cease to belong to the regiment simply because their period of secondment to the regimental depot was at an end.

Now it seems fairly clear that from about 1951 significant changes took place in all three parts of the inheritance, but interpretation of their impact in terms of unification is far from easy. Within the administrative system the introduction of the Indian Administrative Service was in principle devised to avoid any great break in the pattern; the recruitment, training and service of the bureaucratic élite was to continue to be all-India in nature. Further, as the area of state activity expanded both departmentally and through the establishment of public enterprises, so the range and influence of this corps of civil servants extended also. On the other hand, some specialist services which had originally been all-India in character had become provincialized and this tendency was not reversed. Moreover, it appears that the movement of officers to and from Delhi tended to diminish: secondments became permanent for some, non-existent for others, and from this it might be correct to guess that some lessening of all-India consciousness has taken place at the state secretariats.

A further group of changes have had great impact on the actual working of administrators: the introduction of the five-year plans and the Planning Commission; the development of air transport and other long-distance communications; the combined operation of community development and democratic decentralization. Whether these changes work to strengthen or weaken unification is by no means clear. One of the few independent studies of the effects of planning on union-state relations concludes that 'planning . . . practically superseded the federal Constitution . . . this supersession was not legal or constitutional but was by agreement and consent'.[1] In order to please their own party leaders in Delhi and in order to receive the matching grants, state governments have sacrificed their federal status; they accept uniform policies laid down by the centre, they have even surrendered certain taxes to the centre. But this is not the full story. The same author admits that it is much easier to get a promise out of state government than to get performance; in the implementation of the plans — on both revenue-raising and physical fulfilment sides — they have in fact dictated the pace. Moreover, implementation cannot be treated as wholly separate from policy. The Planning Com-

[1] Santhanam, op. cit., p. 47.

mission proposes, but since it knows that the states dispose, it takes states' views in at the formulation stages. Even if it was not administrative good sense to do so, it would be politically necessary: the Commission's master is the National Development Council which includes not only central ministers but every state's chief minister. It is true of course that Pandit Nehru is chairman of both Commission and Council. It may even be true that if some of the important planning staff with private routes to the top can persuade him of a point, he can carry the state premiers. But the latter cannot be pressed too far; a Roy or a Kamraj Nadar or a Chavan who can hold Bengal, Madras or Bombay for Congress is not feebly placed if it comes to the pulls and pushes of bargaining.

The comings and goings of chief ministers to Delhi are but a minute part of the total inter-governmental traffic of men and ideas which air lines and improved telephones have made possible. Out from Delhi go the central ministers and in come the states' ministers — of education, labour, public works, irrigation, agriculture and the rest — for formal conferences and informal talks. And for every ministerial journey there are countless separate ones by officials. (Some states keep a fairly senior man in Delhi almost permanently, helping state 'cases' through awkward departmental corridors.) The centre offers grants-in-aid and policies together and the states would often like one without the other. On the other hand, as fellow-Congressmen they may not disagree strongly on policies, and the states know that even if they may look like agents they are nevertheless without acceptable rivals and therefore indispensable. The discussions are therefore like market operations. But it is not possible to say that one side is in control of the prices. It is disappointing to the student when those on the inside state merely that there is 'a lot of give and take', but this may still be the fairest summary.

An unambiguous generalization is also difficult to obtain in the matter of community development and *panchayati Raj*. Reports on the working of these schemes are becoming almost numerous but they frequently seem to be answering different questions or even to be conflicting in their answers to the same questions. Our particular question here is whether these schemes by challenging the former position of the district officers and changing their role, by emphasizing developmental functions and reviving local elected bodies by injections of finance and authority, have loosened the administrative fabric, weakened the hand of the centre and dimmed the view of the whole. Now in a sense of course this is just what was intended — that the people should be brought to express their needs, to see how through combined effort they could meet them, to look on government as a source of certain technical advice and supplementary aid, in a word to see local affairs as the responsibility of local people. What has actually happened is, naturally, more complex and confused — and even apparently contradictory reports can be true. That the bureaucrats have often treated this as one more scheme to run, that the village leaders have invariably played the game in order to please the authorities, that the rural establishment have scrutinized the new world with a cool eye to economic, political and social gain — all this has been said and no doubt contains truth. It is also reported with equal conviction that new elements are appearing in the local atmosphere, that some younger officials are adjusting themselves to the new conception of the public servant, that the villager notes that he seems to have acquired a new and unwonted importance in the eyes of outsiders, that even the have-nots sense a strength that comes from numbers, that new leaders with new attributes enter, that in consequence relations between government and governed and among the governed are changing. To say that both accounts can be correct is not to be timid but only to recognize the essentially hesitating nature of almost all social change. To the question concerning the loosening administrative fabric the answer must be that in this matter change is at present very slight and overshadowed by the change in scale and kind of government activity. But at least it seems likely that some decentralizing influence will persist and even grow.

It would seem that on balance it is not easy to find in administrative developments any dramatic undermining of unification taking place at the present time. By those who are convinced that disintegration is happening in the Indian polity, it could still be argued that this conclusion only shows how out of gear with political realities an administrative structure can become. (If this were in fact the case, the situation would be grave indeed, for such a disharmony within the body politic frequently constitutes an explosive condition.) We should therefore turn our attention from 'administration' to 'politics' and consider what has happened since 1951 to the political parts of the inheritance. Is disintegration easier to find in this sphere? It will be convenient to take the two political aspects of the inheritance — 'mediators' and 'movement', or parliaments and parties — together. (That it should be convenient to do so is itself significant: it indicates that in this period the two have grown up together; the parliaments have been — for the first time in India — the chief operational front of the parties.) One might have expected that the passing of the crisis years of 1947–50 would have resulted in a shift of the political centre of gravity away from Delhi to the state capitals. After all, most of the subjects which affect the everyday lives of people are the responsibility of the states. The fact that MPs often complain that in the constituencies people are more interested in the members of state legislatures (MLAs) would seem to confirm this guess. Yet the position is not quite so simple. That the centre has not lost in quite this way has something, but not too much, to do with its being the place where Mr Nehru sits. By now almost the sole survivor of the big men of the freedom struggle, he certainly attracts attention; no body to which he belongs can be unnoticed. The political magnetism of the centre has also some connexion with the issues with which it deals; these include foreign affairs, the big planning schemes and large issues of social reform. Probably, however, it would be true to say that what has happened is not a shift of interest (from central parliament to state assembly) on the part of any section but rather the arrival of new sections. The old political classes — the urban-dwelling, educated, English-reading folk — still look on the whole to Delhi and read those debates rather than the local ones. But there are now new political classes — small town and large village people, easily literate only in the local language — and for these Trivandrum, Ahmedabad, Hyderabad and Calcutta are quite far enough.

The distinction between the new and the old political classes is important even if (as I shall try to indicate later) the point of present-day Indian politics is to prevent it from becoming a separation. In a sense the significance of the linguistic reorganization of the states (1953, 1956, 1960) was that it was the outcome of political campaigning which, to a degree unique in independent India, brought together both groups in a common cause. The most sophisticated minister of the central cabinet and the humblest Satara shopkeeper could for once speak the same political language. So far as the results of reorganization are concerned, the usual view may be that it has strengthened this particular form of 'fissiparous tendency'. Some caution is needed here. First, against the idea that increased coherence at the state level must mean increased state selfishness *vis-à-vis* the centre, it has to be said that formerly the linguistically mixed states do not seem to have been noticeably less demanding than the others; perhaps the need to satisfy both 'majority' and 'minority' regions within their own boundaries made them all the more importunate. It might be that the energies available for bargaining with Delhi were reduced by those which had to be spent on internal wrangles, but this cuts both ways: less energy for bargaining with Delhi means also less time to spend on those problems and policies which relate to matters beyond the state limits, less awareness of a wider world. Second, against the notion that linguistic states have opened up routes of influence which permit parochialism to permeate upwards to unprecedented levels must be set the consideration that these routes are two-way. The achievement of linguistic homogeneity (however imperfect)[1] not only removes an obstacle which blocked all other political traffic; it positively effects an introduction between issues of constructive policy and the new political classes.

Party is of course the great agency for all these processes. Nothing is more striking about the last dozen years of Indian politics than that the disappearance of the all-India leaders of the nationalist period has not been accompanied by any widespread replacement of all-India parties by regional ones. Certainly it is true that a few regional parties have made great headway — Ganatantra Parishad in Orissa and Dravida Munnetra Kazhagam in Madras for instance. Also, very effective 'fronts' have been established for purely regional (and

---

[1] The points of imperfection are just those at which the processes of political education get halted at present: notably the Bengali pockets in Assam. To note this is not necessarily to recommend a further search for 'perfection'.

usually temporary) purposes — Samyukta Maharashtra Samiti and, in a different sense, the anti-Communist grouping in Kerala. But on the whole the all-India scale of operations has survived. That this should have happened with Congress could be explained on special grounds; likewise, though on different grounds, with the Communist Party. But the Praja Socialist Party and Jan Sangh are also still there, and the coming of the Swatantra Party means that even the enterprise of starting a new all-India party has not seemed unprofitable to a number of seasoned politicians. Moreover, in a matter of this kind, mere survival has its force. No one should try to deny that the all-India parties (even, it might be, the Communist Party) are now markedly federal in nature and thus require great effort to manage.[1] But every ardent regionalist in an all-India party is engaged perforce in a double-edged activity: on the one hand, he communicates his regional views upwards towards head-quarters and in doing so smudges the tidy ideologies and complicates life for the working committees; on the other hand, he still communicates the party image downwards among his regional fellows and customers. Is there any evidence that in normal times he is less effective in the second capacity than he is in the first?

The separation of 'administrative' from 'political' which has been made in this analysis has a convenience for purposes of exposition, but is in a measure unreal. In relation to unification and disintegration the two come together effectively in the institution of state government. State ministers are simultaneously engaged at key positions in both the administrative and political federal structures, and through these ministers the two structures achieve one of their vital points of interaction. Within their states they are as heads of departments responsible for the formulation of policies and for their implementation by the state-level bureaucracy and local officials. In this work they are called upon to reconcile four streams of influence which are in principle separate though in practice often complementary: their own officials, the relevant departments of the central

[1] Few things are more amusing than the air of alarm and concern with which observers from established federal states note that Indian parties are becoming rather like their own have always been! Could federal politics for long avoid federal parties?

government, the party at the national level, the political circumstances in the state. Often the task requires a display of toughness 'upwards' — as when a central ministry or the working committee of the party has to be told that a certain line cannot wisely be pressed too hard in one region. At other times the lesser of difficulties may be to risk displeasure either in local political circles or among the state bureaucracy by insisting on policies favoured by influential bodies at Delhi. It will naturally happen also that some ministers may be so placed and/or so disposed that they regularly exhibit a bias in their manner of choosing: 'difficult' states or state ministers of more than usual local patriotism will produce a response that leans towards an 'upward' toughness.

It is in this connexion that the changing character of state leaders acquires importance. New state ministers have emerged in most states in the last half-dozen years: Nadar, Chavan, Kairon, and most recently Patnaik are only examples. They have in some measure displaced men of a slightly older generation who have moved or been moved in various directions: Rajaji into opposition, Desai to the centre, Mahtab (perhaps) to the wilderness. It is not easy to be dogmatic or to produce conclusive evidence as to the consequences of these changes in terms of bias and pressures operating on the federal balance. It does seem very probable, however, that the new men will be more sensitive to local political currents than their predecessors, therefore inclined to the solutions which involve an 'upward' toughness. To the extent that this is true (and especially if this is reinforced by an increased 'states' interests' point of view in the state bureaucracy) it does constitute a force working against unitary coherence. But the commentators seem frequently to exaggerate this; the pull of party headquarters, the carrots and sticks of the central government, the larger ambitions of state ministers themselves, their very intimate and confident mastery over local political forces — all these must surely serve as substantial checks on a disintegrative tendency.

It is difficult to do justice to these themes in a few pages and the above analysis makes no claim to be comprehensive. One important deficiency is of course the inadequate treatment of the language issues. Reference has been made briefly to some political effects of the reorganization of states on linguistic lines

but no attempt can be made here to discuss the effects of other
no less important aspects of language policy: the slow shrinkage
of English, the slow development of Hindi and the opposition
aroused in Madras and Bengal against it, the fairly rapid
advance of the regional languages in education. It must suffice
to say here that these factors, while by no means unimportant,
seem less likely to influence substantially the federal balance of
political and administrative factors than to be influenced by it.

III

The discussion of the allegation that India's integration is so
weakened as to be in peril has been conducted in terms of the
regions and states. But of course those who arrive at this pessimistic conclusion do so on the basis of social as well as geographical cleavages. Although it is convenient in this paper to
consider the social cleavages of class, caste and community in
relation to the second of our two themes — viz., the character of
Indian democracy and its supposed shallowness and fragility —
it is to be noted that the social and geographical cleavages are
closely related. Selig Harrison's analysis of 'regional élites' and
'caste lobbies' shows them as aspects of the same changing
political life.[1]

As already mentioned at the outset, much of the uncertainty
and lack of conviction so frequently encountered in Indians on
the subject of the quality of Indian democracy can be attributed
to two things: doubts sown by British writers and administrators
and perfectionism born of the freedom movement. But it could
still be that the uncertainty is warranted by the facts; this is
what has now to be examined. (Let me confess at once that it
seems to me that the burden of proof is heavily on the side of the
doubters. The fairly complete abandonment of democratic
institutions has happened in Asia so frequently and so easily
that it appears reasonable to begin with the assumption that
where they remain they have substantial meaning.)

We may begin with the general lines of pre-war British
scepticism concerning the suitability of democracy for India.
Setting aside such relatively trivial points as the impossible

[1] S. Harrison, *India: the most dangerous decades* (1960).

c

administrative and financial burden of adult franchise elections and the insuperable difficulties of assimilating princely India with the India of the British provinces, three main themes were to be found.[1] First, the great majority of Indian people are at an early 'stage' of social development and cannot yet sufficiently desire or sustain a democratic form of government which demands more voluntary effort from citizens than any other form. In particular, illiteracy, together with a social structure backed by religious sanctions, disposes men towards passive and reverent acceptance of established authority and incapacitates them for critical judgment and active participation alike. Second, India is a country so profoundly divided into hereditarily determined community groups that reliance on majority decisions must always imply the corollary, at every level and in every unit of political activity, of the permanently subordinated minorities. Third, the same fact carries with it the further implication that public life is bound to be dominated by sectional spirit rather than public spirit, by a vivid awareness of and loyalty to the part at the continuous expense of the whole, by the impossibility of discerning a common good.

These themes can first be countered in a fairly direct manner. Apart from an initial questioning of a too ready labelling of 'stages' of social development and a too ready identification of the socially primitive with the politically naïve (and in particular, of literacy with political sophistication), it may be argued that these themes, baldly stated, underestimate the influence of our own régime and of the national movement. The introduction of certain regularities in the processes of government and the normal supremacy of law and established procedures counts for something; at least we can say that many people became

[1] The best general statement of these is probably J. S. Mill's *Representative Government*. This may seem surprising in view of the fact that it is often said that Mill was one of the chief influences on the rise of liberalism in India. But if his Indian readers studied *Representative Government* and not only the essay *On Liberty*, this might at least explain some of the profound caution to be found among the early liberal nationalists. (Mill does not mention India, but it was of course of India that Mill had special knowledge.) On the other hand, it should be noted that there is a good deal of common ground between (a) Mill's account of the conditions that render representative democracy 'inapplicable' and (b) his descriptions of the 'infirmities and dangers' to which this form of government is subject, even in a country like England. This softens the distinction between 'applicable' and 'inapplicable' and could be read in such a way as to give encouragement to a country like India.

accustomed to the idea that not every form in which power is exercised has equal authority, that some are more proper than others. Again, whether or not we were too ready to give political recognition to the social cleavages, we set in process certain long-term movements — in education, industrialization, urbanization — whose effect is certainly to erode at least some of the cleavages in some of their aspects.[1] From the national movement also, several important lessons were learnt. To teach that governments could be criticized, attacked with abuse and even disobeyed with righteousness may not represent the whole of political wisdom, but it was no poor antidote against the supposed disease of passivity. The movement may not have been in fact as all-embracing in social terms as it imagined, but surely it did succeed, through a large number of its adherents who were men of influence, in establishing the idea of the paramount call of service to the national whole. The importance of all these considerations arises out of the relatively long period of time over which 'government' and 'movement' held joint sway over many men's minds.

Another manner of reply would rest on a fairly minute examination of actual political processes in independent India, seeking to show that the gloomy view is exaggerated and not warranted by the facts. It would take electoral processes and show how most of the close studies of this subject have revealed that the importance of caste and community can be over-emphasized and that these factors by themselves are seldom sufficient to account for electoral behaviour.[2] It would take Parliament and show that the facile dismissal of such an institution as a mere Nehru *durbar* overlooks the unobtrusive but cumulatively significant work of discussion and argument that goes on in parliamentary all-party committees and in party committees.[3] It would invite attention to the present party system in the country as a whole and point out how difficult it is —

[1] The cautious formulation is necessary, for there are counter-tendencies here: education can become a battlefield for communal jealousies; urbanization can provide caste with new opportunities and greater organizational possibilities.

[2] e.g. F. G. Bailey, 'Politics in Orissa' in *Economic Weekly*, Bombay, 29 August–7 November, 1959; A. C. Mayer, 'Rural Leaders and the Indian General Election' in *Asian Survey*, October 1961; A. H. Somjee, *Voting Behaviour in an Indian Village* (University of Baroda Political Science Series No. 2, 1959).

[3] See my *Parliament in India*.

with the notable and obvious exceptions such as Muslim League and Akalis — to find community consistently organized as party.

Yet when these and perhaps other kinds of reply have been made, it remains impossible to discount entirely the arguments which stress the differences between an Asian and a Western setting. However, it will be the attempt of the remaining pages to show that to take proper account of these differences may lead not to scepticism or despair but on the contrary to a more profound understanding of the full achievements of democracy in India.

We are to argue that democracy is not rendered illusory or specious by its setting in a primarily traditional society, but we do not need to pretend that there is no traditional society or that it is only insignificantly different in its political implications from the social setting of a modern state of the West. If it has been the case in the past that much writing about Indian politics has ignored the social structure of Indian rural life, this is clearly no longer a possible course. The change is perhaps one in our understandings; more has been brought to light in recent years. Social anthropologists have turned attention away from the origins of caste as *varna* — that is, away from the historical inquiry using literary and religious sources — towards the current characteristics of caste as *jati*. These *jati* groupings, previously regarded primarily as sub-castes of the main *varna* divisions now stand forth in their own right as the basic units of social stratification in rural India. But the change is also one in the real world as well as in our understanding of it. In a large measure Indian political life before independence was indeed divorced from the social setting of rural India. From this point of view the introduction of adult franchise has been more important than the achievement of independence. Even the Gandhian period of the nationalist movement — different as it was from the earlier liberal and extremist phases — can now be seen as having avoided (except in special matters such as untouchability) a confrontation with the traditional bases of rural life. But a mass electorate has challenged the peculiarly élite character of previous politics and has forced the urbanized politicians of yesterday to come to terms with the rural voting power. This is the change that lies behind the changing character of political leadership in the states to which reference has already been made. But the change is manifested not in this alone but throughout Indian political life.

To grasp the significance of the change, it is not enough to label India as a transitional polity. (In any case that label carries the misleading implication that we can know exactly what it will become as well as what it has been.) Rather we have to find terms that will convey the co-existence within one political system of quite different styles of political behaviour. Elsewhere[1] I have expressed this by speaking of India as a country in which more than one 'idiom' or 'language' of politics is in use. This may not be peculiar to India, it may indeed be common among the 'new states', but it is unusual in terms of polities more familiar to the Western scholar. He is accustomed to societies where in general political and social structure have grown up together and have not been suddenly introduced to each other. What perhaps is peculiar to India is the vivid character of the confrontation of political styles — and this for the reason that both the 'modern' world of politics and the 'traditional' are in India highly developed and remarkably 'pure' in character. All new states have modern politicians but how many have a substantial group who for several generations have absorbed the modern style and acquired experience in its use? And allowing that there are a few states in that position, how many have at the same time a system of traditional social stratification so pervasive and powerful as that of the castes in India?

The character and prevalence of modern politics in India needs no emphasis or illustration. Of the other language, perhaps a further brief word would be in place.[2] First and most evidently, it is the language of a host of tiny worlds. *Varna* has all-India meaning but in the little worlds of *jati*, *varna* is only a reference scale relevant in a limited range of relations. The area within which *jati* and village interact is a microscopic box, in principle sealed away from the other boxes. It has — again, in principle — no direct experience or sense of the other boxes or of being part of a larger whole; India, even say Madras State, is merely the vague outside. Second, it is a world in which men

[1] Contributions to *Constitutionalism in Asia*, ed. R. N. Spann (Asia Publishing House) and *Politics and Society in India*, ed. C. H. Philips (Allen & Unwin Ltd.), both to be published during 1962–3.

[2] A fuller discussion of this point and of the ground covered in the rest of this paper will be found in my *Government and Politics of India* (forthcoming).

have their stations and from these stations in the little society they derive exclusively their rights and duties, their whole code of behaviour, even their outlook on things. Here opinions and interests alike belong not to persons but to groups. As there can be group mobility, so there can be shifts in opinions and interests, but these will shift by groups. Third, it is not a world in which influence and power are absent, but they are present only as attaching to the *jati* groups. For one thing, leadership is fragmented, each caste having its own leaders. For another, in so far as there is any leadership common to the village as a whole, it will come from the ranks of the locally dominant caste who will regard themselves and be regarded as the natural hereditary repositories of such political status. Indeed, the furnishing of political services will be a recognized duty to be performed by that *jati* in the same way as it will be that of another *jati* to cut hair, of another to wash clothes. The location of political authority is no question of choice, will or election; it is given — by station in the social structure. Finally, the nature of political operations is clear. The work of the caste leaders is to ensure the conformity of members to the caste code, to maintain the position of the group in the village community, to achieve appropriate readjustments in that position if the relative strength of the caste should, for some reason, increase. The job of the village leaders is two-fold: to produce a 'consensus' — that is, to resolve and settle inter-caste disputes in such a way as is possible to maintain the *status quo* or if necessary to secure a smooth readjustment of positions; at the same time, represent the village as a whole in relation to the outside, protecting it from interference and securing favours from whoever happens to be *Raj*. This too, then, is a comprehensive language of politics — for its own scale. But it may be noted that this language is more important as behaviour than description; it is by comparison with modern politics inarticulate, acted upon rather than spoken about. This is for the simple reason that on questions outside the little world it has nothing to say whereas within those worlds it is so familiar that there is no need for it to explain itself.

But the distinctiveness of Indian politics lies not so much in the co-existence of these contrasted styles of politics but rather in their astonishing but unobtrusive interpenetration. The work of the social anthropologists has revealed the movement 'upwards' of caste into the larger political arenas hitherto reserved for modern-style politics. This movement is not restricted to the post-independence period but it has intensified in these years. India's modern-idiom rulers are no longer protected from the influence of traditional India by the three bulwarks of British administrators outside the caste system, the national movement and a restricted franchise. All three safeguards have gone and the little worlds of caste have been drawn upwards into the big arenas. The top leaders may proclaim the goal of a casteless society, but the newly enfranchized rural masses know only the language of traditional politics which so largely turns about caste. Nor does caste keep outside the city limits. Although the long-run effects of urban and industrial life may be to weaken caste loyalty, the immediate effects are the opposite. Since immigrants from rural areas keep very close economic and social ties with their villages of origin and since also they often tend to settle in district caste 'colonies' within the city, the consequence is greatly improved facilities for organizing. Moreover, cities teach men to forget caste as a co-operative element making for interdependence; caste becomes instead the unit in which men associate for competition against others.

The result is not merely, not even mainly, the rise of particular caste parties. It is rather that in any kind of politics away from the highest levels, caste becomes a category to be reckoned with. So, in the middle and lower reaches of all parties — and in the administration too — realistic men learn what language they have to talk if they are to be understood and effective. What sounds fine in the Delhi Parliament or for the newspaper-reading public makes little sense at the grass roots. Therefore, behind the formal electoral returns, knowledgeable observers discern the intermediaries who join together the ballots of a caste group to the candidate with a party label. Behind the formal lists of party candidates nominated for the contests, there is probably an inside story of careful calculation in terms of caste appeal. Or again, the wrangles of Mysore politics, which the sociologically innocent might describe in terms of relations between parties and between parliamentary and organizational wings of the Congress, come to be seen as a new stage on which is being played an age-old drama of inter-caste rivalry. Likewise, the mysterious moves in Orissa's recent political history may be illumined by a study of shifting caste positions and alignments.

But in the mixing of idioms the effects are by no means all in one direction. For the modern idiom is moving out of its base in the élite just as surely as the traditional idiom is emerging from its hitherto hidden habitat. The agencies which mainly convey the modern idiom are the institutions of political party and representative assembly (including in the latter the electoral system).

Of all the parties, it is of course Congress which displays on the grandest scale the process of interpenetration. Of the modern politics at the top of the party little requires to be said. But recent investigations[1] begin to tell us something of the nature of Congress politics at the lower levels of the party structure. Some investigators seem to have found two kinds of new men inside the Congress machine. First, there are the leaders of the new village establishment. Until the introduction of adult franchise, the politically active sections of rural India were generally men of higher castes than the peasants and for this reason even a mass party like Congress was manned by Brahmins and other high-caste men out of proportion to their numbers in the community. The politics of adult franchise has in many regions raised the influence of the non-Brahmin middle peasants who are at once numerous and — as compared with the hardly less numerous untouchables — economically substantial. Men from these groups seem to be more prominent in Congress than before. The opponents of the party cry out that Congress is courting and capturing the influential leaders of rural life. Of course it is. But it is equally true that such leaders have in their own ways been courting and capturing Congress. Village India, playing its own game of politics in relation to outside *Raj*, has been adjusting itself to Congress power. The men who for economic and electoral reasons count in any area naturally regard it as one of their functions to get to positions from which they can do what is expected of them by their clients and dependants. Secondly, however, there may have arisen an even newer kind of local Congressman — the man who relies not on his local social status as a member of a dominant caste but solely on his political skill

[1] e.g., M. Weiner, 'Changing patterns of Leadership in West Bengal' in *Pacific Affairs*, September 1959; Bailey and Mayer, loc. cit.; some of the contributions to Park and Tinker, *Leadership and Political Institutions in India* (1959).

in the new politics. Whereas the first type would operate in the traditional idiom as a matter of course, this second brand of newcomer is really a modern who is simply able to exploit that idiom. (In addition to both these, there naturally continue to be many party workers who belong to those sections who, while numerically and even economically weak, provided social and intellectual leadership in the past.)

Similar forces work in the arenas of the state Assemblies. If the central Parliament operates largely in the modern idiom the state Assemblies are much more 'mixed' in character. Their members are drawn from social layers much closer to traditional politics. Also they are in the Assemblies for quite a short part of the year; the rest of the time they will be in their home districts which are, increasingly, their constituencies. No one can visit the lobbies of a state Assembly without realizing quite vividly that the MLA is 'in touch with' his constituents; the corridors are full of them, some still bearing the dust of the village tracks if not the earth of the fields themselves. The MLA is thus another critical point in the drama of Indian politics: which language of politics does he speak? He is himself undergoing 'modern' education from his seniors on the front benches, but the 'courses' are shorter and of a fairly 'elementary' nature. Still he learns to think of his state (even if not yet of India) and to talk of power projects (even if the big decisions are taken in Delhi). At the other end there are the pressures from home and in the corridors — to remember that he comes from the Vidarbha part of Maharashtra, or that he is a Mahar or that he must please those who count in his district party. So evidently he becomes 'bilingual'. Even state ministers have to operate in the two languages. Indeed, one might say that the successful chief ministers are those who are equally skilled in both idioms. Chavan of Bombay may be a good example of this kind. But in at least one state, Madras, there is a fascinating division of labour between the chief minister, who speaks little or no English but manages the 'informal politics', and a colleague who handles the policy questions and converses with New Delhi.

The above discussion may be thought not to answer adequately the question put concerning the fragility or superficiality of democracy. On the other hand, if this is a valid account of the nature of the Indian political process, it should be at least the necessary preliminary to an answer. In fact, it may be more, for it shows that the manner in which the question is put is based on a misconception. To say that Indian democracy is merely some kind of façade behind which caste and other similar loyalties operate seems to imply that it would be more genuine if it was immune to such influence. But, given the Indian social setting, is this true? Should we not prefer to say that only in so far as it gave caste opportunities while at the same time changing it could an Indian democracy be genuine? Yet this is precisely what is happening: caste has moved into politics most evidently through the use of the caste association; by working mainly through existing political parties it opens a door to its own modification; by linking the rural mass electorate to parliamentary democracy it makes the latter intelligible to the former and in so doing makes at least possible the survival and development of that democracy.[1]

Thus from this brief examination of the two themes of the sceptics, I return with conclusions far from pessimistic. Federalism, so far from concealing a process of regional disintegration, is the reality of the Indian structure in all its aspects, administrative, political and social; geographical disintegration is thus successfully contained by federalism. In a not dissimilar way, India's parliamentary democracy is no mere outward appearance nor is it merely living on political capital of the past; on the contrary, its penetrative and pervasive influence is now reaching hitherto untouched social areas; in this way disintegration from the factors of caste and community can be regarded as successfully contained by democracy.

In October 1961 the Government of India set up a National Integration Council, thus providing further evidence of the Prime Minister's well known and indefatigable concern about disruptive tendencies. Whatever may be the contribution eventually offered from this high quarter to the solution of this problem, it is to be hoped that the remedies proposed will not prejudice the more unobtrusive and probably more effective work of national integration continuously performed by almost all parts of the present political system.

[1] I have been helped to this particular formulation by a contribution from L. I. and S. H. Rudolph whose reflections have been closely parallel to my own: 'The political role of India's caste associations' in *Pacific Affairs*, March 1960.

Chapter three

THE POLITICAL EVOLUTION OF PAKISTAN: A STUDY IN ANALYSIS

by Percival Spear

PAKISTAN differs from most other Asian states which attained independence after the Second World War in that it is not a merely colonial successor state but the portion of a colonial successor state. Other countries, like India, Burma, Ceylon and Indonesia inherited the whole apparatus of government, and had a continuity of thought and traditions. In the case of Vietnam the southern half retained the government machine and tradition, Western and local, which went with it, while the northern half took over a ready-made set of political values imported from abroad. In the case of Pakistan, it was torn from the colonial successor state, and launched with little administrative or official inheritance, and with none of the mystique of the old state whether of foreign or indigenous origin. It was born, in fact, of what was really a revolutionary movement within the state. Its strength had therefore to come from the inner dynamic or consciousness of that movement. Of all the new states of South and South-East Asia Pakistan was essentially the most revolutionary.

Pakistan began with a constitution tinkered from the 1935 constitution of India.[1] It has now no constitution at all, though one is shortly expected.[2] The Pakistan movement began as an appeal to the Muslim people of India; it proclaimed them a democratic nation. Today the people have received, after fourteen years, a constitution from the authoritarian hand of a

[1] Government of India Act 1935 and Independence of India Act 1947.
[2] Published in March 1962.

field-marshal. That transformation is an index, perhaps, not only of the difficulty of the task which faced the Pakistani leaders, but of the extent of the ideological vacuum with which they were confronted. Before independence it was common to concede the political possibility of a Pakistan state but to question its economic viability. In fact Pakistan managed unexpectedly well (though with ups and downs) in the economic sphere but has so far failed politically. The reason, I would suggest, is not merely a shortage of ideas — there have been plenty of these of a kind — but an inability to translate latent assumptions and pre-suppositions into institutional forms. So the theorists have indulged in what amounted to theoretical shadow boxing while cynics, one genus not in short supply in either part of the sub-continent, asserted that politics were nothing more than a game of competing vested interests in which every minister had his price.

Here we may pause to consider a moment the relationship between constitutional forms and the ideas behind them. It is easy to assume that the ideas implied by the terms of the consti-tution are related to the desires and values of the community as a whole. But this is not necessarily the case in Asian states where a minority has inherited Western political ideas and their corresponding institutions which have grown up in an entirely different social context while the majority, once largely inert but now perceptibly stirring and emergent, have quite another set of political values. Political forms which in the West were the natural expression of community feeling, in the East can easily be regarded as tactical aids in carrying on traditional struggles. Ideas became slogans and safeguards obstacles to be got round by skilful fictions. So the whole of political life can be reduced to unreality with its consequence of apathy and cynicism, the mental breeding grounds of dictatorship. Even in India, the most advanced of the successor states, signs of this can be seen in the faction fights within Congress which have been occurring in Uttar Pradesh, Madras and elsewhere. The inter-state con-ference in October 1961 was much concerned with the intrusion of caste issues into party politics, which was another way of describing the use of Western political forms for caste purposes. It is good that the danger should be perceived, but it is signifi-cant that such a problem should be discussed eleven years after we were told that caste had been abolished by the constitution of 1950. If this is true of India where the government is the expression of a widely based National Congress of nearly eighty years' standing, how much more so of Pakistan, which had no national organization worth the name before 1935 and now has none at all?

Constitutional forms and the ideas behind them are not then sufficient as guides in judging the political progress of a country like Pakistan. Nor are the proclaimed principles or programmes of political leaders any certain guide. We have to go further, and seek the presuppositions which exist among the large sections of the people whose will must ultimately prevail. The national expression of a people must rest on the forces which come up from below as well as on ideas which are handed out from above. It is an encouraging sign that the present rulers of Pakistan are aware of this but an indication of the defects of political judgment in the past is that it has taken fourteen years to reach this perception. In considering suitable political forms for Asian peoples it is no good discussing what institutions they ought to have on democratic theory; we have also to determine what types of institution the current beliefs of the people presuppose. This may be difficult for the Western or Westernized democrat to swallow. It is so easy to slide into the Cromwellian maxim 'What's for their good, not what pleases them', and to impose dictatorship in the name of freedom. In fact both terms may have quite different meanings to those familiar to the Westerner, thus making confusion worse confounded. This tendency to 'bend' Western forms towards traditional practice can be seen all over Asia, but again Indian examples may illustrate it. How much does 'freedom' mean to the Indian villager in a political sense? If the word and idea means anything at all, does it not in fact convey the notion of freedom from this world altogether? The Sanskrit *moksha* is not of this world. Again has not the Indian Prime Minister, in spite of his deep democratic convictions and meticulous regard to democratic form, tended to become an authoritarian ruler in the traditional manner? Is not the Parliament in effect his *durbar* where he listens to the people's petitions and the cabinet his inner council of *Lal Purdahris*, the counsellors who advise him in private. And are not the decisions which come forth universally regarded as his?

May he not be regarded in a real sense as the Akbar of the new régime (though some may whisper Aurangzeb)?

The Pakistan movement grew to strength on a diet of fear of Hindu domination in an independent India and of desire for an Islamic way of life. At once we must consider a qualification and ask if it did not also contain nostalgic memories of empire and a concealed desire to revive it, if only in an attenuated form. Support for this suggestion can be found in the work of Choudhri Rahmat Ali, which contains, as it seems to me, much implicit Muslim imperialism. Muslim memories of and pride in the Mughal empire were keen all over northern India. But in fact the Pakistan practical promoters (Rahmat Ali being a visionary) were Muslim rather than Mughal revivalists. In this they were following a trend started in the days of imperial decline in the eighteenth century by Shah Waliullah. The secular arm had failed; allegiance must be transferred from the agent of God to God himself. Salvation was to be found, not in worldly combat but in inward renewal. This was the doctrine of the scholars. The people clung longer to the empire and their last expression of attachment was the fleeting restoration of Bahadur Shah in 1857. Thereafter the people followed the scholars and placed their hopes on Islamic renewal. Sayyid Ahmad Khan supported the British because he thought that the Muslims would get a fairer deal from them than from the Hindus and would thus have a better chance of revival.

There was, indeed, a bridge between the new Hindus and the new Muslims in the shape of Western secularism and politics. It existed and its relics in India are the Muslim Nationalists; but it was too diaphanous to stand the weight of traditional mass emotion. In consequence, as soon as the prospect of Hindu participation in the government of India became appreciable, Muslim fears took shape in practical form. That moment was 1906 and the form that of the Muslim League. Henceforth the rhythm of increased Hindu power and increased Muslim distrust and demand for safeguards was almost continuous, only smothered for a few years by mass *Khilafat* emotion.

The positive element in the movement, as has been stated, was a desire for a free Islamic society. As popular fear of Hindu domination grew this desire turned into a demand for separation from Hindu society as the only means of preserving a cherished way of life. Here we meet a first dichotomy in the Pakistan consciousness. What did a free Islamic society mean to those who trumpeted it? To the masses, we may suggest, it meant traditional village life minus idolaters and their temples, their moneylenders, and (in the east) their landlords or *zamindars*. To the Westernized leaders it meant the prospect of office and authority, and something they rather vaguely called nationalism. But how nationalism could be attuned with Islamic theory or Western liberalism applied to a society of the faithful they were not at all clear. The most lucid view was that of the leader himself, who envisaged a secular state on the Turkish model. People would be citizens first and Muslims second. The Islamic religion would be maintained because it was the will of the people, not enforced because it was the will of God. The notion of *ijma* or consensus, much used by Sir Muhammad Iqbal in justifying his dynamic doctrine of Islam, could perhaps be used to cover this position. But Jinnah himself was much more a man for exercising *ijtihad* or private judgment than deferring to *ijma*. His position was such that people followed him blindly and discussion was stifled.

The act of partition and the agonies which followed it overwhelmed all other feelings for a time with a mass emotion of militancy. Many felt that they were crusaders for the faith who formerly had thought of Islam as at most a background to their lives. This was specially true for the masses, to whom Western political theories meant nothing. They had to have something to hold on to and what was there but Islam? It may be said that the hope of a Muslim secular state was killed in the civil war with the Sikhs in the Punjab, the massacres in the partition area and the great migrations. The overall effect was to strengthen anti-Hindu feeling and pro-Islamic sentiment. It should always be remembered that nearly every sixth person in Western Pakistan at this time was a refugee.

As Pakistan settled down it was gradually realized that there was no solid basis for the new state. There was an overriding fear; there were conflicting deep-seated feelings which were potential political forces; there were rival theories which divided and bemused the leaders. The real political evolution of Pakistan lies not in the adumbration of successive constitutions, but in the extent to which these mass feelings, instinctive beliefs and expatriate ideas have been welded into a coherent whole. No state is stable which has not got some generally shared beliefs and generally accepted ideas. Until that is achieved constitutions, however finely drawn, are mere lawyers' briefs, and political compromises, however skilfully balanced, mere tactical devices. Let us take each of these elements in turn.

The fear was of the Hindus, whom now we must call Indians. It derived from the deeply rooted aversion to the Hindu way of life, including the Arab horror of idolatry, but also containing much else. This aversion fed the fear of absorption into Hinduism as the prospect of Indian self-government increased. The aversion and fear were kindled into hate in the various pre-partition clashes and the post-partition massacres. This fear has been kept alive by the events of the past fourteen years. The superior strength of India is an obvious factor. There is the existence of extreme Hindu parties who insist that India should be a Hindu state. In their view the only resource for Muslims in the Indian state in order to demonstrate their loyalty would be to become Hindus.[1] Sardar Patel, the second man in India for some years after Gandhi's death, was credited with such views. Who is to tell whether the future, and perhaps the near future, may not bring the holders of such views into power? The broader fear of India as a potentially hostile state has been kept alive by the three controversies of evacuee property, canal waters and Kashmir. The first, though apparently the least important, was the most irritating to the largest number of people, and the second, while it lay dormant for years after the original incident in 1948, was a matter of life and death to the Punjab. Both these issues have now been settled, but in the case of the second much detailed work must be done before the fear it engendered can pass away. Kashmir remains, without apparent prospect of settlement. For the Pakistani it remains a *terra irredenta*, the symbol of Indian hypocrisy and hostility, the concrete evidence of the Indian danger. To this fear of India can now perhaps be added a second, that of Afghanistan. Relations have been frigid from the start and have now reached the pitch of a break in diplomatic relations and tribal raids into Pakistan.[2] But though the actual danger may be more real than that from India, the

---

[1] *The Times*, 5 October, 1961, p. 11, col. 1.
[2] 5 October, 1961. A *lashkar* of 500 repulsed.

awareness of it is less; it is nothing like, for example, the Swiss awareness of danger from their neighbours which induced members of three different racial groups to coalesce into a new nation.

Fear is a powerful force but it is not satisfactory as the sole ingredient of a national cement. It may lose its force or vanish altogether. We have next deep-seated feelings and passions, which though normally largely latent, are potential political forces of great strength. The first of these is Islamic sentiment. There is, both in East and West Pakistan, a deep attachment to what is conceived to be the Islamic way of life. But here a qualification must at once be made. This attachment to Islamic canons is everywhere mixed in degrees which are extremely difficult to ascertain, with attachment to tribal customs. The Pathan will kill his enemy in a blood feud in the name of Allah. Yet the blood feud is no part of the Islamic religion though it may be practised in some Islamic countries. Neither is the cutting off of a woman's nose for unfaithfulness. In East Pakistan there is attachment to much that is animistic or Hindu as well as to Islam. So while there is a basic Islamic sentiment which is a cohesive factor, there is also a customary element which is a divisive one. It shelters under the banner of Islam thus making it possible to oppose any change in the name of the Faith. The accusation of *kafir* or infidel is one of the most deadly smears which can be applied to anyone in Pakistan; the fear of it is a constant inhibitor of liberal opinion. The Islamic faith itself can be a divisive influence, for there are the sects and there are the heretics. In Pakistan the Shias are a minority too numerous to be considered insignificant; there are bodies like the followers of the Agha Khan and the Ahmadiyas or Qadianis which are definitely heretical. Anyone who has had to do with Muslim institutions knows how sectarian feelings can bedevil personal relationships even at the level of highly Westernized Muslims who would tell you that they did not believe in such things. In the Mughal empire these feelings found political expression in the Turani and Irani factions and such a division is not far below the surface of public life today. Orthodox rancour against the heterodox found classic expression in the Lahore riots of 1953 instigated by orthodox Sunni agitation against the Ahmadiyas. It was thought that if the

D

agitation had succeeded in reducing the Ahmadiyas to the status of second-class citizens, the dissident Shias were next on the list. For a few days medieval Islamic fanaticism found political expression.

A further deep-seated feeling and latent political force is that of provincialism. No doubt this is linked at the grass roots with tribalism, but as a conscious feeling it is separate and beyond it. It is a secular and robust emotion made up, no doubt, of many strands, emotive and economic as well as temperamental. But fundamentally it expresses a sense of difference, and has in it an element of what would be called in Europe nationalism. 'We are the people, and for that reason we are more precious than you.' The Panjabi, the Pathan, the Sindhi and the Bengali has each in his mind's eye 'an emerald isle, set in a silver sea, a demi-paradise'. It may not be politic to express the idea in public and specially in English, but it is a potent directive of thought and action nevertheless. This provincial or regional feeling has been a powerful overt factor in Pakistani public life and shows little sign of losing its vigour. The dissonance of East and West Pakistan is an obvious example. None of the West Pakistani regions appreciate the Bengali temperament and the Bengalis resent what they consider to be the interference of uncongenial outsiders in their affairs. The reconstitution of Pakistan as a twin-unit federal state was partly prompted by these disharmonies. In West Pakistan itself regional feeling is also strong. The Panjabi has a feeling of mission to manage the affairs of others who feel that the mission is misconceived. Here again the make-up of the attitude is complicated, but the element of temperament, the sense of national uniqueness, exists in each case. The formation of a single province of West Pakistan was designed to steam-roller these differences as well as to appease East Pakistan, but it may be doubted if it has succeeded. These feelings are something like Scottish and Welsh feelings within the British national complex, only much more pronounced. They will not be removed by ignoring them; they can only be integrated by adding a common loyalty beyond them.

What is this common loyalty to be? One, not yet mentioned, is that of nationalism in the Western sense, a loyalty to a group holding certain values in common. We know that such loyalties can not only exist but can transcend differences of race, language, religion and even residence. We know that the new nationalism is a fact in Asia. We know that no inhabitant of India two centuries ago called himself an Indian while today thousands or millions consider the term of prior significance to caste, tribal or regional distinctions. In Bengal the process by which half-secularized intellectuals created the image of Mother India in place of deities they had lost faith in during the nineteenth century can be traced in detail. Could not a similar process occur in Pakistan? Perhaps this was the Qaid-i-Azam's dream. But I think the answer is that while a few intellectuals have reached this position, the majority of the Western-educated classes as well as masses of the people have not. Pakistani nationalism as a ruling passion is at present a hope rather than a motivating force.

It is thus seen that both fear of India and adherence to Islam have proved insufficiently cohesive forces in the face of tribal custom and regional loyalties and temperaments. Nor does secular nationalism at present offer a way out. We now come to the 'rival theories which divided and bemused the leaders'. First among these are the theories of the West, which may broadly be called democratic. These theories were real to the few, shibboleths to the many. They were valuable rallying cries in the days of the British connexion, for they made a case within the mental framework of the British. They were also useful against the Hindus, because the Congress was using the same arguments against the British. Even if some League members had mental reservations about democracy they could not avow them in public. But while in the Congress ranks there were large numbers who generally accepted these principles, enough in fact to carry them into the constitution of 1950 and maintain them intact so far, amongst the proto-Pakistanis they were few indeed. Jinnah himself was a leading protagonist, but where were the others? They amounted to a very small number of Western-trained officials, both military and civil, and a still smaller number of men in public life. These men included lawyers and were conditioned to the Indo-British pattern of administration and public life. It was natural that they should perpetuate existing forms and elaborate them according to their knowledge; legal deep calling unto deep. It was equally natural that others

like the landlords of Sind and the Panjab should regard these
institutions as so many hoops to be gone through in the eternal
croquet game of office-hunting and jobbery.

Next come the views of the orthodox Islamic doctors of
Pakistan. A compendium of their views will be found in the
Report on the Panjab disturbances of 1953.[1] Their views are significant since it was men of similar ideas who had sufficient
influence to foment the riots. They vary greatly in detail, but
they all treat non-Muslims (including heretics) as second-class
citizens and they are all irreconcilable with secular democracy.
They also conflict radically with our ideas of modern society.
'All sculpture, playing of cards, portrait painting, photograph-
ing human beings, music, dancing, mixed acting, cinemas and
theatres will have to be closed.'[2] Modern Muslims, of course,
indulge in all these things but such views cannot be dismissed
merely as the ranting of medieval reactionaries. Their holders
have demonstrated that they possess a certain power over the
masses, though not as much as they would no doubt wish. They
cannot be dismissed from the reckoning of political forces. On
the other hand they have little hold over the classes.[3] Their
influence has been strong enough to label Pakistan an Islamic
state and to bring the idea of conformity to Islamic principles
into the constitution. It is strong against Western innovations as
in the sphere of women's rights and the position of non-
Muslims.

Between the secularists, who would like to override the orthodox, and the traditionalist *maulanas*, who regard the secularists as
kafirs, there come those who would like to express the principles
of an Islamic state in terms acceptable to Western-trained
intellectuals. In this way a bridge might be built between the
simple and devout traditionalist and the modern leaders of
society. Sayyid Ahmad Khan began this process when he
appealed to reason and nature as the two underlying principles
of Islam. Many old customs could be modified on the ground
that what was fitting in the time of the Prophet no longer
accorded with the needs of the day. From this stand grew up

[1] *Report on the Panjab Disturbances of 1953* (Lahore, 1954), pp. 209–32.
[2] ibid., p. 232.
[3] We cannot say 'none' when the manoeuvrings of Khwaja Nazim-ud-din as
Prime Minister are remembered.

what may loosely be termed a school of Muslim modernism.[1] But these views never spread to the masses and the Sayyid came to be regarded as too pro-British by a later generation. In the twentieth century came the poet-philosopher Iqbal who captured the imagination of the whole community with his Urdu and Persian verse, who gave the politicians the first hint of Pakistan in 1930, and who provided the intellectuals with a new interpretation of Islam as a revolutionary dynamic. Iqbal has been widely regarded as the inspirer of Pakistan as Jinnah was its external creator. His cult is pervasive and persistent. But in fact he has proved to be more a tower of refuge on the intellectual side of the river of division than a bridge to the other side. His writings,[2] which put Islam into a Nietzschean setting, made Islam respectable again to the Westernized intellectuals. But they made no impact on the orthodox *ulema*, nor shook their hold upon the masses. It is noteworthy that he preferred to write in Persian, the language of a rapidly diminishing élite amongst the Muslims.

We have here a group of theories, any one of which would be resisted by some part of the community if it was sought to be imposed by the others. Any apparent acceptance, as of Western constitutions, is a matter of expedience only, to be withdrawn as soon as an opportunity offers. Stable institutions cannot be built upon such intellectual will-o'-the-wisps. There have, however, emerged certain broad sentiments, which, if insufficient as a firm foundation for a modern state, are things which any Pakistan Solon must take into account. If not the binding cement of the nation they are at any rate ingredients which must not be omitted. The first of these is Islamic sentiment in its broadest sense and distinct from Islamic dogma or orthodoxy. A purely secular state would lack an essential root in present-day conditions. The second is anti-Indian sentiment, which may induce a degree of co-operation between groups not otherwise obtainable. On the negative side are regional and tribal feelings and prejudices which can neither be pandered to nor ignored with safety. To these emergent sentiments we may here add two more

[1] Sayyid Amir Ali, author of *The Spirit of Islam*, was perhaps its most distinguished exponent in India.
[2] Specially *Six Lectures on the Reconstruction of Religious Thought in Islam* (Lahore, 1930), and *The Secrets of the Self*, tr. R. A. Nicholson (London, 1920).

which will not have escaped the observant eye of our Pakistan
Solon. The first is the general regard for authority in Pakistan,
as in Muslim communities in general. Islam itself starts with
God, the supreme ruler of the world and the universe, the
supreme disposer of men and events. God is merciful and compassionate no doubt, but he is essentially One whose commands
must be obeyed. Fate, *kismet*, destiny, thoughts so prominent in
Muslim minds, are after all only expressions of the sovereignty
of God. Islam is the religion of submission to the will of God;
Muslims are resigned ones. This theological authoritarianism
was socially strengthened by the patriarchal societies in which
Islam grew up in Arabia. In India Islam was brought in by the
Turks and they too had a strong patriarchal tribal organization.
It is true of course that Islam has certain markedly democratic
features — the brotherhood of all believers, the absence of a
hierarchical church, the idea of consensus of opinion to settle
doctrine. The Prophet intended to carry the principle into the
political sphere by making the leadership of the community
elective. It is just here that we see the strength of the drag in the
other direction, for within fifty years the elective caliphate had
become an hereditary despotism. Since then the Islamic world
has been ruled by an assortment of sultans and emperors and
chiefs, almost all authoritarian. In the twentieth century democratic constitutions have shown a steady tendency to transmute
into military dictatorships. The modernized Pakistani resembles
the Frenchman in his abstract belief in democracy and practical
preference for authority. I have no doubt that the average
Pakistani has been instinctively more at ease under the
authoritarianism of a Jinnah or an Ayub Khan than under the
egalitarian parliamentarism that came between them.

The second sentiment still to be taken into account is the
nature of the Pakistani's attitude to the West. Few approve it
wholeheartedly and many condemn much that they see there.
The spell cast by the West on the Indian sub-continent during
the nineteenth century has been completely broken by two
world wars. Nevertheless there is a widespread desire, strong
enough to express itself in action, to get on to terms with or be
level with the West. It is strong enough to induce the acceptance
of sacrifices, of controls, of demands for greater efforts. Any
attempt to go back to the past would find in this sentiment a

formidable obstacle. We should have to look far to find historical parallels. Perhaps the attitude of the Mediterranean and East Asian worlds to Greek culture in the ancient world resembled it in some degree. But of the present fact there is no doubt. It is a force capable of great constructive use and perhaps the best guarantee for progress in the modern sense in Pakistan.

The history of Pakistan so far has been the result of the interplay of those forces on the organized groups which have sought to control the country's destiny. Any constitutional Solon must take into account these power-wielding groups as well as the intangible and impalpable currents of opinion. In Pakistan as it emerged into independence we may list them as follows. There were first the professional politicians, organized in the Muslim League and all protesting both democratic and Islamic convictions. History has shown that they were for the most part a collection of individuals seeking power rather than a group with any cohesion or strength of its own. A small number had genuine democratic convictions and sought to manipulate the forces at large to this end. They were too few to succeed and will generally be found to have had affiliations with the service groups to be mentioned below. Next may be listed the landlords. Though individuals frequently intrigued against each other, as a class they formed a cohesive power group and an important vested interest. Their power came from their wealth and their control over their tenants; their common object was to keep things as they were, Pakistan for the landlords. Their weakness was that, unlike the English landed interest of the nineteenth century, they had no larger views. Their epitome was the remarkable A. P. Khuhro of Sind. Significantly, the last constitutional Prime Minister was a landlord from the Panjab. Next come lawyers and the professional class generally, with the modern business community. These men possessed influence and prestige, for they were necessary to get things done and they possessed the 'know-how' of the West. But, apart from the men of business, they were more agents than promoters of action. They could draft constitutions they did not believe in and laws they could not enforce. As a class their weakness was that they had no background support, as the landlords had in their tenants. The businessmen had their wealth and skill, but like their brethren in India their outlook for the most part was limited.

Profit was too high in their scale of values. A much more united body were the *ulema*, the Muslim theologians. Their influence was distinct, but, as we have seen, divisive and negative. Their outlook was also limited by their lack of comprehension of the life flowing round them, so that they lived in a half-real world.

We now come to the services. The civil services, in which must be included that most competent body the old Provincial Civil Service, had certain traits and attitudes in common. They were all to some extent acquainted with Western techniques and ideas. They all had a developed sense of public duty, of loyalty to authority, of order and public decorum. They believed from experience in consultation, in representation as well as in the use of force as the ultimate sanction of authority. Their weakness was in the paucity of their numbers, especially from the old Indian Civil Service, and their lack of popular support to add to the general respect in which they were held. Their ranks supplied a governor-general, the first President of the Republic, two prime ministers and many cabinet ministers. After the civil came the military services. At first they kept rigidly out of politics in the British tradition but it was obvious from the beginning that here was a potential political force of great power. We should therefore note their characteristics as a political force. Though the pre-war Sandhurst-trained officers were few in number they imbibed that military tradition so thoroughly that, with some help from British colleagues after independence, they successfully indoctrinated the large number who took commissions during and after the Second World War. So much was this the case that it is not just a quip to describe the present régime as a Sandhurst *Raj*. The army believed in order, discipline, fair-play, clean administration and friendship with the people. It believed in its own hierarchy but its doctrine of non-intervention made it tolerant of others. Unlike many of the other groups it was markedly empirical in its outlook. But unlike the landlords its empiricism was not confined to its own interests; it recognized an image of the public good for which it was prepared to act.

If these were the underlying forces and ideas both cohesive and divisive, within Pakistani society, and these the organized groups through which any government had to act, the vagaries of Pakistani history cease to be surprising. The wonder is that a country lacking a general will strong enough to sustain an effective central authority has survived. In these circumstances it seems to me to be a straining of meaning to speak of the 'political evolution of Pakistan'. Evolution implies an end as well as a beginning, direction as well as movement. There was confusion in the beginning and so far what has been chiefly observable in events has been movements in various directions towards disparate ends. Manipulation has been more in evidence than creation. We cannot yet measure the political progress Pakistan has made in any direction; we can only, on the basis of an analysis of existing forces and a study of their interplay, suggest a possible line of evolution for the future.

The detailed political history of Pakistan is unhelpful for this purpose because so much of it amounts to the jostling of individuals for office. Nevertheless certain features can be discerned which may be helpful in suggesting future trends. The first is a tendency to give an authoritarian tinge to all institutions. Jinnah, a legalist to his fingertips, was also an autocrat by force of circumstances and by temperament. The Muslim League was conducted with impeccable democratic form and with iron autocracy. As Governor-General he used the emergency powers of the office to make himself the real ruler of the country.[1] The premiership never recovered from this invasion; after 1953 its prestige steadily declined and there were virtually two authorities striving for the seat of power. Since there was no parliament worth the name to sustain the premiers, the Cromwellian solution of army rule became inevitable. Secondly the power and limitations of medieval religious sentiment were revealed by the Panjab disturbances and its part in the constitutional discussions. The *ulema* could promote dissension and obstruct, but not dominate and halt. Again, Western democracy just would not work, however well drawn its forms, because not enough people believed in it, wanted it or understood it. On the other hand the surge towards Western innovation could not be stopped. Nothing gave the Pakistani more pride than the erection of jute mills in Chittagong, or irrigation dams in West Pakistan or the opening of the pipeline for natural gas from Sui. The legal

---

[1] See Khalid bin Sayeed's suggestive book, *Pakistan, the formative phase* (Karachi, 1960).

system has been continued intact without question, education is being largely expanded and still looks mainly to the West.

For an estimate of the political evolution of Pakistan in the future we have to consider the basic ideas of right and temperamental characteristics of the Pakistan people in relation to the actual power-wielding groups. For it is the former which in the long run will determine the success or failure of the latter. What, then, are the basic conditions which must be satisfied by any stable policy in Pakistan? What would be the elements of a politically viable Pakistan state? There must first be a strong authority embodying in some measure the leadership principle. The temperament of the people demands it. Their tradition and habit of thought confirms it. The authority must be visible and personal. From this angle I regard the present régime as a step forward, because it has provided just such an authority and is attempting to build up political institutions consonant with the character of the people. Its weakness is its present provisional character, and the narrow basis of its support. But there are conditions to this authoritarianism. It must not be absolutism like that of a Taimur in a conquered country. There must be consultation with representative interests, a modern version of the *durbar* system. A version of it is practised under cover of democratic forms in India today. This is necessary both to fit the character of the people and because no machinery exists by which a Pakistani government could coerce the majority of the people against their will for any length of time. One is reminded of the parallel of Tudor England.

The authority must consult the people, but it must not be merely a static rule. The desire 'to be level with the West' demands movement, development, change. It must be an organizing directing authority; otherwise it will be held to have let the country down in this essential particular and will lose all credit. A *nawabi* Pakistan would be no solution. Next comes the other factor which any Pakistan authority must take into account, the Islamic. The Islamic force or sentiment can be either wholly neglected or fully embraced only at peril. Neither the Akbar or the Aurangzeb method will do, for both would lead to division, bitterness and tumult. The state must be Islamic in general tone, that is to say, it must acknowledge the place of religion in national life and avoid head-on collisions with strongly held mass religious sentiment. On the other hand it must have a secular tinge also. The emphasis must be on citizenship rather than orthodoxy, involving complete toleration for all religions and all sects within Islam. Social reforms must not be shirked even though the approach to them may have to be indirect. Giving them up in deference to the medievalists would offend the get-level-with-the-West sentiment while pressing them on regardless of such feelings would find the government generally branded as *kafir* or infidel.

Granted that some such authority is necessary and that it must respect and express these sentiments, we have next to ask who is to support and sustain it. Since the death of Jinnah there has been no one in Pakistan who could take the part of an Ataturk in Turkey. The adulation of Liaqat (after his murder) betrayed the desire for such a figure rather than the consciousness of having lost one. It is obvious that the parliamentary system failed completely in the effort. Democratic legalism in Pakistani conditions is a broken reed. If we turn to the main national groups we do not get much more comfort. The civil services have some of the qualities and outlook needed. But they are still too few and in their higher ranks too little in touch with the people to receive sufficient support for the exercise of national power. Pakistan is making great efforts to build up her services but is still a long way from producing a modern mandarinate which could rule as well as administer. And would not such a mandarinate, if produced, tend to violate one of our canons of stability by tending to a static view of life?

The landlords, so prominent so far in Pakistani life, can be ruled out because of their obvious incompetence and lack of public spirit. They, more than anyone, precipitated the military coup; to their lack of wisdom is now being added by legislation a lack of power and resources. The lawyers are another unpromising basis of support for a dynamic authoritarian government. As a class they lack cohesion (except in the matter of briefs) and in the country they lack the respect and support necessary for the exercise of authority. Much the same can be said of the *ulema* though for different reasons. Even many of the orthodox would hesitate to follow their *fatwas* on any matter connected with the modern world and few of any persuasion would trust to their judgment of secular matters in general.

Then there is the business community, but this too lacks the prestige or resources to sustain a government. All these, if suitably handled, might be used as props of a régime, but none could provide the necessary firm foundation. The last of the groups is the one which wields power at present, the armed forces. To believe, however, that the army's action was salutary, and its administration so far in many ways constructive, is not to conclude that it should go on for ever. The army provides too narrow a base for the permanent exercise of authority and, it may be suggested, too small a head for permanent direction. An army *raj* could only be maintained at the price of the officers becoming politicians, and unless they unexpectedly became philosophers as well the danger of a descent to the Middle-Eastern type of military revolution would be great.

Conditions in Pakistan demand an élite to support a dynamic authority. It must be an organized one able to maintain itself and to gather strength from the whole society. It must have some roots in the past (unlike the old Bolshevik party) and some vision for the future (unlike the Chinese mandarinate or the modern *ulema*). It must be strong enough to hold in check regionalism, vested interests and medievalism while it gathers support for constructive measures of new life of its own. It must have an acceptable goal of endeavour pursued with such vigour and discretion that the active energies of the country will be gradually diverted from sectional, regional and dogmatic concerns into constructive national ones. For this task the existing groups are unfitted; it is therefore necessary to create such a group. It would appear that the present Government hopes to find a basis for authority by a system of indirect representation starting from the villages. Parties, however, will be banned on the ground that they will go back to their bad old ways of jobbery and corruption. But if parties are banned the result will be an assembly of notables who will express opinions on the *durbar* plan. The administration itself will have no solid support of its own. It would be Tudor government without the new nobility and squirarchy fed on monastic lands. I do not see stability coming out of a political vacuum. Yet the plan so far evolved has a feature which suggests a clue. The system seems to have a close resemblance to the successive tiers of Soviet people's councils. What it lacks is the Communist Party which in fact controls and animates the system. What should be the substitute in Pakistan? Given that an élite is necessary to animate the governmental authority, that political representative institutions require parties to give them life but that Pakistani parties have become shams, it follows that the élite must assume the form of a ruling party. The nature of the authority proposed rules out the rigorism of Russia and of China; the needs of the situation demand something more drastic and closely knit than the Congress Party in India. Once this suggestion is accepted we have to consider how to produce it and what should be its informing principle. The key to producing it, I would suggest, would be in the educational system. Such a system, without being anti-traditional, would be dynamic in character. From it young men and women would graduate into a party cadre who would largely but not exclusively man the state services. Such a party, if it were not merely to be a power machine and so fail miserably in its purpose, would require an ideology and an animating principle. The ideology must be propounded by Pakistanis themselves. For the animating principle a leaf might perhaps be taken out of the book of tradition at its Mughal chapter. The *mansabdari* system, though quite unsuitable for revival today, rested on a principle which is still very relevant. It was the principle of honour achieved through service to the state. Through it the ambitious of all communities could find a constructive way to fulfilment to the benefit of the whole community. Could not such a principle become the basis of a group which could revive and recreate the varied groups of Pakistan into a harmonious whole?

Chapter four

POLITICS IN CEYLON

by B. H. Farmer

UNTIL the elections of April 1956 and the communal disturbances that took place during the ensuing régime of Mr S. W. R. D. Bandaranaike, Ceylon was often held up as a model for colonial territories aspiring to self-government, a model which had made an easy, gradual and peaceful transition from Crown Colony status to complete independence and which appeared to be able to work parliamentary institutions in spite of the plural character of its population.[1]

As early as 1833, only eighteen years after the Kandyan kingdom had come under British rule, a Legislative Council was established in Ceylon as a result of agitation, not by Ceylonese, but by European businessmen. There were, however, nominated Ceylonese members *ab initio*. Throughout the nineteenth century the Legislative Council continued to function as nothing much more than a sounding-board for the Executive Council, which was composed, after the familiar pattern, entirely of officials. In 1912 elections to the Legislative Council were initiated, the European rural community, the European urban community, the Burghers, and the 'educated Ceylonese'

---

[1] Of the 8,098,637 people recorded by the 1953 census, 5,621,332 were Sinhalese, customarily divided into 3,464,126 'Low Country Sinhalese', who had borne the brunt of Western impact, and 2,157,206 Kandyan Sinhalese, whose traditional way of life had been less impaired; 908,705 were Ceylon Tamils, mainly in the north and east, and the descendants of immigrants from South India who had been long in the land; 984,327 were Indians, mainly Tamils, but all recent immigrants or their offspring; 468,146 were 'Moors', that is, Muslims; and there were also representatives of various minor groups.

each electing one member to a council of twenty-one in which there were also eleven officials and six nominated members to represent specific ethnic groups. The 'educated Ceylonese', it should be noted, included only those with a European-type education — perhaps 4 per cent of the population; their first elected member was Sir Ponnambalam Ramanathan, a Ceylon Tamil.

The way in which the colonial Government handled the religious riots between Buddhists and Muslims in 1915 caused a wave of feeling to run through the country and gave popular backing to what had previously been a nationalist movement limited to the European-educated middle class; it also gave some of the budding nationalist leaders a taste of prison, which they were able in the fullness of time to turn to political advantage. The spear-head of the attack which eventually broke through to responsible self-government was formed by Sir Ponnambalam Arunachalam and Sir James Peiris, a member of the Karāva caste[1] and an Anglican, who had had a distinguished career at St John's College, Cambridge. Both had contacts with Indian nationalism (notably through G. K. Gokhale), both were conservative by nature, and neither, it should be noted, were Buddhists or members of the majority Sinhalese Goyigama caste.[2] They were, however, aided and abetted by Sinhalese Goyigama Buddhists like D. R. Wijewardene, a distinguished journalist, D. B. Jayatilaka, and the brothers F. R. and D. S. Senanayake (the last-mentioned, of course, became Ceylon's first Prime Minister). Men like these were prominent in the Ceylon National Congress, which was formed in 1919, and in agitation for political change in the years that followed.

In 1921 the Legislative Council was expanded in size; although the position of the elected members was stronger in the new Council they were still in a minority. But, whereas before 1920 the Tamils had had as many seats as the Sinhalese, they now held only three seats to the thirteen held by the majority

[1] The Karāva were originally a caste of fishers, some of whose members rose to affluence through taking to commerce in Portuguese times and later. See Bryce Ryan, *Caste in Modern Ceylon* (Rutgers University Press, 1953), especially pp. 103–7.

[2] The Goyigama caste of cultivators traditionally comes at the top of the caste hierarchy in Sinhalese society; see Bryce Ryan, op. cit., especially pp. 95–103.

community; communal dissension began to darken the scene, and the Tamils left the National Congress.

In 1923 the Council was again enlarged, and for the first time elected members were in a majority; but they were elected on a restricted franchise, the Council in which they sat had no executive functions, and there was still provision for nominated members to represent minority communities.

In 1927–8 the Donoughmore Commission visited Ceylon and made far-reaching constitutional proposals, most of which came into force in 1931 in the shape of the 'Donoughmore Constitution'. This provided for fifty territorially-elected members and twelve members nominated to represent interests otherwise unrepresented. For the first time in an Asian colony, universal adult franchise was instituted (the Commission had proposed it for men only 'to induce Ceylonese leaders to listen more attentively to the needs of the populace';[1] but Sidney Webb, then Colonial Secretary, extended the vote to women). More important still, perhaps, the State Council (as the new largely-elected chamber was called) had executive as well as legislative and advisory functions. These were carried out under a curious arrangement which is said to owe something to the committee system of the London County Council, and which was the Commissioners' response to the need, as they saw it, to adapt the constitution to the peculiarities of the Ceylon scene (notably the virtual absence of political parties) and to provide executive experience for Ceylonese before they could be conceded the fully responsible government demanded by the Ceylon National Congress. The arrangement in question was the division of the full State Council into 'Executive Committees' each dealing with such subjects as home affairs and agriculture. Each committee elected a chairman, who bore the title 'Minister'. Certain subjects (external affairs, finance and justice) were reserved to officials, known as Officers of State, who, with the elected Ministers, formed the 'Board of Ministers'. The Governor retained powers of veto.

Such was the Donoughmore Constitution. This is no place for an appraisal of its merits and defects, about both of which

[1] W. Howard Wriggins, *Ceylon: Dilemmas of a New Nation* (Princeton University Press, 1960), p. 86.

much has been said already.[1] It is enough to say that, although it was castigated by the nationalists because it fell short of fully responsible government, by the minorities because it gave them less rather than more representation, and by successive Governors for a number of reasons (including its tendency to encourage bargaining between committees for available revenue instead of firm central direction), recent observers have been a little more ready to see it as a useful framework within which Ceylonese politicians received a thorough, if somewhat parochial, training, and within which considerable economic and social changes were accomplished.[2] It is worth remembering, too, that it was the Donoughmore Constitution that provided the framework within which Ceylonese ministers handled, with considerable skill, the complexities of the wartime situation.

Two further points must be made. The first is that under the Donoughmore Constitution power came to reside more and more with the Sinhalese in general and with the Goyigama in particular. After 1936 the elected members of the Board of Ministers included for some years not a single representative of a minority community; and the Board fell more and more under the leadership, able, sometimes inspired, but nevertheless narrow-based socially, of D. S. Senanayake, his family, and his associates (who were mostly, like him, members of the Goyigama caste); though it is only fair to add that Senanayake was no communalist, and the vision of a united nation never left him. Now, in the days of Peiris and Arunachalam it may well have seemed that there was in process of formation a governing élite, united by education, by the English language and by Western political ideas, and undivided significantly by the frontiers of community and caste that ran through it. Indeed, many observers of the Ceylon scene before 1956 tended to underestimate the potential magnitude of communal tensions and to ignore caste as a political factor because they knew only the Western-oriented Ceylonese middle-class of Colombo, in which ethnic origin seemed not to obtrude and caste not to matter. But both have always been more important than they

[1] See, for example, S. Namasivayam, *The Legislatures of Ceylon, 1928–1948* (London, 1950); I. D. S. Weerawardena, *Government and Politics in Ceylon (1931–1946)* (Colombo, 1951); and Wriggins, op. cit., especially pp. 85–90.

[2] Wriggins, op. cit., pp. 88–9.

seemed; it is significant, for instance, that inter-community and inter-caste marriages were and are very few and far between. Given, then, the underlying disunity of the élite and the majority position of the Goyigama in the Sinhalese community at large, it is not surprising that the shift of power to the Goyigama members of the élite should have taken place, especially with the advent of the adult suffrage in 1931; or that, given the family-centred nature of Sinhalese society, D. S. Senanayake should have brought other members of his own family into politics with him.

The second point is that while the Donoughmore Commissioners were right in thinking that there was virtually no party system in the Ceylon of 1927–8 (for the Ceylon National Congress was, like its Indian counterpart, a national movement, not a party), the seeds of the party system were nonetheless being sown. Intercommunity tensions were themselves to produce parties, albeit on a communal basis; while in the late 1920's men soon to be prominent as the leaders of parties on Ceylon's fissiparous Left were learning their Marxism, Philip Gunawardena in the United States, N. M. Perera in London.

The Donoughmore Constitution survived the war years, though the State Council frequently agitated for further reform, particularly in the direction of a Westminster-type parliament and cabinet (anything else seemed to be something less than fully responsible government). In 1944 a commission under Lord Soulbury visited Ceylon. Once again the communal fissions concealed beneath the apparently seamless garment of Colombo middle-class society were laid bare, notably in the unaccepted Tamil proposal that to prevent Sinhalese domination the minorities together should control half the seats in the proposed House. The Soulbury Commission accepted proposals for a representative chamber and cabinet, but added a second chamber, half of its members to be elected by the Lower House, the other half to be nominated by the Governor-General. So, in May 1947, Ceylon came to have a House of Representatives with members elected on a territorial basis (but with constituencies so delimited as to give the minorities rather more than their share of the seats); a cabinet under a prime minister responsible to the House; and a governor-general who retained control of external affairs and defence.

But events overtook the Soulbury Constitution. For when independence was given to India and to Pakistan in 1947 it could not long be denied to Ceylon, which accordingly became an independent member of the British Commonwealth on 4 February, 1948. However, the essential features of the House of Representatives, Senate and Cabinet envisaged by Lord Soulbury and his colleagues continued into the era of independence, and a governor-general has remained as head of state.

During the first eight years of independence the United National Party (UNP) dominated the scene.[1] The UNP was founded by D. S. Senanayake in 1945-6, and in its early days embodied his ideal of a united Ceylon. It brought together his Sinhalese associates from the State Council and from the Ceylon National Congress, a number of Ceylon Tamils, the Ceylon Muslim League, and, to begin with, S. W. R. D. Bandaranaike's *Sinhala Maha Sabha*;[2] in fact, almost all elements except the Indian Tamils and the parties of the Left; in 1948 even G. G. Ponnambalam, the leader of the Tamil Congress Party, joined Mr Senanayake's cabinet. All of the leaders, it should be noted, were Western-educated and upper middle-class. The UNP easily won the elections of 1947 and 1952; and diplomatic and other circles confidently expected it to win the election of April 1956, though, it was prophesied, with a reduced majority.

In the event it limped back to the House with only eight seats, decisively defeated by Mr Bandaranaike's *Mahajana Eksath Peramuna*[3] (MEP) (Bandaranaike had resigned from D. S. Senanayake's Government in 1951). The MEP won a total of no less than fifty-one seats; though, as often happens, the swing in votes was nowhere near as marked: 1,046,362 for the MEP, 738,551 for the UNP.

What had happened to the proud UNP? And what, with the communal disorders of ensuing years, had happened to D. S. Senanayake's vision of a united Ceylon? In the first place, with Senanayake's tragic death in 1952 the party lacked the force of his shrewd leadership and the incalculable asset of his prestige in

---

[1] It is significant that though the party now has a Sinhalese title (*Eksath Jatika Paksha*), it has always been the 'UNP' (in English) even to those who make political speeches in Sinhalese.

[2] Again significantly, a party with a Sinhalese name meaning 'Great Sinhalese Assembly'.

[3] 'People's United Front.'

the country. Secondly, before his death his party had already been weakened by the defection of Mr Bandaranaike (which was due partly at any rate to family rivalries); and after his death came internal wrangles during the tenure of his successors in office, his son, Dudley Senanayake, and his nephew, Sir John Kotelawala. When Dudley Senanayake resigned not only from the premiership but also from the party, the UNP lost the magic appeal of the Senanayake name: and Kotelawala, for all his brisk administrative competence, was less trusted, less astute, and less sensitive to changes that were abroad in the land; and more easily branded as an alien to Sinhalese and Buddhist traditions and aspirations.

Thirdly, Bandaranaike, a highly-skilled politician, had made two important sets of dispositions, trading on the realization among the many small groups and parties hostile to the UNP that none of them singly could hope to defeat the party that had won independence and that was heir to the Senanayake legend. Bandaranaike formed a coalition of elements so disparate that once he was in power factional fighting became impossible to contain: but a coalition, nevertheless, that held together for the purpose of the election. It consisted of his own SLFP (*Sri Lanka Freedom Party*),[1] successor to the *Sinhala Maha Sabha*; which provided by far the largest element; the VLSSP (*Viplavakari Lanka Sama Samaja Party*)[2] the more extreme of Ceylon's two Trotskyite parties, whose leader was Philip Gunawardena; the *Bhasa Peramuna*[3] of Mr W. Dahanayake; and other smaller groups. Bandaranaike's second move was to engineer a 'no contest pact' with other opposition groups unwilling for one reason or another to join his coalition. Under the terms of this 'pact' the MEP, the Communist Party and the NLSSP (*Nava Lanka Sama Samaja* Party)[4] agreed not to fight each other in any constituency, in order to avoid splitting the anti-UNP vote. Bandaranaike thus succeeded in lining up against the UNP almost all the other parties in the Ceylon of 1956, except the Tamil parties.

That he was able to do so reflects, of course, the unpopularity

---

[1] Sri Lanka is the Sinhalese name for Ceylon. Note the combination of Sinhalese and English in the party title.

[2] 'Revolutionary Ceylon Socialist Party.'   [3] 'Language Party.'

[4] 'New Ceylon Socialist Party': a second and less extreme Trotskyite group.

that had accumulated around the UNP. This unpopularity was partly a consequence of having been too long in power (for, after all, though the UNP itself was at the time only ten years old, its dominant families and personalities had been prominent in the State Council since 1931). There is no doubt that the UNP as a group had become lethargic, with few signs of a clearly thought-out policy at home or abroad. And just before the election the Colombo air, at any rate, was full of allegations of jobbery, corruption, interference with the judiciary, and improper accretion and use of party funds. The mass of the people of Ceylon, moreover, did not forget that Dudley Senanayake's UNP Government had, at a time of economic crisis in 1953, removed the subsidy on rice, so that its price in many places multiplied threefold overnight.[1] (The ensuing *hartal* led directly to the resignation of Dudley Senanayake. Mr Bandaranaike, when returned to power in 1956, replaced the subsidies, which have remained a drag on the economy ever since.)

In the Sinhalese rural districts something much more fundamental and more hostile to the UNP was abroad; Bandaranaike had very good links with the country and was astute enough to understand that what was going on was a complex social movement heavy with political implications. This movement had its roots partly in a revival of Buddhism (in turn partly a result of the celebration of *Buddha Jayanthi* — the 2500th anniversary of the Buddha's attainment of *nirvana*); partly in a resurgence of traditional Sinhalese culture in reaction against the West (one facet of which was agitation in favour of Sinhalese as the national language); partly in the economic frustration of a group of vernacular-educated Sinhalese whose lack of a Western education in a country still dominated by a Western-educated élite was a real or imagined reason for their disabilities. The hostility of this group, moreover, was by no means reserved for the Western-educated. Much of it also turned in the direction of the Ceylon Tamils who, it was alleged, held far more than a proportionate share of jobs in government service and so kept Sinhalese out (in point of fact, this is only markedly true of certain departments such as the Public Works Department and the railway; elsewhere what disproportion there is more or less accurately reflects the superior educational standards and more

[1] One-fifth of the Government's total revenue was going on food subsidies.

industrious nature of the Ceylon Tamil community). The group in question, it should be said, consisted of such people as village moneylenders and shopkeepers (*mudalalis*), vernacular school-masters,indigenous('ayurvedic')physicians, and Buddhist priests.

In the village movement at whose head Bandaranaike managed to place himself the religious, cultural, nationalistic and economic strands were intertwined. For instance, Bud-dhism was one of the main characteristics distinguishing village Sinhalese society from the urban middle-class and the Tamils; moreover, the sensitivity of the Sinhalese to their distinctiveness is all the greater because, although in a majority in their own island, they feel themselves to be a minority in the Indian sub-continent as a whole, and, in particular, in the Tamil-dominated south of that sub-continent. Expressions of sympathy with the Ceylon Tamils uttered by the Swatantra and other Indian parties do nothing to allay Sinhalese anxiety.

Again, language agitation arising from a feeling of economic frustration was reinforced by religion, since many Buddhist priests are drawn from just that stratum in Sinhalese society which suffers, or feels that it suffers, economic frustration; and since Sinhalese tends to be, as the vernacular and as the lineal descendant of Pali, the language of Buddhism. Backward-looking romantic nationalism reinforced feeling not only against the modernized, Westernized élite but also anti-Tamil feeling, since some of the great heroes of old won their laurels against Tamil invaders; while the Buddhist priesthood (or some mem-bers of it) also tended to look back to the days of the ancient Sinhalese kings as days when Buddhism held an honoured place in the land and when the priesthood wielded a power that had been lost during the 'four hundred years of foreign rule'. Those who believe that a sheer desire for power was a main motive among politically-active Buddhists find that writers like W. Howard Wriggins tend to idealize and to intellectualize the role of the priesthood.[1]

Bandaranaike and his advisers, then, computed the direction and strength of some at least of the complex system of forces that were creating a second wave of nationalism in the Sinhalese villages; hence the importance in his election campaign of the proposal to 'restore' Buddhism, to stimulate Sinhalese culture,

[1] Wriggins, op. cit.

and to declare Sinhalese the sole 'national language' (a policy to which the UNP was converted too late for their sincerity to go unquestioned). And since the MEP platform had to appeal to Leftists as well, it also contained planks labelled 'termination of military agreements with the imperialists' and 'nationalization of foreign-owned estates'; while Mr Bandaranaike's rather vague socialism also had its own appeal. His own impeccably aristocratic family background won favour with conservative Goyigama; while his associates of other castes brought their own local harvests of votes.

Given hindsight wisdom, it is not surprising that Mr Bandaranaike was swept into power; in fact, what is more surprising is the number of votes cast for the UNP. Nor is it surprising that his improbable coalition soon ran into difficulties: for instance, Leftist ministers slated their Right-wing cabinet colleagues in public and got back as good as they gave. The Minister of Agriculture, a Trotskyite, pursued a policy in some respects diametrically opposed to that of the Right-wing Minister of Lands. In the end, tensions grew beyond control and the Leftists were removed from the cabinet. Shortly afterwards, but not *post hoc propter hoc* (or so it seems), Bandaranaike was assassinated by a Buddhist priest, as the culmination of a conspiracy involving another priest and several laymen.

Meanwhile, as is well known, the excitement created by discussion of the language issue and its related problems led in 1956 and again in 1958 to extremely ugly and shameful communal rioting;[1] and Ceylon became used to 'Government by emergency' and to a situation in which much day-to-day executive power rested in the hands of the Governor-General, Sir Oliver Goonetilleke.

Much might be said about the Bandaranaike régime. It was certainly opportunist, seeking out and magnifying tensions in village society only to find that these tensions, once laid bare, were extraordinarily hard to absorb or to sublimate. Bandaranaike nevertheless had enough of the apparent socialist in him to appeal to the common man and to make him feel, for the first time, the Government was '*ape anduwa*', '*our* Government'; and to make it possible for there to grow up about him after his death a legend as of a martyred friend of the people. But for the

[1] See Tarzie Vittachi, *Emergency '58* (London, 1958).

most part his Government was so preoccupied with the linguistic, cultural and religious issues that it had exploited and
assiduously cultivated, and with the inevitable crop of rioting
and disorder, that it had but little time to address itself seriously
to the grave economic problems of an under-developed country
with a narrow-based colonial-style economy and a population
growing by not far short of 3 per cent per annum. It is to
Bandaranaike's credit, however, that it was during his time that
a ten-year plan, wise in general strategy, though optimistic in
detail, was drawn up by the National Planning Council that he
had organized.[1] Philip Gunawardena, for all his political fire-
raising, had a reputation amongst the officers of the Department
of Agriculture for research-mindedness, which is more than can
be said of some of his predecessors and successors; and other
ministers, too, showed a concern for serious economic affairs.

When Bandaranaike was assassinated after the first irruption
of murderous violence into Ceylon politics, a caretaker government was formed under W. Dahanayake, who had led the
Bhasa Peramuna at the time of the 1956 elections. His brief rule
was not a particularly happy one. The air was full of rumours of
an alleged conspiracy behind the assassination, and of an alleged
'fascist plot'; and for much of the time real power seems to have
been wielded by the Governor-General.

In March 1960 came a general election, this time to an enlarged House of 151 elected members. The upshot is worth
recording and was as follows:

Party	Seats	Votes
United National Party	50	839,636
Sri Lanka Freedom Party	46	632,378
Tamil Federal Party	15	156,948
NLSSP	10	301,640
MEP	10	296,330
Ceylon Democratic Party	4	119,773
Communist Party	3	123,655
Independents and others	13	396,511

(It should be noted that the MEP in this context means, not the
coalition previously led by Bandaranaike and ruptured not very
long before his assassination, but the Trotskyite group, formerly

[1] *The Ten-year Plan* (Colombo, 1959); for a critical review see B. H. Farmer, 'The
Ceylon Ten-Year Plan, 1959–68', *Pacific Viewpoint*, 2 (1961), 123–36.

VLSSP, under Philip Gunawardena. The 'Ceylon Democratic Party' was led by 'caretaker' Prime Minister, Dahanayake, who lost his seat to a UNP candidate.)

The UNP emerged, it will be seen, as the strongest single party and with a clear 100,000 votes more than four years earlier. The sum of the votes cast for the SLFP, for the MEP, and for Dahanayake's 'Ceylon Democratic Party' was almost exactly the total cast in 1956 for Bandaranaike's coalition, which had now, of course, fragmented into these three main parts. Clearly, then, there had been no mass flight of the supporters of Bandaranaike. It is hard to know exactly what was happening in the villages during those troubled times, but the success of the UNP relative to the SLFP is probably to be accounted for by the loss of the former's allies, by some slight reaction from the disorder of the last four years towards the 'party of law and order', and perhaps by some revulsion against political Buddhist priests consequent on the revelation of the part played by two of their number in the assassination. If this is so, then clearly no strong social tides had set in favour of the UNP. Moreover, the Bandaranaike legend, assiduously fostered by his political heirs in the SLFP and by their exploitation of his widow (who addressed a large number of meetings in the cause), did much to win votes for the SLFP.

Because the three Marxist parties between them won only one more seat in the new, enlarged House than they had held in the old House, the election was widely interpreted in the British Press and elsewhere as a decisive defeat for the Left. This was to read false Western analogies into Ceylon politics. The truth appears to be that because the Communist Party and the NLSSP had held out for parity between the Sinhalese and Tamil languages, they failed to hold their own relative to other parties. In fact, so roused is feeling on the language issue in Sinhalese areas today that to raise a voice in favour of parity outside traditionally Marxist constituencies (in many of which support is in any case personal rather than ideological) is to court disaster. It is significant in this connexion that the only Marxist party to register gains in 1960, in spite of its part in the strife inside Bandaranaike's cabinet, was Philip Gunawardena's MEP (formerly the VLSSP) whose policy was 'Sinhalese only'. It is also indicative of the dominance of the communal motives in contemporary Ceylon politics that the three or four small Tamil parties that sent members to the House in 1956 have disappeared in favour of the Federal Party, which emerged in 1960 as the sole champion of the Tamils under the banner of separatism; with ten seats it was, equally with the MEP, the fourth strongest party in the House. It had won only two seats in 1951.

In the event, and allegedly because the SLFP and MEP were disposed to re-form their erstwhile coalition, Dudley Senanayake agreed to form a UNP Government. Clearly, however, he was in a precarious position; for, with Independents and Nominated Members, he could at most command sixty-four seats in the House, compared with seventy-five that could be mustered by the SLFP, the Marxist parties, and other smaller groups in opposition. The Tamil Federalists were, or rather might have been, in a position to hold the balance of the House; and, it might be thought, could have exacted concessions for the Tamils on the language issue in return for their support. But the truth is that no Sinhalese politician today can afford, if he has his eye on the next election, to make many such concessions. In the absence of Federalist support, Mr Senanayake's Government were very soon defeated: in fact on the Opposition amendment to the address of thanks for the Governor-General's speech. Could he have survived a few months he might have followed Mr Diefenbaker's example and gone to the country at a time of his own choosing, and he might well then have returned with more seats and even a working majority. For while social forces in the countryside would have continued to work strongly in favour of the SLFP, Mrs Bandaranaike might well have proved a wasting asset.

With the fall of Dudley Senanayake's Government, fresh elections were held in July, 1960. The results were:

Party	Seats
Sri Lanka Freedom Party	75
United National Party	30
Federal Party	16
NLSSP	12
Communist Party	4
MEP	3
Independents and Others	11

The SLFP thus won easily, partly through another no-contest pact, but relying on the same forces as in 1956, capitalizing on the Bandaranaike legend, and, indeed, persuading Mrs Bandaranaike to see herself as prime minister if the SLFP won the election (though she was not at that time a member of either the House of Representatives or the Senate). The SLFP, moreover, with its satellite ring of Independents and Nominated Members, was able to command an absolute majority in the House which it has retained up to the time of writing. The UNP was once more eclipsed, though not so near-totally as in 1956. A surprise feature was the decline in the fortunes of the MEP, in spite of its 'Sinhalese only' policy; but most of its losses were to the SLFP, and were therefore presumably not indicative of a popular change of heart over communal issues.

Mrs Bandaranaike was sworn in as Prime Minister on 20 July, 1960 and, not possessing a seat in the House, was given one in the Senate. She appears to lean heavily on Felix Dias Bandaranaike, a young nephew of the assassinated Prime Minister, who has become Minister of Finance, who is said to be impatient of parliamentary procedures and who, as an Anglican, has to demonstrate that he is more Buddhist than the Buddhists if his Christianity is not to count against him. But his sway in the cabinet is not unchallenged.

Mrs Bandaranaike's Government, assured of a parliamentary majority, free from the extreme internal dissension that wrecked her husband's cabinet, has pushed ahead with various measures designed to assure the position of Buddhism (for example, by taking over denominational schools) and of Sinhalese as the national language. Language policy not unnaturally has drawn forth a reaction from the Tamils who, in March 1961, organized *satyagraha* (passive civil disobedience) in Jaffna and elsewhere. There was even, for a short time, a separate Tamil-organized postal service. These and other Tamil moves were conceived by the Government as a challenge that could not be ignored; soon there came the proclamation of a state of emergency, Press censorship, the establishment of what amounted to military rule, and the detention of all Federal Party M.P.s, together with other prominent Tamils. At times the Government's measures seemed not far removed from panic, perhaps from fear of a recurrence of the riots of 1958, perhaps for fear of joint action as between Ceylon Tamils and other (Indian) Tamils in Ceylon, perhaps because the activity of Dravidian nationalist parties in South India emphasized the risk of the development of a pan-Tamil movement and hence heightened Sinhalese awareness of minority status within the Indian sub-continent.

Fortunately, and perhaps as a result of horror at the riots of 1958, attempts at rabble-rousing amongst the Sinhalese failed and most of the country outside the Northern and Eastern Provinces remained relatively calm (though there was one moment of acute fear and tension in April 1961, when it looked as though the Indian Tamils on the estates would make common cause with the Ceylon Tamils).

At the time of writing (early in January 1962), 'Government by emergency' continues but public attention has become focused on the country's economic and labour problems. During the last year or so there has been mounting concern in responsible circles over difficulties in export markets and with balance of payments problems; over a monumental budget deficit; over the ever-rising cost of living; and over the failure of development to keep pace with the country's needs. The political consequences are that the SLFP Government has lost the confidence of many of its supporters amongst the urban workers and the urban middle-class[1]; that a wave of strikes has added to its difficulties; and that the parties of the Left have grown in confidence.

THE QUALITY OF CEYLONESE NATIONALISM

As one looks around the other newly-independent countries of South and South-East Asia, one sees nothing quite like Ceylonese nationalism — or so it appears. True, the nationalism of early days, if it can be called such, readily finds parallels; for the quiet desire of Sir James Peiris and his generation for more say in the government of their country, without any specific aspiration towards independence, can be matched in India and elsewhere. As has been seen, national feeling was strengthened by the riots of 1915. Nevertheless, in the thirty years that followed Ceylon slid quietly and quite unviolently towards the

---

[1] An attempted *coup* by police and military took place on 27 January 1962 and in part reflected middle-class discontent.

independence that it finally achieved in 1948 — yet with so little apparent change that, but for the bunting and the speeches, the ordinary man would be forgiven for thinking that nothing important had happened. Then, after nine years of continued gradualness, came the election of 1956 and a period of violence and rapid change borne in on a second wave of nationalism generated from a mixture of Buddhism, Sinhalese communalism, traditionalism, and economic and political frustration. It is the existence, strength and character of this second wave of nationalism, associated with the rise to political power of a new group in Sinhalese society, and the contrast between it and the earlier, gentler wave, that seems to constitute the uniqueness of the Ceylon situation.

Why has Ceylon witnessed two such different and contrasting waves of nationalism? One stands too near the events to be sure, but it is possible to suggest a number of confluent reasons. In the first place, it is perhaps possible to see in the contrasting Indian situation the advantages that accrue from the confluence rather than the diffluence of tradition-oriented and Western-oriented nationalism: Gandhi and Nehru worked together; but Ceylon has lacked leaders with the vision of a Gandhi and the intellectual grasp of a Nehru, and the two traditions have conflicted and not coalesced. In the second place, that this was so seems to owe a great deal to the fact, often commented upon in other contexts, that the Westernized élite in Ceylon was *very* Westernized, at least in a number of important and visible characteristics. The contrast between trouser and sarong was, on the whole, much stronger than that between trouser and *dhoti*. This was particularly so at a time when the trousers were being worn by Sir John Kotelawala, whose insensitivity to village feeling was remarkable. Moreover, a number of factors have tended to bring economic frustrations among sarong-wearers to the boil in recent years; 'the passing of the frontier', due to the exhaustion of easily-colonized Wet Zone land; population pressure; the apparent beginnings of a decline in *per capita* incomes; and the growth of a large class of educated unemployed. Perhaps there is something of a parallel in the situation in Kerala.

In the third place, it may well be that the very gentleness and ease of the transition to independence sowed the seeds of future trouble. Had the Ceylonese been forced to fight the British more vigorously, it is conceivable that they would have closed their ranks, at least where the gap between urban élite and villager was concerned; though it is doubtful whether communal harmony would have resulted. And finally, there is the fact that by 1956 Ceylon had seen twenty-five years of universal suffrage, and people were growing more confident of the power of the ballot box.

The régime of Tunku Abdul Rahman in Malaya seems to parallel, in some respects at least, that of D. S. Senanayake; but no 'second-wave nationalism' has risen to shake his position — indeed, Muslim reaction in Malaya, which might be thought to correspond to Buddhist reaction in Ceylon, seems if anything on the wane. Perhaps a lesser degree of political sophistication is one of the factors that have hitherto held back a second wave of nationalism in Malaya.

THE QUALITY OF CEYLONESE DEMOCRACY

But all this must not be taken to mean that political society in Ceylon is sophisticated relative to, say, that of Western Europe or the United States. What *does* 'democracy' mean in Ceylon; and how widely diffused are political interest and power?

There is no doubt that the Ceylonese as a whole are now convinced that governments really can be changed by means of general elections. It is not surprising that in 1956, when it was clear that the UNP was losing the election, it was doubted whether Kotelawala would resign; or that similar doubts were expressed in respect of Dahanayake in 1960. For, quite apart from what was known of the personalities of these two leaders, voluntary renunciation of power is not in the Asian tradition; nor, in spite of efforts to show that democracy in Asian countries has deep roots in the *gansabha* and similar village institutions, is there really any tradition of shifts in power accomplished by electoral means. But, with demonstrations in 1956 and 1960 that prime ministers really do resign when defeated at the polls, confidence in the ballot box has grown.

Moreover, Ceylon, with thirty years of universal suffrage behind it, has shown itself fully capable of organizing and conducting quiet, orderly elections, relatively free from intimidation, thuggery and the grosser forms of influence.

But that is not to say that in Ceylon today votes cast at a general election are universally the result of completely free decisions reached by each of the host of individuals who collectively form the electors; or that political power resides in the masses. '*Ape anduwa*', they may have said, claiming the Bandaranaike Government in 1956; 'People's Parties' there may be; interest in Parliament and in politics there certainly is amongst many groups in Colombo. But the truth is that in many but not all rural areas (and for that matter in many urban constituencies as well), the popular grasp of most political issues is generally feeble,[1] though popular emotions are all too easily roused on religious and communal issues, and the villager is not without a grasp of what is in his own local interest. There is very little doubt that over much of the country real political power rests with the group of Buddhist priests, village merchants and moneylenders, ayurvedic physicians and Sinhalese school-masters who have already been described. It is people like this who have insinuated themselves widely into office as presidents, secretaries and treasurers of co-operative and rural development societies, village committees and so on. Through these organizations, through their moneylending activities, through appeal to religion and communalism, people of this sort have risen to positions of great influence and power in the village and, through the villagers' vote, in national politics; often they have been in conflict with the hierarchy of government servants, particularly with village headmen who tend (or have tended until recently), to be drawn from traditionally important families rather than from the group under discussion. It is true that few members of this group have actually entered the House; but it is perhaps not an exaggeration to say that some MPs, at any rate, are virtually nominees of local members of it. Certainly many MPs find it necessary to listen carefully to such people.

In other words, no politician can afford to ignore what is happening in the village; and no student of politics can afford to concentrate on happenings in Colombo to the exclusion of what may be learnt by anthropological, sociological or other study in the villages. Nor is it possible to generalize about politics over the

[1] See, for example, Bryce Ryan, 'The Ceylonese Villager and the New Value System', *Rural Sociology*, 17 (1952), 9–28.

whole country, or even over the whole of the Sinhalese part of it.

One footnote must be added here; for no examination of the extent to which Ceylon is a 'democracy' can neglect the fact that, because of the operation of Ceylon's citizenship laws, most members of the large Indian Tamil community are disfranchised: only 125,477 have so far been registered as citizens of Ceylon.

The picture that has just been sketched of a public opinion influenced largely by a powerful group in the villages is, of course, too simple; if it were a perfect model of the situation, all rural Sinhalese votes would presumably be cast for the SLFP. But there are many complications: caste, the personal standing of candidates because of their family connexions or because of work they have done in the locality, the influence of locally powerful figures hostile to the SLFP, those and other things are important; but none of them subtract from the general judgement that the mass of the people of Ceylon do not yet participate in politics to the extent and with the motives that characterize 'democracy' in the West.

THE WORKING OF THE CONSTITUTION

It has been seen that the Ceylon ministers of the 1930's were insistent that their new constitution must be on the full Westminster model, anything else being regarded as something short of full independence. And the Westminster model Ceylon has indeed been working since 1947, with a Governor-General to carry out, broadly, the powers of the Sovereign in the United Kingdom, a Senate (or Upper House) and House of Representatives (or Lower House); and with a Cabinet, and an independent judiciary and public service.[1] How has the functioning of this machinery, as distinct from its design, conformed to that of Westminster?

There is no doubt that the Governor-General has in many respects behaved with propriety and in a thoroughly constitutional manner, notably in the acceptance of the resignations of prime ministers and in the issue of invitations to form governments; though Lord Soulbury, when Governor-General, was

[1] See Sir W. Ivor Jennings, *The Constitution of Ceylon* (1949). There are, of course, proposals to convert Ceylon into a Republic within the Commonwealth.

faced with a ticklish situation on the death of D. S. Senanayake.[1] Sir Oliver Goonetilleke, Lord Soulbury's successor, has succeeded in making himself *persona gratissima* to successive prime ministers, whatever their party, in spite of the fact that he himself was so much a UNP man that his original appointment can be criticized as a not impartial one. No doubt part of his indispensability is perfectly constitutional; one doubts if all of it is. Certainly during the emergency of 1958 he virtually took over the government when Bandaranaike seemed to be losing his grip.[2]

As for the Senate, the original intention (not, it is true, exactly copied from Westminster) was to create a chamber to prevent 'hasty and ill-considered legislation' and to interpose delay 'for the purpose of giving time for reflection and consideration'. It was intended, too, that its members should be eminent individuals of high intellectual attainment and wide experience of affairs. On the whole these intentions have remained markedly unfulfilled. With exceptions, Senators have not been notable for their intellectual eminence, nor have the debates of the Senate been on a high level. Little if any revision of legislation has been undertaken, and nothing of significance has been done to protect the minorities (as was hoped). In fact, the Senate has in general acted as a rubber stamp for the Government and a convenient way for introducing non-elected ministers into Parliament (Mrs Bandaranaike, it will be remembered, is a Senator). Not surprisingly, there has been much hostility to the very idea of a Senate.

The House of Representatives has on many occasions comported itself with a dignity worthy of Westminster; on such occasions all the constitutional proprieties have been observed and on some of them debates have been of a high order. On other occasions, violent scenes have taken place in the House, usually centring on one or more of a small number of colourful personalities who are not slow to wrath.

But more important than behaviour in the House is behaviour in the countryside. Here (and this is, after all, not surprising in a society used to authority) it seems that the MP has tended, and

[1] Wriggins, op. cit., pp. 94–5.
[2] These words were, of course, written before the resignation of Sir Oliver following the attempted coup of 27 January 1962. His successor is W. Gopallawa, a relative of the Prime Minister.

F

is tending, to take on the mantle of the older colonial hierarchy of Government Agent, Assistant Government Agent, and Ratemahatmaya or Divisional Revenue Officer. He has great influence in his constituency, he holds court in it when he visits it, he tends to behave in government offices as though he were in a position to give orders. He frequently conflicts with the government service, and tends these days to win (which does not improve the morale of the service). The implicit concept here, of the MP as a local chieftain, while perfectly under-standable in terms of Sinhalese society, hardly conforms to the Westminster model; but one gathers that there are Indian parallels. (The MP's wielding of power and influence is, of course, complementary to that exerted at village level by the group so frequently discussed in this paper, in spite of the fact that he may hold office virtually at their pleasure.)

To return to the House, there is the problem of the Opposi-tion. Ceylon has, of course, a properly selected Leader of the Opposition; and successive Leaders have shown some mastery of most, but not all, of the tactics familiar at Westminster. But on the whole Oppositions in Ceylon have tended to criticize details, to the relative neglect of matters of policy (though there have been debates of which the contrary was true). Sir Ivor Jennings has shown how the Opposition failed to press for a debate on a most important report that was highly critical of the Ministry of Health;[1] and to the list of undebated policy docu-ments may be added the Report of the Land Commission that appeared in 1958. But the fault does not lie entirely with the Opposition or in its disunited and disjointed nature. The years 1960 and 1961 have seen most of the members of the Tamil Federal Party in detention, from which they can hardly be expected to oppose effectively.

Cabinets in Ceylon have not found it easy to conform to the doctrine of joint responsibility. Even in the relatively homo-geneous UNP cabinets this was so, especially after the loss of the dominating personality of D. S. Senanayake. But cabinet disunity rose to hitherto unparalleled heights in the days of Mr Bandaranaike, when, as has been seen, it was common for ministers from opposing factions of his unhappy cabinet to slate each other from public platforms. Not infrequently, moreover,

[1] Jennings, op. cit., pp. 128–9.

ministers have ascribed blame to named public servants instead of taking responsibility themselves (though there have also been cases of ministers defending their civil servants).

It is broadly true to say that the judiciary in Ceylon has maintained the independence required by the constitution; though attempts have certainly been made to tamper with it. And, at the time of writing, the Ceylon Government proposes to bring in retro-active legislation which would condemn to death men who were found guilty of conspiracy in the Bandaranaike assassination case but who, the Supreme Court has ruled, cannot lawfully be executed since the reimposed death sentence applies only to murder and not to conspiracy to murder. This, clearly, amounts to gross political interference with a judicial decision and a gross breach of the principle, often claimed to be essential to the rule of law, that no man may be convicted except under laws previously enacted by Parliament; and the fear is that it will create an unwholesome precedent. The Civil Service[1] and the Public Service generally have been allowed much less protection than is required by the constitution and by practice at Westminster. The Public Service Commission seems to have allowed its independence to be whittled away, there have been numerous cases of political interference with transfers and promotions, and there have been many recent complaints of discrimination on communal grounds. The Public Service in Ceylon was, like that in India and Pakistan, one of the most valuable legacies of British rule; but its morale and standing are being undermined and its effectiveness diminished.

Such, then, are some of the ways in which it appears that the Westminster model has been followed or modified or departed from. It must be understood, of course, that to put matters this way is not meant to imply that one expects a society so different from British society to work an imported constitution without modification.

IDEOLOGY AND OPPORTUNISM IN CEYLON POLITICS

The present writer does not pretend to be a professional student of political theory. Perhaps because of this, because for

---

[1] The Ceylon Civil Service properly so called is the approximate equivalent of the Administrative Class of the United Kingdom Civil Service.

him, not being a cobbler, there are other materials besides leather, there is always to him something unrealistic or even amusing in attempts to see Ceylon politics wholly or mainly in terms of the application of political theory.

It is true that Sir James Peiris and other pioneers of the move towards independence were keen and able students of Western political thought, classical and modern; and also that a strong motive with them was the desire to give their own people the advantage of the political systems in whose theory they had become steeped. But political theory had but little influence on the practical men who succeeded them. D. S. Senanayake in particular was a plain, completely unintellectual man who hardly ever read a book and who was as innocent of political theory as he was adept at political practice. (It was, however, otherwise with his son Dudley, who has recently written two perceptive articles on democracy in an Asian context.)[1]

It is also true, of course, that the politics of the Left in Ceylon is based on Marxist theory, which has not been without its practical influence on Ceylon affairs (for example, on industrialization) even though the source has not always been acknowledged or even recognized. It is true, too, that the frequent splits within the Left have often ostensibly been on doctrinal grounds or as a result of differing interpretations of the correct Marxist line when faced with situations like the German-Soviet Pact of 1939.

But, as seems to have been true of ostensibly doctrinal splits among the early fathers of the Church and in contemporary Russia, deep personal antagonisms and disagreements have often been the real cause of splits on the part of the Left. And, as has already been remarked, rural support for Leftist politicians has owed much to personal influence and popularity.

If one has lived in and with the political scene in Ceylon over the last few years it is hard to escape the conclusion that political opportunism has been the main motive with those who have attained power. Bandaranaike may have talked of socialism but there is little to indicate that he had much of a grasp of socialist ideas, whether Marxist or otherwise. He was, on the other hand, the astutest of opportunists, veritably all things to almost all men.

[1] See *Ceylon News*, 21 and 28 September, 1961.

Chapter five

PARTY AND GOVERNMENT
IN NEPAL

---

by John E. S. Driver

I

A 'REVOLUTIONARY SITUATION'

NEPAL's internal evolution naturally reflected the momentous events in her post-war neighbours: India's independence in 1947 (with which she inherited Britain's suzerain role, and many unwelcome imperial problems); the Congress agitation in Nepali-populated Sikkim, in 1949; Peking's 'liberation' of Tibet in 1950. Here we shall consider, rather, those forces within Nepal that one might have expected to make for change.

The peasantry had no few grounds for complaint, if they could but be made aware of them. Most of the land they tilled was owned by Ranas, as tax- and rent-free *birta*, and the proportion of his crop a tiller must hand over unduly high. They were poor, unlettered, 'backward'. They were also inert. Into the farthest backwoods of the country returning Gurkha soldiers brought echoes of the distant world in which they served; but not, it would seem, any notion of questioning the Government that ruled them from far-off Kathmandu.

This task was left, as often elsewhere, to the intelligentsia, in this case largely trained in India, and largely expatriate. Such were the embryonic statesmen of the new Nepal, as the Koirala half-brothers (Matrika Prasad the elder, and Bisheshwar Prasad) and the rest of their family; Surendra Prasad Upadhyaya (a former secretary to the Rana Minister of Education) and mem-

ber of the Nepali Congress Executive in 1950); Dilli Raman
Regmi (historian of Nepal and moving spirit of the Nepali
National Congress); and perhaps also Konwar Indrajit Singh
(another doctor, this time of Ayurvedic medicine, which he
practised during a long residence in Burma) who later, as Prime
Minister, came to regard the intelligentsia as his enemy. Though
tiny numerically and without material resources of its own, it
was this group, exiled when it was not in jail, that led and
organized the revolutionary movement under the slogans of
democracy, modernization and nationalism. Their indignation
was boundless regarding the plight of the peasantry — milked
for land revenue or dues for the upkeep of Rana-owned forests
and elephants, ejected from their holdings on trivial pretexts —
of the exploited mill-workers, and of the very coolies, on whom a
tax was imposed. But above all their indignation sprang from a
burning shame at what they felt as the backwardness of their
country, which could not plead foreign plunder and oppression
as an excuse. The bitter disillusionment they experienced when
rapid solutions and short cuts proved 'unable to deliver the
goods' (a phrase not uncommonly used by Nepalese politicians
of one another) can well be imagined.

Outside the feudatory states, the non-Rana aristocracy had
been pretty thoroughly eliminated. But the Ranas themselves
were a far from uniform group. Between the world wars they
had been divided into three categories: Class A Ranas, of the
impeccable parenthood that put them in the direct line of
fraternal succession for the premiership; Class B, a very small
group of postnatally legitimized children of Ranas; Class C —
who constituted the majority — offspring of a Rana's numerous
concubines. Though all higher army posts were reserved for
Ranas, those of the last category could not reach the rank of
General or hold the more important civilian posts, and B Class
Ranas had no hope of becoming Prime Minister, Commander-
in-Chief, Senior Commanding General or other dignitary in the
direct succession. The number of A Ranas never exceeded a
hundred. Thus was created a fertile source of discontent, for
social custom obliged a Rana to maintain himself in great
magnificence such as his *jagir* (revenue from an allotted portion
of land which an office-holder must collect in lieu of salary)
might barely suffice to support, 'and the fun of it is', remarks

Dr Regmi,[1] 'that a Rana is always needy even with millions because he leads a spendthrift life, and has to maintain and look after a large family and retinue'. In practice, these responsibilities left some possibility of putting a little aside, however, and even the under-privileged Ranas had considerable holdings in India which they were able to draw on when opposition drove them into exile, to finance the activities of the revolutionary intellectuals.

While the dissident Ranas, individually more or less progressive-minded, were bent on removing from power those who had used them less than justly, or whose posts they felt they could themselves more appropriately hold, the King (H.M. Maharajadhiraja Tribhuvana Vir Vikram Jang Bahadur Shah Bahadur Shamsher Jang Deva), who had reigned but not ruled since 1911 when he was five, doggedly continued seeking allies against a bondage that stultified his existence. The revolutionaries realized that to be democratic they must support the King — since loyalty to the divine ruler was the one political sentiment that had any great currency in the kingdom — and their speeches and manifestos of this period often refer to the Ranas as 'usurpers'. The King for his part had ambitions political as well as personal to which the Ranas were an obstacle. Though sedulously guarded from influences of this kind, he contrived to maintain contact with opposition forces operating clandestinely, and was implicated, it is said, in the 1940 plot against the Prime Minister's life, on which occasion Tanka Prasad was sentenced to life imprisonment (as a brahmin, he could not be shot) from which he only emerged after the revolution.

Attempts had been made to unite some of these and other aggrieved classes. As often as not they met with apathy; unacquaintance with concepts like 'democracy', political freedom; or jealousy and suspicion between the different groups — Newars did not trust Gurkhas, nor lower-caste intellectuals the brahmins, and the C Ranas continued to feel superior to any one outside the Rana family.

In 1935 Tanka Prasad Acharya and four other young men founded the Praja Parishad (People's Assembly) or Nepal Praja Parishad (hereafter referred to as NPP) with headquarters in Kathmandu. In 1940 it first formally elected office-bearers and

[1] *Whither Nepal?*, p. 29.

issued a few posters criticizing the administration; but even now
its total membership was less than twenty and with the un-
masking of the gunpowder plot (real or alleged) already
mentioned, in that year, and the executions and imprisonments
that followed, this party lapsed and was not heard of again till a
decade later.

Other conspiracies and agitations involving Newars and
Class C Ranas took place about this time, but no new party was
founded until after the war. A political school of a very different
kind was provided by army service, and in particular by the
Indian National Army formed under Japanese auspices to profit
by anti-British sentiments among servicemen. Former INA men
were said to figure prominently amongst the contingent led by
Dr K. I. Singh on the Western sector of the 1950 insurrection.

The main stream of Nepalese political activity was represented by such individuals as B. P. Koirala, S. P. Upadhyaya,
and Dr D. R. Regmi, who gravitated towards the Indian
National Congress and with them sought imprisonment during
the 'Quit India' movement of 1942. When they gathered in
Benares in January 1946, to found the Nepali National Congress,
they had the support of Indian socialists like Jaya Prakash
Narayan and Dr Ram Manohar Lohia. The Rana régime was
regarded as an extension of British *Raj*, to be overthrown by a
single movement. The slogans of constitutional government,
civil liberties, and an end to Rana autocracy were raised. Tanka
Prasad, still in prison, was the following January elected President of the party, but this function he never actively assumed.
He was in fact considerably to the left of his colleagues at liberty,
whilst the somewhat academic Dr Regmi represented, or
constituted the strictly non-violent wing.

II

RANA REFORMS UNDER PADMA AND MOHAN

At the beginning of March 1947, the Prime Minister,
Maharaja Padma, announced a programme of 'nation-building
activities' — the beginnings of an education programme, a
twenty-year plan for the improvement of agriculture, and the
establishment of industries. With Indian independence in sight

it was a natural precaution to establish diplomatic relations with other nations than British India and Tibet, to whom Nepal's intercourse had hitherto been restricted. First approaches were made to China and the U.S.A., and the latter recognized Nepal's independence in a diplomatic and commercial agreement concluded in April.

Meanwhile, expatriates meeting at Jogbani in Bihar, under the Nepali National Congress (henceforth NNC), decided to start a *satyagraha* movement of non-violent disobedience almost at once (13 April, 1947). It was stated in advance that only Nepalese would take part. The purpose of the agitation was limited to 'the achievement of civil liberties at present and not responsible government', and the party's aim, once such liberties existed, was to 'acknowledge His Majesty the King of Nepal as the constitutional head of the State and establish responsible government'. The technique was to send batches of five volunteers at a time into Nepal to get themselves arrested. This went on at Biratnagar (where a strike of jute-mill workers had been in progress), Birganj and Janakpur — all close to the Bihar frontier.

In the midst of this agitation, the Rana Prime Minister, Padma, announced on 16 May that constitutional reforms were proposed for the country, starting with the following:

An eminent Indian constitutional lawyer to be invited to advise the Government.

Forty-one municipalities and district boards to be set up to whom local authority will be transferred.

Extension of education and introduction of education for women.

The national budget to be published (annually).

Freedom of the Press, speech and association to be guaranteed.

This move in no wise placated the NNC, whose Acting President, Matrika Prasad Koirala, demanded that the reforms should only be adopted after consultations with 'the leaders of the Nepalese people', in which capacity the NNC should be officially recognized. But on 10 June the *satyagraha* was called off in view of advice from Pandit Nehru and of the promised reforms.

In pursuance of those promises it was announced on 13 June that a start had been made with the municipality of Kathmandu, which was divided for this purpose into twenty-one wards returning one councillor each. All males over twenty-one could vote and, over twenty-five, stand. The elections were said to have taken place on 11 June, and it appeared that seven of the twenty-one seats had been uncontested. Nothing else seems to be known of this earliest of Nepalese elections, and it may be questioned how much the electorate themselves knew at the time.

Further reforms were announced on 10 February, 1948 by the Rana Prime Minister Padma who had already publicly decided to relinquish office afterwards and retire to Ranchi, in Bihar. Important features were:

The granting of fundamental rights (freedom of speech, etc.). Adult franchise.

Establishment of *panchayats* throughout the country as the nucleus of a representative body.

A bicameral legislature at the centre, comprising elected and nominated members.

Inclusion of elected members in the Council of Ministers.

An independent judiciary.

The creation of administration committees.

The establishment of a Public Service Commission to supervise recruitment for state service (hitherto on a family basis).

A constitution embodying the above and other excellent proposals was promulgated on 9 March, 1948.

By 1 May Padma had tendered his resignation to be succeeded by General Sir Mohan S.J.B.R. The retiring Maharaja prided himself on having been instrumental in ending autocratic rule in Nepal. He claimed that in some respects the reforms took Nepal to the stage India reached with the 1935 Act. His successor was more concerned with economic plans and spoke of his firm determination to put down disorder and indiscipline.

The year ended with the deliberations at Calcutta of a new political party, the Nepal Democratic Congress (NDC), founded by liberal C Ranas. Resolutions condemned the 'barbaric conditions' of 200 political prisoners and demanded the immediate setting up of a sovereign, elected Constituent Assembly to frame a constitution, and the formation of an interim government. These resolutions were not very different from those of any of the dozens of parties that subsequently sprang up amongst the Nepalese, differing chiefly in the identity of their president: in this case, Mahendra Bikram Shah, a member of the royal family. The NDC was to be fiercely attacked by Dr Regmi[1] (before it merged with the NNC in March 1950) as a party of fake reformers interested only in countering Communism. The NDC President was even prepared to consider Nepal's merger with India: this could only be decided after a democratic government had been set up with the King as constitutional head.

B. P. Koirala was again in Kathmandu jail. On 7 March, 1949 his party, the NNC, from its headquarters at Raxaul, India's nearest frontier post for Kathmandu, called on the people to prepare for a non-violent movement to 'replace the present autocratic government by a popular one'. The agitation was launched on 1 June and suspended on 18 June following the release of B. P. Koirala who brought news of talks with the Prime Minister. In August 1949 Dr Regmi of the NNC was appealing to the Government of India for 'moral and material aid', but in the coming struggle India's official policy was of strict neutrality, accompanied by strong pressure behind the scenes, and it was left to individuals and parties to render more belligerent aid. The Indian Government urged B. P. Koirala in September to co-operate in introducing constitutional reforms in his country; but he refused any dealings with the Government of Nepal until the remaining political prisoners were released and parties allowed to function openly. Koirala was not opposed to the 'continuance' of the King and Prime Minister, provided they delegated all powers to a parliament of representatives of the people. If this were not done, rising political discontent might lead to 'the liquidation of the ruling class of Nepal'.

On 15 February, 1950, Dr D. R. Regmi, who had for a time been President of the NNC whilst B. P. Koirala was in prison, announced that he would found a new party which would represent peasants, dispossessed labourers, and the lower middle class — the *duniyadar* of Nepal, as distinct from the *bharadar* nobility. It would join a united front with all anti-imperialist,

[1] In *Whither Nepal?* (Kathmandu, 1952, but written in 1950), pp. 66–74.

anti-feudal democratic elements, and have as its goal a progressive democratic government. In the outcome, however,
Regmi remained a lone campaigner.

Also in February 1950, B. P. Koirala was negotiating with
Mahendra Bikram Shah of the NDC with a view to forming a
united front for the new 'mass movement' against the Ranas
which he proposed holding by April. With the recently formed
Communist Party the NNC had 'differences' but not as far as
the immediate aim was concerned. On 9 March the presidents
of the NNC and NDC announced that their parties would
merge for the nation's 'supreme effort', and at a conference of
about 500 members in April at Calcutta the new body —
named simply the Nepali Congress (NC) — elected M. P.
Koirala as its president. The conference had the blessings of
Indian Congress President Dr Sitaramayya and other Congress
notables. The NC, announced M. P. Koirala shortly afterwards,
would soon launch a national movement for 'a full democratic
government' with the King as constitutional Head of State, and
if this demand were not fulfilled 'the Government of Nepal alone
will be held responsible for the consequences'.

Whilst the Rana authorities pursued their leisurely course, the
NC gathered support from all the disaffected sections of the
population. The former Governor of Birganj, Major-General
Subarna S.J.B.R., a C Rana who had accompanied his uncle
ex-Maharaja Padma to India, gave up his rank and joined the
party. The authorities at once took military precautions at
Birganj in response to rumours that Subarna was about to
arrive with a large *satyagrahi* following. Forty-five political
leaders, including all members of the NC Working Committee,
were outlawed. Pandit Bhadra Kali Misra and other members
of his Lok Sewak Sangh were arrested while organizing relief for
5,000 victims of a fire at Jaleshwar, in the Terai. Misra was later
to play a part in the first post-revolutionary cabinet government.

III

INSURRECTION

The first blow fell on 29 September, 1950. The Government
declared that a conspiracy to assassinate Mohan and others

had been uncovered, all those involved at the Kathmandu end arrested, and 'identical confessions' made by them. The plot appeared to centre on the household of ex-Commanding General Hiranya, Subarna's father and himself a C Rana. On the eve of the Government's disclosure, a conference of NC workers at Bairagnia (just inside India), already apprised of the first arrests, decided to transfer their organizational apparatus to Nepal, dissolve the Working Committee, and vest the President, M. P. Koirala, with special powers for 'the last struggle for freedom'.

Suddenly on 6 November, King Tribhuvana, on the pretext that he was not allowed to visit India for medical treatment, but according to some in fear for his life, gave his captors the slip and took refuge in the Indian Embassy. With him were the Crown Prince, Mahendra, the latter's elder son and others. The three-year-old second son of Prince Mahendra had been, by a strange oversight, left behind in the royal palace. Parliament was promptly summoned, declared the throne forfeit 'according to the laws, usage and constitution of Nepal', and proclaimed the infant, sole available candidate, King.

The decision now thrust upon India was whether (*a*) to go on bolstering up the régime for stability's sake, or (*b*) to press her wish for rapid popular rule. In any case, as the Deputy Prime Minister Sardar V. Patel made clear, India could not accept the change of monarch. The Congress politicians at once came out in support of King Tribhuvana. The King's own motives were problematic. Physically weak and of gentle character, yet unconventional and with Western leanings, he had been rumoured to be in disagreement with the 'Ranacracy' over the pace of the reforms they were accused of stifling. He was also said to be shocked by the mass arrests after the 'Plot'. Other observers put matters on the plane of personal ambition: the suspicion that he was trying to revive the dormant powers devolved in 1867 by his ancestor King Surendra.

Mohan yielded to Indian pressure to allow the (ex-) King to fly out to Delhi, when it became apparent that Britain and America would not recognize the change until India did. Events now moved rapidly. A NC group set out from Nautanwa (Indian railhead for the key western Terai town of Bhairahwa) on 9 November. The following day planes scattered revolutionary leaflets over the Terai. Soon (as the King with his suite arrived in New Delhi) fighting was reported by NC sources at nine points on the Indian border; their first gain was the important town of Birganj, three miles across the frontier, and commanding the main route to Kathmandu. In overall command of NC forces was the dissident Rana Subarna. Hundreds of volunteers arrived from Darjeeling, Benares, Patna and particularly Calcutta, where recruiting stations were set up and the Indian Press carried daily reports of their departures for the front. In its first proclamation the provisional Government declared its aim as a 'People's Government' under the King, with distribution of all Rana lands. 'We will establish big industries and will give increased pay to the army, police and other Government officials.'

The non-violent NNC, in the person of D. R. Regmi, declared its full co-operation with the NC in the common cause of democratization. The Indian authorities professed themselves completely surprised by what was called a raid into Nepal territory 'from both sides of the Indo-Nepalese border', and on 12 November instructed the Governments of U.P., Bihar and West Bengal to stop armed volunteers entering Nepal. The insurrection rapidly collapsed as soon as reinforcements could be rushed from the capital. All was over in the central sector by 21 November; it took longer to deal with the more distant sectors since Nepalese forces were denied access to Indian territory, which afforded the only quick route to the East and West.

In late November 1950, in an atmosphere of urgency stressed by reports that the Dalai Lama was about to abandon Lhasa, Defence Minister Kaiser and Director-General of Foreign Affairs Bijaya began talks with Nehru and Patel in New Delhi. The Nepalese were dislodged step by step from their positions (NC forces meanwhile counter-attacked, invested Biratnagar, and captured it on 21 December) until by early January they had accepted almost all India's advice. The Prime Minister was thus committed to the following programme:

A properly elected Constituent Assembly to be brought into being as soon as possible to draw up a constitution.
An interim coalition under the Prime Minister to be established pending a new constitution.

King Tribhuvana to continue as King.

The régime to be liberalized and the Prime Minister's powers reduced by predetermined stages.

The King's statement (10 January) welcoming the reforms put the NC leaders 'in an awkward position', for they were proposing to carry on 'till victory is achieved' and considered the proposed changes unsatisfactory. In particular did they resent a reference to political parties in Nepal, whereas 'there is only one such party in Nepal, namely, the Nepali Congress'. But D. R. Regmi was quick to welcome the proposals, and returning to Nepal after ten years' exile, called off his threatened passive resistance campaign. On 16 January, on Indian governmental advice, the NC ceased hostilities, and began talks with the King. The NC continued its parallel government at Biratnagar, Bhairahwa and Palpa, disorder prevailed and Communist handbills started to appear.

The King in a proclamation to his 'beloved subjects' on 18 February, 1951, three days after his return, announced the appointment of an Interim Council of ten ministers, to assist and advise him. In addition to the Prime Minister (Mohan) this contained four Rana and five NC members. B. P. Koirala held the Home portfolio, and Subarna that of Defence. A Constituent Assembly, based on adult franchise, was to meet before the end of 1952 and frame a democratic constitution.

IV

ADMINISTRATIONS UNDER KING TRIBHUVANA (1951-5)

'Democracy' was handicapped from the outset by serious disorders in the state. The controlled lawlessness of revolution had set an example which less sophisticated tribal populations emulated with less well-defined aims. In January 1951 a 'Free Kirat State' of 6,000 square miles and some 400,000 souls was declared by independent-minded tribesmen in the east. Brigandage, defiance of NC orders, and breaches of the cease-fire spread also in the west of the country. There, units of the Indian Armed Constabulary co-operated with Nepalese State forces in breaking up the forces led by K. I. Singh and Balchandra Sharma respectively, who were now described as 'Nepalese Congressmen turned dacoits'. They were accused of exacting contributions from shopkeepers, seizing all available transport, and committing acts of arson and armed robbery: in a word, of continuing the revolution, with whose results they were not satisfied. Dr Singh surrendered with 360 followers on 20 February, 1951, and Sharma a few days later.

In this situation the Home Minister was a key figure, and the measures B. P. Koirala was obliged to take against disorder won him growing unpopularity. The Gorkha Dal (nicknamed Khukri Dal) a conservative and anti-Indian party started by Bharat Shamsher, a young Rana, received his attention and was accused in April 1961 of conspiring to spread anarchy. Bharat was arrested under a new Public Safety Act with Professor Randhir Subha, the party's President, but angry followers broke into the prison to release them and sacked Koirala's official residence.

It was estimated by May that at least thirty-two political organizations were functioning in Nepal. Tanka Prasad Acharya emerged from prison after ten years, and Khadag Man Singh after twenty-two; they were prepared to join the NC only if they could function as an independent Left-wing within the party, which it would not countenance. The Janadhikar Suraksha Samiti (Civil Liberties Protection Committee) was militant and Communist-inclined. The Gorkha Dal, banned for its implication in the anti-Koirala riots, was later to be revived as the Gorkha Parishad (GP). It had strong support in the Valley, as well as in Pokhra and Gorkha to the west, from upholders of ancient institutions, religious revivalists, and resurgent Gorkha nationalists. The Nepal Praja Parishad, which Tanka Prasad Acharya now resuscitated, was a Marxist 'party of workers and peasants'. Its leader stressed in addition the importance of not disturbing the 'existing balance in Nepal between people of Mongolian and Aryan extraction'. The Terai Congress campaigned by 'non-violent and constitutional methods' for a 'self-governing province within Nepal'. What real support any of the existing parties commanded could not be gauged until national elections had been held. In the event, all important groups had a chance to show their capabilities before there was a poll.

In October the Election Commissioner announced that

elections to the Constituent Assembly (earlier promised for 1952) could be held early in 1953, after a census in 1952. Concurrently, the King nominated an Advisory Council (the Government being moribund), and it was announced that an Advisory Assembly of forty-five members (including the ten ministers) would be appointed. It was held necessary that women representatives be included in this body, 'at least for colour and for a better sense of discipline', in B. P. Koirala's words. When appointed, twenty-eight of the Assembly's members were NC supporters, although the Ranas had urged that other parties be represented.

The Government's collapse was precipitated by police firing, ordered by Koirala as Home Minister, on a student mass meeting (6 November, 1951) when one youth was killed. The Prime Minister's attitude was, complained Koirala, one of 'veiled condemnation' of the Home Ministry. There could be no unity in the Government unless Mohan left, and the five NC ministers handed the King their resignations. The following day King Tribhuvana directed the NC members to remain in office until he had decided on the best arrangements, and not to 'indulge in mutual recrimination'. Koirala ordered the release from various prisons of 200 of his political opponents, notably: Bharat Shamsher and Randhir Subha of the Gorkha Dal; Tanka Prasad (NPP); Shankar Prasad and Rishikesh Shah (NNC); and Agni Prasad Kheral (Nepal Rashtriya Mahasabha, a new party standing for Kirata independence). K. I. Singh and D. R. Regmi were not released. The Rana ministers now obligingly resigned in their turn, and the cabinet stood dissolved.

The King next called on M. P. Koirala who had not yet held office to submit a panel of ministers for a new cabinet. B. P. Koirala announced that he would not join this, but concentrate on party work. The new cabinet, sworn in on 16 November, 1951, contained the other four NC members of the old administration, plus seven more, including M. P. Koirala himself, Mahendra Bikram Shah, and Khadag Man Singh.

M. P. Koirala regarded the Communists as his party's only serious opposition; his younger relative had said as much of the underground Gorkha Dal. The first non-Rana Prime Minister was faced with the new problem of an Army demoralized by the

G

absorption, then in progress, of the Raksha Dal into the regular forces. Another ground for complaint was the NC's proposed halting of recruitment for the British Army. The appointment of ex-Commander-in-Chief General Kaiser S.J.B.R. as Defence Minister was interpreted as a move to counter this discontent.

The new Prime Minister soon ran into dramatic trouble. A. P. Kharel and Ramprasad Rai, leaders of the Kiratist Rashtriya Mahasabha had been arrested and lodged in the Singha Darbar (secretariat building) where K. I. Singh was also held. The Mahasabha had the support of the Raksha Dal in east Nepal, and 1,200 of its members now stormed the Singha Darbar and released their leaders together with Dr Singh, who organized them to storm vital centres in Kathmandu, so that, for twelve hours on 22 January, 1952, he was in control of the entire Valley. He demanded of the King:

An all-party government, excluding the Gorkha Parishad.
Diplomatic relations abroad on the basis of equality and no
　　special ties with any particular country.
An all-party conference to draw up a minimum programme
　　to be implemented before the elections.
A five-year economic development plan.

The King refused to negotiate, and as the army closed in the outcome was clear. Singh slipped out with a band of trusted followers, and was in Tibet by March 1952: his earlier activities had put India out of the question. Hospitably received by the Chinese in Shigatse, he was later taken to Peking, and in absence a legend grew about his name.

The King's response to this *coup* was to declare a state of emergency and arm the Prime Minister, M. P. Koirala, with special powers. The growing Communist Party was held to blame and made illegal, followed by the Rashtriya Mahasabha. At this time the Communist-dominated landless peasants' organization Kisan Sangh was organizing murderous anti-landlord riots in the eastern Terai. The Kisan movement was implacably opposed to the ex-Home Minister B. P. Koirala. Pay strikes and student demonstrations against the Indian mission (which was streamlining the army from 25,000 down to 8,000) added to the administration's difficulties.

The working committee of the NC accused the Government

of inefficiency, and asked M. P. Koirala to reduce his cabinet from eleven to seven, presenting him with a list. When he objected that this infringed the 'gentleman's agreement' under which he had not stood in the last election for president of the NC, he was directed to resign the premiership, and refused. The list would have removed ministers favourable to himself, and installed two NC members associated with his half-brother, with whom he was now in open conflict. Three NC ministers resigned, and those remaining, including M. P. Koirala, were expelled from the party (25 July, 1952). Efforts to organize the Opposition culminated in the National Democratic United Front including the NPP, NNC, NC dissidents and the banned Communists. In place of 'lawlessness, corruption and nepotism', the Front's leaders, Regmi and Tanka Prasad, demanded an all-party government, and hinted that NC feuds were arousing anti-Indian feeling.

In August M. P. Koirala, 'disgusted at the low level to which politics here has sunk', submitted his resignation (10 August, 1952). During his nine months in office, first steps towards a general election had been taken with the starting of a census and the preparation of electors' rolls. From now until June 1953, cabinet government was given a rest and the King ruled in daily consultation with a Council of five advisers (three from the outgoing Government, including two Ranas), none of whom belonged to a party. On their recommendation, the Advisory Assembly was dissolved in September 1952.

In October the United Front dwindled to its Communist supporters when the NPP withdrew. B. K. Misra merged his Nepali Congress (People's Group) with the NNC (Dissident Group) to form a People's Nepali Congress (PNC). It regarded the King's régime as 'a necessary evil'. With the formation, by the NC *ad hoc* Committee in February 1953, of a National Democratic Party of Nepal (NDPN) or Rashtriya Praja Party there were four successors to the NC, including the PNC and NC (Progressive Bloc) which split off the previous year.

In June 1953 'Advisers' rule' ended when the King, who had been told to rest by his ayurvedic physician, administered the oath once more to M. P. Koirala, heading a cabinet consisting of four NDPN members and one independent. The new cabinet, regarded as a product of palace intrigue, was much resented by the NC. Banditry, prison disturbances, peasant riots and pitched battles in the industrial centres made its prospects bleak. Confidence cannot have been improved by the first elections since the revolution, those for the Kathmandu Municipal Board. Communist-sponsored candidates emerged on 8 September as the largest single group, winning six of the eighteen seats. The King, his health failing, was more and more out of the country. B. P. Koirala was interned at Kathmandu for distributing a cyclostyled letter on the country's 'deteriorating condition' to, it was alleged, government servants. His NC, the NNC of D. R. Regmi, and Tanka Prasad Acharya's NPP, formed a joint Council of Action for 'a common minimum programme'.

Returning from Europe in 1954 the King on 13 February issued a proclamation and three enactments to reaffirm his authority. Certain legislation which had been declared *ultra vires* by the Supreme Court was revalidated, the King's inherent prerogatives as supreme executive, legislative and judicial authority were reaffirmed, and the judiciary was in effect stripped of its independence. Five days later the King installed a seven-man cabinet under M. P. Koirala, the latter's third government. The redoubtable General Subarna, who had served in every government since 'democracy', was entrusted with Planning, Development, Agriculture, Commerce and Industry, while Narad Muni Thulung, who came in with M. P. Koirala's first ministry, was given Forests and Revenue. General Kaiser Shamsher, the old Rana Defence chief, D. R. Regmi (Foreign Affairs, Education, etc.), Tanka Prasad (Home) and Bhadra Kali Misra were brought into what was in effect a NDPN-Rana-NNC-PNC coalition.

These developments effectively isolated the NC (Official Group) and left B. P. Koirala at the head of the agitation in protest against the proclamation of 13 February, the 'Black Law'. The King persisted in his efforts to create a forum of popular opinion with a second Advisory Assembly and 67 of his 121 nominees were sworn in on 28 May, 1954. They were drawn from six of the chief parties — NDP, NPP, PNC (of B. K. Misra, whose party is also referred to as Jan Congress, NNC, NC, and Terai Congress. The NC boycotted the new Assembly throughout.

In October, M. P. Koirala promised general elections by early 1956, but there was an atmosphere of indifference or hostility towards the Government when the King left for Europe to seek further medical treatment, leaving a Regency Council composed of his three sons to act in his place. A new wave of armed rebellion convulsed western Nepal, and Indian assistance had repeatedly to be called in.

On 31 January, 1955, M. P. Koirala submitted his cabinet's resignation to the Crown Prince. The occasion was the Government's seventh defeat in the Advisory Assembly, the 'indecent' passing of a resolution reducing an item of the Foreign Ministry estimates from Rs 400,000 to Re 1. The cause was evidently the nonco-operation of his cabinet colleagues Tanka Prasad and B. K. Misra. The Regency Council, however, did not consider themselves empowered to accept resignations of heads of government, and adjourned the Assembly for one month, while Prince Mahendra flew to Nice and returned on 16 February, vested with 'all royal authority' for settling the crisis in a democratic spirit. Gaining assurance day by day, the Crown Prince asked M. P. Koirala to make another attempt at a stable coalition; dissolved the Council of State; ordered all political parties and other bodies to submit their suggestions for solving present problems; and on 2 March accepted the Premier's resignation, dissolved the cabinet, and took on direct rule 'for the time being'. On 13 March the King died at Zurich at the age of 48; and his 34-year-old eldest son was proclaimed King within the twenty-four hours that ancient usage dictates.

V

TOWARDS A GENERAL ELECTION (1955–9)

The 'young man of strong character', as *The Times* had described him, who now became King Mahendra, was known for an unassuming taciturnity but believed to favour radical land reforms. He has been described as more traditionally minded than his father, and as less trustful of the West. On his return from Nice, however, he broadcast to the nation that he found Europeans 'well-disciplined and well-mannered which are necessary qualities for any civilized country'. Proclaiming that it was 'inadvisable to do anything in haste to restore a democratic form of rule in Nepal', Mahendra appointed a council of five advisers on 14 April. Unlike its predecessor of 1952–3, this body contained no members of the outgoing Government, but as before none of the advisers was a party man.

Having provided for the day-to-day administration of the country, the new King turned to the consideration of ways of 'consolidating democracy' in Nepal, and to this end called a conference for 8 May, 1955. Invited to it were representatives of 127 political and social organizations who had responded to his earlier call, as Crown Prince, to supply their date of establishment, objectives, constitution and strength, and the names of office-bearers and at least twenty-five members. The presidents of four parties — NC, NPP, NNC, NDPN — jointly refused to participate in the conference because non-political institutions such as *Gaushala* (cattle welfare societies) had been invited, and the objectives not clearly defined. This provoked the scorn of the King but did not prevent the voice of these parties being heard since many of those active in the 'non-political' organizations were their own members, or supporters. The King undertook to fix, within three months, a date for the long delayed general elections; and would in no case allow the country to 'go to ruin in the name of democracy' as it had in the past four years. The representatives were asked for their opinions on the continuance of the Advisory Assembly, the structure of government, and general elections. The proceedings took place on seven days in all, and the consensus was: that the Assembly should be dissolved or reconstituted; the democratic system preserved; early general elections held; and direct rule discontinued — for the King, a 'historic symbol of unity', should keep above politics. Kisan representatives, mouthpiece of the banned Communist Party, spoke of Rana reactionaries back in power, and others stressed the need for awakening the political consciousness of the people.

True to his word, the King announced on 9 August, 1955 that the first general election would be on the Full Moon Day of October 1957, and that the representatives so elected would draft a constitution. But the NC Working Committee sourly replied that this information constituted 'nothing much in itself', demanding an immediate end to direct rule and a clear and authoritative statement on the principles that would guide the holding of the elections. Leaders of the NC, NDPN, GP, NPP, and NNC accepted an invitation to confer with the King on 19 August, and by 26 October the King was prepared to form a coalition of NC, NNC and NPP ministers providing they accepted his formula. This was that he himself should be Prime Minister; two ministers would be drawn from each of the three parties, plus two to four independents; and that the two ministers apiece be chosen from a panel of three only which he presented to each party. After prolonged negotiations, B. P. Koirala, D. R. Regmi and Tanka Prasad rejected the King's formula on 21 January, 1956 as 'undemocratic'. On 27 January Tanka Prasad Acharya was invited to form a government on his own. Three of the five advisers entered the new cabinet, and to them were added Balchandra Sharma and two other NPP members.

After Chinese approaches on the subject of the outlawed K. I. Singh, several politicians asked the King to allow him to return with honour. Singh crossed the border from Tibet in September 1955 and at an outpost of the Kathmandu Valley he was granted a royal pardon in return for a written promise of loyalty and non-violence. This he scrupulously observed, even entering the Valley at midnight, by another route, to avoid a riotous welcome. Amid plentiful speculation on his stay in Peking and the role in which he was now cast, his own account was to the effect that he had been preached to but not converted; had gone on hunger-strike in Peking to get back to Nepal; and was not a Marxist or 'any ist but a Nepalist'. He put forward 'five principal aims' as he entered the political field at the head of his own new party, the Samyukta Prajatantra or United Democratic Party:

To establish constitutional monarchy through elections.
To abolish landlordism, nationalize the forests, and multiply present national revenues by five.
To exploit national wealth for the benefit of the nation.
Harmonious relations among all classes for the national good.
A strictly neutral foreign policy and no involvement in power blocs — 'like Switzerland'.

He claimed he had refused Communist offers to reinstate him by force: and his party would not seek office till it had been tested by the polls. Presently, he was embarrassing India with extravagant praise of her leaders and her 'selfless' assistance. He attacked the Tanka Prasad Government's foreign policy as too Left-wing.

On 8 April the Communist Party decided to launch a country-wide agitation against the ban imposed four years earlier at the time of K. I. Singh's *coup*. General Secretary Manmohan Adhikari announced he and others would defy the ban by addressing thirty public meetings throughout Nepal on 16 April: on the 15th the Prime Minister lifted the ban, and the meetings were held legally. An Act conferring the basic civil liberties 'subject to laws or legislation' had come into force in December 1955, and its provisions were strengthened on 21 May, 1956 when the 'High Court' was abolished and replaced by a Supreme Court with enlarged powers and free of executive control. The country was divided into 100 constituencies by May 1956, and in August an 'election task force' of several hundred officers trekked for a month through the country making preparations for elections the following October. The Election Commission promised that it would finish its work by October and voting would follow a three-phase programme from then until December.

The Tanka Prasad administration's declared order of political priorities was: nationalism, democracy, standard of living. At home, the NPP proposed 'a Welfare State in the true sense of the word', and in foreign policy spoke of the ending of isolation, sympathy for the oppressed, and service to peace. Relations were opened with foreign states including Russia (China's turn came earlier, under the King in 1955), Chou En-lai visited Kathmandu and Tanka Prasad was in 1956 fêted in Peking, whence he returned with what amounted to a free gift of £3½m. On 18 March, 1957, Nepalese armed units stationed by earlier treaties at Lhasa, Shigatse and other Tibetan centres were withdrawn under the agreement Tanka Prasad had reached.

Subarna Shamsher who had stood for the NC presidency on 9 January, 1956, and defeated Ganeshman Singh, stood down 'in favour of a more dynamic person'. This proved to be none other than the previous President B. P. Koirala who, elected at the NC conference in late May 1957, promptly plunged into the controversy that had sprung up concerning the body that was to result from the coming elections. Earlier in the year the Communists said they should be held, not for a mere parliamentary legislature, but for a Constituent Assembly which alone was authorized to draft a constitution. Tanka Prasad Acharya rejected this demand as not guaranteeing retention of the monarchy, without which the country's independence would be threatened. B. P. Koirala now repeated that a sovereign Constituent Assembly should be elected, threatening a country-wide movement if it were not.

Tanka Prasad, on his party's mandate, submitted his resignation on 9 July, unable to maintain co-operation with the three ex-advisers who had been kept on at the King's insistence. He blamed 'vested interests and reactionaries within and without various parties'. King Mahendra accepted the resignation when informed of the Government's inability to hold general elections on the date he had proclaimed, and next asked K. I. Singh, with whom he was said to be friendly, to try to form a coalition, with 'Independents', in fifteen days. No party was willing to join him in a coalition, but the majority reserved judgment on Singh till they had seen how his government worked. He himself promised a foreign policy tailored to Nepal's financial means: China and Russia would not be allowed to open embassies in Kathmandu and foreign contacts would be through the Delhi and London embassies without opening any in other countries. Permission to recruit Gurkhas would not be withdrawn from India and Great Britain. Efforts at a coalition finally failed, and the Government that was sworn in on 26 July, 1957, consisted of eight UDP ministers including K. I. Singh (who also held the Home and Foreign portfolios), and three independents appointed by the King. The Government's minimum programme was to hold impartial elections as soon as possible; to tackle the acute food situation in Kathmandu 'as best we can'; to solve the land problem 'within reasonable limits of time and possibility'; to eliminate corruption, injustice and lawlessness as quickly as possible and increase the national income. The Prime Minister would set up an impartial election board which would give fortnightly reports on the progress of the arrangements. A week later Singh announced that, by a decision of his predecessor, the general elections would be for a Parliament, not a Constituent Assembly, and this would have all powers to draft and amend the constitution, except in certain matters touching the Crown.

On 9 August, 1957, the NNC, NC and NPP formed a Democratic Front to defend civic rights after Singh's appointment, but a group of the NPP, under Tanka Prasad, stood aside unless the three parties accepted his 'buffer state' diplomacy for closer relations with China to counter Indian influence. On the Democratic Front (DF) which it was intended should eventually result in a single party, the NPP was represented instead by B. K. Misra. The DF was to denounce the security force which Singh set up a few days later, as a 'reign of terror' to bolster the new Government. It affirmed also that 'individual acts of the King are never above criticism'. The DF parties also boycotted the Election Commission which was set up early in September, and questioned its impartiality. The Government announced on 30 September that it was 'absolutely impossible' to hold general elections on 8 October as decreed by the King, and blamed the previous Government for failure to help obtain paper for the electoral rolls, ballot boxes and other necessities. The DF decided to launch a nationwide civil disobedience movement in December for general elections, which a 'sincere and honest' government could complete within six months. A new, impartial election commission was demanded.

Singh particularly irritated his rivals who had held office by setting up a committee to investigate what he called the squandering of nearly Rs 100m. of state funds by the previous five governments; and at the end of October by giving amnesty to 500 of his followers in the battles of 1950–1 and 1952. He banned the leading Opposition paper *Samaj* and arrested its editor for a series of articles attacking India. Shortly afterwards, on 14 November, Dr Singh resigned, probably from differences over personnel with the King, who now took on the administration until 'other arrangements are made'. A National Council was now proclaimed and sanctioned by legislation, on 1 December, 1957. Its chairman was the King's youngest brother Prince Vasundhara, and the Prime Minister and Chief Justice were to be *ex officio* members along with six others. This amounted to a new refinement of the Advisers' régime which had already been twice in operation. The DF stepped up their campaign for early elections during the first half of December 1957, with processions, *hartal*, and hundreds of volunteers lying down at the gates of the secretariat. The King fixed the date at 18 February, 1959, eighth anniversary of the birth of democracy, and the DF suspended its *satyagraha*, regarding its demands as 'partially met'.

In the new year, after discussions with B. P. Koirala and General Subarna Shamsher on an executive council to run the day-to-day administration, the King decided to appoint a government 'of Ministers from political or non-political parties without a Prime Minister', and agreed to appoint a commission to prepare the draft for a new constitution; to set up an Advisory Assembly to act as a nominated parliament during the interim period; and to replace the existing Election Board by a new one. Work for the elections had started in earnest by March 1958. Yaks, ponies, helicopters were marshalled to carry officials and ballot boxes to remote areas, in some of which difficulty was experienced in persuading voters to register for fear of incurring taxation. A committee of five was appointed to draft the constitution (whilst in 1951 this was to be done by a Constituent Assembly *after* elections). The services of Sir Ivor Jennings were obtained through the British Government, and during April he was in Kathmandu while the draft was prepared. A Representation of the People Act (2 June, 1958) provided for elections by secret ballot, and set up the necessary mechanism. The minimum age for voters was twenty-one, and for candidates twenty-five. The Election Commission's time-table was announced in September, with nominations beginning on 9 November. It was adhered to. Nine parties were able to contest the minimum number of seats, and therefore eligible to participate, and all had been allotted pictorial symbols (which a 5 per cent literacy rate made necessary) by October. As the parties concerted their election plans and toured the provinces, British and Indian Gurkha detachments arrived from mid-November on with wireless equipment to set up an election communications system.

At this stage the Advisory Assembly of eighty-six members was at last inaugurated, the UDP, however, refusing to participate in anything less than an elected assembly or government. The interim Government (consisting of one minister each from the NC, NPP, NNC, and for the first time GP, with two royal nominees) which under Subarna's chairmanship had been entrusted with the administration since 15 May proposed a number of mild reforms. But now panic seemed to grip politicians in the Advisory Assembly, confronted with the immediate prospect of real elections in which no single party might get a majority and the Communists would surely control many seats. Against the opposition of Chairman Subarna and of D. R. Regmi the Home Minister, the Assembly adopted by 29 votes to 15 a resolution pleading for postponement of the elections. Arguments advanced were that the country's northern and southern frontiers were not yet well-defined, electoral rolls not perfected, and the law and order situation not favourable (all denied by the Government) and that the constitution had not yet been published. The NC, whose strength was clear, stuck to their guns, and their joint Secretary-General Ganesh Man Singh warned that the entire population, executive included, had grown so 'fed up and frustrated' that there was a risk of the type of *coup* that had recently supervened in Burma, Pakistan and elsewhere.

There were now 864 candidates in the field for 109 seats, 339 of them independents. It seemed certain that the elections would be followed by a coalition. Differing programmes would scarcely be an obstacle to this. Each party promised to tackle the land problem with vigour, encourage small industries, undertake public works and alleviate unemployment, and raise taxes to strengthen the economy. The parties of the Democratic Front made no concerted election arrangements. The NC contested 108 seats as a long-term socialist party, whose detailed agrarian programme included encouragement to co-operative farming. The foreign policy outlined in their election manifesto was one of active neutralism. The B. K. Misra faction of the NPP was fielding 40 candidates, and D. R. Regmi's NNC were entering the minimum of 22. The Terai Congress too only produced 22 candidates, while Ranganath Sharma's Nepal Prajatantrik Mahasabha had about 70. Tanka Prasad Acharya, whose NPP faction was represented by 45 candidates, was highly suspicious of the Government's action in withholding

the promised constitution till such a late hour, and threatened
to withdraw if it proved undemocratic. Elections should be to a
British-type Parliament, 'which should possess all powers'.
Tanka Prasad announced that he was receiving Communist
support in the election. Forty-eight candidates were to stand as
Communists, and another 18 had CP backing. K. I. Singh's
UDP, with 86 candidates, issued a manifesto distinguishable by
its opposition to the establishment of an Upper House and its
promise to work for the ending of communalism and business
monopoly. The main opposition was provided by the 90
Gorkha Parishad candidates who represented, according to their
manifesto, 'the nationalist elements, the King and the Army',
as against the 'anarchy, corruption and anti-nationalism' of the
NC. In the countryside, its proposals were radical. For industry,
the emphasis was on promotion of Nepalese enterprises rather
than state ownership.

VI

DEMOCRACY ASSAYED

Almost on the eve of the elections, in a broadcast ceremony of
12 February, 1959, King Mahendra proclaimed the long
awaited constitution, which was received with mixed feelings. Its
seventy-seven articles included provision for five-yearly elections by adult suffrage to a *Pratinidhi Sabha* or Lower House,
representing 109 single-member territorial constituencies, whilst
the *Maha Sabha* or Upper House would contain 36 senators
(minimum age 30), one half of them elected by the Lower
House and the other nominated by the King. The cabinet might
contain up to 14 ministers appointed by the King on the
recommendation of the Prime Minister, at least 2 of whom, and
2 deputy ministers, must come from the Upper House. A sort of
privy council, the *Rashtriya Parishad*, would provide the regency
during a King's minority and in other emergencies. The
executive power of the King was ordinarily to be exercised on
the recommendations of the cabinet. The King would grant or
withhold assent to any bill, 'in his discretion'. He would have
authority to dismiss a prime minister who lost the confidence of
the Lower House, and to rule in his own right if it became im-

possible to form a majority government. The Supreme Court would have power to issue writs of habeas corpus and protect the people's rights to economic, political and religious freedom. A Public Service Commission would recruit civil servants on the basis of merit.

All was now prepared for the poll, which the Commissioner had fixed for eighteen separate days between 18 February and 3 April, due to shortage of personnel. Polling on the first day surprised observers and delighted the Election Commission. Sixty per cent of the electorate voted in some constituencies, and their dignity, intelligence and patience were marked by all. As results came in, it appeared from the start that the NC were gaining a landslide victory. Both Tanka Prasad Acharya and D. R. Regmi (with 618 out of 20,249 votes cast) came fourth, and both lost their deposits. General Subarna was returned from three of the constituencies he contested, necessitating two by-elections. K. I. Singh was defeated by a NC candidate at his home constituency of Doti in far north-west. The final count gave the NC, with 665,000 votes out of 1,800,000 cast, 74 seats in the Pratinidhi Sabha. Over half the remaining seats were occupied by 19 GP representatives. Other parties that gained admission to the House were the UDP (5), CP (4), NPP (Acharya faction) (2), and NPP (Misra faction) (1). Four independents were elected. The NC majority was ensured from 3 April but it was not until 16 May that B. P. Koirala, elected as leader of the NC parliamentary party, was made Prime Minister-designate by the King who would, it appears, have preferred another candidate.

The Government installed on 27 May, 1959, contained eight ministers and eleven deputy ministers (one a woman). The Prime Minister controlled Defence and Foreign Affairs, and the Deputy Prime Minister General Subarna was back in charge of Finance and Planning. The first elected Premier of Nepal, renowned despite his shy manner for impulsiveness and a sharp tongue, had formidable revolutionary antecedents. His father, who was exiled to India for his views, joined the Indian National Congress, and died in prison. 'BP' himself was born at Benares in 1915, and educated at Patna and Calcutta. From the age of fourteen he was imprisoned four times by the British. He felt the Indian Congress not 'Leftist' enough, and joined a socialist group within the party. In his policy broadcast on 28 May he announced that his Government would open new foreign relations, befriend India, Russia and China alike, pursue 'independent neutrality' and join no military bloc. The opposition forces (UDP, NPP, NDC) organized themselves into a National Democratic Front, with Tanka Prasad Acharya as President. They charged B. P. Koirala with abandoning neutrality and converting the country into a 'satellite of India'.

On 30 June, 1959 at 4.59 a.m., the new constitution came into force. On 10 July, eighteen members of the Maha Sabha were elected by the Lower House in exact proportion to its own strength (NC 13, GP 3, CP 1, UDP 1). Two days later the King nominated the other eighteen, non-party save for two NC members. When Parliament met in a joint session of both Houses, legislation was before it to abolish big *birtas* forthwith, put a ceiling on land holdings, eliminate petty principalities, and overhaul the central and provincial administrative machinery.

From early April 1960 the King was abroad on a world tour, leaving B. P. Koirala and his Government to get on with the job. The Prime Minister's biggest problems in developing the country were of personnel, and the vast expenditures necessary to keep up schools or clinics if he built these with available foreign aid of which £50 m. had already been received. His plans were already understood to be inhibited by his relations with King Mahendra, and there were rumours of foreign policy differences between them.

Communist activity was on the increase after drastic organizational changes in the party from late September 1960. Its immediate object was defined as a 'people's democracy' in Nepal, and a national *satyagraha* was planned against the Indian Gandak project. Local elections suggested the NC were losing ground to the CP in some of their urban strongholds. A sectarian tinge was apparent in disturbances put down during the King's visit to Britain when the chief of the order of Guru Gorakhnath attempted to seize power at Gorkha. The Prime Minister scoffed at his claim to be doing the King's will as 'funny'.

Disunity afflicted the NDF. K. I. Singh was trying to forge a new, united party from its constituents, but Tanka Prasad and

R. N. Sharma considered the time and circumstances unsuitable. Singh hoped to launch a unified anti-Government campaign by December. Much depended on the attitude of M. P. Koirala (still a member of the NC Working Committee) who had not yet committed himself beyond appealing for a new party.

More than once, ominously, the King's men in the Upper House had their way against the Government. On the other hand it was alleged that Koirala's administration repeatedly ignored royal directives. The King's move, when it came, was swift and decisive. On 15 December, 1960 all available members of the cabinet were arrested. Mahendra dissolved Parliament and assumed all powers under Article 55 of the constitution. Whole chapters of the constitution were suspended including that guaranteeing basic rights. The royal proclamation[1] declared that the cabinet's economic steps, 'without a scientific analysis and a proper study of actualities and founded on crude theories only, have instead of bringing about worthwhile changes in society merely created an atmosphere of instability and insecurity amongst the people'. The Nepalese Ambassador in New Delhi further specified the reasons for the move: land being taken without the compensation provided for by the constitution; increasing corruption in the administration; deaths caused by the police in suppressing unrest, especially at Gorkha; growing Communist activity and lawlessness. It was explained that the King had acted under insistent popular pressure. Subsequent arrests comprised all important political leaders in Kathmandu. Deputy Premier Subarna Shamsher, who had accompanied the King on all his recent travels, found himself on business in Calcutta at the time. Most of the Opposition leaders were released within a week. Three newspapers banned by the Koirala Government (Tanka Prasad's daily *Samaj* and two UDP weeklies) were allowed to reappear on 17 December. It was claimed that the royal intention was to 'safeguard the true spirit of democracy'. The Kathmandu Press and the released opposition politicians supported the King's action.

On 26 December a new Council of Ministers, mostly independents, was installed under the King's chairmanship. A key

[1] Full text in *The Hindu,* 17 December, 1960.

figure was Tulsi Giri (earlier a close associate of B. P. Koirala) who had resigned the post of Deputy Foreign Minister on 1 September, and now received both the Foreign Affairs portfolio and a new creation, that of Palace Affairs. On 5 January, 1961 the King proclaimed a ban on all political parties. Attempts to develop democracy from the top had failed, and he would now try to develop a new awareness in the people through 'panchayat democracy'. This represents not merely a harking back to the techniques proposed by Maharaja Padma fourteen years earlier, but an attempt to 'Asianise' democracy along the lines Pakistan had been making fashionable. The NC made preparations for a new satyagraha campaign. More arrests were made, and measures against the press began with the closing of two newspapers on 6 February. With the demonstrations for the release of the imprisoned leaders continuing, a Government decree (6 March, 1961) ordered all landlords, civil servants and pensioners and executives of state-aided organizations to inform the police of any one they knew to engage in anti-Government activities, not sparing their closest relatives, on pain of confiscation of land, dismissal, or forfeiture of pension as the case might be. The King cast further light on his motives by explaining that Koirala had been plotting to merge Nepal with India.

The plans for panchayat government were outlined in July. There would be elections every two years. Tanka Prasad became head of the land reforms commission, but three more NPP leaders were imprisoned in August; B. P. Koirala continued to be deprived of his freedom, and developed cancer. Anger against the King's repressive policy broke out in sporadic violence. The King paid a lengthy visit to China in September and October and, back in Kathmandu, reported that Everest continued to be in Nepal 'as usual'; though this did not seem concordant with the text of the boundary treaty. A more disquieting result of his visit was the finalization of an agreement whereby China was to build a road from the capital to Kodari, on the Tibetan border. The leader of the opposition in the former Parliament, Bharat Shamsher (GP) launched a spirited attack on the King's régime, which he described as a police state, on his return from the Socialist International at Rome in November. His party would co-operate with the NC in a struggle for the restoration of parliamentary democracy. He

H

hoped to see the Nepalese exiles politically united, perhaps under the perennial Subarna Shamsher. He said that the King's foreign policy would bring Nepal under Chinese domination. The Foreign Minister complained on 27 November that armed preparations were being made by exiles on Indian soil: and so the wheel appeared to have come full circle. Whether a benevolent despot will be allowed to build up by degrees, from fundamentals, towards a liberal polity, or whether violent intervention from one quarter or another will take the matter from his hands, remains to be seen.

Chapter six

THE POLITICS OF BURMA

---

by Hugh Tinker

ONE of the more meaningful methods of trying to understand
political activity in modern South-East Asia is to attempt to
analyse the traditional pattern of power and influence, and to
estimate how far this is repeated in society and politics at the
present day. In formulating this comparison, the colonial interregnum is both relevant and irrelevant. In Upper Burma the
colonial interregnum was no longer than the life of one man.
The Pyinmana Prince, who was the sole survivor of Thibaw's
massacre of the royal household in 1878, lived on to witness the
occupation of Mandalay by the British, the Japanese, republican
Burmese and Karen insurgents. The values which British rule
sought to impose — the rule of law, administrative uniformity
and efficiency, parliamentary democracy — were therefore
little more than a veneer; which subsequently cracked and
peeled, exposing the native grain of the wood beneath. Yet the
veneer still remains; forming the outer surface of the national
life.

The process of synthesis, of the 'blending and blurring' of
indigenous and imported ideas and institutions — which, one
may argue, was substantially advanced in India during the
period of British rule — has largely to be attempted in the years
after independence, amid heavy pressures, external and internal.
There are cogent reasons for arguing that some form of social
democracy will emerge which is both Burmese and democratic.
This paper attempts to assess the forces, positive and negative,
which are shaping this process.

TRADITIONAL AUTHORITY

Only in the reign of Mindon Min (1853–78) was there any attempt to create a regular administrative structure, with a civil service cadre and systematic assessment and collection of revenue. Traditionally, the King was directly responsible for the government of the middle Irrawaddy valley only. Even here, though he appointed the 'Eaters' of Provinces, local administration and justice was the affair of local, hereditary chiefs. The outer fiefs were ruled by princes and chiefs whose fealty to the King was conditioned by their accessibility to his armies. The idea of the monarchy was the only unifying concept. The Burmese monarchy was compounded of three disparate attributes. There was the Indian concept of the divinely-appointed universal ruler, Çakravartin; the 'South-East Asian' concept of the head of the clan, the warrior-chief of the blood-royal; and the Buddhist concept of the enlightened ruler, protector of the Law.

These aspects of monarchy tended to give it a built-in ambivalence, an instability, which in the absence of a developed system of government continually led to the downfall of the ruler.[1] Because the blood royal flowed in so many veins, pretenders were always appearing. More fundamental was the clash between the roles of the King as divine, above his subjects; the King as personal, tribal leader; and the King as enlightened and compassionate Buddhist. Successive rulers attempted to emphasize one or other aspect: and failed in other respects. The result was the continuing collapse of central authority and the emergence of separatist movements. U Nu has many times dwelt on this theme:

> The evil tradition of wresting power by force. Burmese history is full of instances where a king is overthrown by a contender by force, and who in turn is similarly ousted by a still more forceful rival. Except for the glorious periods of Anawrata, Bayinnaung and Alaungpaya, Burma has always been a battlefield for warring states, each cutting one another's throat.

[1] Of the ten kings who form the last (Konbaung) dynasty of Burma, four only completed their reigns and died natural deaths: one other died of battle wounds, one was murdered, two became insane, and two were deposed.

Loyalty to the King was also conditional on racial and religious ties. His Burmese, Buddhist 'kinsmen' were first in loyalty, and (diminuendo) then Tais and Mons whose beliefs reflected those of the ruler, while last of all were the animist hill tribes. Loyalty largely went along with effective power. In the First Anglo-Burmese War, Shan and Kachin levies fought under Burmese command against the British; in the Second War (1852) the Shans and Kachins held aloof, while Arakanese, Mon, and Karen forces fought under the British flag; in the Third War (1885) the Shans and Kachins were in open revolt against Thibaw. Patriotism, which united the Burmese[1] in loyalty to their king and to the Golden Land, was conceived in narrow terms.

The instability which characterized the monarchy had its counterparts in society. As is well known, every youth passed a period as a novice in a monastery: but it was also customary for young men to be members of gangs: *damya*, 'Sword blades', were accepted as part of rural life. The two poles of compassion and violence competed in attracting the mind of traditional Burma.

THE COLONIAL EXPERIENCE

Burma provides almost a laboratory experiment in the 'plural society' and 'plural economy'. As a minor, backward British-Indian province, Burma was exposed to a dual form of economic imperialism (British and Indian) while traditional Burmese patterns of government and society were crammed into the procrustean frame of Indo-British administration. (The Shan States were excluded; and in remote valleys the simulacrum of the Burmese court lived on. Similarly, the Karen, Chin, and Kachin frontier areas were left to follow immemorial ways.) J. S. Furnivall in *Colonial Policy and Practice* (C.U.P., 1948) argued that this economic and political subordination to India was the cause of social disorder and breakdown. He

---

[1] In this paper, 'Burmese' is used in the narrow sense of a language group and 'Burman' for any citizen of the Union of Burma. This is not a particularly satisfactory distinction: in fact there is no generally acceptable term to describe all citizens, irrespective of language group.

ignored the long-term centrifugal forces within the system.[1]
However, we must agree that the effect of incorporating Burma
within an Indian Empire where social change, consequent upon
Westernization and British rule, was already advanced, was to
place the Burmese at a disadvantage in the new colonial
structure. Indians predominated in many sectors of the public
services (particularly the army, and military police), in the
social services (e.g. medicine, secondary education), in communications (the railways, posts, telegraphs) and in commerce
and industry. The Burmese who continued to fill 'middle rank'
posts in the administration, and who began to come forward as
lawyers, were drawn almost entirely from the small group of
official families who had served the Burmese kings, and who
transferred their services to the new British administration. This
group was curiously isolated from the pressures of everyday life,
absorbed in a search for status conceived in terms of British
titles and decorations, membership of European clubs, and pre-
ferment as deputy commissioners and district judges. Unlike the
middle classes of Bombay, Calcutta, and Madras (and to a
lesser extent, in the mofussil) these status-seekers did not become
Westernized in any essential form. Behind the façade, they
largely remained dignitaries of the court of the kings.[2] In Akyab
and Moulmein, where British rule first took root, and where
Arakanese and Mons were less in thrall to Burmese-Buddhist
values, a more fundamental transformation of values did take
place among the few families who emerged as counterparts of
the literary and professional upper middle class of India. As one
example, we may cite the banking family founded by Rai Thra
Gyaw at Akyab, which numbers among its members the
statesman and financier, Sir Htoon Aung Gyaw, and Kyaw
Min — the only Burman to succeed in entering the ICS by open
competitive examination.[3] Another Anglicized family produced
May Oung, founder of the Young Men's Buddhist Association

[1] As one example: Furnivall makes great play with the appalling crime statistics
of Tharrawaddy District in Lower Burma as evidence of the disintegration induced
by British rule. He nowhere mentions that Tharrawaddy was a penal colony under
the Burmese kings, and that all the most unruly elements in the population had
been deported thither.

[2] An unintentionally revealing portrait of this Burmese official milieu is given by
Ba U, *My Burma; the Autobiography of a President* (New York, 1958).

[3] Other Burmans entered the ICS by the side-door of nomination.

(YMBA), and Member of the Governor's Executive Council, before his untimely death, and his daughter, Mya Sein, historian and feminist. But in general the professional Burmese middle class was too small, too isolated, and too little imbued with a spirit of public service to provide a counterpart of the type of leadership which in India dominated the national movement from Ram Mohan Roy to Jawaharlal Nehru. Because this upper middle class group was unable to take hold of political initiative, even when it was placed in their hands, power rapidly passed to men whose political sophistication (in Western terms) was very limited, but who were able to establish effective contact with the electorate in the transition period towards representative government which came with the 1930's.

Although a Legislative Council was set up in 1897, this remained a vehicle for the foreign mercantile communities until 1923, when the introduction of a ministerial form of government for certain 'transferred' subjects came about as a result of the 'December Boycott' of 1920. The British were taken by surprise by this quite limited display of national feeling, and, in the aftermath of the Indian 'Dyarchy' reforms, conceded similar reforms to Burma: in the same casual way in which in 1947 Burma was given independence in the wake of India.[1]

Politics in the 1920's witnessed a series of somewhat pointless manoeuvres between the British administration, the British mercantile community, and small Burmese political cliques. Political demands were formulated in the shadow, and to some extent under the wing, of the Indian Congress, in the successive phases of its struggle.

These manoeuvrings were overtaken by the Galon rebellion which broke out in 1930 in Lower Burma under the leadership of Saya San. This revolt had something to do with agrarian discontent and the world slump, but it was essentially a 'Primitive Rebellion' (in the definition of E. J. Hobsbawm), drawing its impetus from the Burmese underworld of astrology and magic.

---

[1] As one example of lack of forethought, there was no machinery to compile electoral registers for the first election of 1922; it was therefore decided to utilize the poll-tax registers, and as this tax was levied on males from the age of eighteen years, the franchise was awarded to youths of eighteen — probably an extension of the franchise unique in modern times.

The political basis was the traditional claim of a pretender to the *Min-laung*, the blood royal; the setting up of a traditional court and capital, and the mobilizing of the traditional territorial levies to eject the wrongful usurpers of the Golden Land.

The Westernized middle classes professed their complete disassociation from the rebellion; but after its suppression, two men earned publicity and popularity from their defence, in the courts, of the Galon rebels: Ba Maw and U Saw. Neither had previously been able to earn much of a living at the Bar, but both possessed considerable shrewdness and sense of opportunity. Both now realized the political advantage which could be obtained by exploiting superstition and ignorance (judged from the standpoint of Western political sophistication). These two, from opposing positions, dominated the politics of the 1930's. They presented issues to the electorate in semi-traditional terms; they evolved crudely effective positions of management in the legislature; and they demonstrated a mastery of political in-fighting. Ba Maw did attempt to formulate a political programme, based on peasant needs (the *Sinyetha* or 'Poor Man's' policy); U Saw never moved out of the politics of opportunism.

In 1936, one of the dominant themes of modern Burmese politics was first sounded: the Rangoon University Students' Strike. The Student Union Committee was to provide the political leadership of Burma for the next quarter of a century, and the lines of friendship and animosity which evolved at the coffee stalls and on the trips to the pagoda, have remained the basis of political alliances and feuds right down into the 1960's. The student strike underlined the paramountcy of violence as the arbiter of politics in Burma. After leaving the university, the student leaders continued their association in the Thakin Party. Although the politicians still continued their manoeuvres in the legislature, the liberal, parliamentary tradition had been virtually discarded, untried. The ideologies of the mob leaders, who now claimed whatever mass following there was, were derived from Fascism and Marxism. The Fascist inspiration was most obvious, in the marching private armies, the screaming of slogans, and the cult of force and hatred. Marxism was absorbed as a curious kind of variant.

There was no direct Comintern influence.[1] Ideology was imported via the Gollancz Left Book Club literature.

Throughout the Dyarchy period, religion was invoked by almost all political leaders. Variations included the gentle social reform movement of May Oung, and the YMBA; the mobilizing of the fringe of the monastic order in a Gandhian campaign of non-violence (bordering perilously on violence) by U Wisara, the rabble-rousing monk; the cabbalistic theology of the Galon rebels; and the cynical invocation of monastic jingoism by Ba Maw (by appealing to fears of 'foreign' religions). The only politicians to eschew the appeal to religion were the Thakins: Thein Pe wrote *Tet Pongyi*, lampooning the monkhood, and Aung San frankly spoke of the monks as redundant in modern Burma. Yet even among the Thakins, many adapted the parables of Buddhism to facilitate communication with the masses.

THE JAPANESE INTERREGNUM

These three years consolidated the movement of Burmese politics away from liberal, parliamentary ends towards totalitarianism. With the departing British Government went virtually all the sophisticated, 'London Returned' political class. U Saw was removed by chance.[2] The field was left to Ba Maw, the Thakins — and, of course, the Japanese. Ba Maw became dictator (Prussian tunic, jackboots, and all). His one-party state was called the Greater Burma Front, and its slogan, 'One Blood, One Voice, One Command'. The state mobilized the people through two arms: the Blood Army and the Sweat Army.[3] The Blood Army or Burma National Army (BNA) was almost entirely officered and led by Thakins, with Aung San as

[1] John Thomson in Frank Trager (ed.), *Marxism in Southeast Asia* (Stanford, 1959), confirms (p. 23) that Burma was outside the systematic build-up of Asian Communism.

[2] The chance of his being prematurely discovered in communication with the Japanese, January 1942.

[3] There were two other armies: the Army of Wah (or National Service) and the Army of the Asiayone — the political front. These were symbolic rather than actual forces. For a popular account of this period see U Hla Pe's *Narrative of the Japanese Occupation of Burma* (edited, with a Foreword by the present writer), Cornell Data Paper, 1961.

Major-General and Minister of Defence. The Sweat Army, a forced labour corps, was composed of luckless villagers who were packed off to toil on the Death Railway. A few idealistic Thakins (notably U Win) went along as welfare officers. Ba Maw arrogated to himself all pomp and majesty, but he was largely cut off from actual events. Tiring of Japanese promises deferred, the Thakins decided to foster a 'Resistance Movement'. They were not by any means the first of the 'underground'. In Arakan, Communist cells, in contact with Thein Pe (who had opposed the Japanese from the start), became centres of resistance. In the eastern hills, the Karens formed the largest and most aggressive movement. In March, 1945, Thakin Than Tun, Ba Maw's Minister of Agriculture, 'went underground' in middle Burma, and with large supplies of British gold created a widespread peasant movement. Lastly, the BNA seized its chance and defected to the British side. And so, in mid-1945, the pattern of the 'underground' which has persisted to the present was already in being: (1) Red Flag Communists, as cells in Arakan; (2) White Flag Communists as large-scale peasant force in middle Burma; (3) Karens in eastern hills; (4) Thakin army (later called People's Volunteer Organization, and then People's Comrade Party) down lines of commmunication.[1]

THE BASIC PATTERN, 1946–62

The writer has told the story of the winning of independence, and the politics of subsequent years, in detail elsewhere.[2] The principal phases may be described as follows:

The Search for a Party of National Unity — I (September 1946–March 1949). Both the pre-war Marxist 'Popular Front' policy, and the wartime 'Greater Burma Front' Government influenced the Thakins to work for a nationwide rally in their resistance movement, named the Anti-Fascist Organization. Quite rapidly, this Popular Front cracked; with the Communists, the guerrilla PVO, sections of the new army, and lastly

[1] Native revolts were reinforced by the Chinese KMT invasion from 1949 onwards.
[2] In *The Union of Burma; a Study of the First Years of Independence* (O.U.P., 1957; 3rd ed., 1961).

the majority of the Karen leaders, breaking away. U Nu continually worked to bring back the rebels into the Government (still regarding them as comrades, as in Student Union days) but while he was on tour in Upper Burma in March, 1949, his Socialist colleagues took fright at the deteriorating situation and offered to hand over power to the Communist rebels. Nu repudiated the offer, and his colleagues resigned *en bloc*, leading to:

Government of National Emergency — I (April 1949–January 1950). Nu formed a small cabinet of independents, in which his principal lieutenants were Justice E Maung (Foreign Minister) and Lieut.-General Ne Win (Deputy Premier, Minister for Home Affairs and Defence). This cabinet succeeded in restoring confidence, both at home and abroad, but Ne Win pressed to be allowed to return to his regular duties. Nu therefore reconstituted his cabinet, bringing back the Socialists and others.

Government of Compromise (January 1950–January 1958). This period (by far the longest) rested upon an uneasy stability dependent upon the agreement to differ which existed between the Nu group and the Ba Swe-Kyaw Nyein group. The Premier recognized that the Socialist Party represented an organized entity within the AFPFL coalition, and allowed them a monopoly of certain cabinet posts (including Industries). The Socialists, in turn, gave the Premier a free hand regarding Religion and Education. The compromise was strained over planning, especially as the Socialist-influenced five-year plan of 1953 collapsed; and on the level of mass influence and power the division became increasingly open as the mass organizations — the trade unions, the Peasants' Organization, etc.— were consolidated on lines of rivalry. At length, U Nu chose to make the division public.

Disruption (January–June 1958). At the third All-Burma Congress of the AFPFL, Nu reiterated the role of Buddhism as the basis of the welfare state, and concluded, 'The AFPFL rejects Marxism as a guiding philosophy or as the ideology of the AFPFL.' The Swe-Nyein group attempted to undermine the Premier from within the Government, but finally withdrew.

Search for a Party of National Unity — II (June–October 1958). Nu reinforced his Government from the Right, bringing in Justice E Maung; from the minorities (the Arakanese bloc); and from the rehabilitated PVO. He sought, also, to 'bring into the light' all the underground Communists, and others. Protracted negotiations led to deterioration in the security situation, and, under pressure from senior army officers (who favoured the Swe-Nyein group), General Ne Win stepped forward to take over the reins of power.

Government of National Emergency — II (October 1958–February 1960). Ne Win entered office by overwhelming vote of Parliament. The constitution permitted the General to exercise emergency government for six months. At the expiry of this term, he went through the motion of resigning, and securing a constitutional amendment from Parliament, extending his tenure for a further twelve months. He then supervised the holding of an election, and handed over power to the choice of the people.

Government of Unity in Diversity (March 1960–February 1962). It was anticipated that a 'Centre' and 'Left' grouping would emerge from this election. Instead, there was a landslide vote for Nu. The extreme Left disappeared; the Socialist Party was decimated. Nu discarded the now discredited name of AFPFL, and called his new 'rally' *Pyidaungsu Apphwe-gyok* or Union League. He was required to honour two election pledges: to make Buddhism the official religion of Burma, and to create new constituent states for the Arakanese and Mons. Having received a mandate demonstrating a broad degree of national support, Nu was committed to two measures strongly calculated to stimulate parochialism and particularism.

Despite introducing a 'Budget for Democracy' followed by a 'Budget for Development', Nu's Government incurred the growing suspicion of 'the colonels', the politically-active group which surrounds General Ne Win. Nu's failure to act against the secessionist activities of the Shans led to an army *coup* on the Thai or Pakistani model.

Army Rule (February 1962– . . .). By setting up a Revolutionary Council and dissolving Parliament, the army went far beyond its 1958 course of action. The trend appeared to repeat the pattern of 1935–45, with a rejection of liberal, parliamentary methods for totalitarian concepts of 'One Voice, One Command'. Interest lies in whether General Ne Win can maintain control, and keep open the possibility of a return to

constitutional methods; or whether he will play Neguib to the
Nasser of one of the rising colonels.

POLITICAL CHARACTERISTICS

The Continuing Tradition

As in old Burma, politics and political organization are
under-developed. Whereas in Anglo-Saxondom they provide
the skeleton and the nervous system of the body national, in
Burma they are little more than a cloak. Party organization is
inchoate: not till January 1958 (on the eve of its dissolution) did
the AFPFL attempt to frame a constitution for itself. Nu's
Union League has about as much organizational structure as
Bhave's Bhoodan movement. This assessment of politics and
government is providential: thereby, Burma has survived
twenty years of near-anarchy without serious strain. The
essential core of national life is the cycle of festivals, the myriad
pagodas and monasteries, the community of the market-place
and the rice-field. All this has maintained the thread of
continuity: and Burma has survived.

The localism of old Burma remains. Politics among Shans,
Kachins, or Karens has little to do with national issues, such as
Socialism or neutralism. It has everything to do with local
leadership, ancient loyalties, parochial grievances. Irredentist
movements among the Shans and Karens have attracted solid
support. Little has occurred since independence to ameliorate
the historic divisions between the Burmese and their feudatories.

The poles of violence and compassion still exercise their
attraction. Violence has been the driving force of the rebellions,
and has recurred in the threats and extortions and murders of
'constitutional' politics. Violence — or, at any rate, force — has
demonstrated its potency as a political principle in the military
government. Compassion has its chief exponent in the political
techniques of U Nu: in the charity and tolerance which he has
extended to opponents (such as the Karen rebels), in his programme of public welfare (*Pyidawtha*) and in his foreign policy.
Compassion is illustrated in the reluctance of Burmese politicians to sever their ties with those from whom they disagree
witness the duration of the compromise between Nu and the

Socialists, 1950–8). Even after twelve years or more 'underground', the rebels are not entirely beyond the pale.

The traditional pre-eminence of religion remains. Politicians know that if they can formulate their messages within the linguistics of religiosity they are more likely to be listened to. The Left — including the Communists — attempt to exploit this medium, but, not surprisingly, their efforts are less well-received than those from politicians whose religious approach is more fundamental: notably, U Nu. Nu stands forth as protector of the *Sangha*, purifier of the *Damma*, devotee, and mystic: he combines public and personal religious eminence, as only an honoured few of the old kings did.

The Advent of Democracy

The prospect for some adaptation of democracy into a Burmese mode will be briefly considered under two heads: the formal working of political institutions, and the influence of the social milieu.

Since independence, Parliament has been going through the accepted forms of activity prescribed from Westminster. It has never been the locus of power: this has rested with the party caucus, or with the army: but it has gained prestige, and general acceptance among all parties as the institutional symbol of democracy. During the disruption, the struggle was fought out in the chamber, and was resolved in terms of the views indicated in the chamber. Three general elections have been held (1951, 1956 and 1960) and though there have been plenty of individual cases of wrongful practices, the contest in general has been fairly conducted and the results were accepted by all parties as embodying the people's will. The third election produced a result distasteful to the military junta in power, but they made no attempt to dispute its consequences. The orderly and unquestioned transfer of the premiership from Nu to Ba Swe and back (in 1956) and from Nu to Ne Win and back, has few parallels elsewhere in South or South-East Asia.

Despite efforts to revitalize institutions of local self-government, it is not possible to detect any growth in constructive 'grass roots' political activity. Local 'boss' politics has become less oppressive than in the early years of independence, as the army and civil administration have re-established some sort of law and order in the countryside. Corruption and 'fixing' are probably less systematically applied than in any other South-East Asian country.

The cultural milieu is (it may be argued) more favourable to democracy than to the old kingship or to modern authoritarianism. First, there is the relative homogeneity of the Burmese. The class structure is fluid. Status is still determined more by classless attributes (such as age, or the wearing of the Robe) than by wealth or (more doubtfully) by rank. There is a common tongue, and a common cultural idiom. The Burmese political tradition of near-anarchy permits a remarkable amount of criticism and comment among press and public.[1] Freedom of speech is almost excessive, in terms of responsibility and restraint. The resilience, good humour, and tolerance of the Burmese enable them to distinguish between party political attitudes (where no holds are barred and a dagger is concealed in every palm) and the amenities of personal and social relationships. The hatreds which destroy democratic associations in Middle-Eastern countries are almost entirely absent.[2]

CONCLUSION

Despite the near-chaos which has persisted in Burma since independence, and although a military régime has been imposed since this study was first drafted, this writer adheres to the view (first stated in 1956) that of all the South-East Asian countries, Burma is most likely to create a social democracy in the years ahead.

One factor in the situation remains a mystery, and may nullify any judgment — the role of the younger generation. Burma is still in the hands of the student strike leaders of 1936. The development of any movement of opinion among those under forty has been almost entirely checked by the continuing grip of these men on politics, government, the army, and all other institutions. How do the post-war products of Rangoon

[1] There have been attempts to impose censorship, but only under the military régime has this been accepted.

[2] Aung San, singular in many ways, was the only political leader of his generation to be utterly ruthless in deed as in word. He was capable of committing murder himself, when this was a political desideratum.

University, the men and women up to forty, really view affairs? Student political feeling has been sharply Left-wing: but how far was this merely the politics of protest against an immovable Establishment? What is the influence of the hundreds of Burmans who have received training in Britain and the United States? Are the younger generation religious or rationalist, traditionalist or modern minded? Do they look East or West? Probably not one of the pundits on Burmese politics has even the rudiments of an answer to these questions: questions which will determine the political future of Burma.

Chapter seven

THAILAND
— A CONSERVATIVE STATE

---

by Stuart Simmonds

IN EVERY modern account of South-East Asia reference is made, sooner or later, to the fact that Thailand maintained her political independence during the century or so of European colonial rule on the mainland. It is important to consider how far this situation has affected the nature of political evolution. Economically Thailand has made general progress for a considerable period of time. Politically this process has been aided by the long continued existence of a strong central government. What loosely may be called 'national' unity has been sought after as the chief political desideratum for many hundreds of years. This theme can be traced even in the historical inscriptions and in the literary epics of the medieval period. This unity has not been sought for its own sake but the understanding of the need for it has been forced on Thai rulers by their experience in a climate of unceasing foreign pressure. The strict necessity of avoiding fatal disunities which might lay the way open to foreign interference has produced a tendency to conservatism in domestic political attitudes. When internal changes have taken place they have frequently been occasioned by foreign policy requirements and here the successful maintenance of flexibility has demanded the rapid re-establishment of stable government after an upheaval or, if possible, even the keeping of an apparently untroubled front to the outer world.

There is also an innate resistance to change to be met with among the people, about eighty-five per cent of whom are countrymen, concerned with the agricultural production which is vital to national prosperity, but sheltered in their still largely traditional village society, in a country firmly ruled and at peace, from the impact of political change that has affected even the farmer elsewhere in Asia.

This conservatism among the rulers and the ruled is an important constant attitude and, since the years 1945–61 have not been remarkable in terms of political development of a progressive kind, helps to explain why the reasons for slowness of movement in this field cannot altogether be found within the period itself.

It is necessary to look back over a hundred years to see how Thailand, determined on maintaining independence, has moved, under external pressures, from a country whose foreign policy outlook was limited, in the main, to the matter of relations with her own immediate neighbours, and who domestically did not question in any way the nature of her political institutions, to a nation who sees herself, and is seen to be, fully upon the world stage.

DEVELOPMENT OF ASSOCIATIONS WITH THE WEST, 1850–1932

In 1850 Thailand had been, for some time, in expansionist mood and though the motives for this expansion were to some extent defensive in nature the result was to give Thailand control over large areas in Laos, Cambodia and the Malay Peninsula. Though Western nations were beginning to seek special privileges in terms of freer trade, relations with the West were kept to a minimum under the influence of unimaginative elder statesmen with personal interests in the traditional organization of commerce.

King Mongkut[1] (1851–68) attempted a fundamental modification of Thai attitudes. He had few illusions about the potential threat to his country created by the arrival of Britain in Burma and the Malay states and of France in Indochina. Thailand's tributary relationship with China was allowed to lapse and an outward-looking policy of improved relations with the new forces in the area was adopted. The opening of the

[1] Transcription according to the general system of the Royal Institute of Thailand.

country to European contact, first in the field of commerce and mainly with Britain, inevitably led, as Sir John Bowring had forecast, to internal administrative changes.[1] Ability to adjust in part was essential to the survival of the whole. It was the impact of the West that caused the Thai to become critically conscious for the first time of the nature of their forms of government. Both King Mongkut and his son and successor King Chula-longkǫn (1868–1910) wrote much about traditional Thai government, and on history, religion and related subjects: something which had never been done before. Even in the narrow literary sense this was an advance, for in these books and essays a new use for the medium of prose developed.

By no means lacking in justifiable pride in their own culture these rulers clearly saw that the new kind of relationship with the powerful outside world created a need for internal changes. These they began to make. King Mongkut's major contribution was in foreign policy and in religious reform and that of King Chulalongkǫn in the fields of education, training, administration and finance. Schools for princes and other selected future administrators were set up to broaden the basis of education in government that had theretofore been provided by the court page system. A few students, mainly of royal blood at first, began to be sent abroad. Foreign advisers were employed in many government departments and care was taken to maintain a balance of foreign influence, in this as in other ways, by selecting advisers from a number of different countries. Slavery for debtors and prisoners-of-war and state labour obligations for the people were abolished, and reforms were instituted in methods of tax-collection, provincial government and the administration of justice.

Though her independent status was maintained Thailand was forced to acquiesce in the loss of considerable amounts of territory, some 90,000 square miles in all, over which she had claimed suzerainty or had exercised direct administrative control. By 1909 she held no territory east of the Mekhong river and had surrendered her influence in Cambodia and four Malay states. Moreover the imposition of unequal treaties and other manifestations of alien power that resulted from Western capital

[1] Sir John Bowring: *The Kingdom and People of Siam* (London, 1857), vol. II, p. 226.

investment meant that true independence was compromised to some extent. The fortunate rivalry of Britain and France and the foreign policy of the kings in the second half of the nineteenth century, which might be characterized in modern terms as a species of 'positive' neutrality, did, however, leave Thailand with more than nominal freedom. Internal policy resulted in the maintenance of stable centralized government and the promotion of a slowly developing economy which was able to keep on terms with the outside world during the colonial period.

Yet the lifting of a nation from a medieval to a modern condition is a prodigious task and, perhaps inevitably, the adoption and adaptation of Western ideas did not change the basic patterns of social organization. The monarchy retained the vital attributes of its particular form of absolutism. Reforms in the administrative structure, particularly in the provincial sector where Western colonial models had an influence, resulted in an even higher degree of centralization than had existed before. The administrative élite had always been fundamentally bureaucratic in nature. This bureaucracy, looking inward towards its royal patrons, was not absolutely exclusive. It was penetrable from below to a limited extent. But it was separated by the nature of its functions from the mass of the people who continued their country life still relatively unaltered by the educational reforms which began to bring new secular schooling to them from 1921 onwards.

Trade was in the hands of aliens, either Western or Chinese, and the Thai hardly took part in this aspect of the national life, though the Government continued to take profit from commercial operations as it had done throughout the centuries. This non-participation in trade was, above all others, the limiting factor in social development because it meant that no strong non-alien middle-class grew up creating, through its own self-made wealth, a permanent stake in the prosperity and progress of the nation. The individual rice-farmer had his own stake — the rights he held over a small plot of land — but this was essentially local, not national, in character. He participated in no nationally important activity beyond the actual growing of the vital rice.

THE 'REVOLUTION' OF 1932 AND ITS RESULTS

The *coup d'état* of 24 June, 1932 was effected by a group of civil and military officials who called themselves the People's Party, little more than a fashionable name, and who have come to be known as the 'promoters'. Many of them had been educated in Europe under the auspices of the royal Government. The most prominent was one of the younger men, Nai Pridi Phanomyong (Luang Pradit Manutham), a lawyer and university teacher. He was the political theorist of the movement. Among the causes of the 'revolution' were general factors, such as dissatisfaction with the absolute monarchy as being a system of government that left the law-givers above the law. Government economies which fell mainly on the civil service and armed forces, involving dismissals without prospect of other employment, and the imposition of a salary tax were the immediate causes of irritation to the group that carried out the revolt. But the aspect of political idealism ought also to be taken into account. This may not have affected many of the promoters but it was certainly a factor with at least one of the foreign-educated — Pridi. He had acquired radical ideas in Paris and was a strong enough character to attempt to put them into practice in his own country on return. The fascinating paradoxical contradiction between innate Thai regard for tradition and the willing acceptance of, and indeed positive seeking after, new foreign ideas results in an ever-changing synthesis. In this lies much of the secret of political flexibility that has aided Thailand to survive in a harsh world.

In 1932 Pridi was as much ahead of his time as King Mongkut had been in 1855. Like the latter he was at first almost alone in promoting new ideas but he was a lawyer not a king and he had to beat the system from outside not redirect it from within. The system beat him in the end and there are many Thais who would argue that this was just as well. The economic policy which he planned to introduce was dominated by its theoretical aspect. The original proclamation of the People's Party had promised peace, freedom, equality and education for the people but the most important clause was the third which read:

The new government promises to promote the economic welfare of its citizens by providing remunerative employment for everyone and by promulgating a national economic policy designed to end poverty.[1]

Pridi's attempt to pass the national economic policy into law in March 1933 at first gained considerable support but it caused irreconcilable differences to arise both in the People's Assembly and the State Council. The plan itself was revolutionary enough. It involved the nationalization of land (except house-plots), industry, capital and labour. The vast majority of the people were to become salaried pensionable state employees. Pridi was accused of trying to introduce Communism but the document, formidable in length and style, is a remarkable theoretical exercise in the application of welfare-state socialism in Thai conditions.[2] Changes were to be effected with compensation not by expropriation and, with foreign pressure in mind, alien business interests were provided with safeguards. Pridi described himself as an agrarian socialist and the plan as a combination of capitalism and socialism. There was an authoritarian air about the plan and indeed it could hardly have been put into operation except by force in a nation of politically unemancipated land-holding farmers.

On 2 April, 1933 an Act making Communist activities illegal was announced. Pridi left the country on a foreign visit. The definition of Communism in the Act was wide enough to embrace any form of state socialism. Pridi's political intentions had administered a shock to the more moderate promoters and the assembly was dissolved due to the deep division among its members. On 20 June, 1933 army and navy leaders, under Phraya Phahon Pholaphayuha and Luang Phibun Songkhram, arrested the members of the Government and took control on the grounds of the need to counter a Communist danger to the state. This convenient precedent for direct military action in the political field was to be remembered and used again in Thailand when the word 'Communism' became a useful panic-promoter among her allies.

The Government had its own far less radical economic plans which stressed advances in the agricultural field and assistance

[1] Quoted in K. P. Landon, *Siam in Transition* (O.U.P., 1939), p. 262.
[2] Full translation, ibid., pp. 260–93.

for the farmer by the formation of co-operative credit and land-purchasing societies. The abundant energies of Pridi were employed between 1934 and 1939 in the Ministry of the Interior where he began the establishment of local municipal and rural district government, an important advance in decentralization, in Foreign Affairs where he negotiated a set of equitable treaties with foreign powers, and in Finance.

The constitution of 1932 placed strong restrictions on the power of the monarchy, which lost its absolutist character, and on the power of senior members of the royal family to engage in political activities. Three separate branches of government were established; executive, legislative and judicial. The People's Assembly was given two categories of members, those elected for a four-year term, at first by indirect suffrage through village and district representatives, and those appointed, in practice, by the government in power. The institution of second-category members favoured the development of self-perpetuating governments. Originally, provision had been made for a completely elective assembly after ten years or when more than half the electorate had completed four years' primary education, whichever was the shorter period. The establishment of political parties was not permitted and there was censorship of press and radio.

The Phraya Phahon Government gave considerable and increasing support to education particularly in the primary sector to establish widespread literacy. Ĉhulalongkǫn University was already in existence and, in 1937, Thammasat University (University of Moral and Political Sciences) was founded by Pridi. This institution, which was designed to train a politically sophisticated intelligentsia to complement the literate voter, provided Pridi with a group of followers in the years to come, an important factor in Thailand where political loyalties are directed to persons rather than to parties.

The effect of the 1932 revolution was, therefore, to set up a form of constitutional government which, however, did not turn over power to the people. King Prachathipok, in his abdication statement of 2 March, 1935, already foresaw that power had fallen firmly into the hands of the promoters themselves.[1] The lack of knowledge of democracy and interest in national govern-

[1] ibid., pp. 257–8.

ment on the part of the mass of the population made this inevitable. In any case all sections of the promoters envisaged at least an interim period of authoritarian constitutional rule. Nevertheless the revolution had created conditions for possible political advance. Its inspiration was based on Western democratic ideas imbibed by a very small number of foreign-trained students.

The attitude of mind which inspired Pridi to revolt and reform, impatience with the traditional local world and admiration for the active materialistic principles of the West, as expressed by him implicitly, and sometimes explicitly, throughout the text of his national economic policy proposals was not so very different from that of non-Marxist nationalist leaders in other South-East Asian countries, for example, Sutan Sjahrir.[1] However the absence of a local colonial régime and the relative prosperity of Thailand, though it admittedly lay within the economic framework of a colonial South-East Asia, provided no strong tensions on which a natural and widespread nationalism could be built. The overnight collapse of the absolutist state left the promoters with no alternative but to impose their would-be democratic institutions. This was attempted both at the levels of central and local government but the forms which were established were too weak to take root in the poorly prepared soil. They could not function because they were not understood by the people. The impossibility of obtaining genuine popular participation at this stage was demonstrated by the elections of 1933 and 1937 when less than a tenth and a fifth of the electorate voted. What should be noted, however, is that the number of voters doubled as between the two elections and that while officers of the armed services constituted a large majority of the second, appointed, category, the elected members of the Assembly were mainly respected civilians. Nevertheless natural conservatism from below and, soon, from above in the form of military government held in check even the hope of democracy which, in any case, existed only in the minds of a few.

[1] e.g. Sutan Sjahrir, *Out of Exile* (New York, Day, 1949).

THAILAND AND JAPAN

Luang Phibun Songkhram, who as Minister of Defence since 1934 had begun to build up the army, succeeded as premier on 15 December, 1938. Without disrupting connexions with the West, Phibun gradually led Thailand into a closer association with Japan, first of all commercially and then in political terms. The military leaders were as adept as the royal governments had been at estimating shifts of political power abroad and their probable effects on Thailand. Phibun was well aware that a southward move by Japan would involve his country. When Vichy France was unable to resist Japanese demands in Indochina (from which Thailand drew some benefit) and Britain was too weak to offer military support in the crisis days of December 1941 it was not only opportunistic but also wise of Thailand to seek an accommodation with Japan. The aim was that of keeping fighting off Thai soil and it is doubtful if local British intervention would have been welcomed, even if it had been forthcoming. Some form of alignment with Japan could only have been checked if the West had been able to halt her well short of Thai frontiers. It might have been open to the Phibun Government to adopt an attitude analogous to that of Denmark towards Nazi Germany, but, in the event, it offered or was coerced into a greater degree of co-operation which culminated in declarations of war against Britain and the United States on 25 January, 1942.

The receptivity of Thailand's leaders to foreign political ideas led, in the late 1930's and early 1940's, to the Government's acquiring the appearance of a Fascist-type dictatorship. The military assumed a major role in national life. Economic and political nationalism was encouraged and, with Japan's aid, the pan-Thai chauvinistic policies were crowned with temporary success when Thailand took control over areas she had lost in Indochina and Malaya and gained a new sphere of influence in the eastern Shan states. The conservative attitude of the people did much to nullify the effectiveness of rather silly cultural decrees inspired by nationalistic motives but paradoxically expressed in terms of superficial Westernization.

In the field of domestic politics this first Phibun régime paid lip service to constitutional government but the war-time emergency situation provided a plausible excuse for not implementing the provisions for a fully elective assembly, due to come into force in 1942. The Assembly met throughout the period but its members, fairly independent at first, were gradually brought to heel by a mixture of threats and patronage and found themselves doing little more than giving *ex post facto* approval to government measures. They did not succeed in bringing down the Government by a vote of no-confidence until mid-1944 by which time general political sentiment, even in the services, was in favour of a flexible re-adjustment towards the Western allies in view of their imminent victory. Such a policy meant that Phibun had to retire from the field. Seen in terms of conservative Thai political attitudes, whose first consideration is strong government and the presenting of an acceptable united front to the outer world, Phibun had become a liability and he went without resistance. In the same terms his rise in the late 1930's was an asset to Thailand because his nationalist revival offered prospect of immediate gain and also provided the certainty of firm government in an increasingly difficult foreign policy situation.

AN OPPORTUNITY FOR LIBERALISM

It is often said that Thailand came out of the war well. This is true to the extent that no fighting took place on her soil and that she was left with the pre-1940 frontiers when the inevitable post-war territorial adjustments were made. But her economic condition had deteriorated. Export trade, of vital importance, had been mainly with Western markets via the British-controlled entrepôt centres of Singapore, Penang and Hong-kong. There was a great decline in exports which led to large unfavourable balances of trade from 1943 to 1947 contributing to budgetary deficits. The production of rubber, tin, and timber was reduced to small percentages of the pre-war levels. Much rice land went out of cultivation. Forced loans to Japan, the tying of the baht to the yen, high local wages and other factors led to a serious inflationary situation.

There was need for a government in Thailand which would treat with the Allies in a spirit of concession in the hope of obtaining a peace settlement that was not too harsh and opportunities for co-operation to restore the economic position. The sympathies of the United States, who had refused to accept Thailand's declaration of war and who had regarded her as an occupied state, were engaged to help moderate the less lenient demands of Britain and France.

Pridi, wartime regent and organizer of the Free Thai resistance movement, was the obvious leader with whom the West could deal. A peace treaty was rapidly concluded (signed on 1 January, 1946) though a settlement with France was delayed until November 1946. Thailand became a member of UNO in December. Pridi himself had become Prime Minister in March 1946 following the resignation of Khuang Aphaiwong, a liberal leader and associate of Pridi, who had become a potential rival in terms of popular support.

The external political situation, now dominated by the Western democracies, as well as the inclinations of the civilian leaders newly come to power, made a move towards a democratic government likely. Political parties were established and elections to replace the second category members with elected Assemblymen were held on 6 January, 1946. A higher proportion, about a third, of electors took part and supporters of Pridi, organized in the Sahachip (Co-operative) Party, won a sweeping victory. After the elections a re-alignment of opposition groups in the Prachathipat (Democratic) Party, under Khuang Aphaiwong, took place. They were determined to oppose any attempt to reintroduce radical economic policies.

A new permanent constitution was drafted and came into force on 9 May, 1946. It removed the restrictions which had prevented members of the royal family from taking part in political life. The provisions for the legislature were revised. The Assembly was to be fully elective by popular vote but the Assembly itself was to choose the members of an Upper House. This Senate was to have power to initiate legislation and pass votes of confidence. It could check legislative measures from the Assembly but could not pass votes of censure on the Government. This bi-cameral system, as Vella has pointed out, marked a regression, in theory, from the provisions of 1932.[1] Like those

[1] W. Vella, *Impact of the West on Government in Thailand* (University of California Press, Berkeley, 1955), p. 389.

provisions at an interim stage of development, which is all they ever reached, the new system with its long-term Senate provided, in practice, for self-perpetuating government. But it is doubtful if it was framed as a deliberately retrograde measure.

The general political atmosphere was more liberal than had ever before been the case. Until difficulties for the Government began to mount there was considerable freedom for the Press. Even a Communist publishing house was allowed to exist, and, after the repeal of the 1933 Act concerning Communism in 1946, a Communist member was elected to the Assembly. A statement by Pridi on the question of repeal is interesting because he made it clear that the main motive in this was diplomatic rather than political and was one of the conciliatory moves made to the Soviet Union to avoid a veto on the issue of Thailand's entry to the UN.[1]

Trade union organization of a sort was attempted by the formation of a Central Labour Union with the support of the Government. Its leadership was mainly Thai, its membership Chinese.

Pridi showed understanding and sympathy for the post-war independence movements in South-East Asia. His proposal for an eventual union of South-East Asian states was evidence that he was thinking in terms of alignment with a new set of forces which might be expected to develop in the area.

Asylum was given to the Lao independence movement and a South-East Asia League, later to become Communist dominated, with membership among Left-wing Thai, Vietnamese, Lao and Cambodians had its headquarters in Bangkok for a time in 1947.

Pridi himself attracted a good deal of popular support particularly in the navy, among civil servants, and the students of 'his' Thammasat University. His reputation as a Free Thai leader and his general success over the peace settlements stood him in good stead. But after the sudden death of King Ananda Mahidon on 9 June, 1946 insidious rumour connecting him and close associates with the event began seriously to affect his popularity. It was said that he intended to establish a republic. That general sentiment for the monarchy was strong enough

[1] David A. Wilson, 'Thailand and Marxism' in F. N. Trager (ed.), *Marxism in Southeast Asia* (Stanford University Press; O.U.P., 1960).

for accusations of action against it to bring him into disrepute is
an indication of the underlying strength of traditional attitudes.
His personal position was greatly weakened and his Government was compromised by involvement of its members in
financial scandals. Strikes and Thai-Chinese riots caused a
threat to public order.

On 24 August, 1946 Pridi was succeeded by an associate,
Rear-Admiral Luang Thamrong Nawasawat. The internal
situation did not improve under his administration. Financial
scandals increased. Profiteering, smuggling and inflation grew
in spite of measures taken against them. Critical debates in the
Assembly became frequent and, in May 1947, caused the
resignation and re-constitution of the Thamrong Government.
Phibun Songkhram was reported to be the force behind a new
political group known as the Thammathipat (Right is Might)
Party. The Government through its failure to provide firm and
stable rule was thereby, in Thai terms, in a position of considerable danger.

THE MILITARY RÉGIMES

The end of the quasi-liberal civilian rule came on the night of
8–9 November, 1947 when Phibun Songkhram carried out a
military *coup d'état*. The army justified its action on the grounds
of the inefficiency and corruption of the Government, its
ultimate responsibility for the death of the King, and of the
seditious behaviour of some of its Free Thai members in selling
arms to the Viet Minh and storing them for use in connexion
with future political action.

It was frankly admitted that the *coup* was unconstitutional.
Field-Marshal Phibun said:

> Public opinion wanted the change and, as it could not be done
> by constitutional means, the former government having a
> majority in Parliament, the Army decided unanimously to get rid
> of it.[1]

It may be added that during the seventeenth and eighteenth
centuries dynastic changes had on several occasions been
carried out by military leaders using the method of *coup d'état*.

[1] Vella, op. cit., p. 391.

Phibun's declared intention of returning to politics, made earlier in the year, had already caused hostile comment abroad and the need for international approval of the new régime persuaded him to act with caution. He now disclaimed all desire to take over political control and within a few weeks accepted the post of Commander-in-Chief of the army in place of that of Commander-in-Chief of all armed forces which he had assumed on 9 November. The opposition Democratic Party was invited to form a provisional government and Khuang Aphaiwong became Prime Minister, a situation which was confirmed by elections held on 29 January, 1948. By co-operating with the military the Democrats gained at least the appearance of power which would not have come their way otherwise. But this does not fully explain why they were prepared to compromise their liberal principles; it was partly due to a patriotic feeling in favour of national unity.

After the elections the régime obtained international recognition in a matter of hours and then, on 8 April, the Khuang Government was forced to resign by extremist officers and it was replaced by one led by Phibun himself.[1]

This Government also was soon recognized, for the prospect of a stable régime in Thailand was attractive to the Western powers, particularly France and Britain, whose difficulties in Indochina and Malaya were becoming more acute. During the Pridi era Bangkok had shown signs of becoming a centre of Left-wing activity whereas Phibun took an uncompromisingly anti-Communist line. This policy was motivated not only by purely opportunistic considerations. Thai sympathies for the national independence movement in Vietnam were tempered by the suspicion that a Communist victory there might increase the eventual influence of China in the region. The Thai were already alive to the probability of Communist victory in China itself and feared Communism as an efficient vehicle for the spread of Chinese power. The powerful Chinese Communist leadership of the revolt in Malaya was regarded with anxiety in view of the separatist tendencies that had long existed in the southern provinces of Thailand with their large Malay and Chinese minorities. The situation in the unstable north-east

[1] Full accounts of the period are given in *Survey of International Affairs, 1947–8* (R.I.I.A., O.U.P., 1952), and in Vella, op. cit.

provinces was complicated by the presence there of some 50,000 pro-Viet Minh Vietnamese. Such factors led Thailand to seek Western support.

The post-war economic recovery dates from 1948. The increased efficiency of the new Government, in which a number of able civilians continued to serve, certainly played a part in initiating the favourable movement towards prosperity which continued generally in spite of some less good years in the later 1950's. The overall financial and economic situation has remained sound and this in itself has been a check on any tendency to violent political change.

The Phibun administration produced three revised constitutions, the last of these being the permanent constitution which came into force in November 1951. On the legislative side this constitution returned to the provisions of 1932 and thus the bicameral legislature was replaced by a single chamber assembly. The system of two categories of members, appointive (ten-year term) and elective (five-year term) was retained for a period of ten years. Provision was made for the gradual replacement of appointive by elective members as literacy among the electorate increased. The elective members did not outnumber the appointive until 1957 when the Government at once attempted to raise the second category total to parity by the appointment of thirty-seven additional members. They were overruled by the Constitutional Tribunal.

The executive power of the Council of Ministers was safeguarded by constitutional provisions such as authority to dissolve the Assembly and call for new elections, to remain in office before and during elections, and to issue decrees of an emergency nature without the Assembly being in session.

The power of the throne was again subjected to stronger limitation probably because the King was a potential focus for liberal opposition. The law banning political parties was reintroduced after the 1947 *coup* and anti-Communist legislation was passed in 1952.

Two aspects have been important in internal politics between 1949 and 1961. First, the overcoming of resistance from groups supporting Pridi who attempted counter-*coups* in February 1949 and June 1951. Action had also to be taken against certain army officers who threatened the régime.

The second aspect was the development of a major power struggle within the military group. In 1952 twenty years had passed since the original revolution, and younger men, not members of the group of promoters, were coming into the field. Prominent among these was Police-General Phao Siyanon. As Minister of the Interior and Director-General of Police he commanded, by 1954, a para-military force of 42,000 men equipped with tanks and armoured cars and with commando and paratroop units. Phao and General Sarit Thanarat, an army commander, were stepping up to challenge the leadership of Phibun. All three had become rivals in the economic as well as in the military sense as they were all heavily involved in commercial enterprises. Phao became an unpopular figure because of the high-handed actions of the police and their open dependence on the profits of opium smuggling which had become an extremely lucrative business.

In 1955, when Sarit became Commander-in-Chief of the army, Phao began to lose influence. In the same year Field-Marshal Phibun went on a world tour. On his return he began to introduce experiments of a democratic nature. The establishment of political parties was permitted from 25 September, 1955 in preparation for the 1957 elections. When in London Phibun had been intrigued by the orators of Hyde Park and he instituted a similar idea in Bangkok. The result was astounding, for crowds of many thousands thronged the open space outside the walls of the Grand Palace to hear Saturday afternoon speeches highly critical of the Government.

Seeing military power slipping from his personal grasp Phibun had hoped to swing public opinion behind him by means of democratic reform but the situation got out of hand and the 'Hyde Park' experiment in free speech had to be curtailed before the elections.

Twenty-three political parties came into existence. Some five of these were of significance but the only nation-wide challenge to the Government was provided by Khuang's Democratic Party. The elections of 26 February, 1957 were carried out in an atmosphere of unusual tension. After the declaration of a result which favoured the Government more definitely than had seemed to be probable at intermediate stages of the count, charges of ballot-rigging were made.[1] The main responsibility was fixed upon Phao but Phibun shared in it. Public indignation was extremely strong and culminated in spontaneous student demonstrations on 2 March. Tactful handling of this situation by Sarit made him into something of a popular hero and eased his subsequent rise to supreme power.

One may recall at this point the reference made by Phibun in 1947 to public opinion and the demand for a change of government.[2] In 1957 a situation had again arisen in which sections of the public interested in national affairs were disturbed by the growing irresponsibility of the Government in power. A new leader was looked for and accepted in Sarit Thanarat just as Phibun Songkhram had been accepted ten years before. To this extent public opinion, though not making use of many of the usual forms of democratic expression, may be said to have an influence. Public views seem to provide a sort of safety-valve for the blowing of which an astute would-be leader listens and, by using it as his cue, assumes power by means of his own devising. Thus, at one and the same time, autocratic rule is prevented from becoming unbearably extreme and yet the autocracy is preserved. It is not too far-fetched to interpret the chronicles for the years 1781–2 in a similar way. The fall of King Tak Sin to Ĉhao Phraya Chakkri, the military leader who became King Rama I, did not take place until there had been widespread public dissatisfaction with the rule of the former.

Sarit Thanarat delayed his move for several months. He declared his loyalty to Phibun and supported the new Government formed on 2 April in which he was Minister of Defence. During the summer it became clear that action against Phao would also have to include Phibun. On 20 August Sarit and his closest associates Thanǫm Kittikhaĉhǫn and Praphat Ĉharusathian, future Minister of the Interior, resigned from the Government and on 16 September Sarit carried out a military coup as a result of which Phibun and Phao left the country. Sarit's move had the support of the King. It had generally good reception in the press, including the liberal newspapers. Hope for better things was the prevailing tone.

---

[1] See 'The Siamese Elections of February 1957', *The World Today* (1957), v, pp. 220–6.
[2] See above p. 131.

K

An interim government under Phot Sarasin, the Secretary-General of SEATO, was installed until new and more honest elections held on 15 December confirmed the military group in power. General Thanom then became Prime Minister and Field-Marshal Sarit himself finally took over on 20 October, 1958. Martial law was then declared, the Assembly dissolved and the constitution abrogated.

Sarit has ruled through an interim constitution promulgated on 28 January, 1959. Special powers in matters of state security and for the dismissal of members of the ministerial council were reserved for the Prime Minister. A Constituent Assembly of appointed members was set up which had a quasi-legislative function and also the duty of drafting a new constitution. The Constituent Assembly was made up of service officers and the inclusion of a considerable number of able civilians drew on a wider range of talent. An interesting provision of the interim constitution is that which separates the executive and 'legislative' functions by laying down that members of the Council of Ministers shall not also be members of the Constituent Assembly. This seems to limit the latter to a mainly advisory role.

Field-Marshal Sarit's rule has been chiefly remarkable for the steady economic progress and development that has taken place. In foreign policy a firmly anti-Communist line has been followed. Thailand has been a consistent upholder of UN policies and actions. She was the first country in South-East Asia to obtain a loan from the International Bank and has enjoyed strong support from the United States since 1950.

The apparently uncompromising nature of the American alliance has drawn forth the expression of considerable disquiet in Thailand, all of which cannot be ascribed to the result of successful Leftist propaganda. The rise of Japan in the 1930's to challenge Western domination in South-East Asia produced a response from Thailand which showed that the changing balance of forces was understood. The rise of China as a potential influence in the area in the 1950's has not caused Thailand to make significant policy re-adjustments. Why is this so?

Ideological considerations are not of prime importance in Thai politics. It is impossible to imagine that there could be a spontaneous move towards Communism on ideological grounds. The internal conditions in the country do not warrant it and, in any case, the number of Leftist political thinkers is small and none have been members of the ruling group in recent years. This situation may be contrasted with that of Burma and Indonesia, not to mention Vietnam, where an interest in Marxism, if not in Communism as such, formed a natural part of the political education of the post-war leaders for a decade or two before they came to power.

Yet the very firm and frequent declarations of opposition to Communism might also be unexpected. Neighbouring Cambodia, also with an authoritarian anti-Communist leader, has been much more accommodating if not to the doctrine then at least to its exponents — the Soviet Union and China.

Any considerations of crude self-interest, which may well be far from the most important, can be disposed of first. American generosity, which is naturally enough related to support for United States policies, has made the association a profitable one for Thailand. The ease and promptitude with which Thai governments have scotched the many 'Communist-inspired plots' which have been discovered has no doubt been noted with gratitude. Furthermore a memory remains of the influence that Thailand exerted in Laos and Cambodia; the last manifestation of this was, after all, less than twenty years ago. Thailand may well have appreciated United States encouragement for her attempts to increase her political influence in these countries by liaisons with local factions. As in former times defensive rather than offensive motives are paramount in such apparently expansionist tendencies.

For a number of reasons the challenge of China is seen as being particularly dangerous and co-existence with her more difficult to accomplish than was the case with Japan.

First there is the presence of an economically dominant Chinese minority in Thailand numbering over two million. The problem of assimilation is great and while its solution is in doubt there is hesitancy even to accept a diplomatic mission from the People's Republic of China. From this stems Thailand's reluctance to see the People's Republic as a member of the United Nations.

The existence of the Thai autonomous region in South China and the Thai-Meo autonomous province in North Vietnam is a matter for concern. Though little indication of aggressive tendencies is apparent these two régimes contain an estimated

9,000,000 people ethnically and linguistically related to the Thai of Thailand. The re-appearance of Pridi in China since 1954 and the difficulty of estimating how far he still has political influence in Thailand itself is a cause of particular anxiety because it introduces a challenge to the ruling group in terms of personalities.

In addition, the north-eastern region presents a security problem to the Thai Government which exists quite apart from the presence of the Vietnamese minority there. This region is composed of provinces with a high population which are economically less rich than other parts of the country. Time is needed for the present Government's plans for economic improvement to take effect. From these provinces have come a number of Pridi's associates. Moreover there has been almost a tradition of opposition to the Government in this region and many Thai with Leftist sympathies have been north-easterners. The Lao-speaking population has close affinities with the trans-Mekhong Lao and they are the descendants of people brought across the river during the military campaigns of the nineteenth century.

For this reason and, too, because of a clear understanding of the need for political unity and a complete lack of confidence that the Laotians of Laos can achieve it, and the stability that would derive from it, the Thai Government has consistently advocated a more determined policy in the Laotian crisis than any of her allies and associates.

It seems likely that Thailand will maintain her association with Western policies unless a complete collapse of the Western position appears imminent. Her economic position depends on continued trade with the non-communist world whatever additional arrangements may be made. Since China and Communism together are a daunting combination any adjustment towards neutralism is far more likely to involve the distant and less threatening Soviet Union.

CONCLUSION

The preservation of political independence in Thailand has had three important indirect effects.

The threat from the West came at a time when Thailand was enjoying considerable success against weakened local rivals and so the imperative necessity for strong but flexible government was made plain at a time when good fortune at home might have led to an intensification of internal power rivalries. Dangerous external pressures were then maintained long enough for an experienced reaction for them to mature. The outward look and the gradualist methods of change thus came into being.

Thai contact with foreign powers has been more within her own control. The student from Thailand has not been bound to associate himself with a particular Western language and culture because knowledge gained in its terms would provide him with the key to a successful career in a colonial régime. He has been free to choose and it is interesting that in most fields, for example, the law, constitution-making, the armed forces and police, education, literature, agricultural development, traces of a number of foreign systems can be found in the syntheses created by the Thai. Thus Western contact has moved the Thai to adapt rather than to adopt. This is in any case in line with the nature of his own creative genius.

The absence of a colonizing power inhibited the rise of a militant anti-Western nationalism, inevitably directed towards progressive political thought, and easily able to gain widespread influence among the people. Resentment certainly existed and exists at the encroachment on what have been widely advertised as Thai frontiers but this has produced a 'pro' rather than an 'anti' type of nationalism — pro-Thai nationalism which showed itself markedly in the 1930's and which, to a lesser extent, is again emerging today. In modern conditions this needs a backer; in the 1930's this was provided — by Japan. Nevertheless the emotional pressures have never been high enough to involve the whole people. It is a politician's nationalism.

All these factors work in a conservative direction, in favour of the preservation of authority among a people with healthy individualistic tendencies it is true, but with whom the autocratic tradition is strong and respect for age and leadership ingrained; in favour, since the nature of the Thai is also to be receptive and flexible, of gradual adaptive change, for Thai conservatism is by no means obscurantist.

Even in the ex-colonial countries of South-East Asia democracy of the Western parliamentary type has not proved to be a suitable model which can be adopted without modification. Experiment in these countries continues. In Thailand, the attempts to introduce an effective political and economic system of an advanced Western type made in 1932-3, and, to a lesser extent, after the Second World War, were particularly short-lived because the conditions of urgency provided by a colonial or ex-colonial situation did not exist. The authoritarian element was not foreign and gratuitously imposed but was native and with its roots in tradition. Paternalistic in intention, in practice sometimes severe but without sustained harshness, it provided an authority that was understood. There was no demand from below for revolutionary change.

Steady political evolution has found expression in matters of detail, for example in the progressive liberalization of the electoral laws since 1932. Certain important ancillary features such as the relatively enlightened educational policy of successive administrations ought also to be taken into account.[1] But fundamental principles of government have been less affected. The principle of authoritarian rule was indeed modified by the change from absolute to constitutional monarchy but authoritarianism survived nevertheless.

A nationalist motive can be traced in the political changes introduced by most governments since that of King Mongkut. The rulers of Thailand have accepted their responsibility for the preservation of national identity. To this end they made use of such foreign ideas that came their way. King Mongkut opened the country to Western commerce and his son introduced his extensive administrative and legal reforms and effected some social changes such as the abolition of slavery. King Wachirawut founded his nationalist youth corps, initiated the attack on local Chinese economic power and led his country into the First World War and the League of Nations with the object of demonstrating that Thailand was a nation to be given consideration in world terms and not just a small state in a predominantly colonial region. The promoters established constitutional government. Phibun Songkhram turned away from the weakened Western democracies in the 1930's and 40's and attempted to introduce something of the dynamism that he felt

[1] The furtherance of education was a requirement of the 1932 constitution.

the Fascist powers possessed. Field-Marshal Sarit was attracted to the new forces expressed by de Gaulle in France and Nasser in Egypt. The recent and hitherto unprecedented move of Thailand to associate formally with other South-East Asian states is a further demonstration of flexibility in foreign policy attitudes.

The paramount considerations have been not only the preservation of power in the hands of a few but also the protection of the state and the people. This is a highly traditional function of Thai government. The continuing influence of this traditional concept of government as protection and the acceptance of government service as a valued activity by the individual are factors operating against radicalism and in favour of a high degree of public consent to authoritarian rule. The rulers have looked outward towards a threatening world and, though Thai political methods have not stood still, change has been largely controlled by what has been required to ensure the survival of the nation amid external pressures.

Even the idealistic and daring Pridi Phanomyong was affected by considerations of foreign policy, though, in the context of 1932, he saw the external threat in economic rather than in political terms:

> The fundamental aim of the government should be the administration of all kinds of agricultural and industrial enterprises with a view to rendering the country entirely independent of all foreign nations. This should be done to protect the country from dangers arising from trade restrictions of various sorts.[1]

Nevertheless Pridi was perhaps the one man who made a definite attempt to create a new basis for political authority very different from the traditional. It is likely that the idea of eventually establishing a socialist republic with a parliamentary form of government was consistently in his mind. He was far from being able to realize it.

Since Pridi's time support for private initiative in economic matters has become a constitutional provision.[2] But policies of economic nationalism with massive government participation have been continued and intensified. This is a marked feature of

---

[1] *National Economic Policy*, Pt. VIII, Landon, op. cit., p. 283.
[2] 1952 constitution.

the Sarit Thanarat régime and genuine development in the economic sphere has been significant. Fundamental measures to increase rice production have been undertaken. Planned diversification of agriculture is already showing results. An important industrial sector is in being. Greater involvement of Thai nationals in commerce is foreshadowed. The consequent rise of an urban proletariat and technical, managerial and professional classes together with the increasing impact of education will produce demands for more direct representation in government from wider and better organized sections of the people.

The elections of February 1957 were a sign of the times. The direct rule of the present day has been the response. It has achieved its immediate aim: strong government in a threatening foreign policy situation.

But February 1957 may prove to have been only a beginning. When internal demands and tensions become fully operative a new dimension will have been added to political life in Thailand and a new set of problems posed to test the skill of her leaders.

Chapter eight

DYNAMICS OF POWER
IN CAMBODIA

---

by Philippe Devillers

AMONG the five 'Buddhist nations' of South and South-East Asia Cambodia occupies a very special place. It achieved independence in 1953 without war or violence and has subsequently set out upon an original political path which has no equivalent in Ceylon, Burma, Siam or Laos. It is true that in comparison with at least three of those countries Cambodia enjoys the undoubted advantage of not being an ethnic mosaic and not being acquainted with 'communalism'.

The recent political evolution of Cambodia has just been the subject in France of an excellent study,[1] so this paper will only aim at marking the outstanding points of that evolution and at formulating in a summary and unintegrated fashion some reflections evoked by the Khmer experience to consider whether or not it has the value of an example in Asia.

I

Cambodia has not experienced a popular independence movement analogous or comparable to those which were seen in countries like India, Vietnam or Burma. Perhaps one may find an explanation of this feature in the origins of the French protectorate in Cambodia. That protectorate had not been imposed by force. French help had been requested by the Cam-

---

[1] Ph. Preschez, *Essai sur la Démocratie au Cambodge*, Paris, 1961, Centre d'Étude des Relations Internationales (Fond. Nat. Sciences politiques).

bodians themselves who felt themselves threatened by the rival ambitions of Vietnam and Siam. That alliance for safeguarding the independence of the kingdom has not lost its *raison d'être*. The Khmers still remain today very conscious of their relative weakness in face of their dynamic neighbours and of their need to rely upon a power which is capable of inspiring fear and respect.

The absence of a nationalist movement may perhaps also be explained by two other facts. The first is the manner in which the colonial authorities generally respected the traditional Khmer institutions (the rebellion of 1885–7 had demonstrated that it was dangerous to try to touch them). The reality of political and economic power was certainly transferred to French hands but all the appearances in relation to both the monarch and the Buddhist religion remained. The traditional framework of Khmer life was scarcely affected. National self-respect and patriotism were not affronted. The relations between French and Cambodians were generally good.

The second fact that some would advance as an explanation of the first is the slight importance of French public and private interests in Cambodia: no substantial agricultural colonization apart from some large rice-growing estates (Battembang) and some big rubber plantations (created out of deserted forests), no industry worth the name, a competent administration but insubstantial and remote. Cambodia was a part of that somewhat forgotten Indochina where the pleasantness of living, the sparseness of the population, the absence of pressing social or political problems had the effect of producing a kind of torpor. It is rare for a virulent nationalism to develop in such circumstances.

II

No serious social tension resulted from the European impact. The economic activity of the Europeans only affected the population indirectly and, except on the plantations, in an almost invisible manner. In Cambodia the French traded mostly with the Chinese and relied for administrative work on immigrant Vietnamese. No class of the Khmer population was tied by any economic interest to the 'colonizer'. Granting that at some stage the latter might arouse, by their attitude or their policy, an opposition, it could only take a nationalist character and could not be diverted to more revolutionary methods of struggle and include among its objectives the elimination of foreign 'puppets' or 'agents'.

The foreign grip which was most resented was not that of the French. The presence of ethnic minorities of Chams and Phnong did not present any serious problems. That was not a question of foreigners but of Cambodians of different race. On the other hand the position which had been secured by the Vietnamese (in the administration and as artisans) and by the Chinese (in commerce and industry) created fears that one day or other the Cambodian people might no longer be completely masters of their destiny, and the only visible resentment that some Cambodians showed sometimes towards the French presence was directed at their having too much favoured the Chinese and Vietnamese grip on the economy and the administration. To this the French replied that they had not any choice and that the Khmer 'nonchalance' had compelled them to have recourse to more dynamic personnel.

The Khmer people remained profoundly attached to their customs, to their ancestral way of life and to their framework of traditional institutions. They retained a respectful loyalty to their monarchy and their rulers. The Buddhist religion left a deep imprint on personal and collective life. The monks (*bhikku*), grouped in two orders, enjoyed undoubted consideration and respect. In the villages the pagoda was the real centre of the community, the meeting place for everybody where matters of common interest were discussed.

The country did not experience over-population (quite the contrary), nor special difficulties resulting from the infertility of the soil or from lack of space. The population, nevertheless, suffered from ills which were also traditional resulting from national sociological conditions and not from the French presence: a chronic agrarian indebtedness, prohibitive interest rates (usury) exacted by the Chinese moneylenders, some peculation and corruption by civil servants, high and low, poor production techniques, high infantile mortality rate, and so on. The efforts of the colonial administration had achieved some results but much remained to be done.

III

Political awakening in Cambodia is a very recent phenomenon. It dates in fact from the last war and its origins go back
to the ferment in religious circles provoked in 1941/2 by some
measures of modernization ordered by the French administration (adoption of the Gregorian calendar, attempt at Romaniza-
tion of Khmer writing). A small group of laymen who were
associated with the Buddhist Institute and whose leader was the
young Son Ngoc Thanh took an active part in this agitation in
which there was also some Japanese influence. The stifling of
the movement (almost in embryo) and the subsequent flight of
Son Ngoc Thanh to Japan produced a respite of three years.

The Japanese *coup* in March 1945 by cutting off the top of the
French administration opened out other possibilities. On 12
March, 1945 the Japanese arranged the proclamation of the
independence of Cambodia by the young King, Norodom
Sihanouk, who had come to the throne in 1941, and a certain
number of responsible political and administrative posts were
transferred to Cambodians (who were assured of the enlightened assistance of Japanese counsellors). But the political
character of Cambodian public life only assumed real breadth
with the nomination as Prime Minister in June 1945 of Son
Ngoc Thanh who had returned from Japan, and the collection
around him of a small group — more anti-Western than
nationalist — who were determined, mainly for personal
reasons, to oppose a return to the previous régime.

IV

However, the re-establishment of French authority in Cam-
bodia was accomplished without great difficulty shortly after the
Japanese surrender. When the Japanese had been disarmed and
repatriated by the British, Son Ngoc Thanh was arrested, taken
to France and placed under surveillance. His followers — the
Khmer Issarak or free Khmers — took to the jungle or fled to
Siam. A new pro-Allied government, headed by the uncle of the
King, Prince Monireth, was established.

France had declared herself ready to grant internal autonomy to Cambodia immediately and a Franco-Khmer *modus vivendi* signed at Phnom Penh on 7 January, 1946 laid down the framework. Essential political and administrative responsibility remained in Cambodian hands.[1] The French theoretically held the position of counsellors, yet France still retained very extensive powers going well beyond the reserved field of foreign affairs and defence and including practically everything which should in principle belong to future federal institutions (currency, economic planning, customs, telecommunications, immigration, the protection of minorities and so on). Nevertheless a long step had been taken which would allow new forces to make their appearance on the Cambodian political scene.

V

The political movement quickened with the return from France at the beginning of 1946 of a small group of young Cambodians (not more than thirty) who were animated by a keen desire to modernize the kingdom by providing it with, above all, institutions of a Western type. Since King Sihanouk for his part indicated his intention to put an end to the absolute monarchy and to grant a constitution, the main topic in the speeches and discussions of Khmer ruling circles was the 'next' constitution.

In fact, behind the more or less theoretical discussions about the value of such a type of régime or about the amount of 'civil liberties' which could be conceded to the Khmer people there was immediately to be discerned a conflict of forces, a struggle for power between the upholders of the traditional order on the one hand (the noble families, the high religious dignitaries, largest landed proprietors, the senior civil servants) and those on the other hand who, often with a thought for their career, placed their hopes in a change (junior and middle civil servants,

---

[1] It is interesting to note that at the time (January 1946) well informed observers estimated the number of Cambodians who had received a modern secondary education and were capable of taking a certain amount of responsibility at 150. Compared with the population of that time (about 4 million) this figure highlights the terrifying lack of cadres from which the kingdom was suffering and the magnitude of the task to be accomplished.

students, educated elements among the personnel of the agricultural, industrial, and commercial enterprises). The former
grouped themselves mainly under the banner of a 'Liberal
Party' of which the leader was Prince Norindeth. The latter
came together in a modern-type party, the 'Democratic Party'
which was formed in April 1946 by a group of young men returning from France and was organized with masterly skill by
its dynamic general secretary, Chhean Vam (who was also
headmaster of the Phnom Penh High School). Its supreme head
was Prince Youthevong, a man of great culture, very Westernized, with numerous relations in France where he had lived for a
very long time.[1]

The Democratic Party discovered in a few months how to
inject politics into Khmer public life and provoke a general
agitation. It was able particularly to make use of the profound
desire for modernization which animated the younger generation (which had been marked by the youth organizations of the
Admiral Decoux régime and the Japanese period) and the coolness of the civil servants towards the régime set up by the
Franco-Khmer *modus vivendi*. The civil servants for the most part
were on the side of the Democrats and their influence on the
countryside swung the balance heavily in favour of that party
which emerged triumphant from the elections of September
1946. From the summer of 1946 to the summer of 1955, that is to
say for nine years, the Democratic Party was to dominate
continuously the Cambodian political scene, though under
various forms.

VI

For five years, from 1947 to 1952, the scene was occupied by a
conflict, more or less open at different times, between the Palace
and the Democratic Party.

The clear victory of the party at the elections in September
1946, the fact that the government was entrusted to it at the
beginning of 1947, destroyed for a long period the equilibrium
which it had been hoped would be established between the
forces of tradition and the forces which we may call progressive.

[1] He had also been a member of the French delegation to the IPR conference at
Hot Springs in 1945.

Apparently given an overwhelming majority by an electorate dominated by the civil servants, and controlling the Assembly, the Democrats were quickly to transcend the framework in which some had wished to confine the first Assembly. The constitution of May 1947, which was to be granted by the King, was in fact their work. Largely inspired by the French constitution of 1946, it was to bring Cambodia from absolute monarchy to constitutional monarchy much more quickly than the King, though liberal, had wished, and to give it moreover parliamentary institutions hardly corresponding to the stage of the country's political and social evolution.

The powers of the sovereign were ostensibly preserved. According to the constitution all powers theoretically emanated from the King but he exercised them by the intermediary of the Council of Ministers. All the acts of the King had to be countersigned by the Prime Minister. The Prime Minister was nominated by the King but he could only constitute his government after receiving the investiture of the Assembly to which the Government was responsible.

The preponderance of the Democratic Party in the Assembly was such that the régime under which Cambodia was to live could be compared with that of a single party. For an underdeveloped country this was not in itself a bad thing provided that it brought the country stability, unity and firmness of direction, mobilization of energy, co-ordination of effort, participation of the masses, efficient economic and social activity and so on. Cambodia did not enjoy any of these advantages under the Democratic régime.

The Democratic Party was quickly weakened by the death in July 1947 of its leader, Prince Youthevong, who headed the Government. It was unable to preserve its unity. While the Left-wing adopted blustering anti-colonialist attitudes which were desperately negative and showed itself very susceptible to the influence of the *Khmer Issarak* and the followers of Son Ngoc Thanh, the Centre and the Right-wing indulged rather in activities of a less political but often more profitable nature. The rivalry of persons and clans and the 'auction' which resulted from it made any political definition or serious action impossible. The quasi-sovereign Assembly was to make and un-make governments and ministerial instability was to become one of

the principal characteristics of the new Cambodian democracy.

King Norodom Sihanouk, who had allowed the experiment
to begin and develop without resisting, in spite of pressure which
was exerted upon him by conservative circles, became gradually
conscious of the reality of the danger. The Democratic Party,
besides, systematically blocked legislation proposed by the King;
so he decided to enter the fray and to profit by the dissensions
of the Democrats for the progressive re-establishment of his
authority.

The Government of Yem Sembaur which was formed in
February 1949 was no longer the kind of government which the
framers of the constitution had envisaged. Yem Sembaur was a
dissident Democrat who enjoyed only an intermittent and
limited confidence in the Assembly which he had alarmed by
his temperament and his taste for authority. In fact, conflicts
were numerous but ended this time not in the overthrow of the
Government but in the dissolution of the Assembly. Insecurity
did not permit the holding of fresh elections and the Government continued to govern without Parliament.

From 1949 to 1951 therefore, the Democratic Party lost its
hold on power to the profit in the first instance of one of its own
members who had gone over to the camp of the King, and then,
when parties had multiplied, to a government of National
Union which the King even presided over for a month. In spite
of the absence of an Assembly the conflict between the King and
the main party continued behind the scenes, made sharper by
the fact that the Democratic Party criticized strongly the
Franco-Khmer treaty of 1949 (which recognized the independence of the kingdom but enmeshed it in a multiplicity of
obligations) and reproached the King and Yem Sembaur for
playing the French game.

The victory of the Democratic Party in the elections of
September 1951 consequently resulted in a return to the parliamentary régime, the results of which were no better than during
the earlier period. The dissensions within the ruling party and
the obstruction produced were of the same kind. The Democratic Party, now strongly organized with a hierarchy, governed
in a partisan fashion, penetrating and disorganizing the administration where it tried to appoint its friends and so arousing

much dissatisfaction. Another factor also intervened: the return to Cambodia of Son Ngoc Thanh who was freed by the French in October 1951 on the request of the King who was trying to appease the Opposition. Almost at once Son Ngoc Thanh became the rallying point of a virulent nationalism. He re-grouped the whole of the Left-wing of the Democratic Party and renewed contact with the *Khmer Issarak* of the maquis, leading Cambodia progressively towards an open conflict with France.

On 15 June, 1952, the King, in weariness, dismissed the Democratic cabinet of Huy Kanthoul and took upon himself the executive power. In a message to the people published on the same day as this 'legal *coup d'état*' he allowed himself three years to obtain full and satisfactory independence, accomplish the pacification of the country and its unity and clean up the finances and ensure economic recovery.

The underground opposition of the Democratic Party to the new policy was to lead the King to take still more radical measures; in fact to put an end to the parliamentary régime. The Assembly was dissolved on 13 January, 1953, and the nation was declared 'in danger'. All the regulations for the summoning of electors to elect a new Assembly within a given time were suspended.

So the conflict which had been foreseeable from the start between the dominant party which claimed to represent the people and the sovereign, ended provisionally in the victory of the latter. The artificial character of political activity born of parliamentarism became evident to almost everybody. In fact, the parties whose nature, significance and objects still remained practically foreign to the peasant masses had established themselves mainly as new privileged castes, as associations for furthering careers. The parties had made the constitution, but in their thirst for power, believing that they could keep the control of affairs for a very long time, they had neglected the fact that the monarchy remained, in the hearts of the people, the very essence of the nation — the great refuge, the great protector — and that it was to the monarchy and not to the parties that popular hopes turned in the end. In opposing the monarchy it is probable that the Democratic Party sealed its own fate.

VII

An important factor in the opposition of the King to the Democratic Party was the denunciation, made implicitly by the party and explicitly by its attachments abroad, of the 'collusion' between the King and the French. The Democratic Party was basically trying to do what the Viet-Minh was doing in Vietnam: by discrediting the monarchy, by showing what an outworn institution it was, a mere instrument of the colonial power which consequently could not have any desire to achieve real independence, the Democratic Party (or its Left-wing) had touched the King to the quick and awakened in him a lasting and personal animosity against the people who had dared to cast doubt upon his patriotism.

This surely explains why the King came forward as the champion of nationalism and devoted most of his energy during the first two years of the 'royal mandate' to obtaining independence. After a series of solemn warnings, diplomatic journeys, dramatic reversals, and spectacular withdrawals to half-dissident areas which marked the year 1953, he succeeded in obtaining the treaty of November 1953 which really marks the recognition by France of the 'full and satisfactory' independence of Cambodia.

That independence was to be internationally acknowledged in the following year by the Geneva agreements (July 1954) which put an end to the war in Indochina. Cambodia was the most successful at the Geneva conference through knowing how to exploit cleverly the Anglo-Indian anxiety for the external security of Malaya and Burma, and Chinese and Soviet haste to conclude with M. Mendès-France a satisfactory arrangement of a kind which would exclude any American intervention. While Vietnam emerged from the war exhausted, war-torn and partitioned and the internal unity of Laos was gravely damaged, Cambodia emerged little weakened, neither ravaged nor divided, independent and accepted (or recognized) by the two blocs, free from all ties, having been able to obtain from it opponent unconditional evacuation.

This unexpected result was due essentially to the policy of the King and his team, among whom Sam Sary was prominent

Among the basic facts in the Cambodia of today the first is this: it was the King who personally restored to the Khmer people their independence: ninety-nine per cent of the electorate recognized this in 1955. The prestige of the monarchy, which had appeared for a moment to be somewhat weakened, was completely restored.

During this decisive period the King became aware of his role as the real leader of the nation, and of his ascendancy over the people (contact revealed it to him and this new role inspired him more than the one to which he had been destined, that of remote and hieratic sovereign), as well as of his international audience. It was clear thenceforward that he would not reconcile himself to resuming the background functions of a constitutional monarch. He had suspended parliamentarism and reverted to a tradition of an active monarchy, which was probably that of the Angkor kings, and anyway that of all enlightened Buddhist sovereigns. The King was very deeply impressed by this experience. The 'royal mandate' marks a real turning-point in the history of modern Cambodia.

VIII

By the end of the war, the Geneva agreements contained in embryo (and perhaps with still more danger than before) the revival of the party system, and this time probably of parties still more 'popular' and demagogic than the Democratic Party. The agreements did indeed envisage an amnesty for the rebels and their re-integration in national public life, the restoration of democratic liberties and fresh elections. The nation was no longer 'in danger'. It was going to be necessary again to take account of the parties and Parliament. In view of the favour with which anti-colonialist movements (Democrats or others) were regarded by the international bodies (especially the Supervisory Commission) the King foresaw that in spite of his prestige there was a risk that he might be outflanked.

He immediately set to work to oppose a return purely and simply to the previous constitutional régime; on 19 February, 1955 he proposed a constitutional reform of which the main feature was to make the cabinet responsible no longer to the

Assembly but to the King. This proposal had very little democratic appeal, and for that reason was received with coolness and reserve not only by Cambodian 'political circles' (where the Democrats were again dominant with Son Ngoc Thanh back from the maquis) but also in diplomatic circles.

This time the King threw himself into the arena with the knowledge that it was the best method left to him of preventing the Democrats' return to power. He abdicated in favour of his father (2 March 1955) and soon afterwards with Sam Sary and some others formed the Popular Socialist Community (Sangkum Reastr Niyum) henceforward known by the name of Sangkum. The scheduled elections were postponed to September. They gave the Sangkum an overwhelming victory: 82 per cent of the votes, as against 12 per cent for the Democrats and 3 per cent for the Communists (Pracheachon), and almost all the seats in the Assembly.[1] From that time Cambodia has lived under the Sangkum régime.

IX

More illuminating than an analysis of the form and functions of present-day institutions in Cambodia would be an inquiry into the intentions and motives of the Samdech (prince) Norodom Sihanouk. This seems the best way to approach an understanding of the dynamics of power in Cambodia.

In the first place, the formation of the Sangkum accords with a clear and simple aim enunciated by the King at the time of his abdication, that of 'making democracy comprehensible to the people'. Of recent years the parliamentary game has been played out on a plane wholly inaccessible to the masses. The Prince intends to restore real, effective, and live contact between leaders and populace.

There is considerable sincerity in this declared aim, but an element of political calculation also enters into it. The new structure of the Sangkum had for its object not only to allow the people to express themselves but also to resolve finally the conflict between the throne and the parties, or rather the party. The Sangkum itself was not a new party, it was the grouping of all

[1] Out of 761,958 votes cast the Sangkum obtained 630,625; the Democratic Party 93,919; the Pracheachon 29,509; the Liberal Party 5,488.

active patriotic Cambodian citizens who wanted to work for the greatness and prosperity of their country; but to be admitted to the Sangkum it was necessary not to belong to any political party (Article 6 of the Statutes).

By creating the Sangkum the Prince outflanked all the parties, broke through the screen which they had set up, and aimed at establishing direct contact with what he called 'the real people, the great mass of the little people who symbolize the Khmer nation'. He was not wrong in thinking that his personal prestige, the confidence that he inspired and the contact which he knew how to establish and foster with those who listened to or spoke with him, would guarantee an overwhelming victory for the Sangkum. The majorities which were obtained enabled him to say that the Sangkum alone represented and interpreted the Khmer people, and that the parties which remained represented practically nothing. Plebiscitary régime with a single movement? The problem was not there. The essential fact was that therewas no longer a duality or dyarchy or dichotomy in Khmer political life. 'Communion' was re-established between the people and the throne. The Prince was the incarnation of that union. His person still had a sacred character yet very human, and he wanted to take the leadership of the great popular grouping. He also took from the Democrats their main trump: the support of the class of civil servants. Having scented the wind they rallied massively to the Sangkum, of which they constituted more or less the framework, and they contributed much to the remarkable penetration of the movement among the masses. Whether through idealism, enthusiasm or opportunism, the fact is that the civil servants played the Sangkum card and consequently any possible opposition could only show itself with difficulty.

However, Prince Norodom Sihanouk did not lose sight of the fact that to prevent his opponents (the Democrats) from getting the upper hand or from benefiting by popular support was not enough. He had to go further and outflank both the Parliament and the bureaucracy if he was not to fall into their hands.

When in India several weeks after his abdication, the Prince declared that he felt that his duty as sovereign had come to an end once independence had been achieved, and that the task for the future was

the solution of social problems and the fostering of a truly democratic régime to put an end to a situation in which the powers of
the government were concentrated in the hands of a small group
of privileged people who one could not say represented, in any
sense, the real interests of the people whom in fact they exploited,

and he added 'My object is to see to it that those powers are
exercised by the people themselves'.

In its statutes the Sangkum described itself after April 1955 as
a 'national rally which fights against injustice, corruption,
exaction, oppression and treason which are committed against
the people and the country'. It was in order to supervise from
below (that is to say, by his allies 'the little people') the 'exploiters' that the Prince introduced new institutions and rules:
the possibility for electors to recall their deputy (by a majority
of three-quarters), personal responsibility of civil servants (whom
the people might question in certain circumstances and even
have transferred or dismissed), popular provincial assemblies,
election of *Mekhums* (chiefs of basic local groups) by universal
suffrage. Finally and above all, the National Congress where
twice a year the assembled people came to hear the record of
Government action, to discuss with the Prince affairs of state, to
question ministers and senior civil servants and so on. It was a
variation on direct democracy recalling the *Landesgemeinde* of
the small Swiss cantons.

X

To what extent did the Popular Socialist régime (SRN)
remedy the ills from which Cambodia had suffered during the
preceding period?

It appears to have succeeded largely in enabling the people to
participate in political life, in giving them at least the
illusion of a kind of sovereignty. Also it created an outlet for
grievances or complaints of all kinds and that contributed very
much to clearing the atmosphere — all the more since the
Samdech, leader of the Sangkum, undertook in some sense, and
this time more closely, the fundamental royal function of protector of the people, of great dispenser of justice and redresser of
wrongs.

It has also brought about a real mobilization of popular

energy for the purpose of collective improvement of the standard of living and of economic development. A journey to People's China revealed to the Prince the efficacy of voluntary manual labour practised on a large scale. This idea adapted to Cambodia took the form of digging pits and wells almost everywhere, the building of roads, bridges, dykes and barrages and of hospitals and schools, etc. The Khmer people were aware that under the aegis of the Sangkum and the Prince they were making progress and modifying little by little the aspect of the country.

There were there some very positive elements. But the record also showed some darker spots.

Contrary to what might have been expected the new régime did not bring the country ministerial stability. One might have thought that with the overwhelming majorities obtained at the elections of 1955 and 1958 the Sangkum would have a stable ministerial team putting into effect a definite policy without having to worry about parliamentary harassment or demagogic bidding. That hope was disappointed. Numerous Sangkum governments followed one another and were overthrown or compelled to resign by the Assembly.

It must be recalled here that the parliamentary régime continued and that the Government was still responsible to the Assembly. In the first legislature (1955–8) the Government had been composed of members with little experience and often of a mediocre quality. But the better quality of the chamber elected in 1958 did not prevent it from falling into the same bad ways: personal rivalries, clannishness, submission to narrow particular interests and so on. All the deputies, or nearly all of them, belonged to the Sangkum so there was no room in Parliament for ideological debates, and it became clear that there is no real Parliament without parties and without ideas. The parliamentary experience of the Sangkum period was unhappy. But one should not conclude from that, as some have done, that there was a duplication between the Assembly and the National Congresses. The two institutions had their value and their utility. It is correct to think that the efficacy of the Khmer Parliament would have been very much improved if the Sangkum had a better constructed executive committee with a sounder doctrine capable of imposing strict discipline on the parliamentary group. The Assembly would then have exercised, during the interval between the National Congresses, the necessary supervision over Government action.

Rivalries and corruption continued, opposing clans were not disarmed, but the opposition, being unable to succeed by parliamentary manoeuvre, adopted the classical method employed in a more or less unanimous régime, of plotting. On several occasions since 1955 plots have been discovered in which there were implicated elements belonging either to evicted parties, like the Democratic Party, or to groups more or less manipulated by foreign services. It was here that foreign policy intervened. Its relationship with internal policy was indeed close.

XI

At the Geneva Conference of 1954 Cambodia had refused any neutralization of her territory. She wanted to preserve complete liberty of action which at that moment had a very precise significance: it was a matter of being able to continue to benefit from American aid and to have whatever relations she wished with the United States.

The following year, in 1955 at Bandung, Cambodia discovered the virtues of neutrality. A certain number of facts led her rulers to proceed to a fresh analysis of the situation. It was realized at Phnom Penh that American aid was not unconditional. It implied on the part of the recipient an alignment on certain fundamental positions, in the first place consistent anti-Communism. In this context the Khmers understood that between South Vietnam and Thailand, both of them anti-Communist and large beneficiaries of American aid, they would never have more than crumbs, and above all that the interest of South Vietnam or Thailand would always take priority, almost certainly, over those of Cambodia.

Prince Sihanouk who had already been very sensitive to the campaign of the Democratic Left which in 1949–51 had depicted him as a tool of the French, showed himself in 1955 no less sensitive to the campaign of the Pracheachon (Communist) Party and certain Democrats who now accused him of being the instrument of the Americans and of sacrificing the independence of the country for dollars. The Indian seduction (the visit to New Delhi) also contributed to modify the outlook of the Prince.

The result was that Cambodia publicly affirmed her desire to be neutral and to pursue a policy totally independent of the two blocs, declaring herself ready to accept help from anybody providing that it was unconditional. Certain American pressures only resulted in reinforcing Cambodia in that determination. After being admitted to the UN in November 1955, Cambodia, supported by France, was able to pursue with success this policy of total independence which she wanted.

However, the establishment of diplomatic relations with Moscow, Peking and the European satellites of the USSR cooled the relations of the kingdom with the USA and strained its relations with South Vietnam. The visits of the Prince to the USSR and China and the visits of Russian and Chinese personalities to Phnom Penh, the economic and technical aid which the Communist bloc began to give Cambodia from 1957, soon led Bangkok and Saigon to regard Khmer neutrality as the Communist Trojan horse in the region. Pressure to put an end to this orientation which was regarded as dangerous has scarcely ceased since 1956–7. The various plots that have been disclosed have shown that behind the groups which proposed to overthrow the Sangkum régime there were always Siamese or Vietnamese shadows. As in the nineteenth century, before the French intervention, Cambodia found herself thenceforward threatened, within the régime itself, by intrigues fomented by her neighbours who wanted to secure a *de facto* protectorate at Phnom Penh.

The influence of foreign policy on Cambodian internal policy was complex. It was above all in order to disarm the Left-wing Opposition that Prince Sihanouk turned towards neutrality. But that neutrality brought with it, among other advantages, the power to neutralize, at least provisionally, Communism in Cambodia. China and the USSR had no interest in supporting the handful of Cambodian Communists (for that would drive the Prince back towards the USA) so long as Khmer neutrality allowed them to demonstrate to good account, right in the heart of the SEATO zone, their generosity and pacifism.[1]

[1] The USA and France for their part continued to give substantial aid.

The policy of Prince Sihanouk obtained in this respect results analogous to Mr Nehru in India or Colonel Nasser in Egypt (until recently): anti-Communism was tolerated by Moscow provided that it was not, or was no longer, 'Atlantic'.

On the other hand this neutrality provoked sharp reaction from the Siamese and Vietnamese (and also Americans). There, too, it was the Sangkum which was the real beneficiary of the situation. The proof which it provided of the intervention of Bangkok and Saigon in Khmer affairs enabled it to intensify to the utmost the traditional Cambodian distrust of their neighbours and to discredit all groups or individuals who worked in liaison with them. All the adversaries of the Sangkum could now be classed as foreign agents or enemies of the throne, of religion, or of the country. Thus foreign policy (including foreign economic aid) continued powerfully to raise still higher the prestige of the Prince and to consolidate, at least in appearance, the régime.

XII

The policy of Prince Sihanouk and the Sangkum was not pure empiricism. Nor did it merely aim at altering the balance of forces in Cambodia. If in its appearance it closely resembled the policy of certain French kings who invoked the aid of the people to defeat or subdue the feudal powers, it was anchored basically in the Cambodian past. The ideology of the Sangkum existed. It was 'Khmer Socialism' and it now found for itself some antecedents which enabled it to place its activities in the process of evolution of the Khmer nation.

Certain theorists of the Sangkum, after specifying that for them Marxism was only one form of socialism and not the whole of socialism which 'has existed in one form or another for centuries and in all human societies', explained why they had chosen socialism and oriented the Sangkum towards it. They accepted as a definition of socialism the following:

the system in which the state assumes the direction of the national economy and protects the citizen from the exploitation of his labour by a privileged class and assures him his existence and dignity and aims at giving him the material means to find happiness.[1]

If the Sangkum chose socialism it was because 'this path is a continuation of that which was followed by our kings for a thousand years, corresponds to our Buddhist ethic and alone will permit us to advance our country and give greater well-being to our people'.

This Khmer socialism, according to these theorists, was not Marxist, first because it was national and because the Khmers could not accept that 'a philosophic doctrine and even an ethic could take on a character of universality', and then because Marxism was almost inapplicable to Cambodia, taking into account above all the class structure. Cambodia created 'without difficulty' its own socialism which was essentially pragmatic and adapted itself gradually to the evolution of the country.

The roots of Khmer socialism went back, they said, as far as the Angkor kings who immortalized their names by great works of economic and social value. Buddhism was besides both 'the most precious guide in the elaboration of this socialism considered from the moral and philosophical angle' and also a 'corner-stone'. Buddhism taught indeed that 'man must rely on his own powers to reach the truth and the liberation from all alienations. . . . Buddhism is socialist in its aspect of struggle against evil and social injustice. . . . Buddhism is also struggle against suffering in all its forms'. Thus it may be seen that Khmer socialism derives from profoundly religious sources.

For the theorists of the Sangkum, the Cambodian people and particularly the rural communities were already living and applying socialism in their daily lives: they had the habit of working in common (for example there was no other way of achieving irrigation works), of helping one another and of living in an atmosphere of equality. The tools of this 'natural' socialism would be perfected by the new régime, but the spirit was to remain.

As for economic development it was to be sought in the framework of a plan of which the essential objective would be to harmonize efforts. Taking into account the state of the country

[1] 'Considération sur le socialisme khmer', 1961, 14 pp. (Cambodian Embassy, Paris).

the co-existence of private and public enterprise would be permitted for a long time.

Khmer socialism, impregnated with Buddhist thought, is opposed to violence. It does not think in terms of 'revolution'. It chooses to realize itself by means of persuasion and not by authoritarian measures or by constraint.

As may be seen the new Cambodian régime did not neglect the ideological field but it did not go much further than giving to an essentially national reality a name which was well known and enabled it to take a better position on the world's ideological chess-board and to describe as 'reactionary' and 'anti-popular' any opposition. Moreover, it only wanted to modify that reality cautiously because it considered that it had no basic structural faults and that it needed above all to be developed and modernized. Here again Prince Sihanouk had an insight into what would please both the people and the élite, by loyalty to the best national traditions and also through the desire to progress and to reach an equal footing with more advanced nations.

XIII

The new Cambodian régime presented the original feature of being the only one in Asia where the King himself took direction of the Democratic movement. It may be wondered whether in doing so he did not modify the traditional image of the monarchy in the minds of the Cambodians. The fact that he was no longer king but at the same time head of the state, head of the Government (for the time being) and head of the Sangkum, showed to what extent power in present-day Cambodia was personalized. Indeed there was something like a reversion to ancient forms of power in that country. The Angkor kings, to whose glory there is such frequent reference today, also exercised personal power, it is said, and through their ministers, counsellors and civil servants, they had — at least some of them — a real contact with the people.

However attractive it may appear (particularly through the spontaneous, direct, sympathetic and relaxed character of the frequent encounters between power and the people) the Khmer experiment, nevertheless, leaves with observers an impression of fragility. It is impossible to avoid the thought that in reality its success or failure depends on the fate of one man, Samdech, Prince Sihanouk. Would the machine operate without him? Has the Sangkum penetrated deeply enough among the masses, has it inspired them to the point where they are now capable of producing cadres and élites dynamic enough to take over from the 'mandarins', the civil servants of the old school or of the democratic school? Will powerful personalities arise in the shadow of the Prince to whom the supreme responsibilities of the Sangkum and of the state may one day be entrusted without conflict or deadly rivalries? There are so many questions posed by the internal situation in Cambodia today.

But there are others. In Asia where ancient rivalries and hatreds which had been more or less stifled by the Western presence are reappearing on all sides, and where the recourse to force is more and more attractive (particularly against the weak) can neutral Cambodia resist for long the pressure of her threatening neighbours? Prince Sihanouk is so conscious of this danger that he has already taken practical steps to prevent it: his recent *rapprochement* with Communist China constitutes his response to a more distinct menace. In the years to come will China succeed France as guarantor and protector of Cambodian independence? This would be a serious matter with grave consequences for the whole of South-East Asia.

If external threats oblige the Khmers to close their ranks about the throne, they also set up a tension which is harmful to the success of the task that has been undertaken. The new democratic experiment, to succeed, needs peace. For there remains a great deal to be done internally to free the people from injustice, from exactions, from exploitation and from suffering, to bring them a better life.

Chapter nine

INDEPENDENCE AND POLITICAL
RIVALRY IN LAOS 1945-61

by Stuart Simmonds

HISTORICAL BACKGROUND

IT IS no accident that the preamble and the first article of the
Lao constitution insist upon the unity as well as the independence of the state. During her history, recorded, in a fashion,
since the middle of the fourteenth century, Laos has existed in
her own right only when a sufficient degree of unity has obtained
among her small constituent principalities. Internal dynastic
and regional quarrels have, from time to time, broken up
temporarily established centralized control but, more important
than this, regional rulers have attempted to further their ambitions by seeking political association with neighbouring
states, or, because of their weakness, have been forced into such
arrangements, in either case threatening the existence of an
independent state. Laos has always been plagued by neighbours more powerful than herself. Of these the most dangerous
have been, traditionally, Burma, Annam and Siam. Historically, the conditions for the survival of an independent Laos
have been the presence of a ruler sufficiently powerful to attract
the allegiance of the regions inwards towards himself and the
existence of a balance of power or of a condition of relative
weakness among the neighbours.

A relatively unified Laos can be said to have existed in the
fourteenth century, during the latter half of the fifteenth and
part of the sixteenth, and from *c.* 1645–94 under Soulinga-

vongsa.[1] Long periods of dynastic struggle coupled with foreign interference preceded and followed these interludes of unity. The final disintegration of the kingdom into its constituent principalities from 1711 meant that no unified state existed for almost two centuries until, from 1899 onwards, the French created a unity without independence during the colonial period.

From their conquest of Vientiane in 1828 the Siamese set about establishing direct control there and in the barely administered territory immediately to the south of it. Luang Prabang and Champassak were ruled through commissioners. The north-eastern principality of Xieng Khouang, which had become subservient to Annam, was penetrated by the Siamese but further effectual expansion was interrupted, especially after 1874, by the incursions of armed bands representing the remnants of the Taiping and Panthay rebellions in China and by local Tai dissident groups.

When firmly established in Annam and Tongking the French began to look westwards towards the Mekhong. Taking advantage of Annamese claims to suzerainty and of the fact that the Siamese were unable to pacify the region, the French forced Siam to acquiesce in their annexation of large areas in north-eastern Laos in 1888. In 1887 Luang Prabang had become a French protectorate and the next phase of French expansion resulted in the relinquishment by the Siamese of all territory east of the Mekhong. After a series of Franco-Siamese treaties between 1893 and 1907 the frontiers of Laos became what they are today.[2]

Under French control Laos was the least exploited and therefore the least developed region of Indochina. A system of road communications through the difficult mountain country was planned and the skeleton of this was more or less complete by 1940. Tin was mined in central Laos and the planting of such products as coffee and rubber was encouraged on a small scale in the south. For the most part the people continued their peaceful existence as subsistence rice farmers in the plains or as practitioners of slash-and-burn agriculture in the hills. The French

---

[1] Entirely systematic methods of transcription for Lao and Thai terms have not been adopted. Generally accepted forms are used.

[2] As a result of the Franco-Thai war of 1940-1, areas of Laos west of the Mekhong were absorbed into Thailand. These were restored to Laos in 1946.

allowed the settlement of considerable numbers of Vietnamese in
the Mekong valley and, by 1945, these totalled between 30,000
and 50,000. They were employed as minor functionaries in the
administration, as labour in the tin mines or as artisans. Others
engaged in shopkeeping or market-gardening. At the same time
small numbers of Laotians were gaining some experience of life
in other parts of Indochina, principally in Hanoi where they
went for further education. A few, mostly members of the
princely houses, went to France.

The pattern of small heterogeneous élite groups who, sometimes in alliance, more often in rivalry, were to dominate the
post-war political scene was already forming during the colonial
period. There were the several branches of the royal house of
Luang Prabang with a small court of non-hereditary nobility,
while, in the south, the princely family of Champassak maintained itself within the system of French administration. In
Vientiane, where no king had been for a hundred years, and in
the newer Mekong valley towns of middle Laos, an administrative class, only a few families strong, began to grow in wealth
and influence. In the hills were the leaders of the Tai, Mèo and
other minority communities.

The north-eastern province of Houa Phans was attached to
Luang Prabang in 1933 and, in 1941, by a treaty between
Marshal Pétain and King Sisavangvong, the provinces of
Vientiane, Xieng Khouang and Houei Sai were added.

An early move of the Japanese after taking over direct control
in March 1945 was to press King Sisavangvong to proclaim the
independence of Laos as a whole. In effect his proclamation of
8 April maintained the *status quo* by claiming only those
territories designated by the 1941 treaty.

LAO ISSARA — THE INDEPENDENCE MOVEMENT

Japan capitulated on 14 August. By the provisions of the
Potsdam conference the Chinese gained access to Laos down to
the 16th parallel to take the surrender of the Japanese troops.
British forces assumed temporary control in south Laos where
Prince Boun Oum of Champassak had been engaging in
resistance activities in collaboration with the French. Japanese

troops in Laos were relatively few in number and they tended to move south, preferring to surrender to the British rather than to the Chinese. There was little established authority in central Laos in August and September and in this area, which included three of the five chief towns, Prince Souphanouvong brought out into the open the militant resistance movement he had organized. In the south the French soon regained control, moving into position more quickly than the Chinese who did not reach Vientiane until early October. At the beginning of September French officials had been parachuted into Vientiane and Luang Prabang.

In Vientiane, on 1 September, Prince Phetsarath, as *maha oupahat* (viceroy) and Prime Minister, proclaimed the rupture of ties with France as exemplified by the 1941 treaty and declared the independence of the kingdom of Luang Prabang under Sisavangvong. The limits of royal jurisdiction were extended on 14 September to include the four southern provinces. A provisional national assembly was appointed and work on a constitution was commenced. An independent and unified Laos now had a nominal existence but these arrangements, though supported by public acclaim in Vientiane, were not accepted by the King whose final announcement of the continuance of the French protectorate reached Vientiane on 17 September.[1]

The King dismissed Phetsarath from his offices on 10 October but this merely confirmed him in his opposition. Two days later Phetsarath set up a provisional government in which the princes Souphanouvong and Souvannaphouma held important posts.

Fear of pressure by the Chinese and the presence of the French group in Luang Prabang moved the King to decide on his declaration of loyalty to France. In Vientiane, however, the French had to deal with less Francophile figures than the King and Crown Prince and the Chinese presence there was an encouragement to the Phetsarath group to develop their policy of independence from France. Thus foreign interests can be seen once more in general alignment with rival internal dynastic groups. Prince Phetsarath, with his brother Souvannaphouma and half-brother Souphanouvong, are members of a cadet branch of the royal family of Luang Prabang. The senior

---

[1] A confusion of dates exists here. See Katay D. Sasorith, *Le Laos* (Paris, Berger-Levrault, 1953), p. 60. This work contains a full account of the Lao Issara period.

M

branch, which has provided the ruling line, was represented by
the King and Crown Prince. They and the cadet branch princes
are descendants of the elder and younger sons respectively of
King Anourouth of Luang Prabang (*c.* 1791–1815). The
southern principality of Champassak of which Prince Boun
Oum is the head lay, in 1945–6, fully within the French sphere
of influence. The present Champassak princes, like those of
Luang Prabang, trace their descent from King Soulingavongsa
of Laos (1645–94).

Lao troops loyal to the provisional Government placed the
King in house arrest in October 1945. The deposition of Crown
Prince Savang Vatthana as heir to the throne was announced in
Vientiane and, on 20 October, the dethronement of the King.

A logical further step would have been the assumption of
royal power by Prince Phetsarath but this did not follow,
though it is probable that his more extreme advisers urged him
to take it. A compromise was arranged. King Sisavangvong
accepted the position of a constitutional monarch and he was
enthroned as such on 23 April, 1946. The provisional Government was legitimized and the provisional constitution of 12
October, 1945, adopted as the constitution of the kingdom.

During this period, however, the French had been active.
Having firmly established themselves in the south, French forces
moved up the Mekhong during the dry winter season of 1945–6,
harried by the guerrillas of the resistance who were already
supported by Viet Minh cadres. At Tha Khèk a decisive and
destructive pitched battle took place on 22–3 March, 1946, in
which the Lao Issara forces were severely defeated and Prince
Souphanouvong wounded. French troops occupied Vientiane
on 24 March and reached Luang Prabang on 13 May, a mere
three weeks after the final declaration of an independent Laos
Prince Phetsarath and his Government retired to Bangkok
where a national resistance movement was set up under the title
of Lao Issara. In addition to the three cadet branch princes of
Luang Prabang a large number of Lao leaders and potential
leaders, drawn from all parts of the country, were now in exile
in Thailand.

The movement did not remain united during its four-year
period of exile. Prince Souphanouvong visited Ho Chi Minh in
Hanoi in July 1946 and established closer ties with the Viet

Minh. He represented the extreme nationalist wing of the movement, dedicated to violent resistance to the French re-occupation of Laos. He held at this time the position of Foreign Minister in the Bangkok organization and was commander of the Lao Issara forces. The increasing closeness of his contact with the Viet Minh began to arouse the doubts of his colleagues in the resistance Government, traditionally suspicious as they were of Vietnamese motives towards Laos.

The moderates in the Lao Issara movement soon began to think in terms of a negotiated settlement with France and the royal Government. Some like Nhouy Abhay, then and later the holder of important ministerial posts, returned to Laos within a few months. Most, including the later prime ministers Prince Souvannaphouma and Katay D. Sasorith, continued the organization of Lao Issara and the dissemination of propaganda for independence.

The French, having taken all the Mekhong valley towns by mid-1946, then attempted to regain control of the more distant provinces. An important difference between the valley and mountain regions of Laos lies in the ethnic distribution of the population. The Lao, a Tai people, cultivators of wet-rice, live mainly in the Mekhong valley and its immediate offshoots. The three most important groups of hill peoples are the Tai tribes of the northern and north-eastern valleys, of which the Black Tai and the Lü are the most numerous; the Mèo, found at a greater altitude in the same areas, a people who have migrated into Laos from the north in the course of the last hundred and twenty years; and the Kha,[1] mostly Mon-Khmer tribes, who occupy the mountains and plateaux of the centre and south. The hill areas have never been completely controlled by any central government and in pre-colonial and colonial days its peoples were not infrequently in rebellion against all authority except that of their own local chiefs and sorcerers.

Prince Souphanouvong devoted his attention to organizing resistance with the hill peoples. Among the Kha and Mèo leaders were the descendants of chiefs who had paid with their lives for their struggle against French control during the colonial

---

[1] Mèo and Kha are Lao terms applied to the tribes but not used by them. They are somewhat pejorative and are used here purely for convenience. Equivalents recently introduced are Lao Xung and Lao Thoeng.

régime. Some of these and their followers were intransigent enough to provide fertile soil in which to plant seeds of renewed resistance. Prominent among them were Phay Dang of the Mèo and Sithon Kommadom of the Kha people, both of whom were to become important members of the central committee of Pathet Lao.

The militant resistance thus relied for its indigenous support mainly on the hill peoples and it is interesting to note that the later success of Pathet Lao, both militarily and politically, has been precisely in those provinces where the Lao people proper are in a minority.[1]

Prince Souphanouvong also engaged in the activities of the South-East Asia League with its headquarters in Bangkok and Rangoon. Although the Lao Issara in Bangkok had welcomed some careful association with the Viet Minh, having in mind, for one thing, the sympathies of the important Vietnamese minority in Laos, Souphanouvong appeared to be leading them too fast and too far to the Left. He was officially removed from his post of Foreign Minister in the exiled Government and of commander of the resistance force on 16 May, 1949, though relations between the two parties had really broken down a year earlier. It is worthy of note that Souphanouvong worked in the French administration as an engineer in Vietnam before and during the Second World War and married a Vietnamese with Left-wing sympathies in 1947. These facts play a part in explaining his attraction towards the Viet Minh. It is probable that he spent some time in China during 1949–50.

NEGOTIATIONS WITH FRANCE AND THE RETURN OF THE EXILES

In the political sphere France had proved reasonably conciliatory and a *modus vivendi* of 27 August, 1946, confirmed the unity of Laos under the constitutional rule of King Sisavangvong. An attached protocol defined the position of Prince Boun Oum of Champassak who renounced his hereditary rights and became Inspector-General of the kingdom. One possible source

---

[1] For percentages of ethnic groups in provincial populations see the useful table in F. M. LeBar and A. Suddard (ed.) *Laos* (HRAF Press, New Haven, 1960), p. 239.

of disunity was therefore removed, in theory, by the Prince's generosity. On 15 March, 1947 a Lao commission with French advisers began the preparation of a constitution which was promulgated on 11 May. General elections of a sort were held and a Legislative Assembly came into being.

During the next two years France attempted to create stability in Indochina by offering independence within the French Union to the constituent states. Paralleling the Auriol-Bao Dai accords of 9 March, 1949 France entered into an agreement with Laos — the general convention of 19 July — which, together with the revised constitution of 14 September, established the status of the kingdom. Laos had gained much. The constitution emphasized the democratic nature of government and the unity and independence of the state. France undertook to sponsor the admission of Laos as a member state of the United Nations and she was eventually voted in on 14 December, 1955. Nevertheless much remained to be won. France retained significant fiscal, economic and judicial privileges and was permitted to establish bases and move troops both for the defence of the country and in pursuit of the wider aims of the French Union which, at this time, meant chiefly the war against the Viet Minh.

From the point of view of the moderates of the Lao Issara in Bangkok these arrangements, though not fully satisfactory, represented, nevertheless, an important advance towards independence. Prudence suggested that an appropriate moment had arrived to attempt a reconciliation with the royal Government and a return from exile to share the sweets of office. Lao Issara and its 'liberation army' was formally dissolved on 24 October, 1949, and its members began to return home. Prince Phetsarath had quarrelled with Souphanouvong over the Viet Minh issue but was unable to return to Laos because of his actions aimed at the royal family. He remained in Bangkok until 1957 when he returned home to spend a brief retirement before his death in 1959.

Prince Souphanouvong and a few followers, some of whom were part Vietnamese, soon moved to Vietnam and then, in September 1950, set up a resistance group near the township of Sam Neua in the north-eastern province of Houa Phans. These militant nationalists, who later adopted the name of Pathet

Lao, were unable to accept that Laos was yet truly independent or could become so by means of negotiation. Moreover they were by now firmly in the hands of the Viet Minh and from the point of view of the latter a continued struggle was urgently necessary in Laos in view of the acceptance by the royal Government of terms which would allow French troops and aircraft to use Lao territory in their campaign against the Viet Minh in north and central Vietnam. The Viet Minh, therefore, had immediate reasons for supporting Souphanouvong and, indeed, his group could not have survived as a meaningful political and military force without their aid.

In Vientiane the returned exiles soon began to play a part in government and administration. Their presence strengthened the Lao Government but increased the dangers of divisions arising from more complex local rivalries.

The 1949 Convention had provided that certain governmental functions would be carried out in quadripartite form with France and the other two associated states Cambodia and Vietnam. These included a monetary and customs union and agreements on economic planning, communications and navigation of the Mekhong. The details were left to a conference which met at Pau between 27 June and 29 November, 1950. The Pau Conference did not run smoothly. The Laotian delegation had some reservations about accepting the form of the economic and commercial agreements because of a fear, shared by Cambodia, that increasing independence from France would result in ultimate domination by the strongest of the Associated States — Vietnam.

In these circumstances the Lao Government saw advantages in a continuing association with France. They desired political and economic independence, it is true, but they were not so emotionally concerned about the issue as many emergent nationalist régimes and wished to rely for a further period on French aid for defence and the cushioning effect of economic links with France. They also wanted to have freedom to develop commercial outlets through Thailand to offset a potential increase in Vietnamese control.

United States interest in the area grew rapidly from 1950. American financial assistance enabled France to implement General de Lattre de Tassigny's policy of forming strong national armies in the Associated States. The Royal Laotian Army, later to be supported entirely by the United States, thus came into being.

The Lao leaders, traditionally conditioned to setting up an elaborate system of political checks and balances, were at once aware of this new American factor in the power pressures in the region. Preliminary agreements for economic co-operation were made with the United States Government in September and December 1951. These allowed for the establishment of a technical and economic mission in Laos.

The pressure of events in the war led France to make further conciliatory moves which affected Laos. On 3 July, 1953 the Laniel Government pledged its intention to complete the sovereignty and independence of the Associated States. Prince Souvannaphouma, then Prime Minister, began negotiations on the transfer of powers on 4 October. On 23 October a Treaty of Friendship and Association was signed. Although some of the quadripartite arrangements continued in being, Laos gained virtually full sovereignty but retained her association with the French Union. During the negotiations it was made clear by Souvannaphouma that Laos continued to depend on France in the sphere of defence. Indeed, the serious military situation made this imperative.

VIET MINH INVASIONS OF LAOS

On 11 April, 1953 strong Viet Minh forces crossed the Lao frontier into the province of Houa Phans and occupied Sam Neua, the provincial headquarters, on the 19th. Advancing in several columns they drove the Lao-French forces into defensive positions round an aerodrome on the Plain of Jars near Xieng Khouang. Further columns approached Luang Prabang.

Souvannaphouma asked for aid to resist Viet Minh aggression. It is arguable that the French response with the decision to defend Laos was a major factor in determining their strategy in the closing phase of the war. Acceptance of defence responsibility for the difficult mountain region between the Black River and the Mekong led directly to the recapture of, and later fatal failure to hold, the fortified area of Dien Bien Phu which lies in Tai country on the edge of Laos. From the immediate Lao point of view, however, the episode could be represented as a diplomatic victory and underlines Souvannaphouma's suspicion of Vietnam.

On 27 April Prince Souphanouvong announced that his Government was the only legal government of Laos and on 10 May the Viet Minh radio confirmed the existence of the Pathet Lao (PL) — State of Laos — administration of Souphanouvong and said that new political officials were being appointed in the villages under his control. At this point the Viet Minh began to retire from their extended positions in Luang Prabang and Xieng Khouang provinces and these areas were relatively free from the invader by September. Sam Neua was, however, firmly held. The actual military role played by PL in this attack was undoubtedly a small one but Souphanouvong's organization of the hill peoples provided useful logistic support. Nevertheless the hill tribes were by no means all pro-Viet Minh. A number of Tai tribal leaders and Touby Lyfoung, of the Mèo, whose territory lay in Xieng Khouang province, organized guerrilla forces against them. The suspicions of the hill tribes regarding the Vietnamese were hardly stilled by the propaganda that the Viet Minh strike was a liberation movement. Many feared it as an alien invasion of their territory equally as they had disliked and resisted all Government attempts at pacification in the past.

The large-scale assault on Laos was well planned. Its cause was ostensibly the fact, certainly true, that Laos was being used by the French as a base for their campaigns in the Tai country of North Vietnam. Another declared motive was the desire firmly to establish a 'free' government on Laotian soil. This political motive was probably equally important. The idea of a settlement in Indochina was being mooted and early in December 1953 Ho Chi Minh seemed ready to make a peace offer to the French. In the event these tentative overtures came to nothing but had negotiations begun they might well have led to a general peace. In such circumstances Communist, or, indeed, specifically Vietnamese ambitions in Laos would have been helped by the existence of a Lao resistance government. Such a 'government' for which established boundaries with organized administration within them could be claimed would have had an important effect on the nature of any political agreement over Laos.

On 20 December a Viet Minh strike began from Vinh to Tha Khèk and Savannakhet on the Mekong. A month later further attacks were made in the direction of Luang Prabang. These operations aimed at ensuring the dispersal of French troops before and during the vital battle of Dien Bien Phu.

THE GENEVA CONFERENCE AND THE SUCCEEDING PHASE

Discussion on Indochina at Geneva opened on 8 May, 1954, the day after the fall of Dien Bien Phu. The deteriorated military situation, arising directly from the Viet Minh invasions of 1953, explains why Laos, unlike Cambodia, was unable to liquidate an organized Communist internal threat through the provisions of the Geneva Accords which were finally signed on 21 July. Phoui Sananikone, a man of Vientiane, leader of the Lao delegation, stubbornly insisted that the royal Government was the sole body entitled to represent the country at Geneva. He resolutely opposed Communist, particularly Viet Minh, attempts to seat a rival PL delegation and eventually made his point. He emphasized that Prince Souphanouvong, leader of PL, had been removed from the command of the Lao Issara forces by the resistance Government itself in 1949 because of his complete dependence on foreign (i.e. Vietnamese) elements and powers.

Laos fared better than Vietnam in that the question of partition was not seriously considered, yet she had to accept the allocation of the two north-eastern provinces of Phongsaly and Houa Phans as regroupment areas for PL personnel who did not wish for local demobilization. It was intended that both French and Vietnamese forces should leave the country but the French High Command was permitted to set up a training mission and retain two small military establishments. The Vietnamese, on their part, obtained a possible loophole in the withdrawal arrangements in that a special convention safeguarded the position of those 'volunteers' who had been settled in Laos before the hostilities. A further concession which was to cause great future difficulty was made by the royal Government in its declaration not only that all citizens would be integrated into the national community but also that, in the interval before the holding of general elections, the interests of those who did not support the royal forces during the fighting would be specially represented in the administration of the provinces of Phongsaly and Houa Phans.[1] Moreover the wording of a vital section of the Geneva Agreement itself was none too definite. Article 14 simply stated: 'Pending a political settlement, the fighting forces of Pathet Lao, concentrated in the provisional assembly areas, shall move into the provinces of Phongsaly and Sam Neua (Houa Phans). . . .' This vagueness was unfortunate especially in view of the fact that Pham Van Dong's attitude at Geneva had made it clear that there would be continuing Vietnamese support for PL intransigence.

Yet another source of controversy was the local Khang Khay agreement of 29–30 August in which no mention was made of assembly areas in Phongsaly and Houa Phans but only in the other ten provinces. The Geneva Agreement had stated that twelve assembly areas, one for each province, would be established. Relying on their claim to have organized government in the allocated provinces from May 1953, and on their interpretation of the ambiguities of the several agreements and declarations, PL claimed jurisdiction over Phongsaly and Houa Phans and, from the start, attempted to prevent by force the reestablishment of authority there by the royal army. The royal Government naturally maintained that the Geneva Agreement gave it the right directly to administer the whole country and this right was upheld by the International Control Commission.[2]

The period from late 1954 to 1961 may be divided into four phases. In the first of these, from September 1954 to December 1955, the royal Government, hoping for a successful military solution, made not very whole-hearted efforts to reach a settlement with PL on its own terms. The second phase, from April 1956 to July 1958, was one of attempted reconciliation and democratic coalition government with PL. Then a swing to the

[1] Donald Lancaster, *The Emancipation of French Indochina* (R.I.I.A.; O.U.P., 1961), p. 341.
[2] Memorandum adressé le 13 Avril 1955 à la commission internationale (Royal Government of Laos, Imprimerie française d'outre-mer, Saigon, 1955) Addendum pp. 1–2.

Right constituted the third phase and finally, after the *coup d'état* of Captain Kong Lè on 9 August, 1960, the civil war began.

Negotiations begun in September 1954 were soon terminated because the Souvannaphouma Government fell in October after the assassination, on 18 September, of Kou Voravong, Minister of Defence, who was believed to be the strongest opponent of an aggressive policy.[1]

The succeeding Government under Katay D. Sasorith, a man of the south and relative by marriage of Prince Boun Oum, was based on a coalition between his party and the Vientiane Independent Party of Phoui Sananikone. Clashes between the royal Government and PL continued during the first half of 1955 even though cease-fire negotiations were attempted. The royal Government complained that PL were impeding the negotiations over integration through their insistence on their claim to administrative authority in the two provinces. This round of negotiations was finally broken off by the royal Government on 26 April.

This was the period of the Bandung Conference. The Lao delegation did not hesitate to declare its dislike of foreign intervention in its affairs. By this, Vietnamese support for PL was clearly meant. But Chou En-Lai registered a personal success with Lao as with other South-East Asian national leaders. It was no doubt clear to him that to assume a moderate attitude might attract support for an apparent 'hands-off' policy of neutrality and non-interference.

In June, under International Control Commission auspices, negotiations re-opened in Rangoon between Katay and Souphanouvong and these were continued in Vientiane. PL again demanded that a political settlement should come before elections and proposed changes in the electoral law to allow a revision of voting qualifications, votes for women and mixed supervisory groups to control the elections. PL, who continued to mount guerrilla operations against royal army posts and were intensifying their programme of administrative and political change in the two provinces, would not reduce their terms.

[1] For a Communist account of this incident see W. G. Burchett, *Mekong Upstream* (Seven Seas Books, East Berlin, 1959), pp. 244–5.

On 9 November the royal Government again announced that negotiations were at an end and that the elections, originally intended for August 1955, would be held on 25 December. Voting would take place in ten provinces and in areas held by royal Government forces in Phongsaly and Houa Phans. The policy of the Katay Government had been to establish closer economic relations with Thailand including the setting up of a Lao-Thai trading organization. The gaining from France of full independence in foreign trade and the ending of the quadri-partite monetary and customs union set up at Pau, which occurred at this time, gave Laos a freer hand. Support for the economy was still an obvious necessity and it was hoped that this would be obtained from the United States. An economic co-operation agreement was signed in July 1955 and direct defence aid was provided on a greatly increased scale. The Lao Government wanted to raise the strength of its forces as it still hoped to impose a military solution before the elections. It appears that there was a serious difference of opinion between the State Department and the Joint Chiefs of Staff over this issue.[1] The former believed in continuing the build-up of the Lao armed forces while the latter recommended that the royal army be held at not more than 12,000–15,000 which had been the aim under French planning.

PL boycotted the elections in which Katay's Progressive Party gained 21 of the 39 seats in the National Assembly.

RAPPROCHEMENT

Following the elections, a new Progressive Party government was formed on 21 March. Souvannaphouma, the Prime Minister, was a genuine nationalist, little inclined to compromise with either Thai or North Vietnamese interference. He regarded both nations with suspicion. Such suspicions in the mind of a prince of Luang Prabang are not surprising when the history of the eighteenth and nineteenth centuries is recalled. He was, however, naturally inclined towards the West by background and training and was amenable to French advice. He

---

[1] *U.S. Aid Operations in Laos*, Seventh report by the Committee on Government Operations (Washington, 1959), pp. 2–9.

aimed to maintain the interest and support of the Western powers, without overtly alienating China, and to seek an accommodation with his half-brother Souphanouvong, believing that only a small number of PL party members were convinced and trained Communists and that participation by PL in government might well wean them away from the influence of the North Vietnamese.

Laos, though not a signatory of the Manila treaty, nevertheless lay within its protective 'umbrella'. But doubts about the wisdom of relations with SEATO were widely held among Lao politicians as is shown by unfavourable Lao reaction to Thailand's 'helpful' move to bring the PL threat before the SEATO meeting in July 1955.[1] Renewed insistence by Lao leaders that the PL affair was entirely an internal matter may be thought to have been due to fears of foreign intervention, from whatever quarter it might come. Such fears were based to some extent on considerations of historical experience.

After some preliminary exchanges Souvannaphouma's policy resulted in a conference in Vientiane between PL and royal Government delegations. On 10 August an agreement was announced. PL military activity had been considerable in late 1955 but its cessation in 1956, probably deliberate, contributed to a better atmosphere. A campaign in Vientiane by Bong Souvannavong, leader of the anti-monarchist National Union Party, later to become the Santiphap pen kang (Peace and Neutrality) Party, through his newspaper Lao Mai (New Laos), had an influence on public opinion.

By the Vientiane accords PL obtained many of the concessions for which they had been waiting. The most important of these were the right to form a legal political party, Neo Lao Hak Sat (NLHS) — Lao Patriotic Front — and ancillary organizations, and the agreement, in principle, that they should participate in a government of national union. The Government agreed to follow a neutral foreign policy and declared support for the five principles of peaceful co-existence. Arrangements were made for the holding of supplementary elections to bring in new constituencies mainly in the provinces of Phongsaly and Houa Phans. On their part PL promised fully to hand over authority in the two provinces and to integrate their civil and

[1] LeBar and Suddard, op. cit., p. 149.

military wings with the royal administration and army. Mixed commissions were set up to settle the details of reintegration and here a continuing source of disagreement was found.

Following the Vientiane accords a strong government delegation, including both Souvannaphouma and Katay, visited China and North Vietnam almost at once. The agreements had induced an atmosphere of hope in Vientiane and consequently were popular. The delegation was seen off from the airport by a large crowd which included the heads of diplomatic missions. A notable absentee was the Ambassador of the United States. This incident might be dismissed as too trivial to be included in an account of the period were it not for the fact that such studied discourtesies are long remembered in Laos.[1] Moreover this marked the beginning of a coolness between Souvannaphouma and the American authorities which boded ill for the Western cause in general.[2]

Declarations of respect for Lao independence and territorial integrity were obtained in Peking and Hanoi. In return the Lao Government was not held to definite diplomatic recognition of the Communist countries, nor to the acceptance of aid from the Communist bloc. The Chinese dropped these issues after discussion and left them to be raised by NLHS at a later stage. As if to mark his neutrality in almost traditional form, Souvannaphouma visited South Vietnam, Britain and France. This neutrality, which Souvannaphouma characterized as 'vigilant but absolute',[3] naturally caused concern in the West. As early as January 1957 American opinion began to refer to 'conquest by negotiation', following the confirmation of the Vientiane accords in December 1956.

PL proved tough negotiators over the details of integration and the Souvannaphouma Government fell on this issue in May 1957. But, in default of Assembly support for any alternative, the King had to call on Souvannaphouma again and he formed a new government on 9 August. Negotiations with PL were resumed and agreements on integration were signed on 2

---

[1] See, for example, Sisouk na Champassak, *Storm over Laos* (New York, Praeger, 1961), p. 43; and Souvannaphouma: Laos; Le fond du problème, *France-Asie*, xxii, no. 166 (1961), pp. 1823–6.

[2] A frank statement of Souvannaphouma's grievances is given in *New York Times*, 19 January, 1961.

[3] *Lao Presse*, Vientiane, 13 August, 1956.

November. Prince Souphanouvong formally handed over the powers he had claimed in the two provinces at a ceremony on 18 November. A government of national union was announced in which Souphanouvong held the Ministry of Planning and Phoumi Vongvichit, former PL 'Minister of the Interior', the Ministry of Religions. In December the Government resumed full control of the two provinces.

The supplementary elections of 4 May, 1958, increased the total number of seats in the National Assembly from 39 to 59. Twenty-one seats were contested of which NLHS won 9 and the Santiphap party 4.[1] NLHS and Santiphap gave each other mutual support while the other parties engaged in contests in the same constituencies. This resulted in the Left-wing victory of thirteen seats being obtained with a poll in their favour of no more than 32 per cent of total votes cast. It is interesting that the candidate who gained the largest personal vote was Prince Souphanouvong. The degree of support for NLHS surprised even Souvannaphouma himself and he took immediate steps to create a unified front against growing Leftist influence. In June the nationalist and independent groups in the Assembly united to form the Lao Ruam Lao (Rally of the Lao People) Party. This provided a solid block of thirty-six seats. Up to that time there had been little tendency for more than temporary concerted action between the rival moderate groups and leaders. Now, most of the moderate nationalist leaders who had participated in government since independence were concentrated in the new party. This move was important mainly because it demonstrated a genuinely Laotian reaction to a feared swing to the Left. Immediate experience of the determined way in which Communists pursue their aims was far more valuable to the empirically-minded Lao politicians than the second-hand instruction in such dangers frequently offered, with the best of intentions, by American diplomatists and others. Constant advice-giving was a feature of the American connexion greatly disliked by the Lao ministers. Indeed the Lao, and the Thai too, have never reacted well to gratuitous political teaching. One is reminded of the ironical comment of the Thai ministers on Sir James Brooke in 1850:

---

[1] A normal by-election held at the same time raised the number of seats contested from twenty to twenty-one.

Indeed we ought to praise Sir James Brooke for his great knowledge and skill at negotiation. Since we have been nobles in the
service of His Majesty, some of us for seventy, others for fully
sixty, fifty, forty, thirty and twenty years, we have never met a
man like this, coming to engage in political negotiations as a
teacher giving out directions and instruction — flowing out like a
flood over the forests and rice plains. . . .[1]

The creation of the Committee for the Defence of National
Interests (CDIN) on 29 June brought into the field for the first
time an organization specifically charged with combating
Communist influence. The CDIN drew on army support and
United States encouragement had been influential in its
formation. It had a more youthful and militant flavour than the
Rally and was the first truly Right-wing political grouping in
Laos. Its rapid rise was a sign that the dangerous policy of
polarization was succeeding. Extremism was to be met with
extremism and not with vigilance, moderation, and attempted
social and economic advance.

The Lao Government took the view that the carrying out of
the provisions of the Vientiane accords, which they claimed was
complete by March 1958, meant that the demands of the
Geneva Agreement had been complied with. Consequently the
function of the ICC was at an end. After some wrangling, the
ICC for Laos adjourned *sine die* on 19 July, the Polish delegate
opposing the move.

The Souvannaphouma Government of national union was
about to fall. Its leader was in a difficult position. Although
NLHS was behaving quite constitutionally it was beginning to
exert pressure for closer relations with countries of the Communist bloc. Souvannaphouma was a lone figure. He had been
quite unable to form a strong political group to prosecute the
moderate progressive and reformist policies that would have
been popular. Many of the older group of politicians, some of
whom were his ministers, were tainted with suspicion of corruption and profiteering. Heavy inflation had occurred due to the
American policy of pumping in huge cash grants to pay the
large army, the cuckoo in the nest in Laos. Certainly, CDIN

[1] *Ru'ang thut farang samai krung ratanakosin* (Prachum Phongsawadan, lem 62), pp.
211–12. Translation by the present writer.

was reformist but it was already obsessed with its American-inspired single-minded anti-Communist role and was therefore unfitted to come to Souvannaphouma's aid to strengthen him within a fully representative national government. The holding up of United States aid from 30 June provided the final pressure on Souvannaphouma. He resigned on 22 July and then tried to meet CDIN and American pressures by forming a government without NLHS participation. In this last move he was unsuccessful mainly because CDIN made an unreasonable demand for eight out of fourteen available portfolios even though they had not been concerned as a political party in the recent elections.

THE SWING TO THE RIGHT

Phoui Sananikone, the next Prime Minister designate, was able to form a Government on 18 August in which he did include four members of CDIN, who were not Assemblymen, and also Bong Souvannavong as a concession to the Left.

The first move of the new Government was to initiate a drive against corruption. An essential part of this policy involved the devaluation of the *kip* (from 35 to 80= $1 U.S.) and the reform of the import licensing system which had been heavily abused in conjunction with the unrealistic rate of exchange. The United States Government supported the new *kip* as a fully convertible currency and resumed aid payments in October.

The Communist powers had made frequent protests against the adjournment of the ICC and the formation of the Phoui Sananikone government. Then, in December 1958, a small-scale outbreak of fighting at Huong Lap on the border with North Vietnam led to a further hardening of attitudes on both sides. Charges and counter-charges of frontier violations were made to the Secretary-General of the United Nations, on 16 January, 1959. On the 15th the Prime Minister had received from the Assembly a favourable vote on his request for special powers for a period of twelve months. By this vote the Assembly virtually divested itself of legislative powers for the period. Plans for constitutional reform were announced and it was stated that a general election would be held after the National Congress

N

(National Assembly and King's Council) had approved the revisions.

On 11 February Phoui Sananikone made a policy statement in which he said that Laotian obligations under the Geneva Agreement had been faithfully discharged and that the Government of Laos could not accept the continuing validity of the terms of the agreement which imposed restrictions on Laotian freedom of action pending a final political settlement in Vietnam.[1] He claimed that he would recognize no arbiter but the United Nations.

On 12 February a State Department announcement supported the action of the Lao Government and American officials expressed the view that the United States Government was now entitled to establish a military mission in Laos. This action had not been permissible under Article 6 of the Geneva Agreement. At once China and North Vietnam responded with charges that Laos had repudiated the Geneva Agreement and that American influence had dictated this policy. In reply the Lao Government denied such repudiation and stated that they would not allow foreign bases or the stationing of foreign troops in Laos except as provided for in the Geneva Agreement.

Phoui Sananikone's Government adopted a stiffer policy towards the final integration of the former PL military forces. Although this had been officially carried out in December 1957 many points of detail remained to be settled and meanwhile two PL battalions retained separate existence, a situation much to PL's liking. In April and May the Government's final terms were put to PL. The main point was the reduction to 100 of PL officers and non-commissioned officers who were to retain their ranks and remain operational. PL's policy had been to inflate their officer and N.C.O. totals during the protracted negotiations. On 11 May the two battalions were ordered to lay down their arms and on the 14th they were surrounded by royal Government troops. One battalion accepted integration but the second, at Xieng Khouang, broke the cordon and moved off with their arms into the mountainous jungle country bordering North Vietnam. In July the effectiveness of the political wing of PL was reduced by the placing of the NLHS leaders under house

[1] Further documents relating to the discussion of Indochina at the Geneva Conference, 16 June–21 July, 1954, Cmnd. 9239, p. 42. Document No. 9.

arrest in Vientiane. They were later imprisoned and charged with treason.

At this stage it was clear that the royal Government had managed effectually to block every path by which NLHS could reach power by democratic political means. It could hardly be expected that the Communist powers supporting PL and NLHS would acquiesce in such a firm rebuff, and thus it became very likely that there would be a deterioration to a point at which a military solution would be attempted.

During the early months of 1959 the situation had developed in ways which did not seem characteristically Laotian. The PL battalions might have been expected to accept integration as a tactical move when faced with force. It has been suggested that Souphanouvong issued an order to this effect. That it was only partially complied with might mean that influences stronger than his were at work in PL.

The final forcing of the issue by the royal Government is also difficult to understand in Laotian terms. Negotiations had been successfully protracted since 1956 without causing any absolute rupture, and the relative powerlessness of the PL battalions had been maintained through supervision by the royal army and by limitation of arms and supplies. That a more extreme solution developed at this period suggests that foreign influences were gaining ground in Laos.

A campaign for the return of the ICC was promoted by the Communist powers in mid-1959. Britain and Russia, the Geneva co-chairmen, failed to agree. India favoured return in the hope that Laos might thus be kept from becoming more closely involved in the cold-war struggle.

During the year the American aid programme came under heavy fire in the form of an adverse and very frank Congressional report.[1] The preponderance of military over civil aid was ruthlessly criticized. It was pointed out that only two non-military projects were given regular large-scale support, the police scheme which was, in any case, related to security and the road rehabilitation project which was characterized by irregularities in contract placing, bad administration and poor performance. The report stated bluntly: 'The excessive use of cash grants and

[1] *U.S. Aid Operations in Laos*, Seventh report by the Committee on Government Operations (Washington, 1959).

related laxity in import controls have, in effect, led to the financing of capital flight by the United States aid program in a country where one of the primary needs is for local investment capital.'[1]

The original disagreement over the size of the army was recalled:

'In Laos, the only country in the world where the United States supports the military budget 100%, military judgements have been disregarded.'[2]

'An army too large for the economy to handle was inadequate to perform its appointed mission. Against a much smaller force it was unable to enforce Communist compliance with the Geneva Agreements. . . .'[3]

Finally the report said that the nature of the aid programme itself might have contributed to an atmosphere in which the ordinary people of Laos questioned the value of the friendship of the United States and had provided the Communists with propaganda opportunities which helped their victory in the supplementary elections.

The military policy certainly continued on its appointed path. On 24 July the Lao Government announced that it had requested the aid of American military advisers to assist in the re-equipment and re-organization of the French-trained army.[4] Then, at the end of the month, a series of Laotian communiqués charged that North Vietnamese elements were assisting the resistance of the escaped PL battalion. In August Laotian reports suggested that the situation was worsening and moves to secure a United Nations fact-finding mission commenced. At the same time additional American transport, arms, aircraft and technicians began to arrive in Laos. On 4 September the Lao Government went so far as to request a United Nations emergency force to resist aggression from North Vietnam.

Procedural difficulties of a serious nature having been overcome, a fact-finding sub-committee of the Security Council was dispatched to Laos. Its report was made on 4 November. Fighting, such as it had been, had ceased and though the sub-committee confirmed the long-known fact of assistance in arms,

---

[1] ibid., p. 13.   [2] ibid., p. 8.   [3] ibid., p. 50.
[4] Arranged in this way presumably to circumvent the provisions of Article 6 of the Geneva Agreement.

supplies, and the provision of political cadres by the Democratic Republic of Vietnam, it did not clearly establish whether there were any crossings of the frontier by regular troops of the DRV. Each side interpreted this inconclusive report to suit its own case. A reasonable impartial conclusion might be that at this stage no great political advantage was to be gained by a regular Communist invasion, especially in view of the possibility of SEATO intervention in such circumstances. The important thing from the Communist point of view was merely to reactivate PL resistance and this could be accomplished without greater Vietnamese aid than had normally been given in the past. It seems that this was what was happening, for most observers on the spot were extremely sceptical of reports of heavy fighting during this 'crisis'.[1]

Mr Hammarskjöld visited Laos from 12 to 19 November. From 15 November he was joined by Mr Sakari Tuomioja who was to report on the economic situation of the country and make suggestions for development. His report favoured help from United Nations and the specialized agencies.

Mr Hammarskjöld recommended a policy of neutrality to the Government of Laos. Indeed there had been signs that Phoui Sananikone was by no means in favour of all-out pro-Western commitment and extreme solutions. The trial of the PL leaders, due to begin on 26 October, had been postponed. The Rally of the Lao People's Party demanded a reduction of CDIN strength in the Government and, on 15 December, Phoui Sananikone attempted a reshuffle which left out three prominent CDIN ministers including Phoumi Nosavan. The particular point at issue between CDIN and the moderates was that of new elections. CDIN favoured authoritarian rule and indefinite postponement of elections. Phoui Sananikone, seeing civil war as the probable end to extremist policies, and perhaps thinking of the possibility of increased United Nations aid, was prepared to return to democratic procedures. He tried to compromise by getting an Assembly vote, on 22 December, in favour of postponement of the elections until April 1960. But he had offended the powerful CDIN too deeply and, on the 30th, the army

[1] See Bernard B. Fall, *Street without Joy* (Harrisburg, Penn., U.S.A., 1961), pp. 301–5. This work contains an interesting account of a typical military action of the period (pp. 121–4).

took over. On 7 January a government heavily influenced by CDIN assumed power. The swing to the Right was gathering speed.

Souvannaphouma's policy of *rapprochement* had one definite advantage in that it was clearly designed to carry out the provisions of the Geneva Agreement and therefore could be vilified less easily by Communist propaganda. Moreover a neutral foreign policy was psychologically more readily acceptable locally than one of commitment. Yet a definite risk was involved in allowing PL participation in government, in administration and in the army. But to Souvannaphouma this was a calculated risk and behind it lay the belief that Vietnamese influence in Laos would be reduced by taking it. The chance of course existed that aid would be given by and diplomatic recognition accorded to the People's Republic of China. Fear of this was certainly a consideration in Thai opposition to the policy. But a Chinese presence in Laos would not have been welcomed, for the memory of their behaviour in the zone they occupied in 1945–6 was still green. Souvannaphouma's policy rested on the assumption that Western aid would continue. Even if Western, more particularly United States, hesitancies about supporting this policy can be understood, the further step of preventing Phoui Sananikone from making an effort to return to negotiations with PL from the position of relative strength he had built up in 1959 was highly dangerous.

Constant United States support for the army since 1954 meant that it now had a strength approaching 30,000 men. It had taken the lion's share of $250,000,000 since 1955.[1] Inevitably the army became an internal political force as had happened long since in neighbouring Thailand. Its rising leader, General Phoumi Nosavan, is said to be a relative of Marshal Sarit Thanarat, the Thai Prime Minister. Phoumi Nosavan first became Minister of Defence in the Phoui Sananikone Government and held a dominant political position in Laos from that time. He commanded much foreign but less internal support.

Now that the army was in control of political life its view of the risk of early elections was less unfavourable. By the closing date for nominations no NLHS candidates had been put forward. Prince Souphanouvong and the major PL leaders were in

[1] *New York Times*, 12 August, 1961.

custody, but, at the last moment, NLHS participation was announced. The Government probably allowed the late and irregular nominations because they saw Left-wing candidatures as a divisive factor in the Opposition and anticipated a landslide victory over NLHS itself. PL, more subtle, changed the original boycott plan because they, or their backers, could scent the propaganda possibilities of a heavy defeat.

The elections, firmly controlled by the army, took place without any notable violence on 24 April. NLHS and Santiphap candidates, fourteen in all, failed to gain a seat. Even in areas known to be sympathetic to PL the NLHS vote was ludicrously small. In Sam Neua the NLHS candidate was defeated by 4,500 votes to 13 and this was the typical pattern.[1] The Left-wing in Laos and the Communist world press and radio immediately made violent accusations of ballot-rigging against the Government. In reply Foreign Minister Khamphan Panya, a CDIN leader, said, on 28 April: 'the truth sometimes appears impossible to be true.'[2]

On 3 May CDIN formed a political party, the Paxasangkhom (Social Democrat) Party with Phoumi Nosavan as president. This party claimed 35 out of 59 seats in the Assembly.[3] The remainder fell mostly to supporters of Phoui Sananikone and Souvannaphouma who were linked in the Rally of the Lao People's Party. The real danger feared by the CDIN in the election had not been NLHS but the more moderate Rally Party who might have been expected to sweep the board.

The trend to the Right continued with the formation, on 2 June, of a mainly CDIN government under a compromise Prime Minister, Tiao Somsanith, nephew of Souvannaphouma. On 23 May Souphanouvong and a party which included seven of his important associates escaped from Vientiane prison where they had been held since 28 July, 1959.

---

[1] *Christian Science Monitor*, 25 April, 1960.

[2] *New York Herald Tribune*, 28 April, 1960.

[3] It is not unusual for political parties in Laos to form themselves *after* elections. This provides an acceptable way by which politicians can switch to the winning side.

COUP D'ÉTAT AND CIVIL WAR

On 9 August Captain Kong Lè seized power in Vientiane with a force of 700 paratroopers. Kong Lè is an American-trained officer, twenty-seven years old in 1960. The *coup* was hailed with embarrassing swiftness by Moscow, Peking and Hanoi radios. However, Kong Lè's earlier speeches were by no means entirely couched in obvious Communist terms.[1] A major force behind them seemed rather to be a naïve isolationism. Isolationism is a familiar attitude of the less politically mature Laotian. It would of course condemn Laos to complete stagnation at best and would probably end by the absorption of the country by her neighbours. Neutrality of the kinds advocated by Souvannaphouma or Norodom Sihanouk of Cambodia are much more sophisticated concepts. Sihanouk believes in a 'positive' balance to be achieved by deliberate contact with all political pressures. Souvannaphouma favours declarations of support from the great, and more distant, powers to help to hold in leash the eager nearer neighbours.

Kong Lè gained support from the wave of popular discontent on several counts. The most important of these were dislike of the ubiquity of the American presence in the army and in other government organizations, more because it was foreign than American as such, and resentment that the Rally Party had obtained only one seat in the ministerial council in spite of considerable success at the polls. There was a widespread feeling that the Government had over-controlled the elections and a lack of confidence that the poor position over economic advance would be improved. Charges of corruption were made and distrust of government links with Thailand was strong.

Kong Lè was also probably in touch with Left-wing opinion and ideas. Communist contacts with officers of the armed services date right back to the days when the Polish branch of ICC was in Laos. Kong Lè is a cousin of Sithon Kommadom, the Kha vice-chairman of the central committee of PL, and is a brother-in-law of General Ouan Rathikoun, an army colleague and possible rival of Phoumi Nosavan.

The Revolutionary Committee obtained the somewhat re-

[1] e.g. *Hsinhua*, Hanoi, 13 August, 1961.

luctant support of Souvannaphouma. He formed a council of ministers which included only Touby Lyfoung from the previous Government. This did not take effective power and, on 29 August, he made his first try at forming a coalition which included five of the Somsanith ministers. Kong Lè at once objected to the inclusion of Phoumi Nosavan and it was already clear at this stage that Souvannaphouma's attempt at unification was going to prove very difficult. Power was in the hands of the soldiers.

On 10 September a new revolutionary committee, this time Right-wing, under Prince Boun Oum and Phoumi Nosavan, was formed at Savannakhet. It provided a focus for military moves against the Government in Vientiane. Thailand, greatly concerned at the *coup*, had immediately closed the frontier and began to urge strong action upon the Western powers. Souvannaphouma was already under pressure in Vientiane. The spontaneous enthusiasm with which the *coup* had been received now began to be organized by the Left as a pressure group of students and soldiers. On 2 October Souvannaphouma said that he needed support for the army and police if he was to hold PL in check. This support was not forthcoming. Aid funds including both supplies and army and police pay had not been getting through after 9 August. There was an official suspension by the United States from 7 to 17 October. The move was intended to exert pressure on Souvannaphouma to accommodate with the Right, but not surprisingly, as Norodom Sihanouk had warned as early as 23 August, his weakened position forced him to give way in the opposite direction.[1]

Souvannaphouma gave his support to proposals made at the UN General Assembly by Sihanouk on 26 September that Laos and Cambodia should form a guaranteed neutral zone.[2] It was significant that Thailand and both North and South Vietnam were included among the proposed guarantors. Souvannaphouma was resisting new negotiations with PL at this time and was inclined to go no further than to accept the 1956–7 agreements.

Sporadic fighting along the Mekong from 18 September

---

[1] *Le Monde*, 24 August, 1961.
[2] Full text in UN General Assembly 15th Session. Report of 877th Plenary Meeting, 26 September, 1960.

brought success on balance to Kong Lè's forces. A difference in
the attitudes of Kong Lè and Souvannaphouma became
apparent. The former wanted to inflict a military defeat on the
Savannakhet group while the latter wished only for a cease-fire
to enable him to attempt the formation of a coalition government.

In late October food and fuel supplies were very short in
Vientiane. Thailand announced the re-opening of the frontier
on the 29th but it was constantly alleged from Vientiane that
supplies were not arriving and a Soviet air-lift of food and fuel
began on 4 December following the acceptance of a Soviet
diplomatic mission on 13 October. This arrival coincided with
the visit of the American representatives led by the former
United States ambassador accredited to Laos at the time of the
1956-7 agreements. Conditions for the resumption of aid were
reported to include cessation of negotiations with PL and formal
recognition of the Savannakhet group. A further chance of
settlement had been lost when Sihanouk's proposals at United
Nations had fallen upon deaf ears and now other forces were in
the field. The American conditions were rejected and Souvannaphouma accepted Soviet aid in principle on 26 October.
On the 28th United States aid, in the form of a cheque for
$700,000, was resumed.[1]

During November Souvannaphouma, who had been forced
into accepting a political link with PL in a unity party, continued his efforts to form a coalition which was now to include
both NLHS and CDIN members. The United States, sensitive
to the views of her allies in South-East Asia, strongly opposed an
all-party coalition though most other powers were in favour of
serious consideration of this as the best obtainable solution.
Souvannaphouma's efforts were continued until 3 December
but by then the two extremes were quite irreconcilable.

On 10 December, in the face of an imminent military threat
to Vientiane, Souvannaphouma retired to Phnom Penh with
six of his ministers though he did not resign. On the 12th the
King declared his Government illegal. The attack on Vientiane
commenced on 13 December. It was resisted by Kong Lè who
had accepted the aid of PL forces at the last moment. By the
17th the capital was in the hands of Boun Oum and Phoumi

[1] *New York Times*, 29 October, 1960.

Nosavan. These leaders headed a government of strongly southern complexion formed on the 25th with royal approval and Assembly support. Between September and December, 42 of the 59 Assemblymen had been transferred or had found their way to Savannakhet.

There were now rival governments in Laos. The Communist powers still supported that of Souvannaphouma which, with Quinim Pholsena as acting premier, operated from Xieng Khouang from 31 January, 1961. The Western powers and SEATO recognized the government of Boun Oum now at Vientiane.

A statement of British policy in favour of a genuinely unaligned status for Laos was made on 19 December.[1] The following day Boun Oum rejected British proposals for the reconvening of the ICC and official resumption of United States military aid was announced.

Events to December 1961 concern the fighting in Laos, the attempts of the three princes to reach agreement and diplomatic moves before and during the meeting of the fourteen nations conference at Geneva.

The recapture of Vientiane settled nothing. The build-up of military aid continued on both sides. When the May rains brought an end to easy campaigning the Boun Oum Government had not registered success.

In late December 1960, a few days before a SEATO meeting, startling reports of a Vietnamese invasion also involving Russian troops had emanated from Vientiane. The deliberately exaggerated nature of these reports, on which protests to UN and SEATO were based, was admitted by the Boun Oum Government in late January. The reports had probably been conceived first as a face-saving formula to cover the loss of Xieng Khouang with its vital airfield which was captured by Kong Lè on 30 December. Differences between Laotian and Western attitudes cause gross misunderstanding in cases like this. The West does not appreciate the depth of psychological need for the Lao to manipulate fact into fiction when unfortunate circumstances arise. Conversely, the Western passion for uncritically translating happy thought into disastrous action is not understood in Laos. Had SEATO decided on action the

[1] *Hansard*, Lords 60–61, vol. 227, p. 695.

Laotians would have been appalled since it would have involved the crossing of their frontiers by alien troops, including Thai.[1]

By May, in spite of temporary successes, the Boun Oum Government did not effectively control more than the Mekhong valley towns and their hinterlands of rice-plain. PL-Vietnamese activity was considerable along the Annamite chain and on the Bolovens plateau, probably both to protect infiltration channels into South Vietnam and to harry supply columns moving from that country into Laos. American-supported Mèo guerrilla activity achieved some success behind the lines but an attempt to hold a base at Pa Dong, ten miles south of Xieng Khouang village, failed when it fell on 7 June. The pitched battle there, a type of warfare for which Mèo tribesmen are in any case unsuited, provided a small-scale Dien Bien Phu to mark the opening stages of the Geneva conference which met on 16 May.

The idea of a conference which, in its final form, was to include the participants at Geneva in 1954, the remaining neighbours of Laos and the three ICC countries, was first mooted by Norodom Sihanouk in December 1960. The proposals were coolly received by the West and allies.

The new United States administration accepted officially the need for a non-aligned Laos. Slow progress was made in the attempt to secure the return of the ICC. An American-supported move by King Savang Vatthana, who had succeeded to the throne on the death of his father on 30 October, 1959, for an inspection commission from Burma, Cambodia and Malaya failed to arouse support and at length the ICC arrived in Laos on 8 May.

Both sides adopted delaying tactics over a cease-fire but this held up the Geneva meeting for a few days only. The delay of months in the acceptance of the idea of a conference, occasioned mainly by Western hesitations, resulted in the opening taking place in the difficult atmosphere, for the West, of a seriously deteriorated military situation.

The conference made little real progress between May and November. A major point of difference was Communist, especially Chinese, insistence on substantive discussion of the

[1] See inter al. the statement of Nhouy Abhay, a member of the Boun Oum Government: *New York Times*, 27 January, 1961.

neutrality issue and Western determination to establish the ICC first as an effective supervisory organization.

By mid-December, although two vital matters, the relationship of Laos to SEATO and the reorganization of the Lao army, remained unresolved, patient committee work behind the scenes had agreed a time-table for the withdrawal of foreign troops and reached a compromise on methods of supervision and the question of French military bases and training personnel.

The degree of real concession made by the Communist powers to achieve these agreements was not great, in fact they did little more than show a mere willingness to negotiate, yet, even so, they managed to appear in public more solicitous than the West for Lao susceptibilities over sovereignty.

Serious difficulties continued over the formation of a coalition government. The princes Boun Oum, Souvannaphouma and Souphanouvong agreed at Ban Hin Heup, on 6–8 October, to include four PL, four Boun Oum and eight neutral ministers. But, as at the earlier meeting at Zurich in June, agreement seemed to be a matter of words rather than of fact. In mid-November Phoumi Nosavan was insisting that four of the neutral ministers should be 'his neutrals'.

At the urgent request of the conference the princes met in Xieng Khouang on 14 and in Vientiane on 27 December. Deep distrust was shown on all sides. By making demands for the Ministries of Defence and the Interior the Boun Oum Government showed both its lack of faith in the agreements reached at Geneva and its determination to maintain a dominant role in any coalition. Such obviously unacceptable demands could be interpreted indeed as showing unwillingness to negotiate.[1]

In December 1961, at least at Geneva, the solution of a neutral Laos was offering itself again, though, on the ground, the political and military situation had greatly deteriorated from that existing in 1956–7. In an area where stability obviously depends on a slackening of international tension the history of Laos from 1958 to 1961 recorded a victory for tension-creating forces, for the two extremes. Moderate elements had been progressively weakened and the militant factions had acquired

---

[1] In *Le Monde*, 17 December, 1961, there appears an amusing account of how the opposing views of United States officials have allegedly caused divided counsels to be offered to the Lao Government.

a greatly increased fighting potential. An unstable *de facto* partition of Laos had come into existence producing areas of control closely paralleling the opposing Siamese and Annamese spheres of influence in the nineteenth century. Now, as then, the nature of the terrain made it difficult for either side to attain success by military means alone. Yet the risk of renewed fighting on a large scale existed, as the ICC repeatedly warned, even though, in the words of Souvannaphouma:

'Force of arms will not settle the Lao problem in ten years.'[1]

REVIEW

The events of 1945–61 suggest that there has been little political evolution in Laos if by that is meant the progressive development of forms of government able to master the changing problems of state and society. The changes in the relationship with France, out of which political independence grew, were in a sense evolutionary. But the increased pressures in the area since Geneva 1954 have halted political development in Laos and challenged the very existence of independence itself.

Laos, unfortunately for her, has offered a continuing casehistory for the study of the cold-war struggle. The advent of the United States resulted in the influx of great amounts of unproductive wealth and in strong support for a military solution in a most unfavourable context. Concentration on the build-up of forces from 1954 created the impression, heightened by effective Communist propaganda, that the United States was using Laos as a battleground but that serious efforts were not being made to solve economic problems. These latter, and the concomitant difficulties arising from the nature of Lao society, are of course vast, but sustained token efforts would have had some impact as France has found after several years of attempting to provide the sound economic and technical aid that has not been forthcoming from other sources. The military plan could be represented with some plausibility as being offensive as well as defensive, particularly because of the presence, from 1959, of

[1] *Christian Science Monitor*, 3 March, 1961.

Nationalist Chinese and South Vietnamese diplomatic missions in Vientiane.

The existence of the cold war has led the United States to see Laos in terms of her interests in Thailand and South Vietnam. Thai influence has been considerable, for example in the choice of Lao leaders thought to be worthy of Western confidence and aid. The position of the United States has been unenviable. She has been under pressure from Thailand whose Government understandably is reluctant to accept the risks of a compromise settlement. Thai fears of the spread of Chinese and Communist influence drive her to attempt to ensure a friendly Laos at all costs. United States anxieties have been easy to play upon in view of her emotional attitudes towards China and Communism. From such attitudes the policy of polarization grew. It failed because it involved commitment to the West and the attempted absolute destruction, not merely the control, of a legally constituted Communist Party in a country with Communist neighbours. In addition, the extent of detailed local influence obtained by the United States and her Asian allies became repugnant to the Lao people.

While the military hand has been overplayed, producing a predictable aggressive response, opportunities in the political and economic fields may well have been missed. There is more than one way of spending $250,000,000.

In Laos, with its low population, absence of urban proletariat, and system of small family or group holdings of land or rights of usufruct, the urgent social tensions out of which a natural revolutionary situation could easily be created do not exist. The revolutionary movement, indeed a constant factor since 1944, grew out of the anti-colonial struggle in Vietnam rather than in Laos itself and its whole life has depended on foreign support from the Viet Minh and its successor government. This arouses distrust in Laos where suspicion of the Vietnamese is traditional and strong; its impact on Laotian thinking has been underestimated. PL success has been founded mainly on the errors and omissions of its opponents in political and economic strategy.

Rivalry between France and the United States has weakened the Western position. Greater co-operation might have enabled France to do more to foster the connexion of Laos with the West after independence. It should not be forgotten that Paris is still the centre of the Western world for Laos. Virtually the whole of the small governing élite was conditioned to accept some form of association with the West short of sacrificing their pride in newly-won independence. Only with the Kong Lè group did a non-revolutionary movement with reservations about a basic Western bias emerge in a situation where aid could be extended. The Soviet Union has given support to them while China and North Vietnam, though extending a seeming friendly hand, have continued to advocate the claims of the revolutionary PL. This puts the Soviet Union in a potentially strong position in any future that Laos may have as a neutral state.

Laos and other independent powers in South-East Asia, though psychologically deeply opposed to warlike intervention on their soil, want to ensure against possible domination by a strong China. Unconditional commitment to an anti-Chinese line cannot be expected while a balance of forces exists in the region. Support for neutrality by the general maintenance of Western power and diplomatic skill in the world as a whole, and the offering of political assistance, profitable economic inter-course and effective types of aid could still encourage these states to maintain their Western connexion.

A stable neutral Laos will not be easy to establish. The use of Lao territory for Communist infiltration into South Vietnam encourages Western doubts. But the end of infiltration, difficult for even a Western-aligned Government in Laos to achieve, would not remove the Communist challenge in South Vietnam which exists in its own right. A graver obstacle to effective neutrality as a buffer state is the continued lack of unity in Laos. The geographic, ethnic, and social situations are such that the impersonal attempts of government to weld a single nation out of diversity have had little success. Tribal differences remain, parochial and regional loyalties persist and the country stays divided by its forests and mountains. No single leader of experience has emerged who has been able to attract wide popular support and by this very attraction cause embryonic public opinion to grow into a national force. Prince Souvanna-phouma has made the nearest approximation to such a figure but he lacks charismatic qualities and has suffered on account of the dubious probity of some of his associates. Other leaders,

Prince Souphanouvong for example, are finally compromised by their overt commitment to foreign influences.

Political rivalries in Laos have continued to operate in traditional terms because the society has not yet developed from its traditional pattern. Foreign pressures operating in a three-tier system of action, the cold-war powers upon neighbours of Laos, the neighbours, in turn, on leaders within the country, have enhanced these rivalries in the classical Laotian manner. In reverse some local leaders have attempted to manipulate external forces for their own rather than for national ends. The huge genii thus conjured up are not easily persuaded to return to their jars.

There has been little encouragement for the growth in Laos of a middle force able to temper the clash of extremes. Unlike the situation in Burma, for example, there existed no background of liberal and socialist thinking to enable the formation of a national government able to tackle experimentally the problems of independence.

It will be a sad circumstance if Laotian independence proves to be short-lived yet once more, if, in the end, external powers in rivalry force dissolution upon her and she herself compounds the sin by her inability to lay aside internal dissensions.[1]

[1] Despite wide differences of view and intention between the three factions, a coalition Government was formed and received the royal assent on 23 June 1962. A neutral status for Laos was agreed by the fourteen nations conference at Geneva on 23 July.

The new Souvannaphouma Government faced again, in grossly exaggerated form because of the war, the problems that arose following the 1956 agreement at Vientiane. Chief of these was the urgent need to reduce and re-integrate the armed forces.

It is plain that there is a future for Laos as a unified non-aligned state only if her leaders still their quarrels and co-operate in an attempt to balance and control potentially destructive foreign influences during the lengthy process of nation-building.

Chapter ten

DEMOCRACY AND
THE REPUBLIC OF VIETNAM

---

by P. J. Honey

Since the end of the Second World War a number of formerly dependent states have achieved national independence, and their leaders have been faced with the problem of how best to govern them. Local conditions differ considerably from state to state, but a few important factors are common to most of the newly independent nations. The inhabitants of a state which has, over a long period, depended for its government upon another state, have not usually been burdened with the responsibilities of electing or controlling their own rulers. Consequently, the overwhelming majority of them are without experience in running their national affairs. For them, the government has always been a remote body which takes and executes decisions affecting their own lives, but over which they have exercised no control. Indeed, since the government has collected taxes, punished wrongdoers, and carried out measures not always universally popular, it has not infrequently become an object of suspicion, or even of dislike, for the governed. In the case of these countries, the peoples are without political judgement, without any understanding of the difficulties which have to be overcome by governments, and are difficult to convince that any of the responsibility for the actions of their government could possibly devolve upon them.

The second common factor is the choice facing the leaders, actual or potential, of the form of government best suited to the conditions obtaining in their own countries. The majority of such leaders are men who have been educated abroad in one of the Western democracies. Almost all have conceived a respect and admiration for the political life of the countries in which they spent their formative years and would like to introduce similar régimes to their own countries. Others have never travelled abroad, but even these have read about, or heard about, the Western democratic institutions and, on the whole, share their more travelled colleagues' respect for them. But none of these leaders has played an active part in the working of a democracy. They have been spectators, and have studied the forms and procedures, but in very few cases have they fully appreciated all the factors which are essential to the efficient working of a democracy. These new leaders themselves lack experience in government and all too frequently have not fully understood the difficulties created for its rulers by democracy.

No country, even under the leadership of able politicians, can be well governed unless she is administered by an efficient, honest, and experienced civil service. In the case of former colonies, the more responsible civil service posts have always been occupied by nationals of the colonial power, the native recruits tending to be restricted to posts in which they dealt with routine tasks and were not called upon to take important decisions. India was a striking exception to this general rule and her civil service, more than any other institution, enabled her to overcome the early difficulties of independence. The Indian Civil Service, in which Indian nationals had held some of the highest posts, continued to administer the country effectively while the political leaders acquired the experience necessary for the discharge of their new responsibilities. The majority of the newly independent states have had to create entirely new civil services and to man them with persons experienced in carrying out the low-grade tasks of administration or without any experience at all.

If India commenced her independent existence with the advantage of an efficient civil service, she was adversely affected by another factor common to most countries in the region, fossilized social strata. The hereditary ruling families and the system of caste have proved to be a source of considerable difficulties for the Indian Government. Vietnam, on the other hand, is probably the least affected of all by this problem and the most pre-disposed towards democratic rule by her former institutions.

From the time when Vietnam established her independence of China in the tenth century until the abdication of Bao Dai in 1945, she preserved the institution of hereditary monarchy. The Vietnamese nobility, however, was not self-perpetuating. Titles were granted to some Vietnamese in recognition of their services to the state, and the members of the imperial family inherited titles of royalty by right of birth, but all titles were reduced by one grade when they passed from one generation to the next, and even the highest title became extinct after five generations. Vietnamese administrators, or mandarins, were, for many centuries, selected not by birth but by examination open to all citizens with very few exceptions (criminals, actors, etc.). Thus, the way to advancement lay through scholarship and administrative ability, and the children of mandarins were not guaranteed entry to the mandarinate. This encouraged a great respect for scholarship and rendered the son of even the poorest citizen eligible for the highest post in the mandarinate.

In practice, it was found that the children of mandarins tended to become mandarins themselves. The reason was probably twofold, a combination of inherited ability and a childhood spent in a home where study was encouraged and helped, but unless they could pass the state examinations they were not admitted. The mandarinate, however, never became fossilized because it was an élite based upon merit and its composition was constantly changing. It is interesting to note in passing that virtually all the senior officials in the Communist and non-Communist zones of independent Vietnam are, in fact, the children of mandarinal families, that is to say, families in which the father or grandfather was a mandarin. For the Communist leaders, their origins are proving a growing embarrassment, since the cry to get rid of the 'bourgeois elements' from the control of the state, now being repeated with increasing frequency, means in effect getting rid of themselves.

Other problems facing the newly emerging states, economic, political, security, defence, etc., show wide variation from one country to the next, so that no general statements can be made. However, few countries can have come into existence to face greater military, political, and economic difficulties than the Republic of Vietnam, more generally known as South Vietnam. At the time when France signed the agreements granting independence to Vietnam, the Communist-controlled Viet Minh, which claimed to be the only legal government of the country, was already laying siege to the French and Vietnamese nationalist forces at Dien Bien Phu. The Viet Minh, aided by massive grants of Chinese military equipment, advisers, technicians, and soldiers, appeared certain to destroy or capture the beleaguered garrison, and an international conference was about to meet at Geneva to arrange an armistice and decide upon the future of the country. The greater part of Vietnam was already in the hands of the Viet Minh, and much of the remainder was controlled by three armed groups, each prepared to defend the rights which it enjoyed in its own fief. Of these three, the Cao-Dai and Hoa-Hao were indigenous religious sects, each maintaining its own army, and the Binh-Xuyen was a bandit force which, in addition to holding its own territorial stronghold, controlled most of the vice in the capital city, Saigon, and had acquired the direction of the Ministry of the Interior.

In these inauspicious circumstances, the Vietnamese Head of State, the former Emperor Bao Dai, entrusted the government of the country to Ngo Dinh Diem and granted him full civil and military powers. Shortly after Diem's appointment, an armistice was concluded at Geneva and agreements were signed, under the terms of which Vietnam was divided into two states, North Vietnam falling to the Communist Viet Minh and South Vietnam to the nationalist Government of Diem. Nearly a million penniless refugees fled from the Communists to South Vietnam to become the responsibility of the new Government and to render an already complex situation chaotic. Still further difficulties were caused by members of the French Expeditionary Corps who manifested their disapproval of Ngo Dinh Diem by causing explosions in the capital, supplying arms to the three semi-autonomous groupings already mentioned, and generally creating all possible difficulties for the régime.

It is not the purpose of this paper to examine the methods employed by Diem to resolve this desperate position, but rather to assess the system of government which he subsequently devised. Suffice it to say that he broke the power of the Cao-Dai, Hoa-Hao, and Binh-Xuyen by armed force, secured the return to France of the Expeditionary Corps by negotiation, and rid himself of the troublesome Head of State by means of a popular referendum, the conduct of which has since been much criticized. The refugees were resettled in the south, largely thanks to the monetary assistance and technical guidance of the United States, and, by 1956, Ngo Dinh Diem had secured control of the state which he governed.

With the ending of the difficult initial phase, Diem addressed himself to the problem of creating a permanent system of government for South Vietnam. In order to rid himself of Bao Dai he had declared South Vietnam a republic and had himself been elected President, so that the powers of which he then disposed were wider than when he had first assumed responsibility for the government. Other features of the situation in South Vietnam in 1956 militated in his favour. He enjoyed the full confidence of the United States Government, which accorded him economic and military aid on a vast scale. The National Army, whose loyalty had been suspect, was, in 1956, completely at the service of the President. Communist agents, who had remained inside South Vietnam in large numbers, were denounced by the southern population, so that most were under arrest and the Communist organization had been totally smashed. Refugees had been resettled and had ceased to be a drain on the national resources.

If the credit side of the balance sheet showed some important assets, the debit side was no less weighty. The countryside had been devastated by eight years of war and the national economy was virtually non-existent. The withdrawal of French troops, although politically desirable, had closed an important source of revenue, shopkeepers and tradesmen being particularly hard hit. Although the military strength of the Cao-Dai, Hoa-Hao, and Binh-Xuyen had been smashed, there remained a burning resentment against Ngo Dinh Diem among followers of all three groupings, who represented roughly a quarter of the total population. North Vietnam posed a constant threat to national security, and its Communist Government resorted to every expedient to subvert the south.

Such, then, were the important local factors of the South Vietnamese situation in 1956. In common with other newly independent states, she possessed no political leaders with any experience of government, a small number of civil servants whose experience was restricted to minor posts, and a population which understood little about the rights and duties of citizens in an independent country. These were the circumstances under which Ngo Dinh Diem elected to give South Vietnam a democratic form of government.

Cynics alleged that Diem so decided in order to curry favour with the United States and to continue to enjoy generous American aid. They cite as evidence to support their contention the constitution promulgated in 1956 which is strongly influenced by, if not based upon, the constitution of the United States. But this cannot be accepted seriously as the reason for his choice. The United States, whose principal requirement in the sphere of foreign policy was to prevent the further advance of Communism, could not but grant aid to the non-Communist Government of South Vietnam no matter what system Diem had chosen to adopt. Undoubtedly many observers expected the constitution to be based upon that of France and were surprised that it copied so much from the American constitution, but there are valid reasons for this. Diem was certainly familiar with the constitution of France, but he had viewed French government in practice, as it were, from the most unfavourable angle. As a Minister of the Imperial Court at Hue, he had to resign his high office in protest against it. Throughout the long war in Vietnam he had witnessed one of the worst periods of French political life, with intrigue following self-interested intrigue, corruption and political jobbery being practised on an unprecedented scale. It was hardly surprising that he entertained reservations about a French-style constitution.

During his period of exile from Vietnam, Diem had lived for a long time in the United States, where he had sought to lay the difficulties of his country before the American political leaders and to obtain American help in establishing an independent and prosperous Vietnam. It is highly probable that he was favourably impressed by what he saw of American government and administration, and that this is the reason he promulgated the constitution he did.

It cannot be denied that the Vietnamese constitution is a very liberal document indeed. Its ninety-eight articles provide for the election, by universal suffrage, of the President, the Vice-President, and of a National Assembly at stipulated intervals.

Twenty-one articles lay down the rights and duties of citizens, assuring them of freedom from arbitrary arrest, freedom of movement, freedom of opinion, freedom of the press, freedom of speech, and much else besides. The elected National Assembly is empowered to pass laws, to ratify treaties and agreements, and to approve the national budget. The independence of the judiciary is assured. Indeed, no section of the constitution can be criticized on the grounds of repressiveness or of illiberality.

Threatened from without by North Vietnam and from within by Communist guerrillas and saboteurs, her economy shattered and her agricultural lands devastated by the war, South Vietnam required strong central government if she were to survive at all. Security in the countryside was her prime need, for without it agricultural production could not be restored and the national income assured. As Britain discovered in Malaya, the successful elimination of Communist guerrillas demands that the Government should dispose of very wide powers. A state of emergency was declared in Malaya and whole sections of the population were forcibly resettled in new villages. Yet although all the guerrilla fighters in Malaya were Chinese, a fact which exempted all the other races from suspicion, and although Malaya shared no common frontier with a Communist state, the campaign was long, hard, and costly. In South Vietnam the problem is more difficult because the guerrillas are Vietnamese, so that no section of the population is above suspicion, and because its long frontiers may be easily crossed and recrossed by the Communists. Under the terms of the constitution, the Government simply does not possess the powers necessary to take the type of action carried out by the Government of Malaya.

The Government of President Diem has always been vulnerable to the activities of its opponents in the sphere of politics, for the constitution guarantees them freedom of speech, freedom of the press, and freedom of opinion. In a country where the electorate is as politically inexperienced as Vietnam, irresponsible politicians and political parties could, by exploiting these freedoms to make promises to the people which could not possibly be kept, secure election to office in the general and presidential elections prescribed by the constitution. The electorate is too naïve to be able to discern whether such promises could be kept or not, and such irresponsible parties, once in power, might continue to hold office indefinitely by amending the constitution. Again, a free press with a politically naïve readership might well criticize the Government most unfairly and unreasonably, and thereby contrive to turn public opinion against it.

Economic recovery in South Vietnam depends upon the rebuilding of agriculture and the development of national resources in the most logical and effective way. Clearly many of the Government's actions, while they may be most desirable for national prosperity in the long term, will be unpopular with some of the people directly affected at the local level. Such local antipathies, even if short-lived, could easily bring to a stand-still all progress towards economic prosperity, and the Government would not be permitted by the constitution to take the necessary action to prevent this happening.

These few instances, which are selected as typical examples of difficulties which might arise, will suffice to demonstrate how the Government of Ngo Dinh Diem was hampered and endangered by the liberality of the constitution which it promulgated. The constitution does not accord the central Government powers wide enough to deal with the predicament in which South Vietnam finds herself and it permits a politically naïve electorate the power to overthrow the Government at the instigation of irresponsible newspapers or Opposition parties for reasons which are not valid.

In practice, none of these things has happened, and the reason is to be found in the methods employed by President Diem to govern South Vietnam. One of the most important instruments at the disposal of his Government is the Movement of National Revolution. In theory, this is a political party whose programme, reduced to its lowest terms, consists in supporting fully all the policies and actions of President Diem. The pressures on the people to join this party are very great, and several instances investigated by the author showed that the inducements offered for membership and the penalties for refusal to join are sometimes far from ethical. Government officials at all levels, from ministers, through civil servants, employees of the National Bank, down to the caretakers of government premises, are virtually bound to join if they wish to retain their employment. In the countryside, peasants and farmers frequently find it impossible to obtain loans from the Agricultural Credit Organization or low-priced goods from the co-operative unless they are party members. Villagers find that they are refused permission to travel unless they are party members when permits are granted without questions or difficulties. Shopkeepers and businessmen are induced to join by the withholding of loans or credits for non-members, or the refusal to grant the necessary trading licences.

Pressures of this kind have succeeded in swelling the numbers of party members to a formidable size, and most of the members have a personal interest in belonging to the party. The Government uses party members whenever it wishes and is thus able to produce a 'spontaneous demonstration' for or against any action or policy at very short notice. Still more valuable is the support which the party offers in elections. The author witnessed the 1959 elections to the National Assembly and possesses documentary evidence of how the party was used. Official party candidates were selected for the various constituencies, each chosen for his political reliability more than for his other qualities. A letter was dispatched to all branches of the party, the contents of which were ordered to be communicated to all members. Briefly, it ordered every member to vote for the official candidate, and demanded the resignation of anyone who refused to obey this order. Now in Vietnamese elections, the voter is given a separate slip of paper for each candidate, and it bears the candidate's name and symbol. The voter enters a curtained booth, places the slip of his chosen candidate in an envelope, tears the remaining slips, and places the sealed envelope in the ballot box. The party letter instructed that members were to vote for the official candidate, retain the torn halves of the other candidates' slips, and then present these at the local branch office as proof (a) that they had voted, and (b) that they had voted for the official candidate. Those failing to comply with this order were threatened with immediate expulsion from the party.

In addition to the Movement of National Revolution, which is a mass-membership party, there is a party of the élite with a restricted membership, the Can-lao Nhan-vi or the Party of the Personality of the Worker. The philosophy upon which this party is based is 'Personalism', a philosophy developed by Roman Catholic French philosophers such as Maritain, but its importance is minimal since few, if any, of the party members have any understanding of it, almost all contenting themselves with the learning of a few clichés. The real function of the Can-lao, as the party is usually known, is to act as a secret intelligence network for the Government. The Can-lao is semi-clandestine and the names of its members are not disclosed, although some of its more important members are widely known to belong to it. Members are required to supply confidential reports to headquarters about the conduct, opinions and attitudes of their colleagues whom they encounter in the course of their employment. These reports are scrutinized at the Can-lao headquarters and all which give rise to suspicions are investigated. The underlying purpose is to detect Communist agents who have infiltrated into South Vietnamese organisations, but some instances are known to the author in which the Can-lao member has disclosed his membership and used it to blackmail another Vietnamese into according him some privilege, threatening to submit an adverse report about the latter in case he should refuse to comply. The founder and director of the Can-lao is President Diem's brother, Ngo Dinh Nhu.

The Vietnamese language press is not subjected to censorship, but copies of every edition must be deposited in the Department of Information before it may be circulated. All editors receive daily communications from the Department of Information instructing them what news to publish and, more important, what not to publish. If a paper prints any item which the hyper-sensitive Information Department construes as critical of, or hostile to, the Government, the distribution of the paper is immediately stopped. It is possible to do this because newspaper distribution is the monopoly of the Thong-nhat Agency, which devotes its profits to the care of disabled soldiers. The Agency is directed by a General who can, in a matter of minutes, prevent any paper being sold. Offending newspapers may be closed down or suspended by the Information Department and their editors punished. Foreign language newspapers are subject to censorship, a privilege which is envied by all Vietnamese editors. In the case of an offence by a foreign language newspaper, it is the censor, not the editor, who is punished.

The constitution permits opposition political parties to be formed and to operate freely, but President Diem has decreed that they must first register with the Government and obtain certificates of registration. In practice, these certificates have been granted only to 'puppet' Opposition parties, such as the Socialist Party, which are in reality controlled by the Government. Genuine opponents of the régime never succeed in registering their parties, and these are consequently illegal. The result is that the Government allows its political opponents no opportunity of expressing their opinions. When such persons stand for election to the National Assembly as independent candidates, they are continually harassed by the police for alleged breaches of the electoral law, find it impossible to hire premises for the holding of political meetings, and are unable to make their views known to the electorate. They are generally eliminated from the election before polling takes place, and the few who survive until that date then face the party machine. One such candidate, Dr Phan Quang Dan, actually secured an overwhelming majority in 1959, but was prevented from taking his seat in the Assembly on 'technical grounds'.

The first Presidential election was held in 1961, but only candidates of little worth had their credentials accepted. Dr Nguyen Ngoc Bich, the one candidate who would have posed a serious challenge to President Diem, was not permitted to stand for election on the grounds that there was a 'technical' fault in his application. President Diem was returned, hardly surprisingly, with a large majority.

Concentration camps, euphemistically described as 'Political Re-education Centres', exist in South Vietnam. The number of such camps has never been disclosed, but the author has seen several in the course of his travels, and it is probable that they are numerous. The function of such centres is, according to government sources, to provide a course of political education to arrested Communists and to teach them the error of their ways. No charge needs to be preferred against a person before he is admitted to such a centre, and he may be detained there indefinitely. The author has talked to several former inmates of these centres, and has reached the following conclusions on the basis of the information they supplied. The majority of the inmates are Communists, or Communist sympathisers, who would, if not detained in the centres, give aid to the Communist saboteurs and guerrillas active in South Vietnam. Others, however, are strongly anti-Communist in outlook, and their only crime is to have uttered some injudicious criticism of President Diem's Government. A few are people who have incurred the anger of an official or of a Can-lao member. But the centres also offer a convenient and effective means for disposing of an annoying political opponent.

Much more could be said about the practices and the institutions employed by President Diem to govern South Vietnam, but the preceding examples will provide a sufficiently clear picture of how the Government contrived to maintain itself in office in spite of the liberal constitution. In plain language, President Diem grossly exceeded the powers accorded to him by the constitution and acted in a way for which he had no authority. He resorted to subterfuges in order to achieve results which, however desirable they may have been for the welfare of South Vietnam, he could not encompass with his constitutional powers. Every informed South Vietnamese is well aware of what President Diem has done, and his conduct is almost universally condemned. There are many who would heartily endorse the aims he has set his Government, but who are most vehemently opposed to the methods he has employed in order to achieve these aims. Indeed, opposition to the methods used by President Diem, and by extension to President Diem himself and the whole régime, has grown rapidly and continues to increase.

The overwhelming majority of the South Vietnamese people are openly hostile to Communism. Even the least politically conscious of them is well informed about what has taken place in Communist North Vietnam, and he does not want the south to suffer the same fate. The mass murders which were committed during the Communist Agrarian Reform Campaign, the tyranny of the people's courts, the desperate plight of the impoverished peasantry, the shortage of almost all essential goods, and much more besides is common currency among the people of the south. The hostility towards the northern régime which results from this constitutes a potentially valuable asset to the anti-Communist Government of the Republic of Vietnam.

In even the most efficiently governed state, some of the

people will on occasion feel that the government is wrong, that they have legitimate grounds for complaint because of an injustice suffered, or that they have a useful and constructive criticism to offer. The people of South Vietnam, which is neither the best governed nor best administered of states, are no different from any other people in this respect. Most of them have experienced dissatisfaction with the authorities at one time or another since the coming of independence, some for personal reasons, others for economic reasons, for social reasons, for political reasons, or for any one of a host of other reasons. In the Western democracies dissatisfied citizens may write to the press, or complain to their Member of Parliament, or vote against the government in an election, or even carry banners through the streets if they feel strongly enough. Whatever remedy they may choose, they succeed in airing their grievances which, by some process of catharsis, assume less importance for them once these have been communicated to others.

The rigid control of the press in South Vietnam, the absence of any genuine opposition party, the ubiquitous Can-lao members, and the ever-present police make the voicing or sharing of any complaints or criticisms impossible. It is difficult to describe to anyone who has not lived under such conditions how the importance of even trivial grievances tends to become grossly exaggerated. So bitter have some of the long pent-up grievances against the régime now become that some Southern Vietnamese have felt themselves driven to join the only movement which represents open opposition to Ngo Dinh Diem, the Communist guerrillas, or Viet Cong as they are known locally. Vietnamese who detest what the Communists are doing in North Vietnam and who are not themselves Communists have sheltered the Viet Cong in their homes or have even entered the jungle to swell their ranks.

Viet Cong tactics have been to terrorize the inhabitants of entire regions by wholesale murder. They enter villages, select victims for assassination — these are frequently minor government officials, but by no means always so — execute the unfortunates before the assembled population, and then threaten to kill the remainder if they fail to collaborate. By such methods, they ensure the obedience of the terrified people, whom they sometimes force to fight and to carry out sabotage for them. It is, therefore, impossible to ascertain how many of the South Vietnamese have helped the Viet Cong under duress and how many have done so voluntarily, but there can be no doubt that some of the Viet Cong collaborators have become so of their own free will.

Resentment is also great among other South Vietnamese who have not joined the Viet Cong, as was shown by the revolt of the parachute battalions in November 1960, which almost succeeded in overthrowing the Government. The smiles on the faces of the citizens in the streets of Saigon during the revolt, and the numbers of those who joined the rebels, are evidence enough of the Government's unpopularity.

Towards the end of 1961, President Diem proclaimed a state of emergency in South Vietnam, so that the constitution is temporarily in abeyance. His Government now wields authority enough, under its emergency powers, to take the military, security, and political measures necessary to combat the Viet Cong. Whether President Diem can win public acceptance for the course he is pursuing, and whether he can command a wide measure of support for his enlarged military campaign, it is still too early to judge.

The question remains to be answered, 'Why has the régime of President Ngo Dinh Diem become so unpopular in South Vietnam?' Obviously, a large part of the answer is to be found in the actions of the North Vietnamese Communists, who have attacked him constantly in their propaganda and have sought to overthrow his régime by subversion, sabotage, terror, and warfare. Yet another part must be attributed to the unfulfilled hopes of the politically unsophisticated Vietnamese who, like other colonial peoples, believed for so long that they had only to rid themselves of the foreign ruler in order to achieve a paradise on earth. It is, perhaps, worth while to pause a moment to examine some of the specific aspirations of the Vietnamese people.

South Vietnam, as has already been pointed out, has never had a self-perpetuating élite class in its social structure, so that the demand for equality, so widely heard elsewhere in the region, was not great. Some Vietnamese had become rich landowners under French rule, and the peasants demanded that their large estates be broken up and given to the landless, but this was a very limited sort of equality. The most widespread and deeply felt longing for equality was concerned with the equality of Vietnam, as a nation, with the other nations of the world. This longing expressed itself in the desire for industrialization, for factories, for machines, for tractors, not so much to raise the living standards of South Vietnam as to win her an international standing equal to that of the more advanced countries. The author has discussed the merits of American tractors with rice farmers and formed the impression that, while these farmers found the traditional buffaloes more efficient, they were delighted to have the tractors because they were up-to-date and advanced, a modern Vietnamese status symbol. The most notable expression of this attitude of mind is South Vietnam's decision to spend a large sum of money upon the establishment of a Nuclear Energy Research Centre.

A considerable measure of material prosperity has been achieved in South Vietnam since the coming of independence, and notable advances have been made in many fields, particularly in education — there can surely be no other country in the world where education is so greatly respected as Vietnam — with the opening of so many schools and the establishment of two new universities. Yet in spite of this, the Government has failed to win the enthusiastic support of the people. A not unimportant contributory factor has been the inexperience of the administration and the shortage of able, trustworthy civil servants. Some civil servants have antagonized the public by their dishonesty and by the high-handed manner in which they deal with those under their charge, which is frequently no more than a cloak for their own incompetence.

When Ngo Dinh Diem first assumed power in the summer of 1954, he faced a desperate situation. His efforts to overcome the difficulties besetting South Vietnam enjoyed the goodwill and the active support of the greater part of the population, for he was regarded as the first truly independent leader of Vietnam, without ties or obligations to France or to any other country. He himself was known to be incorruptible and patriotic, a man who would always place the interests of his country first. Late in 1956, however, a distinct change in the attitude of the people towards the Government first became discernible. There was a lessening of President Diem's popularity, a tendency on the part of the Vietnamese to revert to their earlier attitude towards the French-controlled governments. Since then, the Government's prestige has steadily declined, and the public's attitude has passed from one of enthusiasm, to tolerance, and finally to antipathy.

Several reasons for this change have already been given, but the most important one is the change which took place in the Government itself. Until 1956, all its energies were seen to be directed towards the overcoming of the difficulties threatening the very existence of the state, but since that time, the Government has appeared more and more to be directing its greatest efforts towards perpetuating its own period of office. The outward signs of this, the Government-directed political parties, the control of the press, the arrest of political opponents, the 'rigging' of elections, and so on, have been described earlier. No people will freely tolerate a Government whose principal concern is to remain in office no matter what the cost to the citizens in hardship and suffering, and this, more than any other factor, turned the people of South Vietnam against President Ngo Dinh Diem's Government.

To understand how this situation has arisen, it is necessary to examine the political ideas of President Diem himself and the nature of the régime he has created. He has repeatedly expressed his admiration for democracy as a system of government, and it is impossible for anyone who knows him to doubt his sincerity. President Diem does admire democracy but, for the past several years, he has devoted himself with great singleness of purpose to the removal of the Communist threat to his country, which he regards as his most immediate and most important task. Until South Vietnam has been freed from this danger to its independent existence, President Diem is unlikely to direct his attention to the introduction of a working democracy or to other matters which, although desirable for South Vietnam, he regards as less urgent.

President Diem has no very high regard for other Vietnamese politicians. The Communists he condemns as traitors who have sold North Vietnam and its people to foreign masters in exchange for the right to govern as puppet rulers, and who are now trying to bring South Vietnam under the same foreign yoke. Many of the non-Communists he rejects entirely because they have

P

served French masters in the past just as the Communists are
now serving Russian and Chinese masters, and the remainder
constitute for him a serious danger to South Vietnam. They are
dangerous, in the eyes of President Diem, because they lack
practical experience in government and would fall easy victims
if ever they had to deal with the North Vietnamese Communists. It is because he holds this opinion that he has become
convinced the future safety of South Vietnam depends upon his
continuing to hold office. He has led his Government for eight
years and, under his leadership, the country has survived great
dangers. If the other nationalist politicians were sincerely
patriotic and not just self-seeking, he argues, then they would
serve their country under his experienced leadership instead of
seeking to become President themselves. This is the real reason
why President Diem has refused to tolerate a genuine political
opposition inside South Vietnam, why he has 'rigged' the
elections, why he has imprisoned political opponents who are as
opposed to Communism as he is himself, and has forced others
to flee abroad.

Because of his mistrust of Vietnamese politicians in the
present precarious situation of South Vietnam, President Diem
has striven to retain the maximum measure of control in his own
hands and to delegate the rest to persons whom he can trust,
members of his own family, old friends, and the like. His attitude
has not always made for the employment of the most effective
leaders and has tended to encourage yes-men, flatterers, and
persons anxious for the trappings of high office without the
responsibility, which remains with President Diem himself, to
serve under him rather than men of ability and independence of
mind. The presence of such people in some of the highest posts is
not conducive to popular esteem for the Government. Moreover, these men understand full well that if President Diem
were aware of the shortcomings of the Government and the true
extent of its unpopularity, he would make drastic changes, and
they themselves would be the first victims of such changes.
Consequently, they have erected an effective barrier around the
President which shields him from critical reports or unpleasant
news, and makes it almost impossible for those thought likely to
voice criticisms to approach him. Thus, President Diem remains in ignorance of much that is happening in his own

country and is certainly unaware of the full extent of his régime's unpopularity. It is true that he visits different parts of the country from time to time and talks to the inhabitants, but those who surround him so effectively in his capital see to it that all is carefully stage-managed in advance so as to give the President the impression that all is well. As for the people to whom he speaks, they behave towards him in the way Vietnamese citizens have behaved towards their high officials for many centuries. They say only things designed to please and avoid unpleasant subjects. Much of the applause which welcomes President Diem on these visits is sincere, for he himself retains the respect and affection of many of his subjects in spite of the unpopularity of his régime.

In South Vietnam, democracy seems as far away as it ever was despite all the brave words and the promises. It has become a victim of the struggle between the world's two great power blocs. The present political situation, with the Communist insurgents continually building up their forces and discontent with the régime steadily mounting, is explosive. No amount of American military and economic aid is likely to restore the situation while the Government and the people remain so widely divided. But the first steps in democracy have been taken with the promulgation of a democratic constitution and the holding of elections for the National Assembly and the Presidency. If circumstances should so change as to render the constitution a workable document, and if the people of South Vietnam are granted a period of respite from outside attack, the seeds of democracy already planted may yet bloom in South Vietnam.

Chapter eleven

MALAYAN POLITICS

by Victor Purcell

AFTER the Japanese occupation of Malaya in 1942, the British Government seemed to accept the *fait accompli* as if it were a permanent one. Unlike Burma, which had a government in exile at Simla, even nominal British authority over Malaya ceased entirely with the fall of Singapore. The British Government, of course, was fully occupied with matters nearer home, and it was not until late in 1943, when it did eventually seem likely that Malaya would be recovered, that the Colonial Office set up a Malayan Planning Unit (MPU) and those few Malayan officials who happened not to be interned were recalled to London to plan for the liberation.

The MPU was instructed to draw up 'directives' for the guidance of the military Government which was to be established when Malaya had been liberated, and for Malaya's immediate post-war future. These 'directives' were to cover every aspect of government, but when it came to the overall political directive it was found that this had already been drafted and decided upon a higher level. There was, the planners learnt, on the termination of the military Government, to be a 'Union' of all the mainland territory, but Singapore was to be a separate colony. A majority of the planners (including the writer) was opposed to the separation of Singapore from the mainland, and some of the principal Colonial Office advisers also. Who was responsible for the decision must be a matter for speculation — but the motives were undoubtedly political. In the writer's opinion the decision was a mistaken one, and is responsible for the unfortunate political division of Malaya at the present time.

As for the Union, it was generally understood by the planners that this was to be introduced only after full consultation with the Malayan rulers and representative bodies of Malays, Chinese, and Indians. The decision to create the Union immediately on the ending of the military Government was taken by the British Government at some later date — presumably after the liberation of Malaya.

The task of persuading the rulers to sign the new treaties to provide for the creation of the Union was entrusted to Sir Harold MacMichael. He was given explicit instructions by the Colonial Secretary as to the pressures he must exert, and he carried out his instructions to the letter. When the agitation against the Union started he was most unfairly attacked and made the scapegoat of the British Government when it abandoned the Union and established a Federation in face of the widespread agitation of the Malays against the Union. The Federation came into being, replacing the Union, on 28 February, 1948, and under it the rulers were given more powers than they had possessed since the protectorate system started.

In the meantime, the British Military Administration (BMA) had found itself confronted, in September 1945, when the Japanese surrendered, with a situation utterly different from that which existed in 1941. The Chinese Communist guerrillas, the Malayan People's Anti-Japanese Army (MPAJA), had emerged from the jungle directly the Japanese troops had assembled to surrender, had virtually established themselves as a government in the towns and villages of the mainland, and had to be displaced by the BMA. The MPAJA, however, were now the nominal allies of the British by virtue of the agreement which had been signed before liberation between them and Lord Mountbatten, the Supreme Allied Commander, South-East Asia. By this agreement, full liberty of speech and association had been guaranteed to the Malayan Communist Party (MCP) (of which the MPAJA was the military arm) during the period of the military administration, providing that it was not abused.

The intention of the MCP, however, was to make the position of the BMA untenable by means of strikes. This they very nearly succeeded in doing by engineering a mass stoppage in January 1946. But in February they overreached themselves when they attempted to cause another stoppage to celebrate the British surrender four years earlier. This time, however, the BMA and the army were ready for them and the attempted stoppage was a fiasco. The MPAJA had been demobilized in December 1945 so that the MCP was now without a military arm. It now, perforce, confined its efforts to infiltrating labour until June 1948, when the Chinese Communist guerrillas, reformed as the Malayan Races' Liberation Army (MRLA), came out in rebellion against the Government.

Before the war, there were no domestic political parties in Malaya. Membership of the Kuomintang (KMT) in China was legal, but the KMT was not registered in Malaya as a society under the law and its local organization was therefore illegal. It nevertheless continued to operate illegally. The MCP was also illegal. The Malays had shown no disposition to organize politically, while the Indians (if politically minded) were interested only in the activities of the Congress Party in India itself.

Under the BMA, political organization was not discouraged, and it was indeed hoped that other political parties would come into existence to counterbalance the MCP. The first party, however, which did form, the Malay Nationalist Party, turned out to be Indonesian in origin, under Dr Buhranuddin (who is still active in east coast politics), and therefore having no general appeal to the Peninsular Malays. Its eight resolutions passed at its inaugural meeting in November 1945, were very similar to those of the MCP.

The first real Malay party to be formed was the United Malays National Organization (UMNO) under Dato Onn, in April 1946. The agitation carried on by this party against the Malayan Union eventually caused the British Government to replace the Union by a Federation.

The pre-emergency political parties other than the MCP, KMT, and UMNO can receive only passing mention here.[1] The Malayan Democratic Union (MDU) was formed in December 1954, with the declared object of securing representative government for Malaya within the British Commonwealth. This party

[1] A full account of them is given in the writer's *Malaya: Communist or Free?* (1954), Ch. V.

soon came under Communist influence. As an offset to UMNO, a coalition of parties was formed in December 1946 to oppose its policies. In addition to the MDU, there was the MNP, the Pan-Malayan Federation of Trade Unions, the Malayan Indian Congress (MIC), the Malayan People's Anti-Japanese Army (MPAJA) Old Comrades' Association, the Malayan New Democratic Youth, and others including a women's party (Angkatan Pemuda Insaf). This coalition, the All-Malaya Council of Joint Action (AMCJA), did not last long. It split into factions — one the rump of AMCJA (Chinese-dominated) and an organization calling itself the People's United Front (PUTERA), including the MNP, under the direction of Dr Buhranuddin. PUTERA added four more points to the six-point programme of AMCJA — that Malay should be the official language of the country, that foreign affairs should be jointly controlled by the Malayan and British Governments, that the term *Melayu* should be applied to all citizens of Malaya, and that the national flag of the country should incorporate the Malay national colours.

In June 1948, some four months after the Federation succeeded the Union, the Communist insurrection began. The Malayan Governments thereupon declared a State of Emergency, which lasted officially until 1960. The emergency brought an end to the incipient political parties which had come into being since liberation since they were either declared illegal or found it expedient to dissolve. UMNO alone survived. This left a vacuum in Malayan politics. There was, above all, now no party or organization representing the Chinese community of Malaya. Before the war, the KMT had been largely supported by the *towkays* (heads of businesses), but these had lost their leadership of the Chinese during the occupation on account of their collaboration (enforced or voluntary) with the Japanese, and the KMT suffered eclipse in Malaya as a political force. In any case it had never been really 'Malayan'. To fill the gap, the Malayan Chinese Association (MCA) was now (February 1949) formed under the leadership of Mr Tan Cheng-lock (later Dato Sir Cheng-lock Tan) and received official blessing.

The basic idea of the MCA was the combination of the Chinese — not only in the interests of racial unity but with the object of bringing about Sino-Malay friendship. But Sino-

Malay friendship seemed a very remote possibility at this time. Separated from one another by race, language, religion, and economic interest, the Chinese and Malays were far apart and the emergency had separated them even further. The Communist insurrection was almost exclusively a Chinese one, and the guerrillas fighting the Government in the jungle were ninety-nine per cent Chinese. Opposed to them were the security forces — the British troops, the Malay Regiment, and the police and the home guard, (the last two numbering over 100,000 and nearly all Malays). The Communist MRLA in the jungle received its support from the majority of the half million or so Chinese 'squatters' — the rural Chinese who had been collected together in some hundreds of 'new villages' to prevent them supplying the guerrillas with food, ammunition, etc. Since the Chinese guerrillas were thus the enemies of the Malays who suffered many casualties at their hands, and the Chinese squatters were, generally speaking, the allies of the MRLA, it was very hard for the Malays to distinguish Chinese friend from Chinese foe. The feeling between the two communities was thus worse than it had been even during the occupation when the Japanese had done their best to foment hatred between Malays and Chinese in the interest of 'dividing and ruling'.

No doubt the divisions between the two principal Malayan communities had assisted the British in their task of administering the country, and since over 80 per cent of the Malayan Civil Service learnt Malay, a handful learnt an Indian language, and only some 10 per cent learnt Chinese, the sympathies of the MCS as a body tended to be 'pro-Malay'. But this did not mean that the MCS encouraged jealousy between the races. On the contrary, their influence was instrumental in bringing about the harmonious relations which existed between all communities before the Japanese war.

In order to defeat the Communists, the British had to secure the support — or at least the effective neutrality — of a majority of the Chinese as well as the support of the Malays. The Chinese squatters were the crux of the situation. Either willingly or under threats they were supplying the MRLA guerrillas with food and manpower, and to prevent them doing this was therefore the prime task of the British authorities. To this end, General Sir Gerald Templer, the High Commissioner from 1952–54, attempted to subject them to greater penalties for supplying the terrorists than the latter could impose upon them for refusing their demands, but unfortunately the General's use of armoured cars, cuts in the rice ration, curfews, and destruction of villages were less effective than the methods available to the Communists. Directly the General and his armoured cars had driven off, the guerrillas emerged from the jungle to murder anyone who had succumbed to his pressures. The MRLA remained fully active, and the 'incidents' increased.

This period (1952–4) was one highly critical for Malay-Chinese relations. The assumption of the administration seemed to be that the Malays were the friends of the Government and the Chinese community, as a whole, its enemies. If this assumption had been founded on fact the final consequence might well have been civil war between the Malays and Chinese — and, in view of the fact that the Chinese (except for the 3–5,000 MRLA guerrillas) were unarmed, things would have gone ill with this community. Such an outcome, needless to say, would have been a great calamity, and one fatal to the idea of a unified Malaya.

The year 1953, however, saw a remarkable phenomenon — the bridging of the yawning gap between Malays and Chinese and the formation of an alliance between the UMNO and the MCA with the united aim of starting independence for Malaya. Nevertheless, the administration continued to act as if this alliance had no existence.

UMNO, it should be mentioned, was now under the leadership of Tunku Abdul Rahman. Dato Onn had made the political mistake of trying to open UMNO to the membership of other races besides the Malays — a course unacceptable to the latter. Then, in 1951, he formed a new Independence of Malaya Party (IMP), with the support of the British High Commissioner, Sir Henry Gurney, with the object of creating a united Malaya, but his failure to gain the support of his own creation, UMNO, for his new IMP, led to his loss of the UMNO leadership.

In April 1954, a joint UMNO-MCA mission went to England to request an unofficial majority in the Federal legislature — in opposition to the recommendation of a committee of the existing legislature appointed by General Templer. At first, Mr Lyttelton, the Colonial Secretary, refused to receive the mission, but later did so — only to refuse their request. The consequence was that all members of the UMNO or the MCA in the legislature walked out of it and those serving on boards and committees resigned. There was a period of hesitation by the British Government, and then its policy was reversed. Negotiations between the new Colonial Secretary (Mr Lennox-Boyd) and the UMNO-MCA Alliance resulted in a concession whereby the unofficials would have a majority of five over the officials in the legislature. Thus the Alliance, in order to have a narrow working majority of 5, would have to win all the fifty-two elective seats in the new Assembly.

In the event, at the elections of 1955 the UMNO-MCA Alliance won fifty-one out of the fifty-two seats. With this narrow majority of four seats the Alliance paved the way to independence and were now assisted in this course by the British Government which had reversed its previous policy. Independence was granted to the Federation of Malaya in September 1957.

Federal Union Citizenship, created after the formation of the Federation in 1948, had conferred citizenship on all those of Malay race automatically (even if they had only recently arrived from Sumatra, Java, etc.), but others could qualify for citizenship only by satisfying certain conditions (the birth of both parents in Malaya, a knowledge of Malay, etc.). Thus of those qualified to vote in the 1955 elections the Malays were in the great majority. The Alliance allotted a quota of seats (15/52) to the MCA, besides 1 Indian, and 1 Ceylonese. The conditions for qualification for citizenship were subsequently amended to include more Chinese, but the Malay advantage has been continued.

Under the treaties between Britain and the Malay rulers, and the citizenship laws passed in the British period, the Malays enjoyed a political advantage which would become greater once elections were held. The Chinese, on the other hand, had the economic advantage. A minority of Chinese possessed considerable wealth, but the bulk of the Chinese community possessed superior earning capacity to the Malays, most of whom were peasants. The tacit agreement upon which the Alliance was based was that the Malays should continue to enjoy their political advantage and the Chinese should continue their economic advantage. The Chinese, however, would have to submit to taxation which would permit the progressive raising of the standard of living of the Malay peasant.

After 1957, the Alliance was reinforced by the addition of the Malayan Indian Congress (MIC) representing some 800,000 odd Indians in the Federation.

New parliamentary and state elections were held in August 1959, two years after independence. In the parliamentary general election the Alliance won 74 of the 104 seats.[1] In 1955, Alliance candidates obtained approximately 80 per cent of the votes cast, and in each of the fifty-one constituencies in which the Alliance was successful their candidate obtained twice as many votes as any of his rivals. The only seat lost by the Alliance was in a three-cornered contest in the Krian constituency of Perak, when the Pan-Malayan Islamic Party candidate finished just ahead of the Alliance candidate. Dato Onn's new party, the Party Negara (stressing Malay rights), contested more than half the seats, but its efforts were most unsuccessful, and 13 of its 30 candidates lost their deposits. The Pan-Malayan Islamic Party (PMIP), with a programme of a Malay-dominated Islamic State, had 11 candidates — 3 in Kelantan, 3 in Perak, 2 in Selangor, and 1 each in Kedah, Pahang, and Penang. Four of the PMIP candidates lost their deposits. The total electorate in 1955 numbered 1,280,000 — largely Malay. It was estimated that 84 per cent of the electorate was Malay, 11 per cent Chinese, and the remaining 2 per cent mainly Indian.

In 1959, the total electorate had increased to 2,177,000, and the proportion of non-Malay electors was very considerably larger than in 1955. It was estimated to include 750,000 Chinese as compared with the 155,000 of 1955. Approximately 57 per cent of the increased electorate was Malay, 36 per cent Chinese, and 7 per cent Indian.

It was understandable that despite its tacit agreement with the Malays the MCA would want a larger number of candidates than in 1955. UMNO wanted 75 Malay, 27 Chinese, and 2 Indian candidates to be nominated, whereas a large section of the MCA wanted at least 35 Chinese candidates. The final compromise reached was — UMNO 69 candidates, MCA 31, MIC 4. This solution, however, was approved within the MCA by only a small majority, and a number of members resigned in

[1] See T. E. Smith, 'The Malayan Elections of 1959', *Pacific Affairs*, March 1960.

consequence, some of whom stood as independent candidates at the elections.

Even before the parliamentary elections were held there were indications of the opposition that the Alliance would have to meet when the state elections took place. To begin with, the Alliance promised to repeat the 1955 landslide in their favour, capturing all the seats in Kedah and Perlis, but then came the débâcle in the east coast states of Kelantan and Trengganu. In Kelantan, the PMIP won 28 out of the 30 seats in the State Council, and in Trengganu it won 13 out of the 24 seats — 7 going to the Alliance and 1 to Dato Onn's Party Negara. In all other states, the Alliance had clear majorities in the State Councils, but in Perak it met strong opposition from the People's Progressive Party (PPP) and in Penang from the Socialist Front.

Then came the parliamentary general election. But before I summarize the results let me give some idea of what the parties other than the Alliance stood for.

The PMIP called for Malaya for the Malays in an Islamic theocratic state. The party promised to 'restore' Malay sovereignty by changing the constitution and it proposed to establish friendly relations with all Muslim countries. All treaties permitting the stationing of foreign troops in Malaya were to be revoked. The leader of the party was the Dr Buhranuddin who had founded the MNP (it was later proscribed by the Government before independence), and who was the advocate of a 'Greater Indonesia' with Malaya as a part.

Dato Onn's party, Party Negara (PN), also stood for the extension of Malay rights, but in less extreme a way. PN had not recovered, however, from its crushing defeat in 1955 and was not a force in Malayan politics.[1]

The PPP made its appeal primarily to the Chinese voters and attacked Malay nationalism. It demanded also 'one class of citizenship' and multi-lingualism, and condemned the existing educational policy (instituted by the Alliance Government) which favoured the Malay language. It also demanded the nationalization of rubber and tin, and increased taxation for companies and the higher income groups. The leaders of PPP were two Indian lawyers, the brothers Seenivasagam.

[1] Dato Onn died in January 1962.

The Socialist Front (comprising the Labour Party and the Party Ra'ayat (Peasants' Party)) in its manifesto spoke of 'planned Socialist economy', the replacement of 'middle-men' by agricultural co-operatives, the elimination of racial 'separatism', etc.

The result of the general election was that the Alliance won all the seats in Kedah, Perlis, Johore, and Pahang. In Negri Sembilan, it won 4 of the 6 seats, the other 2 going to independent Chinese candidates who had resigned from the MCA in July. The PPP won 4 of the 20 seats in Perak, and another seat was won by a Chinese independent. The Socialist Front won 4 of the 8 seats in Penang and 5 of the 14 seats in Selangor, the remainder going to the Alliance. The PMIP retained its hold in the east coast states of Kelantan and Trengganu, winning 13 of the 16 seats in the two states. PN had a solitary success in Trengganu where Dato Onn himself won a seat, and the Malayan Party (of purely local significance) won a seat in Malacca.

The net result was that the Alliance was back in power with 73 seats out of the 104 (52/69 of its Malay candidates, 19/31 of its Chinese candidates, and 3/4 of its Indian candidates having been elected). The Alliance poll, however, had dropped from 80 per cent in the 1955 elections to 55½ per cent in the 1959 elections. It seemed probable that in the course of the next five years the Malay vote, though remaining predominant, would continue to diminish slowly in importance.

Let us now turn to Singapore which in spite of its comparatively small size and population (1,600,000) received more attention in world news in the early 1960's than has the Federation (pop. 7 million).

Singapore is in a special position (a) because of the importance attached to it in Western strategy, and (b) because of the great preponderance of Chinese in its population.

After the resumption of the civil government in 1946, plans were made for granting Singapore a certain measure of popular representation. The new constitution, however, did not meet with the approval of the local Chinese who boycotted the elections of 1948. In the elections of 1951, the Progressives and the Independents were opposed by the Labour Party, which had a programme based on that of the British Labour Party and demanded immediate union with the Federation. Out of 9 seats, the Progressives obtained 6, Labour 2, and the Independents 1. But out of about 300,000 persons qualified to register votes, only about 20,000 actually voted.

In view of the indifference of the Singapore populace to the existing constitution, the British Government in 1953 appointed a commission headed by Sir George Rendel to recommend a new constitution. The commission in due course recommended a legislature with twenty-five elected members out of a total of thirty-two. Six of the elected members were to be members of a Council of Ministers (replacing the Executive Council), the Chambers of Commerce were to be deprived of political representation and the names of those entitled to vote would be automatically included in the registers. Brought into operation in 1955, these measures led to a vote of more than fifty per cent of the new electorate.

A schism had taken place in the Labour Party in 1954 when one faction had formed the Labour Front with the newly formed Socialist Party. Then in November 1954, still further to the Left, there appeared the People's Action Party (PAP) under Mr Lee Kuan-yew, which had the support of the Chinese trade unions. (It was believed that the PAP also enjoyed the support of the Communists.) The conservatives were even more divided — the Progressives having to compete with a new democratic party and with a branch of the MCA-UMNO Alliance. Of 25 seats, the Labour Front obtained 10, the Progressives 4, the PAP and the Alliance 3 each, the Democrats 2, and the Independents 3.

There was no one party with a sufficient majority to form a government, but the leader of the Labour Front, Mr David Marshall, was able to do so with the assistance of the Alliance. Scarcely had he assumed power as Chief Minister when he was confronted by a crisis caused by a strike of the employees of the Singapore Bus Company, and made worse by an agitation among the pupils at the Chinese secondary schools. Then arose the question of the future relations of Singapore with the British Government. In August 1955, following a visit by the Secretary of State for the Colonies and discussions between him and Mr Marshall, it was announced that, except in the event of the suspension of the constitution, the Governor of Singapore would nevertheless act in conformity with the recommendations of the Chief Minister, thus recognizing the existence of parliamentary government, and that the following year negotiations would be opened in London on the question of self-government for Singapore.

When the promised discussions took place in London in April 1956, the Singapore delegation would not accept the conditions for self-government imposed by the British Government. The latter would recognize internal sovereignty only on condition of its power to suspend the constitution in any situation where the contemplated Committee of Security and Defence might consider it impossible for the High Commissioner (the British official who would replace the Governor) to carry out his responsibility regarding defence and external affairs. No agreement seeming to be possible, Mr Marshall resigned as Chief Minister on his return to Singapore. He was succeeded by another member of the Labour Front, Mr Lim Yew-hock, a Malayan Chinese who had formerly been the Secretary of the Union of Government Employees.

Mr Lim Yew-hock, being much more representative of Singapore opinion as a whole than his predecessor, was able to obtain better results than he in the struggle against Communist-inspired agitation which had previously caused riots, and conditions were therefore better for the re-opening of negotiations with Britain. A new conference was called in London in March 1957. This time agreement was reached regarding the internal government of Singapore and on the composition of the Defence Committee which it was now agreed should consist of three British representatives (with the British High Commissioner as Chairman), three Singapore ministers, and a representative of the Federation who would have the casting vote. The Legislative Assembly would consist of fifty-one members, elected by the universal suffrage of all adults, male and female, on a common roll irrespective of community.

Under the new constitution, the self-governing State of Singapore came officially into existence at midnight on 2–3 June, 1959. The Governor, Sir William Goode, ceased to be Governor but was sworn in the next day as *Yang di-Pertuan Negara*, or Head of the State, representing the Queen. In December he was to be succeeded as Head of State by a

Malayan-born person. He temporarily also was UK High Commissioner, but in December he would be succeeded in this capacity by a UK Commissioner for Singapore and South-East Asia.

At the first elections held on 30 May, 1959, under the new constitution the PAP, under Lee Kuan-yew, won an over-whelming victory in the elections for the new Legislative Assembly. Of the 51 seats, 43 were won by PAP, 4 by the Singapore People's Alliance under Lim Yew-hock, and 3 by UMNO-MCA, and 1 by an independent.

In a post-election statement, Mr Lee Kuan-yew said that the PAP did not 'propose to be, or even appear to be, the handmaid of the Communist Party', adding that 'a PAP Government is quite capable of taking its own steps to ensure the security of the State and the survival of democracy'. The PAP emphasized that it would not take office until the release of eight of its members who had been detained after the riots of 1956 by the then Chief Minister, Mr Lim Yew-hock.

Before proceeding to take stock of the record of the PAP Government to date, it is appropriate to note that although Singapore is eighty per cent Chinese, there is a considerable Malay minority which, while normally quiescent, on occasions asserts itself sometimes violently as it did in the case of the Maria Hertogh riots of 1956. On 11 January, 1961 the Singapore Minister of Culture, Mr S. Rajaratnam, announced in the Legislative Assembly that on 6 January the Government had foiled a plot by an extremist organization, known as the Soldiers of the Muslim Revolution, to bring about clashes between Chinese and Malays. The police had so far arrested fifteen persons including Abdul Ghani bin Hassan, the president of the organization, and had discovered in an unoccupied hut jungle-green uniforms and shoulder badges bearing a white crescent and star on a green background, as well as flags with Arabic (Jawi) inscriptions.

In the existing situation, any government in Singapore had to be 'anti-colonial' to enjoy popular support, and Mr Lee Kuan-yew's programme was regarded (especially by the European merchants) as decidedly to the Left. But Mr Lee made a great feature of the 'Malayan' nature of PAP, accepting Malay as the official language for Singapore, and insisting on the need to come to terms with the Malays of the Federation. The question was, however, whether Mr Lee would be able to control the communistically inclined elements inside his own party.

On 3 August, 1960, Mr Lee Kuan-yew declared in the Legislative Assembly that a collision was bound to take place between the 'adventurers of the Left' (the Communists) and the 'colonialist imperialists'. PAP, however, would allow the two factions to tear one another to pieces. Both the British and the Communists, he said, were quite prepared to use the PAP as a battering-ram in their operations against one another. The Communist Party was the only organization which could challenge the Government in the struggle for power. In the fourteen months that had elapsed since the elections the Communists had increased their power in the trade unions, thanks to the underground cadres bringing pressure on the workmen. Since the Communist Party was clandestine, it was impossible to stop the formation of several pro-Communist groups with differing outward ambitions. The least clever among the Communist partisans were those leftists who tried to exploit the Ong Eng-guan incident.

This reference was to the principal thorn in the side of the Prime Minister. Mr Ong Eng-guan, a Malacca-born Chinese who had studied in the University of Melbourne (aged thirty-four in 1960), had, as Mayor of Singapore, called considerable public attention to himself by banning the use of regalia inherited from the British period and having the Union Jack removed from the Council Chamber. He had been a PAP minister, but had been compelled to resign after a personal attack made by him on the Prime Minister. He now came out in overt opposition to the Government, attacking what he called the 'controlling clique of the PAP' — namely Mr Lee Kuan-yew and the Minister of Finance, Mr Goh Keng-swee. His contention was that the existing constitution did not confer real self-government on Singapore. The powers of the Security Council, he said, were too great; the British forces occupied too large an area in return for a nominal rent.

The issue now turned on whether Mr Lee Kuan-yew, whose most solid support came from the English-speaking government servants and the teachers in the University of Malaya in Singapore, could retain trade-union support or whether it would be wrested from him by Mr Ong Eng-guan and other opponents.

At a by-election held in Singapore on 29 April, 1961, Mr Ong Eng-guan was elected by a majority of 4,927, winning 7,747 votes against the 2,820 won by Mr Jek Yuenthong of the PAP. Over 90 per cent of the electorate voted. Mr Ong claimed that the result was a 'triumphant victory of the people against a government which had so disappointed them, and also a victory for the people of Singapore'. Once again Ong Eng-guan was a force in Singapore politics. Mr Lee admitted his success as a 'set-back'.

A second set-back was to follow only about two months later. On 15 July, at another by-election in Singapore, PAP again lost the seat. The victor this time was Mr David Marshall, the former Chief Minister of the Labour Front Government and now leader of the Singapore Workers' Party, by a majority of 546 votes over the official PAP candidate who polled 3,052. (Other contestants were MCA-UMNO, 1,482 votes; Liberal Socialists, 104; Singapore Congress, 69.) When his victory was announced, Mr Marshall waved a hammer, the symbol of his party, and called for the immediate resignation of the Prime Minister in no measured terms. The PAP Government in its two years of office had surprised its opponents, he asserted, and shocked and disturbed its supporters, who had expected 'stirring extremism', by its moderation. In token of this attitude the by-election campaign had been fought on the issue of a merger with the Federation of Malaya (desired by PAP) which Mr Marshall described as 'the Colony of Malaya'.

The PAP Government was now facing other difficulties as well. It still held 39 of the 51 seats, but at least 8 of its members were in active disagreement with its policy and there might be other waverers.

This question of a merger between Singapore and the Federation was without doubt the leading issue in Malayan politics early in 1962. The original objection of Tunku Abdul Rahman and the Peninsular Malays to the merger was the obvious one — namely that if a single equal citizenship were adopted it would threaten the special position politically which the Federation Malays at present enjoyed. Tunku Abdul Rahman's proposal for counteracting the greatly enhanced voting power of the Chinese in the event of a merger was his concept of a 'Greater Malaysia', to which he made his first public reference on 11 July. This was a few days after his visit to the territories of British Borneo where he had discussed with officials and political leaders the possibilities of forming a Malayan federation. He said that the sooner this objective was achieved the better it would be for all. In his Borneo visit, he said, 'I stressed that it would be to the mutual advantage of both the United Kingdom and Malaya and the territories concerned if those states could be brought into federation as soon as possible, because there are elements working hard to prevent it.' One of the biggest elements opposing the plan were the Communists who felt that once the Bornean territories joined the Federation they would have less reason to attack Britain for being imperialistic in this part of the world and would have no further grounds for making insinuations against Malaya, as those territories would be members of the Federation of Malaya. Tunku Abdul Rahman saw no difficulty in bringing the territories of Borneo into the Federation. The argument has been put forward in some quarters that those territories are not ready for independence, but once they joined the Federation they would be independent and enjoy the same prestige and privileges as the various Malay states in the Federation.

As the year 1961 moved towards its close the question of the 'merger' became more and more a matter of urgency. Both Tunku Abdul Rahman and Mr Lee Kuan-yew favoured it, but with the precarious PAP majority in the Singapore legislature it was doubtful whether it could be arranged on terms which the Tunku could possibly accept. Singapore now had a new party, the Barisan Socialis (Socialist Front), a coalition in opposition to the Government, which was willing only to accept a merger on its own terms (e.g. control of internal security measures, Malayan citizenship for Singapore citizens, proportionate representation in Parliament, etc.). However, on 8 October the Federal House of Representatives agreed in principle to the scheme, and on 16th Tunku Abdul Rahman flew to London to discuss conditions with Mr Macmillan. Agreement was soon reached, but as to the terms on which Britain would be able to continue to use the Singapore base there was a difference in interpretation (which could only be resolved in the event). Before leaving London after the discussions with the British

Government, the Tunku declared that if a merger of the Federation, Singapore, and the Bornean territories was not quickly accomplished, it would fail because of the onslaught of Communist imperialism.

When the White Paper setting out the terms agreed for the Federation between the Tunku and Mr Lee was debated in the Singapore Legislative Assembly on 20 November, the issue was not whether or not there should be a merger but the terms on which it should take place. Dr Liew Siew-choh, leader of the Barisan Socialis (in a record speech lasting seven and a half hours over two sittings), moved an amendment to the Government motion asking for a 'genuine merger' with Singapore citizens automatically becoming Federation citizens. But in the words of another member of the Opposition, 'merger must be resisted without giving the appearance of resisting merger'. In the end the Government motion was passed, since 13 Socialist Front, 3 United People's Party (Mr Ong Eng-guan and his colleagues), and the one Workers' Party member (Mr David Marshall) walked out. The Alliance Party members (Mr Lim Yew-hock's 4 and the 3 UMNO representatives) voted with the Government. One Independent member was absent from the division and the motion was thus carried by 33 votes to nil.

So far as it was safe to prophesy the future early in 1962 in a rapidly changing situation, one might venture to predict that the Alliance in the Federation would retain a sizeable majority at the next elections and that consequently there was likely to be a stable government for some years to come. The state of affairs in Singapore, however, was quite different. In accepting the leadership of a Government subject to constant pressure by the Communists who at any time might gain the upper hand, Mr Lee (to use a Chinese idiom) was 'riding the tiger', and (as the saying goes) 'He who rides the tiger dare not dismount'. Mr Lee, however, was a very adroit and determined rider and it was still possible that he would continue to be able to manage his dangerous steed until the Malaysian Federation rendered it obsolete.[1]

[1] In mid-1962 the PAP lost its remaining majority of one by the resignation of a member.

Chapter twelve

THE POLITICAL EVOLUTION OF INDONESIA: THE FAILURE OF PARLIAMENTARY DEMOCRACY

---

by C. D. Cowan

ON 17 August, 1961 the Republic of Indonesia celebrated the completion of its second *windu* of independence. The *windu* is a period of eight years of special significance in traditional Javanese historiography, and independence in Javanese eyes dates, of course, from the proclamation of the Republic of Indonesia in Java by Sukarno in 1945. Outside Indonesia its independence is more usually dated from the inauguration of the Republic of the United States of Indonesia under United Nations auspices on 27 December, 1949. The point is one of importance apart from the somewhat academic necessity to establish an agreed chronology of independence. The political experience and the forms of government of the Republic during the four and a half years of its struggle against the Dutch became once more live issues after the final collapse of parliamentary government in 1957. It was then contended that the Republican constitution of 1945, with the very wide powers it gave to the President and his ministers, provided a better means of grappling with the basic political problems of Indonesia than did the constitution of 1950, with its emphasis on the party system and the sovereignty of Parliament. Before proceeding to discuss this proposition and all that lay behind it, we can best begin by reviewing the basic political problems with which Indonesia has been presented since her independence.

THE BASIC POLITICAL PROBLEMS OF INDONESIA

Many of the political problems of Indonesia arose in part from the way in which independence was achieved, and in part from the nature of government and society in the colonial era which preceded independence. Thus governments have had very limited resources in terms of administrative capacity and coercive authority because of the small number of trained civil servants available, the breakdown of respect for civil authority during the Japanese war and the War of Independence, and the fact that they did not inherit a nation-wide functioning administrative machine from the Dutch. They have had few resources in economic terms because of the physical destruction and dislocation of the war period, and because the psychological heritage of nationalism and the parting in anger from the Dutch have made it difficult to expand production for the international market, even when managerial and technical competence was available.[1] Again, apart from difficulties on the production side, the political legacy from the revolutionary period led to very heavy spending by governments unable to prune the over-large salary rolls of the military and civil services. The result has been inflation, and continuous budget deficits and balance of payments crises. Again, Indonesian governments have been sustained in only a very limited way by popular consent and guidance throughout the country. The pre-war Dutch régime imposed its administration over the archipelago, but it did not create a state or a nation there. Its policies were inspired and sanctioned from outside; they did not rest on the demands or consent of the governed. Independent Indonesia has therefore been faced with the problem of devising constitutional forms which produced not only an efficient executive but also provided channels through which the largely inarticulate masses could be associated with government. The almost total lack of experience of operating such a system, combined

[1] For example, addressing a trade union meeting at Semarang on 23 November, 1961, the Minister of Labour, Erningpradja, declared that while strikes were not really permissible under Indonesian socialism, it was necessary to take into consideration against whom they were directed. Strikes against large foreign concerns could be justified. In the case of state enterprises deviations from the course set by the Government should be opposed, and if representations were unsuccessful strikes could be resorted to.

with the low literacy rate and the fact that most of the available educated talent and ability was in any case already integrated in the higher ranks of government and civil service, has made the running of a parliamentary democracy of the Western type, with political parties, a hazardous experiment. The only significant reservoirs of such talent not in some way connected with and compromised by the disaster of 'liberal democracy' were in the higher ranks of the services, and of the Communist Party. The possibility that either of these two groups might attempt to take over the running of the state has therefore been for some time a potential threat.

Most of these problems are in essence similar to those encountered by many other newly independent states in South and South-East Asia in this period. But in Indonesia they are conditioned and exacerbated by several other basic factors, historical and geographical in origin, which are peculiar to this area. Before 1949 the peoples of the archipelago had never been united in one independent state. The creation of such a state rested on two propositions, one practical but negative, the other ideological and positive. The first was that those who had driven out the Dutch should succeed to their heritage, and take over as one state all the territories within the Dutch-created frontiers of the former Netherlands India. The other was that, the Dutch having been defeated, the opportunity should be taken by the Indonesian peoples to create their own democratic state, free from outside control, which they could develop in their own interests. On the surface these two propositions, so far as they go, do not clash much. The first would bring Irian Barat (Western New Guinea) within Indonesia. The second might or might not do so, depending on how far its inhabitants may be said to be 'Indonesian'. It could more easily be held to provide for the inclusion of the Muslim and Malay-speaking peoples of Malaya, North Borneo, and parts of the Southern Philippines at a later stage, if this should become practicable. More fundamental, however, is that implicit in these two propositions are the two main political themes which have run through Indonesian political life since 1949. On the one hand a unitary state with a high degree of direction exercised from the centre of control in Java, and with power resting in the hands of those who had led the predominantly Javanese nationalist movement against the Dutch, or those who succeeded subsequently in wresting that power from them in Java. On the other, a state in which the peoples of all the islands, whether they had taken the lead against the Dutch or not, could play an effective part in determining the policies of government, and be left a reasonable amount of autonomy in local affairs.

This brings us to one last general point: the way in which the most fundamental Indonesian problems spring from her geography. The broken nature of the physical relief has produced a corresponding particularism and separatism in the peoples of the archipelago. They have developed very strong local identities, each with their own political traditions, customs and languages. And this fragmentation has made it easy for significant religious minority groups to survive in particular areas, Hindu in Bali, Christian in the Batak country of Sumatra, in Ambon and in the Menado area of Sulawesi. This particularism was preserved by the Dutch, who accepted the traditional political units and made much use of the device of indirect rule. And severe as these political and cultural obstacles to unity and agreement are, geography has also produced an economic obstacle by the way in which she has endowed the islands differently in terms of physical resources. Java, with the archipelago's largest and most fertile rice-plains, has also the largest and most rapidly increasing population, which in 1958 was estimated at 53 millions out of Indonesia's total population of about 82 millions. But with 65 per cent of the population she accounts for only about 15 per cent of the country's export income. For it is the other islands which have been endowed with the bulk of the mineral deposits and the staple export crops. It is the foreign earnings of the other islands, therefore, which have to pay for Java's imports of food and consumer goods, and to finance her economic development. This again makes for tension between Java and the other islands, and is a severe obstacle in the way of the development of a political system satisfying all.

The first phase of Indonesia's attempts to grapple with these problems was an endeavour, from 1949 to 1957, to organize government by consent, Western style.

THE FEDERAL STATE, TO 1950

The state recognized as independent by the United Nations in 1949 was named the Republic of the United States of Indonesia. It was a federation of sixteen states, the largest of them the Republic of Indonesia, whose territory in Java and Sumatra had a population of more than 31 million; the other fifteen states were the so-called autonomous states created by the Dutch between 1945 and 1949, four of them in Java and Madura, the remainder in the outer islands. This constitution was regarded by the Republican leaders as tainted by its Dutch origins, and the leaders of the 'autonomous' states as little more than Dutch puppets. In any case the Republican leaders saw clearly that it would be difficult for the central Federal Government and Legislature to enforce a coherent policy in the constituent states. Within seven months the Federal state was therefore dismantled, despite armed opposition at Makassar and Ambon, and replaced by a unitary constitution, since known as the constitution of 1950.

THE UNITARY STATE, TO 1957

The constitution of 1950 brought the whole of the archipelago under effective control by dismantling the sixteen federal states, and replacing them with ten provinces whose boundaries were drawn on rational grounds rather than those of local tradition, so that local particularisms would be assimilated within larger units. Local leaders lost their power to provincial governors appointed from Djakarta, and many local officials were replaced by men from Java. These were either Javanese or men from the outer islands who had fought for the Republic in Java and who, whilst local men, were not members of traditional ruling castes but 'new' men, so that their loyalty to the central government and the nationalist revolution was stronger. This strengthening of the authority of government in the provinces was, however, accompanied by a reduction of authority at the centre. Sukarno was confirmed in office as President, but his ministers were no longer responsible to him, as they had been under the Republican constitution of 1945, but to a parliament made up of the representatives of political parties. These were initially nominated though their authority was confirmed by a general election in 1955. Neither before nor after the election, however, did any one party hold more than twenty per cent of the seats in Parliament, so that party groupings and politics generally were inevitably unstable, and short-lived coalition governments were the rule.

The parties themselves were in general loosely organized, and in their ideologies and attitudes ranged over a wide spectrum of political ideas. It is not possible here to discuss the large number of small parties in existence in this period. Many of them were not much more than the followers of individual leaders, tied to them by their patronage, and by their nuisance-value in Parliament enabling their leaders to secure office and advance their own interests. One may for practical purposes distinguish three main groups, typified by the major parties, the Masjumi (Muslim) Party, the Communist Party, and the Nationalist Party. The Masjumi was the largest and the most loosely organized of the major parties. It was originally a grouping of almost all the Islamic organizations in Indonesia, and its influence extended down through society to the peasantry wherever there were mosques and practising Muslims. By 1952, however, several groups had hived off as separate parties (notably the Nahdatul Ulama — the Muslim Teachers Party — a group associated with traditionalist religious and social attitudes, little influenced by modern ideas, and strong in East and Central Java) and Masjumi itself had become dominated by the so-called 'religious socialists', who reconciled modern Islamic ideas with socialism, and saw the need for economic and political co-operation with the West. The ideas of such Masjumi leaders as Muhammad Natsir, Sjafruddin Prawiranegara (Director of the Bank of Indonesia) and Burhanuddin Harahap were in the economic field very close to those of Sjahrir's small but tightly knit Socialist Party, and of the other 'religious' parties, the Christian (Protestant) Party, and the Catholic Party. Like the latter it was also regarded as representative of the interests of the outer islands, from which it drew 50 per cent of the votes given it in the general election of 1955.

The Communist Party (Partai Kommunis Indonesia, or

PKI) was throughout the period 1950 to 1957 the very antithesis of Masjumi in character. It was a tightly knit, well-organized and disciplined party, with the great majority of its support coming from Java. Starting with the stigma of the Madiun affair (an attempt in 1948 to seize power whilst the Republic was engaged in the struggle with the Dutch, widely regarded by Indonesians as a stab in the back) the party had so restored its credit by 1955 that it more than doubled its numbers in Parliament in the elections of that year. Its major assets were a group of young and astute leaders, the best-known of which, D. N. Aidit, had been trained in North Vietnam and China, large financial resources derived from the Chinese business community and the support of the Chinese Embassy, and an efficient organization in the trade unions and at village level in East and Central Java. Between the PKI at one extreme and Masjumi at the other was the Indonesian Nationalist Party (PNI), the most important group in the party politics of these years, and the one to secure the largest number of votes in the general election. Like the PKI it drew most of its support from Java; like Masjumi it was a coalition of several groups rather than a well-knit party. The larger part of its active membership was drawn from the new Indonesian commercial and professional classes, and from the civil service, both the old-time aristocratic officials of the Dutch régime, and the new bureaucracy of the Republic. Its greatest asset, however, was the fact that it was associated by the Javanese peasantry with the continuation of the nationalist revolution, and with the personal influence of President Sukarno. It stood more than any other party in their eyes for the encouragement of Indonesian firms in trade and industry, hostility towards foreign enterprises and support for the claims of their labour forces, the liquidation of the Dutch position in the country, and the demand for the speedy transfer of Western New Guinea to Indonesian control.

Between the initiation of the unitary constitution in September 1950 and the general election of 1955 there were five parliamentary administrations in Indonesia. In two of these the leading role was played by Masjumi, in one by the Nationalist Party, whilst in the remaining two Masjumi and the PNI combined to form a government. The fact that all these governments were unable to come to grips with any of the fundamental problems of the country was only partly because as coalitions they were inherently unstable and unable to sustain a firm policy on any particular issue. More important was the way in which politics in this period was bedevilled by the impending elections, and the role played by President Sukarno. The parties included in these cabinets tended to think more of advancing their electoral prospects (often at the expense of their allies in the coalition) than of maintaining cabinet solidarity. Party leaders, who were often not members of cabinets themselves, intrigued in the background with opposition parties, so that their colleagues within the cabinet were never sure how far they could count even on their own party to back a joint cabinet decision. In this confusing scene the President was the most important single figure. He personified for most Indonesians the nationalist revolution, and their hopes of a happy outcome to their present problems. He was a national father figure, his prestige was enormous, and he was determined to play an active role in affairs. He was also a President whose constitutional powers were at once limited and practically limitless. The constitution of 1950 assigned the President very few specific powers; but it did not explicitly limit his functions, and it provided no way in which his tenure could be terminated or his actions challenged. In practice therefore he could operate in any field and at any level where there was either no authority specifically charged with responsibility by the constitution, or where such an authority voluntarily allowed the President to take the initiative. Given his political skill and influence, the result was that no cabinet was able to survive for long unless it could count on his active support.

The way in which these factors operated is well illustrated by the course of the Wilopo and Sastroamidjojo cabinets (April 1952–August 1953, and August 1953–August 1955). The Wilopo cabinet was composed of members of the younger and moderate element of the PNI, the 'religious socialist' wing of Masjumi, and the Socialist, Christian and Catholic parties. It attempted to tackle in a rational fashion problems arising from the state of the army, internal security in Java, and the production of export crops. Its efforts in all these directions evoked the disapproval of the President, and proved the occasion for a rift between Masjumi and the PNI, the two major parties in the Government. Its plan to transform the army from a big, expensive and unwieldy body, large sections of which were little more than militia and irregulars raised as local levies during the patriotic war against the Dutch, into a compact, efficient and economic professional body involved the demobilization of many officers and men. Apart from the problems which would be raised in assimilating these men into civilian life, the officers in particular tended to belong to the group of Javanese nationalists associated with the PNI and President Sukarno, and the influence which they exerted both within the army and in society generally by virtue of their rank was considerable. There was therefore considerable obstruction to the cabinet's policy from the President and within Parliament. It hardened into hostility as the result of an abortive demonstration engineered by those officers in favour of change in October 1952, aimed at frightening the President into dismissing Parliament. In the field of internal security the conciliatory attitude of the cabinet towards the Darul Islam movement in West Java was viewed with suspicion as a plot hatched by the Masjumi ministers and directed towards the creation of an Islamic state, or at least an increase in the Islamic element within the state, and thus of their own strength. Finally, in an attempt to increase the production of currency-earning exports and improve the country's balance of payments position, the Wilopo cabinet took the realistic view that since those in the short run best placed to do this were the foreign estate and oil companies, the Government should do their best to assist them. In practice this looked like favouring colonialist exploiters against their potential Indonesian rivals and their Indonesian labour forces, and again provoked intense opposition, from the nationalist-orientated parties represented in the cabinet as well as from those outside it like the Communists. It was in fact their attempt to evict squatters from the concession of a foreign tobacco company at Tandjung Morawa, in East Sumatra, so that acreage under production could be increased, that provided the PNI in Parliament with the opportunity to bring the Government down in August 1953.

Beneath these particular issues there were of course deeper forces at work which explain the downfall of the Wilopo

cabinet, and the nature of the Sastroamidjojo PNI-led Government which succeeded it.[1] In the first place the main body of
PNI leaders outside the cabinet came to see the Masjumi as
their most dangerous opponents in the approaching elections,
and regarded the Wilopo coalition as dangerous because it
retained Masjumi in office and gave it the opportunity to
consolidate its strength in the countryside and in government
through its patronage and policies. The PNI therefore began to
cast around for other allies, and found them in the Nahdatul
Ulama (which had formally cut itself off from Masjumi in
1952), and in the Communist Party. President Sukarno, for his
part, came to regard both an increase in the strength of the
Islamic element in politics, and the policies of rationalization
in the army and co-operation with Western business interests
which the intellectuals of Masjumi and the Socialist Party and
the moderate wing of PNI advocated, as obstacles to the consum-
mation of the nationalist revolution and the attainment of
'Indonesian Socialism'.[2] One may observe from this time his
increasing estrangement from the Vice-President, Mohammed
Hatta, whose ideas were fairly closely allied to those of the
Wilopo cabinet. Both Sukarno and the PNI leaders, from their
somewhat different view-point, seem to have regarded Masjumi
as a greater danger than the Communist Party, which had itself
decided that its best policy was to direct its activities through
the normal constitutional channels, and to try to promote a
popular front government in which it could participate. Beyond these conscious political calculations, however, one may
observe a swing away from respect for the ideas of the largely
Western-trained intellectuals, and an increase in the influence
of the mass leaders who came to prominence during the
Japanese occupation and the revolution. It is true, as Feith has
pointed out,[3] that these were the people who were to be increasingly important as the election campaign developed. But
apart from this factor, there was a growing tendency for Indonesians to associate their discontents with the Western-style

---

[1] These have been well summed up in Herbert Feith, *The Wilopo Cabinet, 1952–
53: a Turning Point in Post-Revolutionary Indonesia* (Cornell, 1958), pp. 191–2, 202–12.

[2] Though so far as the place of Islam in politics was concerned this was probably
based on an incomplete understanding of Natsir's position, as Professor Kahin has
pointed out in *Major Governments of Asia* (Cornell, 1958), p. 554.

[3] Feith, op. cit., p. 204.

parliamentary system, which they did not understand and which was not operating effectively.

The way was thus open for the formation of the first Sastroamidjojo cabinet. Apart from its predominantly PNI membership, this included leaders of several of the smaller nationalist-orientated parties and the Nahdatul Ulama. More important than its overt allies in explaining the strength of this, the longest-lived parliamentary administration in Indonesian history, however, was the continuous support which it enjoyed from both President Sukarno and the Communist Party. With this support, and the lavish distribution of patronage, the Sastroamidjojo cabinet was able to survive for two years. Though reasonably effective in maintaining the political balance in Djakarta, however, neither it nor its successors was able to deal with the much wider problems of the army and of the relationship between the central Government and the outer islands, and this, against the background of increasing economic failure, eventually brought the whole parliamentary régime down. The so-called 17th October Affair in 1952 had left the army divided, and for most of the period of the first Sastroamidjojo cabinet its influence was small. Little by little, however, the two groups of army leaders involved patched up a *modus vivendi* between them. This was cemented by the attempt of the cabinet in 1955 to force on the army as its Chief-of-Staff a nominee of Sukarno and the PNI. The failure of this move not only marked the re-emergence of the army as one of the decisive political factors in the situation, but brought down the cabinet in August 1955. The Masjumi-led cabinet which succeeded it was little more than a caretaker government, since the elections held in the second half of 1955 showed that most of its member parties had lost ground to their rivals the PNI and the Communists. The unexpectedly good performance of the Communists in the election, however, alarmed many of the PNI leaders, who were now forced to revise their image of Masjumi as their most dangerous enemy. The post-election Government (the second Sastroamidjojo cabinet) which was eventually formed in March 1956 was therefore a PNI, Masjumi and Nahdatul Ulama coalition. It was completely ineffective, basically because after the bitterness which the preceding years had generated between them, the PNI and Masjumi members were quite unable to co-operate. The

Communists now resumed their role as a parliamentary Opposition, but refrained from attacking those aspects of government policy associated with the Left-wing of the PNI or with President Sukarno, thus exacerbating divisions in the cabinet. Most important of all, the cabinet lacked the support of the President himself, who was more and more frustrated by the operation of the party system and his inability to get his own ideas carried out, and who still saw the Masjumi group rather than the Communists as the most dangerous element in the situation.

INDONESIAN 'GUIDED DEMOCRACY'

As the result of the complete inability of this series of incoherent cabinets to grapple with the basic problems of the country, parliamentary government in Indonesia was liquidated at the beginning of 1957. The immediate causes of its downfall were on the one hand the refusal at the end of 1956 of several of the outer provinces to acquiesce any longer in a system of incompetent central control in which their own interests were subordinated to those of Java, and on the other, the determination of President Sukarno to sweep away or, as he said, to bury a system which was now discredited, and to replace it with one more suited to Indonesian conditions. In this he carried with him ultimately the Communists, the majority of the PNI and Nahdatul Ulama leaders, and the bulk of the army. The more important Masjumi leaders and some of the Socialists, however, cast in their lot with the dissident provinces, the most important of which were Central Sumatra and North Sulawesi (Celebes). So did a number of high-ranking army officers associated with them, and those army units stationed in (and mostly drawn from) the provinces concerned, who took the lead in setting up local administrations and without whose support no action would have been possible. The declaration on 14 March, 1957, of a nation-wide State of War and Siege, and the simultaneous resignation of the Sastroamidjojo cabinet marked the end of parliamentary government in Indonesia and the assumption of full powers by Sukarno as President and Commander-in-Chief.

With some of the discontented provinces Sukarno was able to

patch up compromise agreements. But in Central Sumatra a rival provisional government (to which North Sulawesi subsequently adhered) was established in February 1958. This demanded as the price for reconciliation the formation of a new central government under the leadership of Hatta (who had resigned the vice-presidency at the end of 1956), constitutional reform to give the provinces greater autonomy with adequate financial backing, and the elimination of Communist influence from government. Sukarno's reaction was to undertake the military suppression of the two provinces, and proceed with his own prescription for the re-organization of government.

The President's ideas fell into two parts. On the one hand he was concerned to restore to government authority and the power to act. As he said, 'what is the use of being called President, Supreme Commander of the Armed Forces, Prime Minister, Chairman of the Supreme Advisory Council, and even the great leader of the Indonesian revolution, if my commands are ignored?'[1] On the other hand he saw that the executive must be informed by the will of the people, and the people in turn educated by government. A parliamentary party system had failed to bring this about. He wished to develop an alternative system based on the three traditional Indonesian concepts of *gotong rojong* (mutual assistance), *musjawarah* (mutual discussion) and *mufakat* (mutual agreement).

The first step towards turning these ideas into practice was taken in 1959, when the President secured the abolition of the constitution of 1950, and a reversion to the principles of the Republican constitution of 1945. Under this constitution, which was originally drafted to provide for a situation in which the Republic was at war with the Dutch, the President had far wider powers than he had possessed since 1950. He exercised supreme power over land, sea and air forces and had the right to make laws with the agreement of Parliament, except during a state of emergency, when he was empowered to act alone. He appointed and dismissed ministers, who were responsible to him as individuals, and not to Parliament as a cabinet. The place of the cabinet as the chief policy-making body was taken by a small Supreme Advisory Council, which Sukarno had already

[1] In a speech to the Grand 1945 Revolutionaries' Conference' in Djakarta, 15 March, 1960.

R

appointed, appointment to which was by the President, and which was not restricted to ministers. The power of the President and those with whom he chose to work was not limited by any obligation to co-operate with responsible ministers, and Sukarno made it clear that the Advisory Council, under his presidency, would lay down lines of policy for Parliament to discuss and the ministers to carry out.

The next step, in 1960, was the 'freezing' of the existing Parliament, and the creation of a new *gotong rojong* Parliament, whose membership would not be based solely on the existing political parties, and whose decisions would be taken not by majority vote, but by *mufakat* — mutual agreement, or the sense of the meeting. The composition of the new Parliament, announced in April 1960, falls into two sections. The first is composed of members of approved political parties (which do not include either Masjumi or the Socialist Party); PNI (44), Nahdatul Ulama (36) and the Communist Party (30) have an overwhelming predominance over the minor parties, who share twenty seats between them. The second section, equal in numbers to the first, is composed of representatives from what are termed 'functional groups', i.e. the services, farmers, labour, religious groups, women's organizations, and so on.

By these steps President Sukarno had thus secured powers to develop a system of 'guided democracy' along his own lines, and ministers and a Parliament of his own choice with which to co-operate. There was, however, one vital limiting factor. This was the extent to which he was dependent on the power and the co-operation of the army. The initial successes of the army in the campaign against the dissident provinces had given them an increased *esprit de corps* and unity under the Chief-of-Staff, General Nasution. Moreover the declaration of a State of War and Siege had placed in military hands extensive civil administrative powers in Java, as well as extending those which, to some extent, they already exercised in parts of the outer provinces. The pushing through of the President's constitutional changes was only possible because of the support of the army and the prominent part which Nasution played in the negotiations involved. Once the essential framework of 'guided democracy' had been achieved, the continued support of the army was (and is) vital to ensure the maintenance of the *status quo* for it to operate. In Java the army provides for Sukarno the only possible counter-balance to the influence of the Communist Party, which has become with the disintegration of the parliamentary system by far the strongest political party. Outside Java, where by mid-1961 all organized military resistance to the central Government had ceased, the army remains in full control, and its organization is the only means by which national policy can be implemented there.

What President Sukarno needs is a perpetuation of the present state of equilibrium, so that he can demonstrate that his brand of Indonesian democracy works, and can cope with Indonesia's pressing economic problems. He must hope that in time the outer provinces will become reconciled to his system, and that its success will weaken the strength of the Communist Party in Java, so that the role of the army in politics and administration may be gradually reduced. The peaceful settlement of the Western New Guinea issue is of great importance in this context. Any development which necessitated the diversion of a major portion of the army's resources to New Guinea for more than a strictly limited period would upset the equilibrium, and involve the risk either of the weakening of Sukarno's position in Java, and the increase of Communist strength there, or of hazarding once more the central Government's control over some of the outer provinces.

Chapter thirteen

THE POLITICAL EVOLUTION
OF THE PHILIPPINES

by Georges Fischer

IN THE Afro-Asian world the Philippines were probably the first colony in which there appeared a nationalist movement resorting to armed struggle against the foreign colonizers (first Spanish, then American). This is all the more remarkable because the archipelago never had experience of a national state before it fell under foreign domination. The Philippines are also the first colony in the twentieth century to which independence was granted at a date fixed long in advance. Since its accession to independence the new state has maintained many connexions with the former metropolitan power and these connexions have generally survived, which is rather rare, in spite of vicissitudes and minor crises. It should be noted also that although there is no linguistic unity the people of the Philippines have a homogeneous ethnic structure and that 93 per cent of them belong to the Catholic Church and that as early as 1939 about half the inhabitants aged ten or more knew how to read and write.

STAGES OF EVOLUTION

The independence of the Philippines was proclaimed on 4 July, 1946 in accordance with the terms of the Tydings-McDuffie Act which was passed in 1934. The proclamation of independence did not constitute a qualitative change or sharp break with the past. The politics of the Philippines are characterized by stability, by the continuity of institutions and of political and social structure. The strata which were economically, socially and politically dominant at the time of American sovereignty still exercise a preponderant influence. The basic features of the political institutions were already found in the Jones Act of 1916. On the other hand, in accordance with the Tydings-McDuffie Act the people of the Philippines, if they wanted independence, had to approve in 1935 the constitution which was put before them and which incorporated certain conditions which were specified in that Act. This constitution could only be altered during the transitional period of ten years — the period of the Commonwealth — with the consent of the American authorities. This ingenious method made it possible to ensure that the new state would have a constitution as soon as it acceded to independence and that the constitution would already have been 'run in' since it would have been operative for ten years.

The war almost upset this continuity and stability. It should be remembered that the history of the Philippines is marked by peasant outbursts which are sudden and violent and without lasting effect. The Huk movement which was born during the resistance to the Japanese repeated this tradition and joined it with another, that of agrarian reform which had been the objective since 1924 of the Peasants' Union, an organization which was at first influenced by the Socialists and then, a little before the war, by an alliance of the Socialists and the Communists. As soon as they returned to the archipelago the American military authorities showed their hostility to the Huks. At the same time General MacArthur gave a certificate of good conduct to Manuel Roxas, a veteran politician who had appeared to collaborate with the Japanese, and insisted that President Osmena, who had come back from the United States, should convene the Congress, the majority of whose members had collaborated with the occupying Japanese.[1]

Manuel Roxas was promptly elected President of the Senate. The Congress declined to approve certain persons nominated by President Osmena who were known for their activity in the

[1] *Seventh and final Report of the High Commissioner to the Philippines*, pp. 6–9, 26–7, 63–5, 74–83, 110–41; Chapman, *Pacific Affairs*, 1946, pp. 193–8; D. Bernstein, *The Philippine Story* (New York, 1946), pp. 91–2, 250–5; Vinacke, *Journal of Politics*, November 1957, p. 728; Rovere and Schlesinger, *The General and the President* (New York, 1951), pp. 80–4; Dalton, *Far Eastern Survey*, 30 July, 1952; Vinacke, *Far Eastern Politics in the Postwar Period* (New York, 1956), p. 386; Hartendorp, *History of Industry and Trade of the Philippines* (Manila, 1958), pp. 206 ff.

resistance. The forces in the field took up their positions with a view to the elections of 1946. In January 1946 Roxas and his supporters split away from the Nationalist Party (which had been in power from 1907) and formed the Liberal Party. American interventions designed to obtain a compromise between Osmena and Roxas were a failure. The candidature of Osmena was supported by the Nationalist Party and by the Democratic Alliance in which there collaborated representatives of the peasants' movement, of the intelligentsia and of the middle classes and which was undoubtedly regarded favourably by the Huks and the Communists. The point of view of the peasants' movement appears in a document of 1946 recently re-published.[1]

The conceptions behind this document were far from dogmatic. It is stated that there are two classes in the Philippines: on the one hand the landed proprietors and on the other the peasants and landless tenants. The troubles in the Philippines are explained by the continuance of the agrarian problem, by the return of collaborators and by American imperialism. However, this last is no longer an inevitable phenomenon. The system of free enterprise has been transformed; F. D. Roosevelt realizing this and renounced imperialism whilst increasing the purchasing power of the American masses. The Huks are said to aim at real independence for the Philippines without economic, political or military links with the former metropolitan country; the struggle against Fascism; the purchase of great estates by the state and their resale to their *bona fide* tenants; the creation of home sites; the abolition of the system of tenancy and its replacement by leasehold; revision of the fiscal system; extensive and systematic state aid to agriculture; respect for the four freedoms of President Roosevelt; the disbandment of the civil guard; recognition to the guerrillas; the right of citizens to bear arms; and the adoption of a system of social security and minimum wages.

In the elections of April 1946 Roxas was elected by 1,333,006 votes against 1,129,884 for Osmena but the new President only obtained from Congress approval of the amendment of the Philippine constitution demanded by the American Bell Act of

[1] 'The Peasant war in the Philippines', *Philippine Social Science and Humanities Review*, June–December 1959, pp. 373–436.

1946 (parity rights of American citizens) by obtaining the invalidation of ten members of Congress belonging to the Opposition. So the years of 1945/6 were of crucial importance. The inclinations towards change were stifled and continuity, which had been threatened for a time, persisted.

Roxas died in 1948. Vice-President Quirino succeeded him and was elected President in 1949. The Liberal administration was characterized by corruption, falsified elections and economic and financial difficulties. The Huk movement spread and was consolidated. Then in 1950 the United States sent to the archipelago the Bell mission whose report was a formidable indictment against the régime. The Bell report proposed that the United States should contribute considerable financial aid on condition that the new state adopted a certain number of financial, economic and social reforms.

To make an impression the new course needed a new man; and he appeared. Magsaysay had worked in the resistance with the Americans. In 1945 he had been nominated military governor of Zambales by the American military authorities and was then promoted to the rank of Commandant. He was elected to the House of Representatives in 1946, then to the chair of the National Defence Committee of the House and was sent by Roxas to the United States to obtain concessions in favour of Filipino veterans. In April 1950 Quirino asked the United States for additional military assistance and for that object sent Magsaysay to Washington. In September 1950 he became Minister of National Defence and according to some authorities his nomination was requested by the American Ambassador.[1] When he took office Magsaysay endeavoured to ensure the freedom of the 1951 elections which turned out unfavourably for the Liberal Party which was in power. At the same time Magsaysay continued his struggle against the Huks with increased military resources; but those resources he declared to be insufficient because, as he said, he realized that only economic and social reforms could eliminate the Huk menace. The agrarian problem therefore became the centre of his preoccupations. It appears that during the whole of this period up to the elections of 1953 there was a parallelism between the views of Magsaysay and those of the Bell, Hardie and MacMillan reports. It would

[1] Douglas, *North of Malaya*, p. 110.

appear that the last two reports were published in 1952 to indicate the unsatisfactory character of the Government's agrarian policy.[1] Magsaysay came into open conflict with Quirino and resigned two months later. He became the candidate of a coalition between the Nationalist Party and the Democratic Party (a group which had split away from the Liberal Party) and was elected President in 1953. Although the new President succeeded in establishing contact with the countryside and the villages he did not manage to impose his programme of reforms which was emasculated by the Congress. However, the interests of the producers and exporters of sugar and coconut oil destined for the American market were satisfied by the conclusion in 1954 of a new agreement with the United States.

The presidency of Magsaysay was characterized by a new style but it did not constitute the turning point in the politics of the Philippines that it promised to be at first sight. The man upon whom the succession devolved, President Garcia, was a retiring personality representing the old guard. He inherited many problems and brought no new solutions nor proposals which might displease the ruling élite. Corruption spread again and in the elections of 1957 the campaign expenditure as a proportion of the national revenue was four times as much per head as the American campaign expenses of 1956.[2]

The elections of November 1961 had once more as their main theme governmental corruption. The new President, Diosdado Macapagal, represented the Liberal Party. He had been elected Vice-President in 1957 and so was able to profit from the obvious failures of the Garcia régime. During the election campaign he presented himself as the champion of the rights of the people, as the protagonist of honesty in politics and as the instrument of an easier and better life for the masses. He made a great many promises to the electors which sometimes appeared difficult to reconcile with one another.

STRUCTURE AND PROBLEMS

To understand the political situation in the Philippines, two features should be constantly borne in mind. First, the continuity

[1] Coquia, *The Philippine presidential elections of 1953* (Manila, 1955), pp. 67ff.
[2] Wurfel, *American Political Science Review,* June 1959.

with which the same social élite has held on to economic and political power since 1907. These *caciques*, these *ilustrados*, very often of mixed blood, have really feudal powers. Their authority was accounted for originally by the traditional structure, but then, after the American conquest, it was legitimized politically by representative institutions and confirmed economically by the part that this élite plays in the production and export of raw materials which are absorbed by the American market. In addition, the vote was restricted to those who could read and write so that only about 50 per cent of the adult population voted in 1957.

Secondly, the internal politics of the Philippines, even after independence, was affected by the influence of the former metropolitan country. Several illustrations have been given above. Senator Laurel, a prominent leader of the Nationalist Party, adduced in support of the candidature of Magsaysay in 1953 the fact that the latter was a great friend of the United States and the only man able to obtain considerable American aid.[1] The fate of agrarian legislation under the Magsaysay régime depended on the fluctuations of American policy and even more on the individual opinions of the American personnel who were stationed in the Philippines.[2] Generally, this influence of the former metropolitan country was accepted without too much resentment because of the links which had so long been established between the élite of the archipelago and the United States. It was the peasant outbursts (Sakdalist or Huks) which were anti-American. Some politicians, such as Senator Recto, displayed a certain nationalism. It was at the time of the elections that recriminations about this or that American intervention became more frequent.

As regards the party system it should be remembered that it made its appearance in the archipelago shortly after the American annexation. The Federalist Party was in power from 1900 to 1907 and all the political and administrative cadres were recruited from its members. The occupying power thus contributed towards the identification of the party with the administration and the Government. From 1907 began the

[1] *Philippines Free Press*, 7 November, 1953.
[2] Starner, *Magsaysay and the Philippine Peasantry* (Berkeley and Los Angeles, 1961), pp. 137–9.

reign of the Nationalist Party, the reign of a single party in effect, which was disturbed only by the opposition of individuals. The establishment in 1946 of the Liberal Party was due, as we have seen, to a historical accident rather than to any internal necessity. Besides the two parties were indistinguishable from one another and did not have any ideology of their own, and their electoral programmes reverted constantly to the same generalities and the same accusations of corruption.[1] At most one might say that the Democratic group which split away from the Liberals in 1953 and allied itself with the Nationalists (although one cannot consider that alliance very durable) represents the interests of the sugar-cane planters.

In point of fact the parties were characterized by their fluidity The leaders and the elected representatives changed their party according to their personal position or changes in circumstances, sometimes performing a veritable ballet during the course of a single legislature. Conflicts took place within the parties rather than between the parties. Changes of label assumed a perfectly respectable character in the life of the archipelago and one could say that this showed to what extent political life still bore the imprint of family and private interests of which the politician made himself the interpreter first and foremost, being assured of the loyalty of his personal group of retainers through all vicissitudes.[2]

The parties in the Philippines have very few permanent cadres and few regular members. Funds do not come from subscriptions but from occasional gifts, voluntary but interested contributions on the part of rich men and non-Filipino (American and Chinese) businessmen. Nevertheless, the party in spite of, or because of, its fluidity absorbs and exhausts the whole of

---

[1] Mr Meadows in *India Quarterly*, 1961, p. 35, considers that after the elections of 1953 two categories of interests were opposed to one another. Magsaysay thought that agrarian reform should take priority, which would in no way harm American interests, while the Liberals and Quirino gave priority to industrialization, an attitude which was less favourably regarded by the Americans. I think that this view is mistaken and that explanations of this kind are ill suited to the political realities of the Philippines. The programmes of the two parties were very little different and in effect the Liberals went further under the heading of agrarian reform than the Nationalists, among whom several prominent representatives were in favour of industrialization. See also Coquia, op. cit., and Starner, op. cit.

[2] Corpuz, *Philippine Social Science and Humanities Review*, June–December 1958, p. 141.

political life which is not yet sufficiently differentiated to offer a field for pressure groups since the dominant interests are directly represented inside the party. However, it may be said that the Catholic Church has a considerable influence which is exercised, generally speaking, in accordance with the interests of the landed proprietors and of the élite. But it also opposes, and often with success, certain *ilustrados* who defend secularism in the schools or birth control. The trade unions and the peasant unions have no real strength and are largely under the influence of the authorities and of the traditional élite.

There has been much talk of the personalism of political life in the Philippines, of 'personalismo'. It undoubtedly exists in a pure state without an institutional framework — bearing in mind the fluidity of the parties — to canalize it. Thus since the Second World War the 'spoils system' has existed in the administration of the Philippines, but the spoils are reserved not for party members on the basis of services rendered but for the personal relations of Congressmen. As has been shown, a real spoils system would be an improvement on the actual state of affairs and would undoubtedly contribute to strengthening the institutional framework of the party.[1] Having said that, it must be observed that in spite of the presidential system set up by the constitution of 1935, personal dictatorship has not been able to establish itself in the Philippines. Two very strong personalities have emerged in the political history of the archipelago: Quezon and Magsaysay. Neither of them was able to set aside the *ilustrados* and the élite. Magsaysay tried several times to rise above the parties, to free himself from them and to base himself on a new movement created outside the parties (Magsaysay for President Movement); he did not succeed. So power was concentrated in a group and dispersed within the same group. At the same time the personalization of power at the presidential level made it possible both to nourish the hope of the masses for change and to contribute to the maintenance of stability of the social structure and confirm, to a certain extent, the power of the dominant group.

Nevertheless, there are signs of a certain evolution. In the presidential elections of 1957 the young candidate of the new Progressive Party obtained more than one million votes. This

[1] Riggs, *Philippine Journal of Public Administration*, October 1960, p. 311.

succeess was confirmed in 1959 but without leading to tangible results.[1] Thus there is to be seen the manifestation in politics of a new and urbanized middle class. The Filipino First policy — from which hitherto the Chinese have been the main sufferers, being literally made to pay ransom for some time past — has contributed to the shaping of that class.[2] Since 1945, that policy has been expressed in numerous legislative measures designed to give Filipino businessmen facilities and privileges as against their foreign competitors (with the exception of the Americans whose parity rights have been guaranteed until 1974). But it must be observed that this new class is far from homogeneous, that it is recruited largely in the tertiary sector of the economy, and that it contains a rather high proportion of traders and men of straw of foreign interests. Industrialists are relatively few, and it is difficult to assess the political and economic evolution of this class as well as its political influence.

In the field of economics one of the great problems that is posed is to estimate the consequences of the Filipino First policy. To this question are inevitably tied others concerning the rhythm of industrialization, the rate of increase of employment, the possibility of absorbing unemployment and under-employment. The solution to these problems may provoke conflicts within the Filipino society as well as between Filipino and foreign interests.

In agriculture it would be necessary to introduce new measures, from the point of view of economic as well as of social and political progress, which would this time really be applied with the object of effective agrarian reform and redistribution of land, suppression of tenancy, and above all a realistic land assessment and progressive land taxation.[3]

With regard to institutions, the presidential system, contrary to appearances, has not shown itself altogether suited to the needs of a country like the Philippines. The late Senator Laurel had proposed the introduction of a semi-parliamentary régime,[4] but there is little chance of changes of this kind occurring in the near future. On the other hand, the problem of decentraliza-

---

[1] Manglapus, *Foreign Affairs*, July 1960, p. 613.
[2] cf. Lim, *Far Eastern Economic Review*, 20 October, 1960.
[3] On this point see Jacoby, *Agrarian Unrest in South East Asia* (London, 1961), p. 220.
[4] *Manila Times*, 14 May, 1954.

ion is on the agenda. Magsaysay earlier attempted to break through the rigid centralization of public life in the Philippines by providing representative organs for the *barrios*, but the multiplication of real centres of decision has so far come up against the opposition of Congress. Indeed the election of its members depends partly on the leaders of local communities, and for this reason particularly Congressmen want to preserve their means of pressure on those leaders.[1]

A last point concerning foreign policy and relations with the United States. Unless there is considerable political and social evolution, the Philippines will continue in the path they have followed until now, that is to say, co-operation with the United States and with the anti-Communist countries of Asia. The declaration made in 1959 in Malaya by the Philippine Minister of Foreign Affairs, which envisaged the entry of his country into the sterling area, appears rather to have been designed to bring pressure on the United States. Between the Philippines and the former metropolitan power, in the present state of affairs, there are, and will be, only secondary questions concerning financial claims or the rights of the Philippines under the agreement relating to American bases.

With regard to the countries of South-East Asia the foreign policy of the Philippines is ambivalent.[2] An expert in South-East Asian affairs has well said that the Philippines are in Asia but not of Asia. The leaders of the archipelago, considering the social structure of the country and mindful of the Huk menace and the presence of a considerable Chinese element, are attempting to join the group of Asian states which are most anti-Communist and also most conservative. So on 18–19 June, 1961, in Quezon City there was a meeting of representatives from the Philippines, Formosa, South Korea and South Vietnam. The communiqué which was published violently opposed Communism and the Peking régime, and supported the régime of Prince Boun Oum in Laos.

But, at the same time, the leaders of the Philippines recognized the relative isolation to which this policy led them in Asia. So they have been trying to broaden their contacts and to increase

[1] cf. Mariano, *Philippine Journal of Public Administration*, October 1957 and January 1959.

[2] cf. Fischer, *Un cas de décolonisation, les États-Unis et les Philippines* (Paris, 1960).

their links with the Asian countries. This tendency is not new –
it was already apparent at the time of the Baguio Conference (
1950 — but has again been manifested recently in an interestin
way. In June 1959 President Garcia while visiting Malay
thought of concluding a political and economic treaty with tha
country; but Malaya envisaged a wider collaboration compri
ing particularly Indonesia, Burma and Cambodia. Presider
Garcia was attracted to this idea, the realization of which wa
inconceivable on a political basis.[1] So on 13 February, 1961, a
Kuala Lumpur representatives of Malaya, the Philippines an
Thailand proclaimed their willingness for 'close co-operatio
which would be non-political in character, independent in ever
way of any power bloc and essentially one of joint endeavour fo
the common good of the region in the economic and cultura
fields'. On 13 July, 1961 the Bangkok declaration announce
the creation of the Asian States Association (ASA) designed t
provide a 'machinery for friendly consultation, collaboratio
and mutual assistance in the economic, social, cultural, scien
tific and administrative fields'; and Tunku Abdul Rahma
expressed the 'hope that the whole of South-East Asia woul
join the founding members.'

So the Philippines are attempting to rejoin Asia, to becom
'of Asia'. One may wonder about the extent of the success of th
attempt which has been received with a great deal of interest b
certain Asian socialists.[2] It is sufficient to recall that to begi
with it was a political idea which in ripening has had to b
emptied of all political content. It is a manifestation of a kind (
splitting of the Philippines' personality as regards interstat
relations in South-East Asia.

[1] cf. *Relazioni Internazionali*, 18 March, 1961.
[2] *News Bulletin of the Afro-Asian Council* (Delhi), 1961, No. 7, p. 3.

Chapter fourteen

POLITICAL IDEAS AND IDEOLOGIES
IN SOUTH AND SOUTH-EAST ASIA

by Francis Carnell

I

THE PRICE OF MODERNIZATION[1]

THE acute social and political conflicts about the very basis of
society, which were once the subject matter of Western politics,
now seem to have taken possession of Asia. In the new states, as
in the early days of the Western nation state, men living in an
age of revolution feel the need of serviceable practical philo-
sophies. Hopefully, fearfully, with much bewilderment, they
face the great political predicaments about freedom, authority,
legitimacy and social justice. This would seem to be the substance of politics in the classical sense. Everywhere, men living
in rapidly changing societies are trying to square modernization
with the achievement of social harmony. As Nehru has said, 'All
our schemes and planning, our ideas of education and of social
and political organization, have at their back the search for
unity and harmony'.[2] Tiny Westernized élites of politicians,
bureaucrats and army officers are groping tentatively and
experimentally for appropriate ways of substituting national
consensus and rapid economic growth for a fragmentary,
traditional social structure and a backward rural economy. But
modernization and political freedom, despite their promise of a

---

[1] For a general discussion of the problem in terms of Western political philosophy,
see John Plamenatz, *On Alien Rule and Self-Government* (London, 1960).
[2] M. N. Das, *The Political Philosophy of Jawaharlal Nehru* (London, 1961), p. 44.

fuller, richer life for the individual, seem to have brought with them only new conflicts and new anxieties.

In these transitional societies, as in Western Europe in the past, uprooted men have suddenly harvested a new freedom which is so novel as to be both a prize and a burden. Men are perplexed by conflicting versions and visions of 'the good life'. The various definitions of freedom and democracy to which we have had to become accustomed in the West are now matched by as many Asian definitions. Western democracy and Communist democracy compete with Indian democracy, Indonesian democracy and Pakistani democracy. In some cases, there is an obvious clash between the claims and values of modernization (dare we still call it 'Westernization'?) and the claims and values of an idealized traditional social order. Only too often, the price of revolution seems to be established disorder and acute social disharmony. Furnivall's analysis of the plural society, devoid of a 'social will', may not have won the approval of all the sociologists, but for sociological imagination it has yet to be improved on.[1] States which have genuinely tried to make their imported Western institutions an integral part of their political systems find themselves increasingly divided by cultural and ethnic pluralism, by communalism, provincialism, regionalism and casteism. Almost everywhere, the harassed political leaders of socially atomized societies are seeking ideologies which will give them the key to meaningful social and political reintegration. There is a feeling that both liberal democracy and Communism are still on trial in a largely uncommitted Asia. Of all the ideologies, the easiest to adopt as a means of fostering social and political cohesion is a xenophobic nationalism which casts all the blame for both disunity and poverty on to 'colonialism'. Indeed, it might be argued that all the political ideas and ideologies of South and South-East Asia are simply various aspects of the one overriding ideology of nationalism. But nationalism, as a state of mind, is just as porous in meaning as political concepts like liberty and democracy. An analysis of the anatomy of nationalism would demand not only a definition of nationalism but of equally subjective states of mind like 'communalism' and 'provincialism'. We prefer therefore to approach the problem

[1] J. S. Furnivall, *Colonial Policy and Practice* (Cambridge, 1948), Chs. 8, 11, 12.

by way of ideas about government, despite the obvious inadequacies of the vocabulary of politics.

The kind of questions we have in mind might be listed as follows. How should we, as Westerners, study the social and political ideas of Asians? Can we distinguish between democratic and undemocratic states? Does democracy in its various Asian manifestations differ from Western democracy? How far is preoccupation with 'progress' (i.e. economic growth brought about by modernization) compatible with political freedom? Where 'guided democracy' exists, does it differ in essentials from what we understand by totalitarianism? What is the role of ideology in new states? To what extent has Asian dissatisfaction with both liberal democracy and Communism fostered the growth of significant alternative Asian ideologies more suited to Asian conditions? What political theory or theories best explain or justify the emerging political systems of the new states?

It is far easier to ask such questions than to answer them because all of them raise both the problem of values and the problem of the validity of ambitious generalization. Our questions seem to demand not only premature generalization about how a great variety of contemporary Asian governments actually work, but also some speculation about the ends and purposes of those governments. We might as well admit at the outset that political theory in this sense of political philosophy is now much disparaged.

II

THE PROBLEM OF VALUES

Western political philosophy, that is to say, systematic thinking about political ideals, has virtually abdicated to the assaults of the Marxists, the sociologists and the linguistic philosophers. It is not so much a question of what meaning is to be given to terms like 'socialism', 'liberalism', 'Right-wing', 'Left-wing' and so on. Though these terms still have to be used for want of something better, they are political catchwords and slogans by now almost empty of meaning. It is rather a question of whether we now have any satisfactory tools left for the analysis of the basic political conflicts underlying the crude myth-

s

making of the major political ideologies. In an age of revolution, dominated by the conflict of Western ideologies in Asia and Africa, we are told that political philosophy is dead; that the term democracy can no longer be used with any accuracy in political theory; that questions such as 'What is liberty?' are meaningless.[1] If this is so, then what is the purpose of trying to discover what Asians mean by freedom and democracy? Is such scepticism to be dismissed as yet another example of the foolish fantasy worlds of the political philosopher? This uncertainty about political ideals is strangely out of line with the optimism of Western governments which have sought to convince Asians that the Western form of democracy is the best, and the Communist form the worst, on the market.

Within the West, men have temporarily ceased asking the fundamental (and unanswerable?) questions about the nature of social and political obligation, because affluent societies with a high degree of national consensus have for the moment eliminated the major social and political conflicts which used to divide them. Whether rightly or wrongly, ends are now more or less agreed. Ideology is dead or dying. The only debate, at least outside countries like France and Italy where ideological disputes still flourish, is about means. And these are regarded as technical matters to be settled by the 'know-how' of the expert.

American and British political theory, in their different ways, thus concentrate on being 'realistic'. Drawing on sociology and history, they seek to give plausible explanations of how actual governments actually work. Glittering generalities based on deductive thinking about human nature are quite discredited. At one end of the scale, we have a brash (largely American) political sociology which seeks the will-o'-the-wisp of a 'value-free' political science reduced to statistical propositions about empirically observed 'political behaviour'.[2] The state as a political concept, as well as its formal political institutions, is increasingly pushed aside in favour of purely fact-finding studies about political parties, elections, élites, leadership, decision-making and so on. Political ideals are simply 'belief systems' or

---

[1] Peter Laslett (ed.), *Philosophy, Politics and Society* (Oxford, 1956), pp. vii–xv and J. D. Mabbott, *The State and the Citizen* (1958 ed.), p. 178.

[2] See, for example, G. A. Almond and J. S. Coleman (eds.), *The Politics of the Developing Areas* (Princeton, 1960).

'interests' to be weighed and measured by sociological techniques. At the other extreme, there is a conservative brand of
British empiricism deriving from Burke that sees political theory
merely as complacent meditation about the impact of the past
on the present. 'Wherever politics begin, they cannot begin in
ideological activity' because political ideologies are no more
than abstracts of a tradition of national political behaviour.[1]
Thus, it is argued, there are no prescriptive political principles
other than the experience and prudence taught by historical
reflection about past (British?) political activity.

What is inescapable about all this is that whether current
political theory stresses 'science' or history as the key to political
understanding, whether it adopts the fashionable behaviourist,
power-élitist or group approaches, political ideals in the old
sense are dropped as too slippery to handle. Political philosophy
is forced to restrict itself to the exposition and elucidation of
linguistic muddles or to the history of political ideas. And it goes
without saying that, being a culture-bound discipline, Western
political theory generally excludes the notion of any worth-while
political ideas that have not been Western in origin.

We should seriously consider whether current Western attitudes to political theorizing are especially well adapted to help
us understand the social and political predicaments of the
peoples of the disunited new states of Asia. The major characteristic of these states is their lack of national consensus, the fact
that men are *not* in agreement about the ends and purposes of
government. There is dispute amongst the intellectuals about
the very basis of society. Can it be otherwise when new states
emerge? Men who successfully throw off colonial rule will still
want to reassure themselves that they are living in the 'right'
state, under the 'right' kind of social and political system, with
the 'right' ends and purposes. But how can we transpose the
admittedly confused language of Western politics so as to
enable us to understand what Asians are talking about? What
'conceptual framework' should we avow or take for granted?
Are we universalists, relativists, historicists, pragmatists, or
what? How do ideologies differ according to race, nation,
religion and social group? If history is one of the keys to political

[1] The view taken by Professor Oakeshott in his 'Political Education', reprinted in
Laslett, op. cit., pp. 1–21.

understanding, how far back do we need to go, and whose version of the past (especially the pre-colonial past) are we to accept? Are Asians asking Asian questions which require Asian answers? Are Asian answers ever likely to satisfy Western questions? If a political ideology is a theory or set of ideas devised to legitimize political authority, where do we look for what are likely to be the dominant ideologies? To the speeches and writings of leaders now in authority? To the manifestos of the dominant political parties? To alienated intellectuals?

III

ASSUMPTIONS

The assumptions, preferences and prejudices on which our analysis is based might be roughly summarized as follows:

1. Asian modes of thinking may well be different from those of Westerners. Asian logic is not necessarily our logic. There may thus be a genuine problem over the communication of ideas.

2. By a democratic state is meant a state which provides regular constitutional (i.e. peaceful) opportunities for changing the government. This implies, as a minimum, free elections, the legal recognition of more than one political party, a free press and an independent judiciary.

3. By a totalitarian state is meant a one-party dictatorship or 'police state' led by a vanguard or élite which has a near-monopoly of the means of mass communication and which claims it has a mission to transform totally a given society into what it conceives to be a perfect society.

4. By an authoritarian state is meant a state which is neither democratic nor totalitarian. Though there is no opportunity of changing the government by free elections, there is equally no wide-ranging effort on the part of the governing élite to transform totally the traditional structure.

5. By an ideology is meant the dominant belief system which gives social cohesion to any community. By a political ideology is meant the dominant ideas or beliefs which legitimize the organized force of the state.

6. Political typologies of new states are likely to be misleading because their emerging political systems are too amorphous and fluid to be categorized.[1] Though some can be provisionally accepted as democracies (i.e. India, the Philippines, Ceylon and Malaya) only one (North Vietnam) can be recognized as an orthodox totalitarian state. All that can be said of the rest (i.e. Burma, Indonesia, Pakistan, South Vietnam, Laos and Cambodia) is that they occupy a no-man's land for which the map-making political scientist has as yet few reliable charts. It is the particular feature of such states that they occupy an intermediate position between democracy and authoritarianism, with some aspects of both systems. Their 'guided democracy' or fluctuating oligarchy ranges from the more or less democratic system of Burma, which, despite a military interregnum, still persists with free elections, to the frankly authoritarian 'basic democracy' of the Pakistani army officers. These crisis-ridden states, dominated as they have been by intense power struggles between competing élites and personalities, have tended to drift in emergency towards the type of 'guided democracy' they learnt from the British. This system rested in the last resort on the power of a strong and uncontrolled executive in times of crisis to suspend or modify constitutional rule. When new states adopt such methods we should therefore be chary of condemning the 'guided democracy' they set up as deplorable deviations from what we think we taught them.

The second kind of government, which may well prove attractive to the South-East Asian states which were once ruled autocratically by the French and the Dutch, is some form of indigenous authoritarianism encased for the sake of respectability in a veneer of Western democratic forms. We have a working model in the Thai system of benevolent military despotism with the comparatively bloodless *coup d'état* as the regular method of changing the government.

[1] An ambitious typology is attempted by Almond and Coleman, op. cit. They divide all the new states of Asia and Africa into democracies, tutelary democracies, modernizing oligarchies, totalitarian oligarchies, conservative oligarchies, etc.

Some of the more crisis-ridden states like South Vietnam and Laos, if they can escape a Communist take-over, may drift towards this type of government.

7. Since some selection is inevitable in such an enormous area, we have chosen for special treatment those states in which there is an articulate consciousness of conflict between Western and Asian ideologies. We have not considered states like the Philippines and Malaya where the conflict of ideologies is accepted by Asians themselves as a straight issue between an imported liberal democracy and an imported Communism. It might of course be argued the Filipinos and Malayans are living in a fool's paradise; that both liberal democracy and Communism are inimical to their 'real' interests, and that they should be seriously trying to think up alternative Asian political solutions; or, at the very least, they should be prepared with an Asian ideology which will enable them to feel that they have made the imported system their own. But the fact is that they have not felt it necessary to do so. Malayans and Filipinos seem to get along very well with imported political ideals. They are none the worse for that.

It is one of our major assumptions that the acute consciousness of a specifically Asian predicament, which has led either to a search for satisfying syntheses of Asian and Western ideologies or to a search for alternative Asian political ideologies (what we might call Asian romanticism), has been strongest in countries like India, Pakistan, Indonesia and Burma. Here Westernized élites have felt obliged to invoke the myth of 'a glorious past'. It is in these countries 'with a history' that the discontinuities between modernization and the traditional order have been most keenly felt.

IV

LEADERS AND ÉLITES: WESTERNIZERS, ROMANTICS AND MODERNIZERS

Before considering special cases, we first need some sort of perspective view of the political psychology of the Asian leaders, particularly in its bearing on the key issues of Westernization, modernization and the traditional order.[1] And since much of what follows relates to élites, we also need to consider whether some sort of élitist theory can be advanced as the general political theory which best fits the facts in the new states. Élitist theory is attractive both because it is 'scientific' and because the élites have fulfilled such key political functions. This is not to argue that such a theory will in fact be wholly serviceable. Élitist theory, in the sense of 'Who Gets What When How?', is, at the best, a limited participation theory; at its crudest level, it is simply a power theory of politics which identifies actual power holders without explaining how power is legitimized into authority.[2]

This difficulty cannot be avoided in Asia. It is clear that, simply as a matter of political fact, some of the key power holders in the new states are merely traditional élites who have been clever enough to adjust themselves to modernization. Traditional leaders like the Brahmins in India, the soldiers in Pakistan, the Goyigama caste in Ceylon, the princely families in Malaya, Cambodia and Laos and the mandarin bureaucracy in Vietnam, have managed to get hold of a good deal of what there is to have. But only too often, we have to explain how and why a particular leader acquires a dominant authority over competing élites and peasant masses. To say that he has 'charismatic authority' and that all men instinctively follow him in troubled times because, as Max Weber says, he has the 'gift of grace', still leaves very open the question of how such natural leaders both acquire and lose this kind of authority.

Turning to the élites, we should first consider the Westernizers, the men who secured the transfer of power. These men, in the colonial period, had never been disposed to haggle about the price demanded by technological Westernization. They had adopted the scientific, rationalist, secular, individualistic world view of the West. Though some were more ambivalent than others, in the main they decisively rejected the religious, custom-bound, organic world view of the disintegrating traditional order. They looked forward, not backward. They sought

[1] For India, see Myron Weiner, 'Some Hypotheses on the Politics of Modernization in India' in R. L. Park and I. Tinker (eds.), *Leadership and Political Institutions in India* (Princeton, 1959), pp. 18–38.

[2] For a criticism of American élitist theory, especially that of H. D. Lasswell, see Bernard Crick, *The American Science of Politics* (London, 1959), Ch. 10.

the enemy to 'progress' in imperialism and in 'the burden of the past' weighing down their own allegedly static societies. The most ruthless Westernizers were the Communists who, though politically unimportant before the transfer of power, were dedicated to the extermination of Asian 'feudalism' as well as Western capitalism and colonialism. But political leadership in the freedom struggles (and this applied particularly to India, Indonesia and Burma) lay with non-Communist Marxists like Nehru, Sukarno and Aung San, whose eclecticism prevented any total commitment to Communism. This was because a nationalist organization, in order to create a mass movement, had to provide an umbrella under which men of the most diverse outlook could shelter. The dominant ideology outside India (where ends as well as means were held to be important) was an opportunist nationalism. If Communist intellectuals accepted that ideology they were welcomed. But at the transfer of power, the anti-imperialist alliance between the Communist and non-Communist Westernizers was severed. Owing to their subservience to the Soviet Union and their misjudged attempts to seize power by insurrection, the Communists were everywhere indicted as traitors. They had dared to challenge the mystique of nationalism.

Though the nationalist movements, on the whole, had encouraged authoritarian rather than democratic ways of thought (India again was the exception), the non-Communist Marxists at the transfer of power turned to Western political institutions. They knew no others and they could find no others in their own societies. In so doing, they allied themselves with their own 'liberals' whom they had so often condemned as colonialist in outlook. The Western-style constitutions which were adopted reflected the complete ascendancy of Western political ideas.[1] The constitutions imported Western political theories about Western political predicaments. In India, a typically Indian effort was made to synthesize the 'best' devices of the 'best' liberal constitutions of the world. The only acknowledgement of a traditional institution was a perfunctory reference to *panchayats*. In Ceylon, a particularly rootless group of Westernizers inevitably insisted on the unadulterated British model, having

[1] Saul Rose, 'Constitutions in South-East Asia' in G. F. Hudson (ed.), *St. Antony's Papers Number 7, Far Eastern Affairs*, No. 2 (London, 1960), pp. 24–36.

previously much resented being fobbed off with the one really original non-Westminster type of constitution the British ever gave a colonial territory. The Indonesians seem to have had some inkling of the possible advantages of a presidential over a parliamentary system of government, but they were in a hurry to give themselves any kind of political certificate which would prove to the world and to themselves that independence had been won. The Burmese, in order to protect their minorities, tried to combine the British system with a Soviet-style chamber of nationalities. The Filipinos probably made the wisest choice of all, taking over from the United States the presidential system. Only the Pakistanis made a serious attempt to find a place for an Asian concept of government.[1] They tried hard to incorporate into a Western constitution the elusive concept of the Islamic state. But after nine years of fruitless discussion about the proposed Islamic constitutional provisions, no agreement could be reached about the precise way in which an Islamic democratic state differed from a Western democratic state.[2]

The dominant Western political ideas, either explicit or implicit, in most of these Western-style constitutions, are fairly easy to identify. First, there was a liberal or Fabian socialism of the Laski kind. Directive principles of state policy envisaged welfare states founded on a positive concept of freedom. Human personality, in order to be developed to the full, demanded extensive state interference in the economic and social fields. But such interference was to be limited by due respect for individual rights. Bills of Rights reflected an American negative concept of freedom naturally attractive to Western-educated élites whose experience of the police power under colonial rule had led them to be highly suspicious of an unbridled executive. The second dominant political doctrine was a tentatively held political pluralism which found expression either in quasi-federal constitutions or in decentralized unitary systems which it was hoped would provide adequate safeguards for minority

---

[1] I am not overlooking the fact that the Vietnamese constitution might possibly be considered to have an Asian slant in that it recognizes duties as well as rights (Article 29).

[2] For the argument about the Islamic State see W. Cantwell Smith, *Islam and Modern History* (Princeton, 1957), Ch. 5; G. W. Choudhury, *Constitutional Developments in Pakistan* (London, 1959), Pt. 2 (5); and Leonard Binder, *Religion and Politics in Pakistan* (Berkeley, 1961).

groups. 'Unity in diversity' was the national motto from Karachi to Djakarta. This preoccupation with the problem of how to limit or contain group conflict (i.e. communalism, provincialism and regionalism) in the interests of national unity implied a Western equilibrium theory of politics.

Thus, at the transfer of power, there was no room for Asian romanticism. The few who were hostile to Western social and political ideas, who sought their utopias in myths of an idealized Asian tradition, were voices crying in the wilderness. Backward-looking Asian romanticism in this sense had always been an important element in Indian nationalism, expressing itself in Gandhian and Islamic concepts of society. But the Indian Westernizers were political, not ethical Gandhians. They were glad to use Gandhian (i.e. Indian) techniques of non-violence to win independence. Yet radical reformers like Nehru who wanted power stations and dams within a Western-style planned welfare state regarded the anarchical social order which the Mahatma called *sarvodaya* as pure moonshine.[1] In Pakistan also, the anti-Western *ulama* got short shrift from the Islamic modernizers who held all the strings of political power. Though the latter were much concerned about how to establish a truly Islamic state, they were frankly appalled by the argument that a theocratic state was the only means of achieving it. Outside British India, with the possible exception of Indonesia, Asian romanticism nowhere took root before the achievement of independence. The revolutions were carried through by leaders and élites who assumed it to be axiomatic that Western political ideas should be used to overthrow crumbling Western political régimes.

Since the transfer of power, both internal and external pressures have significantly modified the former undiscriminating ideological receptivity of some of the more important Westernizers. The gnawing suspicion that neither Western democracy nor Communism may be appropriate for economically backward countries, which wish to achieve rapid economic growth without prejudicing their newly won independence, has bred a

[1] Most of Gandhi's social and political ideas can be found in his *Hind Swaraj* (reprinted, Ahmedabad, 1958). See also: Joan V. Bondurant, *Conquest of Violence: The Gandhian Philosophy of Conflict* (Princeton, 1958) and B. B. Majumdar (ed.), *Gandhian Concept of State* (Calcutta, 1957).

much more pragmatic approach to politics. In a revivalist Asia the Westernizers have necessarily had to become 'Modernizers', prepared to take some account of traditional social forces like religion which were formerly contemptuously spurned. The hazardous pursuit of the national interest under the shadow of over-mighty neighbours has led to ideological non-alignment or neutralism. There is the growing feeling that Asian problems demand Asian solutions.

Old-guard leaders in order to survive have had to become effective reconcilers of conflicting group interests. The revolution of rising expectations has seeped down to the grass roots via party propaganda, electioneering and community development schemes. Mass politics has set off the explosive forces of communalism, provincialism, linguism and casteism. In some places, new provincial élites are appearing who, by reason of their Asian approach to politics, present a challenge to the Westernized leaders.[1] Fears of foreign intervention and the needs of national defence have fostered the growth of other and much more unpredictable élites — the politically minded army officers whose obsession with efficiency makes them hostile to all political ideologies. Thus, under such changing conditions, charismatic leaders must be effective intermediaries between all sorts of competing élites as well as between those élites and the 'politicized' masses. They must be not only astute opportunists but sophisticated men of two worlds who, by reason of being firmly rooted in both Western and Asian cultures, can make the necessary bridges between widely varying 'styles' of political behaviour. Faced by the factionalism of élites, families, castes and other groups, the function of the national political leader seems to be that of go-between or compromiser. He has to be able to speak and act in a number of different political idioms. For the support of the peasant masses he relies on his charisma; for the more literate urban workers rousing party slogans need to be invented which will successfully clothe modernizing ideals in emotive Asian language; for the intellectuals some sort of sophisticated Asian ideology may have to be evolved which seeks to rationalize factionalism and conflict into harmony.

[1] See, for example, Selig S. Harrison's pessimistic analysis, *India: The Most Dangerous Decades* (Princeton, 1960).

Is there then a dominant style of political thinking? Nationalism, in the sense of the pursuit of the national interest, is clearly the refracting prism through which every political idea, whether foreign or indigenous, has first to be filtered. But this nationalism may be defended in different ways according to different political experience, past history or tradition. There is a pragmatism which accepts liberal democracy and rejects Communism as in Malaya and the Philippines; there is the pragmatism of the Pakistani army officers who have decisively rejected *both* the intrusive Western ideologies after having ousted an eclecticism which sought unsuccessfully to synthesize liberal and Islamic democracy; there is an eclecticism which rejects Communism but which seeks to make authoritarianism respectable behind a façade of Western democracy, as in South Vietnam; there is an eclecticism which seeks to reconcile all ideologies, Western as well as indigenous, as in the case of India; and there are attempts to formulate alternative Asian ideologies of the kind put forward by the ethical Gandhians and Sukarno.

In the light of actual political experience, and under the continual threat of internal political breakdown, imported Western ideologies have increasingly to be defended or rejected by reference to refurbished Asian values and concepts. Some of the peculiar syntheses which are emerging might no doubt be dismissed by Western logicians as ideological rag-bags. But for all that, Asian romanticism has to be taken seriously. The belief that every people, if it is to accept its political system as legitimate, must search its own past for its own tradition of political behaviour is poles apart from crude revivalism. The disenchanted Westernizers are in a sense trying to do what so many of their former colonial rulers said Asians ought to do — develop 'along their own lines'. And since Asian disenchantment so often springs from a basic uncertainty about the suitability of both liberal democracy and Communism, we should now briefly consider the kind of case which might be made out against each.

V

THE CASE AGAINST LIBERAL DEMOCRACY[1]

A general mass of Asian criticism might be summarized something like this. Liberal democracy postulates the socially atomized society of Western economic liberalism — the mass of fragmented individuals, the lonely crowd. It is based on an individualistic, acquisitive psychology, and a purely mechanical view of the state. It is so unsystematic as not to amount to an ideology at all, for it has no agreed set of beliefs. It is thus quite out of line with the organic and communitarian character of Asian societies. For untold centuries, the individual in the hierarchical social and political systems of Asia was always in subordination to the group. The idea of the 'worth of the individual' was quite unknown; with minor exceptions, men had duties, not rights. For centuries, the theory and practice of divine kingship prevailed.[2] But despite the 'oriental despotism' of royal courts, the mass of men lived in a small-scale 'good society' — the organic community of the village with its satisfying face-to-face relationships.

Colonial rule did two things. First, by substituting contract for status, it let loose the unrestricted forces of economic liberalism. In the soulless new cities and towns, it placed uprooted men at the mercy of the icy blasts of Western individualism, making them faces in a crowd devoid of the old sense of community. Secondly, most colonial governments always relied (and this applied to Britain for a good deal of the colonial period) on authoritarian methods of rule. The Viceroy sat in the seat of Asoka. Government was autocratic, centralized,

---

[1] For recent critical views of the prospects for representative government, see Rupert Emerson, 'The Erosion of Democracy', *Journal of Asian Studies*, November 1960, pp. 1–8; Werner Levi, 'The Fate of Democracy in South and Southeast Asia', *Far Eastern Survey*, February 1959, pp. 25–9; and Asoka Mehta, 'The Opposition in the New States' in *Representative Government and Public Liberties in the New States*, Rhodes (seminar paper), 1958. For the most persuasive and comprehensive defence of democracy in India, see W. H. Morris-Jones, *Parliament in India* (London, 1957).

[2] The best short analysis is R. Heine-Geldern, *Conceptions of State and Kingship in Southeast Asia*, Cornell Univ. Data Paper no. 18 (Ithaca, N.Y., 1956). For India, see D. Mackenzie Brown, *The White Umbrella* (Berkeley, 1953), and 'Traditional Concepts of Indian Leadership' in Park and Tinker, op. cit., pp. 1–17.

bureaucratized. It is therefore not surprising that liberal demo
cracy has failed to maximize consensus. British 'guidec
democracy', even when injected in small doses, as in Britisl
India, invariably exposed the cleavages in deeply dividec
societies. But it could always avoid disaster by the undisputec
powers of colonial governors either to modify or put an end t
the system whenever occasion demanded. Seeing that th
nearer the Asian dependencies approached self-government th
more disunited they became, what justification could there b
for thinking that there was any inevitable connexion betwee
freedom, democracy and national unification?

The new states have lacked the ideologies and social realitie
with which to support the imported forms and mechanics o
liberal democracy. In most cases, it has never been more than
political façade. It has failed disastrously in Pakistan, Indonesi
and Nepal; as a working system, it has been periodically on th
brink of disaster in both Ceylon and Burma; in South Vietnam
Cambodia and Laos it is mere authoritarianism disguised by th
institutional veneer of democracy. Only India and the Philip
pines emerge from the testing experience of a decade of inde
pendence as stable political structures. Everywhere, the Wester
system has brought in its train purposeless faction and conflict
Majority systems of voting and majority rule have pointlessl
divided the élites, accentuating communalism, provincialism
and casteism. The Western democratic theory of a peacefu
competition for power, on the basis of a moderate tension be
tween contending political parties whose leaders are agreec
about the foundations of society, is as out of place in Asia as i
has been in France. Liberal democracy in Asia has resultec
either in dictatorial single-party systems which are virtually
denial of democracy or in unworkable multi-party system
which threaten a general paralysis in government. Almos
everywhere the stubborn anti-government mentality inheritec
from the colonial struggle has proliferated political partie
(often with identical programmes) whose leaders oppose simpl
for the sake of opposition. As a result of a purposeless factional
ism ranging from central to village level, there has been a lack o
political stability which has invariably impeded the imple
menting of urgently needed economic development programmes

VI

THE CASE AGAINST COMMUNISM[1]

Communism has proved to be even more of an exotic plant in this region than liberal democracy. Though the Communists' techniques have ranged from 'constitutionalism' to armed insurrection, they have so far been able to capture only one new state in this enormous region — North Vietnam. And there, as in North Korea, they had the advantage of an exceptionally good geographical position. As a further asset, they had the imaginative leadership of Ho Chi Minh.

Communism has been unsuccessful because, more often than not, it has stood in opposition to the basic forces of nationalism. If, at the transfer of power, the Communists had been prepared to free themselves from their subservience to Moscow and Peking and come to terms with what, for want of a better word, we might call 'Asian national socialism' they might well have carried everything before them. As ruthless Westernizers, the Communists had much in common in the colonial period with the present old-guard political leaders of Asia, particularly when they pursued the 'Rightist line' of alliance with bourgeois anti-imperialist nationalism. Moreover, Marxism attracted the uprooted intelligentsia because it offered a secular religion. Unlike liberal democracy, it seemed to have the logical consistency of a system. Though poles apart in its tenets from the integrated philosophic-religious systems of Asia, it resembled them in that it offered a comprehensive view of the world, providing alienated intellectuals with a complete explanation of their predicament. No other ideology so systematically repudiated everything against which the intellectuals were in revolt. On top of all this, has been the plausible argument that, in the economic field, Communism is the only ideology likely to deliver the goods. The demonstration effect of its material achievements in formerly economically backward countries like the Soviet Union and China has been profound. It is hard to

[1] For Communism, see J. H. Brimmell, *Communism in South-East Asia: A Political Analysis* (London, 1959); Frank N. Trager (ed.), *Marxism in Southeast Asia* (for Burma, Thailand, Indonesia and Vietnam), (Stanford, 1960); and G. D. Overstreet and M. Windmiller, *Communism in India* (Berkeley, 1959).

refute the argument that only the total mobilization of resources and unified central direction achieved under Communist planning can produce the economic 'take-off' and thus narrow the widening gulf between poverty-stricken Asian countries and Western affluent societies.

Yet despite these advantages, the Communists squandered their opportunities. Outside North Vietnam, where they acted with imagination, they have never really recovered from the crucial mistake they made at the transfer of power in falling foul of Asian nationalism. By their submissive adoption of Stalin's disastrous 'Leftist line' which entailed switching to uncompromising hostility to bourgeois nationalism, by concentrating on internal class struggle instead of anti-imperialism, above all, by the violent insurrectionary methods to which they resorted, the Communist parties were quickly condemned as Trojan horses by the nationalist leaders. They brought schism and conflict precisely at the moment when there was a widespread craving for national solidarity. And in those South-East Asian countries with influential Chinese minorities, the deep hostility of the indigenous peoples to a Chinese 'imperium in imperio' was reinforced wherever Communist parties were Chinese-led.

It might therefore be argued that unless the Communists can accept some new form of Asian revisionism 'or polycentrism' — Communism without outside strings attached and adapted in each case to a specific national environment — they are unlikely to make much headway against either Asian chauvinism or Asian neutralism. Maoism, which was once thought to be the form of flexible revisionism which would best enable the Communists to come to terms with nationalism in peasant countries, has not won the support which was at first anticipated. Nor have the Indian Communists' attempts to develop an 'Indian line' by a reassessment of Gandhism deceived very many Indians. Though there has undoubtedly been a marked receptivity to Communist ideas in certain parts of the region (Vietnam, Kerala, West Bengal, Malaya and Java) the real measure of the Communists' inability to come to terms with nationalism as a social and political force has been their striking failure, outside North Vietnam, to throw up a charismatic leader with a widespread popular appeal. So it might be argued they are old-fashioned Westernizers who have been unable in the new Asia to keep up with the times. The prisoners of imported Marxist dogma, their opportunism has always had to be practised within the straitjacket of a rigidly held ideology which restricts the notion of deviationism. They have thus lost the initiative to more eclectic Marxists who have managed to combine Marxism with nationalism.[1]

VII

THE QUEST FOR ASIAN POLITICAL IDEOLOGIES

Let us now look briefly at the eclectic ideologies on which some of the existing régimes are actually founded.

Nehruism or Indian Eclecticism[2]

India is the one new state where sophisticated political discussion flourishes, though there can of course be much dispute as to whether any original political ideas lie behind the smoke-screen of ideological controversy. The major -isms are undoubtedly Nehruism, Gandhism and Communism. All we propose to do is to say briefly what we think Nehruism is and why we think it has won acceptance as the dominant ideology, not overlooking the fact that there are many, including Nehru himself, who would deny that it amounts to an ideology at all.

Nehru wants a modernized, secular, democratic state resting on the pillars of parliamentary government, central planning, large-scale industrialization and the 'socialistic pattern of society'. In essence, Nehruism is an attempt to combine the government by discussion and rule of law of liberal democracy with Communist-style central planning and some aspects of the specifically Indian approach to politics of the Gandhians. It is, in effect, the politics of reconciliation, and expresses itself

[1] For the argument that Communist advance is likely to be limited to East Asia (i.e. China, Korea and Vietnam) because its cultures are basically more authoritarian than those of South-East Asia, see Richard Harris, *Independence and After* London, 1962, pp. 7–11.

[2] For Nehru's approach to politics, see M. N. Das, op. cit.; Michael Brecher, *Nehru: A Political Biography* (London, 1959), especially Ch. 20; and Tibor Mende, *Conversations with Mr. Nehru* (London, 1956).

T

particularly in neutralism, the mixed economy and the emerging pattern of Indian democracy. The present Indian experiment is based on the belief that radical modernization *can* be achieved without Communism and that such modernization need not be totally inconsistent with Gandhian ideals. India *can* have both more goods and more freedom. Secular Western-style socialism is not incompatible with *sarvodaya*; imported Western democracy is not out of line with indigenous Indian democracy. Single party-government and the centralization needed to bring about economic development are no tyranny and need not stand in the way of decentralization and the achievement of *panchayat Raj*. Steel plants and dams need not push out cottage industries. Gandhian techniques of constructive work in village India supplement the community projects programme. *Bhoodan* and government schemes for land reform may go hand in hand. The use of Hindi as the national language by no means excludes the use of any other languages. Even Communism, in respect of techniques like co-operative farming, may have something to be said for it, if only the Communists would not be so old-fashioned about class struggle. In a word, according to Nehruism, everything can be made compatible with everything else. Where there can be so much reconciliation, why take sides? Why think only in terms of conflicts and disharmonies?

Nehruism has been successful so far because of its eclecticism, because of its technique of reconciliation, of explaining away contradictions, of being all things to all men. For the average man it is all summed up in the political slogan of 'co-existence'. One must always concentrate on the points of agreement rather than the points of disagreement; one must search for the 'middle way'; things are never just all black and all white. It is worth considering the ideas that lie behind this approach to politics. They seem to be partly British, partly Indian in origin. Though one of the few examples of a successful intellectual in politics, Nehru is certainly neither a political philosopher nor an ideologist. By virtue largely of his British education, he is primarily an empiricist suspicious of all ideologies, refusing to cross his bridges until he gets to them. This approach to politics undoubtedly had its advantages in the colonial period when the Congress had to be built up into an all-embracing mass movement bringing into its fold the most diverse elements. As a political party, the Congress today still retains many of the characteristics of a national movement, with the consequent need of a leader capable of reconciling basic antagonisms.

Yet it might also be argued that Nehru's eclecticism is really founded on a specifically Indian mode of thought and that this is why his methods have been found acceptable. This is the doctrine of 'synthesis' — what might without offence be called the Indian sponge trick, the belief, common to the ruling élite, in the infinitely absorptive capacity of Hinduism. It is argued that what look like disharmonies, inconsistencies and contradictions to a Westerner can be made compatible with one another by an Indian. By a comprehensive mode of thought quite different from rigid Western analysis, opposing views are regarded as not mutually exclusive and as not ruling out an underlying agreement. Indeed, they can exist side by side without giving rise to conflict or the urge for a strictly logical solution. The doctrine of synthesis might be advanced as a plausible explanation of India's indigenous social system, its past history under the impact of the West and Nehru's modernizing programme. There is a strong incentive to argue that India has always been unique because it has always been a sponge capable of mopping up all alien intrusions and foreign borrowings and yet remaining as characteristically Indian as before. Some Indian intellectuals undoubtedly justify key political slogans like 'co-existence' in terms of the sponge or synthesis theory of Indian development. As Vice-President Radhakrishnan has put it — 'Why look at things in terms of this or that? Why not try to have both this *and* that?'[1]

It can, of course, be easily objected that these esoteric ideas are confined to a tiny intellectual élite within the Congress and that Nehru himself has never systematically expounded them. His all-India political image is so firmly planted amongst the Indian masses that it needs no support from a sophisticated official ideology, even if such an ideology could be expounded in popular terms. For all that, it is hard to deny that the 'this and that' philosophy is, at many points, a convincing explanation of Nehru's political method, that it does reflect an Indian

[1] Cited in Vera M. Dean, *New Patterns of Democracy in India* (Camb., Mass., 1959), p. 2.

style of thought, and that it might conceivably be accepted as an Indian tradition of political behaviour.

Nehruism seeks to explain away the contradictions and disharmonies within a transitional society. The neo-Gandhians seek to expose the contradictions within Nehruism. As their representative, we take Jayaprakash Narayan rather than the politically naïve Vinoba Bhave who recently argued in typically Indian fashion that Gandhism need not be incompatible with Communism. But there is also a difficulty over Narayan. A former Marxist leader of the Indian Socialists and, as such, once a Westernizer quite out of sympathy with Gandhian ideals, he is now committed to neo-Gandhism with the completeness with which he was formerly committed to Marxism. His philosophical anarchism is argued with a Western logic and dogmatism which seem to have a Marxist rather than a Gandhian origin.[1]

Narayan is uncompromising in his belief that India must choose between wanting more goods and wanting more freedom, since these two objectives of Nehruism are quite incompatible. He insists that Nehru's present obsession with rapid economic growth is resulting in an oppressive and tyrannical power structure which is inimical to all real freedom. India will be free only if she follows the Gandhian path and voluntarily limits her wants. There is little to choose between liberal democracy and Communism; each is totally destructive of social solidarity because of the senseless conflict and factionalism they engender. Narayan glorifies the allegedly simple and uncomplicated 'living democracy' of traditional village India — the face-to-face democracy he calls 'communitarian society'. He advocates extreme decentralization of both political and economic power, the substitution of indirect for direct elections, the abolition of all political parties and the delegation of power upwards from groups of *panchayats* to a purely agency centre with minimal functions.

There are two striking features about Narayan's Asian romanticism. First, it seems to be Gandhism with the religious element left out. The Gandhian notion of an oppressor state gradually withering away has clearly made an appeal to a man who was once a Marxist. But religion, which was so important

[1] Mr Narayan has expounded his views in his *Plea for Reconstruction of Indian Polity* (Bombay, 1959; privately circulated).

to Gandhi, seems to play no part in Narayan's ethics. Secondly, he seems to really believe that his anarchical ideas are capable of being applied in modern India. As he sees it, he has not written an essay in social and political philosophy. He has produced a blue-print for a programme of political action. The problem of power in politics is to be solved by ignoring it.

Though these social and political ideas may be dismissed as hopelessly utopian, they cannot be rejected as uninfluential in a country where government by discussion is fully accepted. They serve to expose the contradictions within Nehruism. Genuine political conflicts do exist in India — they are the substance of politics. They cannot be argued away always by a specious concept of 'co-existence'. By no sort of political conjuring can centralization be made to look like decentralization. And in an economically backward country like India the pursuit of political freedom is very likely in the long run to be incompatible with the pursuit of rapid economic growth. To say that India may have both is probably fallacious.

Sukarnoism or Indonesian Eclecticism[1]

The social and political fragmentation of Indonesia has made national consensus more than usually difficult to achieve. As elsewhere in the region, the new state has been plagued by an intense regionalism which has found a vent in a long series of autonomy movements and rebellions. Parliamentary government quickly foundered because of the multiplicity of political parties, the factions within the tiny élite and the consequent inability to secure a stable executive with the power to govern. There was an inevitable see-saw between the claims of parliamentary and presidential government. The sole political force making for national unity has been the flamboyant charismatic leadership of Sukarno. In view of the strength of the centrifugal forces threatening to disintegrate the state, it is not surprising that there should have been a desperate search for a unifying 'concept' or 'national ideology'.

Sukarno's reasons for establishing his *gotong-rojong* system of

[1] The material on which this section is based will be found in: G. McT. Kahin, *Nationalism and Revolution in Indonesia* (Ithaca, N.Y., 1952); G. McT. Kahin (ed.), *Major Governments of Asia* (Ithaca, N.Y., 1958), section by Kahin on Indonesia, especially pp. 529–30; and G. S. Maryanov, *Decentralisation in Indonesia as a Political Problem* (Ithaca, N.Y., 1958), Ch. 3.

'guided democracy' are given in his 'Concept of Government' message of 1957.[1] He maintained that Indonesia had met with 'all the excesses ensuing from the putting into effect of an imported idea, with all the excesses ensuing from the implementation of a democracy which is not in harmony with our personality'. Western democracy had utterly failed because of the disastrous 'idea of opposition'. Being quite alien to Indonesian thinking and behaviour, it had bred opposition for opposition's sake. What was therefore needed was a *gotong-rojong* (mutual aid) system which would put the emphasis on national unity and co-operation and thus enshrine indigenous Indonesian collectivist democracy. Sukarno has therefore virtually abolished the parliamentary system, put restrictions on the activities of some of the political parties and set up advisory national councils based on functional representation and allegedly representative of all shades of opinion.

Sukarno has thus put into effect political ideas which he has been unsystematically developing for the past twenty-five years. His national ideology might be summed up as an attempted synthesis of Marxism with Javanese pre-Islamic tradition. As early as the 1930's he was already advocating his own Indonesian brand of socialism which he called *Marhaenism* (i.e. 'Marhaen' — the people). An eclectic Marxism, this synthesis was described as 'socio-democracy', 'socio-nationalism' and 'socialism adapted to the Indonesian way of thinking'. It made use of the indigenous village concept of *gotong-rojong* or mutual aid. At the transfer of power, as a means of winning the support of both Islamic and Christian groups for his secular state, Sukarno added the *Pantja Sila* to his vocabulary of political slogans. These were the 'five principles' of nationalism, humanism, representative government, social justice and belief in God. But as Indonesia's political and economic problems piled up, Sukarno turned more and more to the idea of 'proletarian nationalism' as expressed in the *gotong-rojong* or mutual aid state. Behind all this manoeuvring was the conviction that nationalism, democracy and socialism needed to be expressed in Indonesian terms.

Sukarno identifies the image of the national self, the national

[1] *Ministry of Information* (Djakarta, 1957). See also Sukarno's long rambling Independence Day speech in *The Times of Indonesia*, 20 August, 1960.

profile, the tradition of behaviour, the political style — call it what we will — with the communitarian society of the old Javanese village. The whole apparatus of Western democracy — majority voting, majority rule, elections, political parties — is condemned because it allegedly crystallized differences and prevented the natural expression of the Indonesian genius for harmonious co-operation. It is argued that until it became faction-ridden under the impact of a socially atomizing Western individualism, the village was an organic community without tensions or friction. It reflected and achieved social harmony because votes were never taken in order to arrive at decisions. Agreement was reached by *mufakat* or the sense of the meeting. During the parliamentary period various attempts were made to achieve consensus within the divided Indonesian élite by the adoption of *mufakat* both in the cabinet and in other national central committees. This technique is now common practice under the new régime of 'guided democracy'.

The *gotong-rojong* state, whereby Sukarno hopes to achieve what he calls 'Socialism à la Indonesia' is defended as a specifically Indonesian system giving 'the purest reflection of the Indonesian soul'. As a political slogan it is widely known and features in all his speeches. The whole purpose of the new system is to try to evolve a political framework for the co-existence of competing groups. Sukarno generally identifies these groups as the Nationalists (i.e. PNI), the Muslims (i.e. the Muslim political parties) and the Communists. But to these should be added the army, the trade unions and other groups. The emphasis on 'co-existence' recalls the 'this and that' philosophy of Nehruism. And an equally respectable Asian origin might be found for it. As has been said, Sukarno's political thinking expresses:

> The syncretism which is a feature of the Indonesian and particularly the Javanese intellectual and religious tradition, the cast of thinking which emphasizes an ultimate mystical and aesthetic unity of things underlying what appear as material conflicts and logical incompatibilities.[1]

Sukarno's position at present seems to depend more on the army than on any other group. But it has not escaped the

[1] Herbert Feith, 'Indonesia' in G. McT. Kahin (ed.), *Governments and Politics of Southeast Asia* (Ithaca, N.Y., 1959), p. 192.

notice of the Communist leaders, who are now included in both the Supreme Advisory Council and the National Planning Council that the concept of *gotong-rojong* could be interpreted as coming near to the Maoist theory of 'coalition government'. If they are prepared to face squarely the consequences of revisionism, the Indonesian Communists might conceivably have an opportunity of riding to power on an indigenous political ideology.

Buddhist Marxism or Burmese Eclecticism[1]

Eclecticism is also the outstanding feature of the social and political thought of the present Burmese leaders. Burma today has been described as a 'nation built upon a combination of Burmese national identity, Buddhist philosophy, British political organization and Socialist economic theories — both Marxist and non-Marxist'. Internal and external pressures have led the Burmese leaders increasingly towards an attempted reconciliation of Marxism with Buddhism. Former doctrinaire Marxists like Ba Swe and Nu, who carried through the Burmese revolution as radical Westernizers, have been searching, by way of such slogans as *pyidawtha*, for Burmese forms of social and political democracy.

The very vagueness of Buddhism as a system of thought (in contrast to Islam, for example) encourages the kind of mental gymnastics common in the Buddhist countries of South-East Asia today. Ba Swe, for example, has maintained that Buddhism and Marxism are not incompatible. Indeed, they 'are the same in concept'. The argument goes like this:

> In the beginning I was a Buddhist only by tradition. The more I study Marxism, however, the more I feel convinced in Buddhism. Thus I have become a true disciple of the Lord Buddha by conviction, and my faith in Buddhism has grown all the more. I now believe that for any man who has deeply studied Buddhism, and correctly perceived its tenets, there should be no obstacle to becoming a Marxist.[2]

[1] For Burma, see Hugh Tinker, *The Union of Burma* (London, 1957); J. S. Thomson, 'Marxism in Burma', in Trager, op. cit., pp. 14–57; Saul Rose, *Socialism in Southern Asia* (London, 1959), Ch. 7. This section was, of course, written before General Ne Win's army *coup* of March, 1962.

[2] Cited in Trager, op. cit., p. 47.

U Nu's rediscovery of Buddhism is also well known. His religion now seems to dominate his political life. No doubt much of this eclecticism stems from a desire of the leaders to get their values straight in the new Asia. But a cynical Western observer might say that the old-guard Burmese leaders have merely realized that in terms of mass politics the collection of the peasant vote demands that good Marxists should also seem to the monks (who wield much influence locally) to be good Buddhists as well. Nobody probably is much deceived. Certainly not the military élite whose brief and successful tenure of office suggested that both efficient government and popular support by no means demanded a parade of Buddhist values.

Personalism or Vietnamese Eclecticism

This élitist ideology is of some interest because it is founded on the eclectic French doctrine of Personalism which condemns both liberal democracy and Communism.[1]

The Western impact on the Far East, particularly as reflected by the effort of a decaying Confucianism to come to terms with Christianity, resulted for a century or more in the proliferation of syncretic religions and bizarre cults. In China they ranged from the doctrine of the T'ai P'ings to Chiang Kai-shek's New Life Movement, and in Vietnam from Hoa-Haoism to Cao-Daism. With the triumph of Communism in both China and North Vietnam, the problem of a disintegrating Confucianism seems to have been settled; an adequate alternative belief system has been found both by scholars and peasants. Communist dictatorship sits neatly on traditional authoritarianism; the scholars have willingly become 'red mandarins'.[2]

This is the remorseless tide of events against which a Vietnamese Catholic intellectual, President Ngo Dinh Diem, is battling in South Vietnam. He wishes to make legitimate, by a set of anti-Communist values, a régime the very survival of which has often been called 'a miracle'. The dilemma is that, President Diem being what he is and South Vietnam being what it is, the range of choice for such a national ideology is

[1] The attempt to make Personalism the national ideology is fully discussed by John C. Donnell, 'National Renovation Campaigns in Vietnam', *Pacific Affairs*, March 1959, pp. 73–88.

[2] The central theme of C. P. Fitzgerald's *Revolution in China*, London, 1952.

very narrow. A revived Confucianism has little to offer; it has proved a broken reed in the past. On the other hand, though President Diem has sought to make his régime respectable in the eyes of his American friends by the promulgation of a constitution and by the holding of elections, he has little confidence in liberal democracy. He is a firm believer in 'guided democracy'. Faced by such a quandary he has imported, and largely perverted for local consumption, the French Catholic doctrine of Personalism. It was presumably thought that this doctrine, which condemns both individualism and totalitarian collectivism, might have its uses as a national ideology for an anti-Communist authoritarian régime. And to give an Asian sugar icing to the new creed, a little revived Confucianism has been added.

Personalism, as expounded by the French Catholic writer, Emmanuel Mounier might be described as a form of Christian or 'humanistic' socialism postulated as an alternative to the major Western ideologies.[1] It emphasizes the extent to which the essential dignity, integrity and personality of man has been shattered by the warring ideologies of liberalism, Fascism and Communism. As a body of thought, it is both unsystematic and eclectic and in some respects comes near to Christian existentialism. It is not surprising that it should have appealed to Vietnamese Catholic intellectuals whose value system was in ruins after the Indo-China war. Their predicament was not unlike that of European intellectuals after the concentration camp holocaust.

The doctrine of Personalism is referred to in the preamble of the constitution,[1] and under the influence of the President's brother, Ngo Dinh Nhu, efforts have been made to win adherents amongst the bureaucracy. It is pointed out that because of its humanistic philosophy and its condemnation of extremist solutions of the 'Right' or the 'Left', Personalism fits in well with the best ethical traditions of Confucianism. The new ideology seems to have been used to condemn 'degenerate' Marxism,

[1] See Candide Moix, *La Pensée d'Emmanuel Mounier* (Paris, 1960) — 'le personnalisme était né pour combattre non seulement le désordre capitaliste et bourgeois mais aussi les monstres totalitaires' (p. 158).

[2] 'Ayant foi en la valeur transcendante dans la personne humaine dont le développement libre, harmonieux et complet sur le plan individuel comme sur le plan communautaire doit être l'objectif de toute activité étatique. . . .'

Western materialism, democracy by the counting of heads, the decay of the family, corruption and crime. It has been used to exalt national solidarity, political obedience, family cohesion, personal discipline and austerity. The emphasis on family cohesion is not without its irony in view of the way in which the President and his four brothers seem to have successfully institutionalized their own kinship solidarity.

If this peculiar ideology has a parallel in this part of the world it is probably Chiang Kai-shek's New Life Movement which was an attempted synthesis of a revived Confucianism with Methodism. And as an effort to manufacture an anti-Communist set of values for a people whose traditional value system seems to have disintegrated, Diem's Personalism seems likely to be about as unsuccessful as the New Life Movement. As an ideology, it has been restricted to a tiny French-educated Catholic élite. It is difficult to see how such an imported and esoteric cult can have any mass appeal.

Pakistani Pragmatism: The Ending of Ideologies?

Pakistan is the last on our list because it may be a possible pointer to what will happen if the military élites in South and South-East Asia win political power. The present military régime in Pakistan has set up 'basic democracy' without bothering so far about an ideology. Revolution has been justified by efficiency, the soldier's criterion of good government.

There was an obvious reason why President Ayoub Khan could not invoke the concept of Islamic democracy — it had become completely discredited by its indelible association with the parliamentary system. One of the first steps taken by the military government after the 1958 *coup* was to change the name of the state from 'The *Islamic* Republic of Pakistan' to 'The Republic of Pakistan'. In his famous broadcast indicting the corrupt and chaotic parliamentary régime, Ayoub Khan pointed out that chronic 'democratic' misgovernment and the so-called 'rule of law' had been justified 'in the sacred name of Islam'. The alleged synthesis of liberal and Islamic democracy had been brought into contempt by factionalism run mad, and 'in the process, all ideals and high sense of values inherent in our religion and culture have been destroyed'.[1]

[1] Mushtaq Ahmad, *Government and Politics in Pakistan* (Karachi, 1959), pp. 236–9.

In a word, since the Islamic ideology had been invoked by the corrupt parliamentarians in order to justify a travesty of democracy, it was not feasible to destroy their régime by an appeal to a revised Islamic ideology. Indeed, as was well known, the only Islamic alternative to the Islamic modernizers' democratic state was the obscurantist theocratic state of *ulama* like Maulana Maududi.[1]

The present military régime, which in its early days was undoubtedly very popular (it seems to be less so now), is thus left with the unsolved problem of what to do about an Islamic ideology in a Muslim state. Can such an ideology be dispensed with? Having separated from India on the score of religion, the two nation-theory would still seem to demand that the Pakistanis, deeply divided as they are by acute provincialism, should continue to try to convince themselves that the good life can be lived only in some sort of Islamic state. But an anglicized army officer régime like Ayoub Khan's has shown little disposition to lean on Islam. Indeed, the present system of 'basic democracy' has been described as 'rather like the British *Raj* in its most authoritarian days before constitutions were thought of'.[2] When tradition is invoked, colonial rather than Asian tradition seems to be meant. When the President says that a governmental system must be rooted in traditions 'of the type that people can understand' he seems to mean the past British system of colonial government. Thus his restriction of political participation to 'basic democracy' at village level is defended not by reference to traditional Asian systems but by reference to British 'guided democracy' at the village level in undivided India.

Can the leaders of a new state in anti-colonial Asia rely for long on colonial tradition in this way? It is just possible all the while the army regards itself as a political caretaker engaged on a mopping-up operation. This phase, however, seems to be passing; unlike General Ne Win in Burma, President Ayoub Khan has shown little disposition to hand power back to the politicians. But Pakistan being what it is — a state built on a

---

[1] For Maududi's views, see Khalid B. Sayeed, 'The Jama'at-i-Islami Movement in Pakistan', *Pacific Affairs*, March 1957, pp. 59–68.

[2] Guy Wint, 'The 1958 Revolution in Pakistan' in Raghavan Iyer (ed.), *St. Antony's Papers Number 8, South Asian Affairs, No 1* (London, 1960), p. 77.

religion — a recrudescence of the Islamic state controversy seems unavoidable in the long run. It is also just possible that the compulsions of an economically backward society may, in the end, result in the present moderate régime being pushed out by a revolutionary young officers' movement with a radical modernizing ideology of the Nasser type.

VIII

CONCLUSIONS

Though we have deliberately limited ourselves to only five new states of the region, it is hard to sum up owing to the inevitable diversities. Our mountain, after all, may have given birth to only a mouse. But a few conclusions must be hazarded.

We might approach the first conclusion by way of a question. Some years ago Professor Oakeshott published a book which brought together for the convenience of the student of Western social and political ideas the classic statements on Representative Democracy, Communism, Fascism, National Socialism and Catholicism.[1] Would it be worth while to try and compile today a similar volume on 'The Social and Political Doctrines of Contemporary South and South-East Asia'? Such an anthology would presumably need to be divided into two parts — 'Western Social and Political Ideas which have influenced Asians' and 'Asian Social and Political Ideas'. But even if we could agree on whom we would need to select from Oakeshott apart from Mill, Marx and Lenin, and whom we would need to add, apart from Laski (who, after all, is regarded by some Asians as a great political thinker), where would we look for what we want from Asia? What would we have, apart from the speeches and writings of a few leaders like Gandhi, Nehru, Narayan and Sukarno? Presumably, in the case of India, we might be able to trace a definite continuity in political ideas by including representative examples of ancient Hindu political thought. But in most of the South-East Asian countries we would draw a complete blank.

It is a common Western assumption that Asian political ideas

[1] *The Social and Political Doctrines of Contemporary Europe* (London, 1939).

are wholly derivative from the West. We are told by Professor Brogan that 'Nothing moves today, no political system, no system of technology, of law, of science, that is not European or American in origin'.[1] Mr Plamenatz assures us that 'where political and other social institutions are systematically discussed, they are discussed in terms of concepts invented in Europe'.[2] A distinguished Indian historian seems to be equally sceptical. According to K. M. Panikkar, even the Indians have made little or no contribution to social and political thought: 'No political leader among us has tried to formulate any theory of social order, inquire into the principles on which we have reared our political institutions, examine the validity of the many assumptions of our public life.'[3] There are many who would dispute such views especially in respect of India. The Gandhian philosophy of non-violence has a claim to be regarded as an original Asian ideology and there are Westerners (as well as Africans) prepared to accept it as a practical social and political philosophy capable of resolving conflicts. (Whether Gandhism could be successfully exported is another matter.) But what is difficult to deny is the obvious poverty of most Asian political thinking.

Yet whatever views we may hold, we should make sure that they are consistent with one another. That is to say, we should not taunt Asians with a poverty of political ideas and at the same time, as 'scientific' political scientists, disparage Asian political speculation as such. It is tempting to regard the social and political conflicts in the new states as the kind likely to foster attempts at original social and political thought. It was under rather similar conditions of rapid social change that the classical European political thought of the Enlightenment was produced. But now that Western affluent societies have for the time being resolved their own social and political conflicts, it is

[1] *The Price of Revolution* (London, 1951), p. 153. See also Sir Llewellyn Woodward's caustic comment in 'Were Our Sacrifices in Vain?', *Listener*, 6 September, 1956 — 'The transformation of Asia and Africa has been due to western initiative, invention and example. The peoples concerned have not contributed in the last two centuries one single political idea of any value to what we rightly call western civilisation. They have acquired the whole external apparatus of modern societies from the west, and though they refuse now to admit the fact, they have acquired it fairly cheaply'.

[2] op. cit., p. 38.

[3] *India Quarterly*, July–September 1956.

also tempting to dismiss all political speculation as either 'unscientific' or 'outmoded'.

What we can say is that in the parts of Asia we have dealt with there has been a significant trend towards political eclecticism on the part of the national leadership, and that such eclecticism seems to be in line with the national interest. In the colonial period, the need for all-embracing mass movements resulted in the emergence of eclectic Westernizers who sought to synthesize the dominant Western ideologies of liberal democracy and Marxism (India was unique because this eclecticism was accompanied by, but never successfully fused with, an indigenous (i.e. Gandhian) ideology). It would be a great mistake to emphasize that this widespread eclecticism within a Western tradition of thought reflected a poverty of Asian political ideas. In practice, eclecticism paid off. It was, in effect, the recipe for success in the freedom struggles. Since independence, all the political pressures, both internal and external — propaganda from the two world camps aimed at committing the new states to one side or the other, disenchantment with the actual working of liberal democracy, ambivalence towards Communism — have accentuated the eclecticism of the Asian leaders. Neutralism in foreign affairs is simply one form of expression of a general trend towards an ideological non-alignment or eclecticism in Asian political thinking as a whole. But it is now felt that Asian ingredients ought to be added to the mixture and that the Western content should be examined with much more discrimination than before.

Thus we get portmanteau ideologies like Sukarno's Javanese Marxism, Pakistani Islamic democracy, Vietnamese Personalism and Burmese Buddhist-Marxism. There is the Asian conviction that Asians are free to pick and choose from both a Western and Asian heritage. Though much of this eclecticism is no doubt confused and unsystematic in expression, it certainly reflects an Asian response to the central political predicament — how to come to terms, either wholly or in part, with the two dominant, intrusive Western ideologies of liberal democracy and Communism. The leaders recognize that political stability will be impossible to achieve without social harmony. And social harmony will be elusive unless they can somehow square what they have been obliged to borrow from the West with what they think is taught by their own idealized tradition. Thus, political eclecticism takes the form of an urge towards a national type of socialism based on humanistic, non-class-struggle values and a benevolent and active *étatisme*. National socialism is considered essential in the interests both of economic growth and the preservation of national independence. Social and political integration has been sought in romantic myth-making about indigenous village government, in a growing pre-ference for organic (i.e. communitarian) rather than mechanistic theories of the state, and in a reinterpretation of the Asian religions which puts the emphasis on newly discovered dynamic aspects of their ethical systems.

In this political re-thinking it is often difficult to disentangle what is Western from what is Asian. This is evident in Asian romanticism's re-discovery of the Asian village. Since indigenous village institutions disappeared long ago, the Asian theorist can invest them with whatever character best suits his type of argu-ment. Thus, when the village is romantically idealized by Sukarno and Narayan in an effort to construct organic theories about 'communitarian society', the argument either explicitly or implicitly rests on the acceptance of Western social and political theories critical of social atomization brought about by individualism in the West.

If one fairly definite conclusion can be drawn from the material here presented, it is that only India, so far, has suc-ceeded in supporting Western ideas and institutions with a serviceable and genuine indigenous tradition of behaviour. This was perhaps to be expected of the one country in the region with a sophisticated social and political thought of its own. The operative ideal behind India's politics of reconciliation is the concept of 'co-existence', a concept deeply embedded in Hinduism and obviously very useful to a new state faced by all the bewildering disharmonies and contradictions of a transi-tional society.

With regard to Pakistan, Indonesia, Burma and South Vietnam, whether we call them 'guided democracies' or 'modernizing oligarchies', most of their élites still suffer from cultural schizophrenia. These people have found it more diffi-cult than the Indians to reconcile their conflicting ideals. The Pakistanis, like Muslims everywhere, have felt they have a serviceable theory of their own in the ideal of the Islamic state. But they have suffered from the frustration of not being able to translate it into modern political terms. The Indonesians, to meet their particular needs, are evolving an eclectic ideology which might pave the way either for a Communist system or for some sort of personal rule of the Latin American type. Much of Sukarno's political thinking, though it now undoubtedly contains an indigenous element in the *gotong-rojong* concept, has been a mere rag-bag of borrowed political jargon. The *Pantja Sila*, for example, are a set of imported political slogans comparable to the 'principles' of opportunist Latin American ideologies like Perón's *justicialismo*. Vietnamese Personalism seems to be much the same kind of borrowed ideology.

It is possible that as time goes on, the leaders and élites of this region, sandwiched as they are between the two power blocs, and striving as they are to give their nationalism a definite social and economic content, will need to resort more and more to peculiar eclectic ideologies of the Latin American type. The difficulty is that, as the élites are educated and the politically conscious masses are largely illiterate, the resulting ideologies may be mere political tools for legitimizing a type of élite government which has deep historical roots throughout this region.

Perhaps we should end with three questions rather than with a conclusion. Do the special problems of new states make it inevitable that their political ideologies should be more than usually eclectic? How eclectic can these ideologies become without looking like mere rag-bags of specious imported political slogans? Are the various ideologies which have been examined here likely to solve the intractable problem of political legitimacy in transitional societies?

Raghavan Iyer

We could broadly take seven different heads under which we could look at political ideas in the region. First of all, there are the justifications of authority by a ruling class — the problem for any élite-identified as the power-holding class in a country of converting power into authority, of securing for its position some kind of political

u

legitimacy or moral assent, a consensus of recognition and approval. In the attempt to do this it is only natural that leaders in power will coin concepts or produce arguments which would be different in these countries from deceptively similar phrases or arguments used by politicians trying to justify their own power in more settled societies where everything is not being questioned at the same time, where there already exists a universe of shared values in the context of which disagreements about priorities and conflicts of interest arise. In other words, we are not here dealing with countries that have already had, as it were, a Renaissance and then a Reformation and then an Industrial Revolution. We are instead faced with societies which have been disrupted socially and economically, partly by colonialism, partly by the attempt to bring together diverse and heterogeneous societies into new and highly centralized nation-states. We have also to consider the tremendous fermentation of thought and cultural disturbance that resulted under alien rule from the impact of the West. It is against this background that we must consider even such nebulous concepts as Sukarno's 'guided democracy' rather than simply view them as opportunistic and meaningless slogans. The increasing distrust of 'representation theory' in modern democracy and the concern with consensus and participation are only natural in the conditions of the countries in the region.

Secondly, we have the political phraseology used to refer to the social goals held out by rulers, rivals, rebels, to justify or condemn particular policies and attitudes to tradition and development. In this category we have, for example, Khmer socialism and Nehru's 'socialistic pattern of society'.

Thirdly, we have the familiar ideological labels for programmes, not actual attempts to formulate social goals under certain broad shibboleths but rather the mere attempt to find a packaged ideological label which could cover a whole programme — this is socialist, this is Marxist, or something else. This category does not create any special problem as it is not really different from what happens in the West.

Fourthly, we have Asian modifications of Western political ideas — Marxism modified by Buddhism, Islamic democracy, Indian socialism as recently expounded by Dr Sampurnanand, and so on. In using such ideological labels as are familiar in the West, people in Asia realize that they are not sufficient to distinguish them from each other or to distinguish them sharply from their Western counterparts and therefore the temptation is strong to introduce some kind of adjective or some kind of modifying phrase which may only represent the beginning of a recognition that more and major modifications would be needed. Our criterion for distinguishing a genuine from a spurious ideology must be the integrity of the national leader in his search for consensus, his loyalty either to traditional culture or to his revolutionary past as well as his actual success in securing mass assent. We must steer clear of the two extremes of outright cynicism and easy-going Whiggery.

Then fifthly we have, or could have, new political theories and systems, and here even the one example we can think of in the region does not exactly come within the period we are considering. Gandhi is the only one in this region who has attempted, not consciously perhaps, to evolve a systematic political theory which, if properly studied and understood, would amount to a new and different way of looking at the basic problems and conflicts of politics, comparable in this sense to the attempt of traditional systematic thinkers, especially daring and dogmatic thinkers like Hobbes or Marx or Hegel. On the other hand those modifications referred to under the fourth category would really represent what Carnell calls eclecticism, the same kinds of reconciling formulae which we find in Aquinas and Locke who are intellectually perhaps less interesting than the extremist thinkers but were nonetheless even more influential. Of course, there is no reason to suppose that there would appear in this region anybody like Aquinas or Locke, but we can see that some of the attempts made to reconcile different political ideas do point in this direction and they would naturally be on a very different level from the attempt to produce a daring alternative theory, for which we have no example yet except the little understood, little studied, much ignored example of Gandhi. If he is not yet taken seriously as a political thinker even in India, it is not surprising that his ideas have not made the impact that we might expect them to have made on the rest of this region. He himself was quite convinced that even if there were a retreat from his thinking after his departure, eventually his own country would return to many of his ideas. This has yet to be seen but we cannot rule it out.

Sixthly, we have the revival of traditional political conceptions like *dharma*, *ijma*, *pyidawtha*, and so on. In all such cases we find certain traditional words being used without explicit redefinition, and yet clearly they are not being used in exactly the same way in which they were used at one time. The most significant example of this that I can think of is the use to which the leader of the Swatantra Party in India is putting the old notion of *dharma* in his attempt to challenge the secular mythology and the dogmatism that he thinks is implicit in Nehruism. His is really an attempt to challenge what appears to him to be a kind of borrowed authoritarianism implicit in Indian planning in terms of traditional notions of natural law.

Then lastly, we have to consider the question whether in this region some kind of different analysis of basic political notions like authority, equality, law, opposition, freedom, democracy and so on is forthcoming. We are familiar with the doubts that politicians in this region have about the very notions of parliamentary opposition, negative liberty and representative democracy. But here again, we cannot rule out the possibility of an original critique of Western concepts in terms of traditional Asian thought, especially if the imported political institutions are found to be unworkable and unsuitable.

On the whole, in considering the political ideas of these regions we would do better to approach them in terms of Bentham and Mill than in terms of Hobbes and Locke, and even more in terms of Saint-Simon and Marx, Proudhon and Godwin and Bakunin, but above all in terms of Plato, Rousseau and Burke. Rousseau's concept of civil religion is particularly very relevant to an understanding of the political dilemmas facing these countries. In the search for consensus and the expression of the general will it is important to the state, Rousseau argued, that each citizen should have a religion which makes him love his duty; but the dogmas of religion are important neither to the state nor its members except in so far as they have a bearing on morals. As the developing states in South and South-East Asia have to exact sacrifices from people which cannot be justified simply in terms of their immediate self-interest, it is only natural that politicians should indulge in myth-making and idealize either their national past or liberal democracy or state socialism in the present. Political myths fulfil a necessary function not merely in a period of continuing decadence but also in a period of rapid development. The dialogues that took place in the nineteenth century about tradition and modernization under alien rule have been extended and not ended with the attainment of independence and may be expected to take new and subtle forms in the foreseeable future.

O. D. Corpuz

In the Philippines the absence of the Asian ideology appears to be very marked. For instance, for roughly the last sixty years now, the lawyers and the courts have dealt with cases in terms primarily of American jurisprudence, although, like those of their American counterparts, their decisions and briefs are occasionally adorned with a quotation from Locke or Rousseau. Now, the question is why they look at Filipino cases, Filipino situations, in terms of Western legal and juristic concepts. The answer, it seems, is in the nature of the problems that go before them — problems involving corporations, the bill of rights, and the powers of the state, etc. — and these are distinctly Western-type problems. In short, therefore, we have not merely an importation of Western vocabulary in Asian minds, but also an importation of Western problems into Asian society. Now, we often hear of the alienated intellectual in Asia; I assume that that means there is something from which he has been alienated. We likewise hear of Westernized leaders — that would suggest also that there are non-Westernized leaders. This implies, on a broader level of conceptualization, that countries like the Philippines comprise two social or cultural sectors: one which is Westernized, West-oriented, and another that is essentially indigenous. Quite naturally, Western political thinking, and Western modes of thought in general, have proved to be very appropriate and useful in the Western sector. Moreover, since it is in this sector that there is a great deal of social change relative to the rest of the community, it is also here that ideological thinking is most articulate; ideology in this regard I take to be a process of putting historical events into an intellectual order or structure. On the other hand, there is not so much of this ideological thinking with respect to the non-Westernized sector, which is, after all, not only stable, but is also familiar and needing no explanation to the Asian mind. This might suggest why Western ideology appears to be prominent in Asia today, although it does not suggest that there is no thinking along Asian — i.e. non-Western — lines.

Wang Gung-wu

So far the optimism about the possibility of originality in political thought in Asia, particularly South Asia, seems to have come from people who have thought about traditional values and traditional political institutions before independence. The examples of Iqbal, Aurobindo, even Ram Mohan Roy, have come from a time when the ruling class was still the British, whom they wanted to resist by contrasting their way of life with the ruling political system. But in the situation where the people are independent, new leaders have taken power and there is no longer the necessity to build up resistance against the Western colonial rulers. It is now possible for them to use methods proved effective by the Western rulers for their own purposes. There is no longer disgrace or shame attached to these methods as there was once, and there is no desire to go back to older and probably less efficient ways. They were certainly proven less efficient by the fact that they were unable to produce viable states to stand against Western imperialism in the first place. I think this awareness, this realization that there is a more effective way of controlling the people, a more effective way of government, has influenced the leaders to a far deeper extent than we or they themselves are prepared to admit.

The positive side to resistance against colonialism — the idea of nationalism — is a Western idea and it is probably one of the most dynamic in Asia. Even Communism cannot compare with its emotional impact and this is something of which we have not yet seen the end. The penetration of this simple idea of nationalism will produce in time very important consequences at all levels of ideas. Whatever the romantic idealism of the present leaders in their backward-looking attitude, they are still seeking ways and means to give a local colour to what is fundamentally a Western concept, and there is no escaping this. We have borrowed without hesitation all other forms of Western organization — industrial, commercial, economic as well as scientific and technological — which are needed to gain for the people the material benefits which nationalism and anti-colonialism had promised them. To deliver the goods it was necessary to persist with at least the scientific and economic borrowing, and I cannot see how, if the leaders persist in trying to deliver the goods on those lines, they can avoid continuing with the political framework which they have already established.

I think originality is not to be laughed out of court — certainly we can expect it — but that originality should not be associated with the kind shown by Iqbal and Aurobindo who were thinking in a completely different era, a different framework. The modern state has already been set up, the institutions are already there, and the ideas will necessarily be derived from institutions long effective in the country and I think they will remain effective for quite long in most of the countries of South and South-East Asia. The originality which may come from political thinkers will still remain in the Western stream of political thinking, whether they like it or not. The fact is, they are responsible for a Western kind of state and they are dealing with Western-type problems which have been created because of the whole process of modernization. All this is experiment and trial, and will be proven one way or the other in time. If it proves right, success makes it no longer spurious, but legitimate. All kinds of experiments will be made but all of them will be made within the Western framework. If we are to be original in Asia I think we will still be taking over, as it were, from where you left off; and if we make any original contributions we will be taking off from there, either along Communist lines or liberal democratic lines or perhaps some new line, but it will still be with the same conceptual framework.

W. H. Morris-Jones

I am not very happy about the view that we must not expect to find novel political ideas in Asia simply because there are no novel problems there. It has been said that Asian politics is still politics and that as Asia imports Western political problems — everything from public sector planning to judicial interpretation of constitutional documents — she is bound to import Western ideas too. But problems undergo change through export, and so do ideas. Perhaps we are in danger of overlooking some of the significant shifts of emphasis which have taken place in Asian thinking about politics. These changes seem unobtrusive because the terms and concepts are mostly familiar Western ones but the manner in which they are used is more novel than imitative.

Consider for instance the stress which Indian thinking about democracy places on the notions of participation, consensus and 'purity' — old ideas but given new weight and place. Only time can test the viability of the new ideological blends, but their eclecticism is perhaps not spurious if it corresponds to experience.

In part these new Asian blends derive from distinctive experience of the recent past. Evidently the idea of participation has an importance because the fact of political participation was important in the national movement. This seems a valid basis. In part, novelty is an expression of a sense of lacking. The stress on consensus — though this too owes much to unity in the nationalist movement — is a reflection of the fact that it is a serious political problem to get agreement and unity in a very heterogeneous society. Was it not Raymond Aron who said that the problem in so many of these countries is not to get an opposition but first to get a government, to get a coherent majority?

A third source of novelty in political ideas is that political leaders have to be able to talk about politics in ways which make sense to their humble electorates. This involves linking politics to those ethical ideas which are held in the traditional society — as Gandhi did so well. This explains the important role in India of the notion of purity as a standard for judging politicians.

Yet another source of novelty is the mere feeling that it is important to try to be different — to think about politics not in an imitative way but as an Asian or as an Indian. Even this is not wholly disreputable. If Indian intellectuals can contrive to speak about India's Western-style politics in Indian accents, they may be helping to make the new institutions take root — by making them understandable and acceptable to the people.

Along these lines one can distinguish spurious from valid eclecticism. Even eclecticism can be valid if it comes out of experience, felt needs and social realities; it will then do its job of making politics more understandable and sophisticated. I think that the 'eclecticism' theme can in any case be overdone: is it really so peculiar to new states or is it not a feature of a political thinking anywhere except at the level of the systematic philosopher?

Chapter fifteen

POLITICAL INSTITUTIONS

---

by Saul Rose

I

WESTERN DERIVATION

ALMOST every state in the region was, until recently, a Western dependency. Each newly independent country required a constitution and tended to refer to the former imperial power as the model with which it was most familiar. Thailand was one of the exceptions but Western influence was evident there too: the right of interpellation for example was taken from France, and Marshal Sarit for his *coup* in 1958 made acknowledgement to General de Gaulle. Nepal also was an exception, but the short-lived constitution of 1959 was drafted with Western advice. In other countries the constitutional system of the erstwhile imperial power was adopted with some modifications. Those formerly under British sway opted for cabinet government substituting in one case an elected ruler, in others a president, for the hereditary monarch. The Philippines adopted substantially the American model. Cambodia and Laos took their constitutions largely from France, putting their monarchs in place of the President. South Vietnam departed from the norm, as its presidential system resembled more the American than the French constitution; but some features — for example, the Economic Council — are clearly of French origin. Nor was the provisional Indonesian constitution of 1950 a legacy of empire, although the Indonesians borrowed more than they would perhaps care to admit from the Dutch: for example, the institution

of cabinet *formateurs*, not contained in the 1945 constitution t
which Indonesia has now reverted.

INDIGENOUS INSTITUTIONS

The most common feature retained from pre-existing insti
tutions was the monarchy. Its survival was a mark of tradi
tionalism which was reflected in other facets, such as the roya
household, Privy Council, and provisions to regulate the succes
sion to the throne which were incorporated in the constitution
of Cambodia, Laos, Nepal and, formerly, Thailand. Similarly
the Burmese constitution for a time upheld the rights of chief
in the Shan and Kayah states. Other survivals can be found
though not in plenty: for example, a reference to *panchayats* in
the Indian constitution.

INNOVATIONS

The Malayan constitution broke fresh ground by retaining
the Sultans and providing for the election of one of them by hi
peers as Supreme Ruler for a term of five years. Another novelty
was the Cambodian institution of a National Congress, held two
or three times a year, where the Government could be interro
gated directly by the people; but this device of government wa
not included in the constitution. The institutions of 'basi
democracy' in Pakistan have an air of innovation but hark bacl
to the British *Raj*.

On the whole the amount of innovation to be seen in the
constitutions of the new Asian states was relatively small; bu
this was not surprising since new departures in political struc
ture are generally infrequent. More remarkable was the limitec
number of indigenous institutions that were retained, at leas
formally on the national level, and the heavy dependence of the
new states upon the examples of countries from which they hac
recently been emancipated.

II

PRINCIPLES

To Western models of institutions there was added the influence of Western attitudes and outlook, notably the whole complex of ideas about democracy, rights and duties of the citizen, the role of the state in economic and social matters, and, to a lesser degree, relations between church and state.

'DEMOCRACY'[1]

As the independence movements had based their claims upon the principles of self-determination and self-government, nearly all the new states expressed in their constitutions their adherence to democracy. The exception this time was not Thailand, for the constitution of that country before it was suspended in 1958 specified the duty of 'preserving the form of democratic government'. It was the constitution of Cambodia, and more recently of Nepal, that refrained from following the democratic bandwagon. Whereas all the other constitutions more or less explicitly stated that sovereignty was vested in the people, the Cambodian constitution only went as far as declaring that the law was the expression of the national will, and reserved sovereignty to the monarch. In both Cambodia and Nepal the constitution was a gift bestowed by the favour of the king and did not emanate from the people.

That democracy in Indonesia is 'guided' and in Pakistan 'basic' illustrates its power of attraction. The same label is attached to a very different article. The lip-service paid to it

[1] It would hardly be necessary to insist on the distinction between the adoption of Western institutions and the establishment of a democratic system of government if they were not often confused. The blurring of this simple distinction between form and content is partly due to the vocabulary of the cold war. Non-Communist countries are described as the 'free world' and there is a tendency to identify 'free' with 'democratic' as reflected in the Manila Treaty of 1954. The Treaty declared the desire of the participants 'to uphold the principles of democracy' and their undertaking 'to strengthen their free institutions': yet in Thailand at the time of its adherence to the Treaty political parties were banned, as they were subsequently in Pakistan.

arises partly from the notion that it is the hall-mark of every modern civilized state and partly from the fact that the claims of the independence movements were based upon it. The two countries which did not make obeisance to democracy were among those in which there was scarcely any independence movement.

RIGHTS AND DUTIES OF CITIZENS

Adherence to democracy was usually accompanied by a declaration of rights, which was also clearly of Western origin harking back to Tom Paine and the Rights of Man. The notion of the rights of citizens was not well established in Asia: it is rather characteristic of Western individualism. A more Asian emphasis was imparted in some constitutions which mentioned duties as well as rights, as in Laos where there was recognition of the duty to perform family obligations and in Siam where family as well as citizen rights were guaranteed. In Vietnam the family was recognized as the foundation of society; but here another concept was introduced, owing perhaps less to an Asian outlook than to the Roman Catholicism of the ruling family.

ECONOMIC POLICY

As a counterpart to the rights of citizens the state was usually assigned an economic function. Although the roles varied, their inclusion was due to the impact of Western ideas. Thus the new constitutions of Asia reflected the arguments about state enterprise and *laissez-faire* which have been prominent in Western discussions during the past half-century. The Thai constitution was clearly Right-wing in the sense of favouring private enterprise to which the state was to give encouragement. The constitution of South Vietnam was somewhat less favourable, conceding the right to set up economic associations provided that they they did not lead to malpractices. The emphasis here was different: the attitude towards private enterprise was permissive within certain limitations and not, as in the Thai constitution, positively encouraging. Other constitutions indicated varying

degrees of Leftward inclination. The Indian constitution prohibited expropriation without compensation, as did that of
Pakistan, but a subsequent amendment facilitated the acquisi-
tion of property by the state. Moving further Left the Indonesian
constitution of 1950 declared that the right to property was a
social function, and the 1945 constitution lays it down that the
national economy is to be organized on a co-operative basis and
that natural resources and branches of production which are of
vital importance are to be controlled by the state. The 1950
Indonesian constitution stipulated that there was to be no
expropriation without compensation, but the Burmese constitution went further and left compensation to the discretion of
the state. It also required the state to give preference to economic organizations not working for private profit such as
co-operatives.

Whereas there is a large measure of agreement on democracy
and rights of citizens there appears a wider range of attitudes
towards the economic role of the state. There is a Leftward
trend with two notable exceptions — Thailand and Vietnam.
The nationalist movements generally were Left-inclined because
their object was to limit foreign rule and take control of the
state; because capitalism was associated with foreign enterprise
and, rightly or wrongly, with exploitation; and because rapid
economic development seemed to demand state enterprise. So
nationalization went hand in hand with nationalism. This was
not the case in Thailand which had experienced foreign rule
only for the brief period of Japanese occupation. In Vietnam
not a little depended upon the personal inclination of President
Diem; but the determining factor — which led to his emergence — was the civil war against the Communists. This was
the *raison d'être* of the Vietnamese régime: hence it is the only
constitution which prohibits Communism, although other
countries have banned the Communist Party by law.[1] In Asia,
still more than in Europe, the Communists are regarded as part
of the Left, and the Vietnamese constitution sought to avoid
any Leftist tinge.

[1] Philippines, Burma and Pakistan.

SOCIAL POLICY

A similar pattern was to be seen in relation to welfare, al
though the constitutions of Cambodia and Laos were silent on
social questions. Of the others the Thai constitution was the
most limited, mentioning only the duty of the state to provide
education and promote public health. With an access of
generosity, epidemics were to be suppressed by the state without
charge. In Vietnam the state was to go further and provide for
assistance in cases of unemployment, old age and natural
disaster; but these activities, it was cautiously added, were to be
within the limits of its capacity and economic progress. How
ever, everyone had the right and duty to work and there was to
be equal pay for equal work; and everybody in work was en
titled to a standard of living consistent with human dignity
(otherwise unspecified). Burma again went furthest in this
direction, requiring the state to aim at securing to each citizen
not only the right to work or maintenance but also the right to
rest and leisure. India and Pakistan also, in their constitutions
laid down 'directive principles of state policy' which were on
similar lines although less categorical.

Admittedly, the principles of economic and social policy
embodied in these new constitutions should not be taken too
seriously, and bear no necessary relation to reality. Although
the economic role assigned to the state is less far-reaching in the
Indian constitution than in some others, in practice India's
successive five-year plans have taken her much further in the
direction of state enterprise than the rest. Nevertheless, even if
those provisions are largely wishful thinking, they do set targets
and establish criteria by which the performance of governments
may be judged. The Indian constitution recognized this in
Article 37: although the directive principles of state policy were
not to be enforceable by any court, it was to be the duty of the
state to apply them in making laws. They have had some effect
even if only to call forth explanations of shortcomings. Their
insertion in the new constitutions reflected prevailing aspira
tions and indicated the direction in which the new countries
wished to advance.

RELIGION

Whereas the principles discussed so far, whether 'Right' or 'Left', show Western derivation and influence (with the possible exception of attitudes to the family), religion and its place in the constitution represents an indigenous influence. In most cases it has been strong enough to overcome the secularist trend from the West. Thus Cambodia and Laos specify Buddhism as the state religion and the Thai constitution required the King to be a Buddhist and uphold that church. In Malaya Islam is the religion of the Federation as it was in the Islamic Republic of Pakistan. No religion was specified for Vietnam: it would have presented a difficult choice between the religion of the President and that of the majority of his countrymen. In Burma Buddhism was acknowledged to have a special position as the faith of the majority of the people, but other religions were also recognized. The last general election was fought very largely on the issue of making Buddhism the state religion, and the use of yellow on the ballot boxes helped the triumph of this cause. In Ceylon religion was inextricably interwoven with the language issue which precipitated the 1958 riots. In Indonesia there was no reference to any particular religion in the constitution but the state was declared to be founded on the belief in Almighty God and the religious issue has been a continuous problem, exemplified in its most extreme form by Darul Islam. The Constituent Assembly was dissolved in 1959 because of Muslim insistence on a specific reference to Islam. The Indian constitution shows a more secular imprint by declaring the right of freedom of religion. Only in the Philippines is there to be found a fully secular clause that 'no law shall be made respecting the establishment of religion', taken directly from the first amendment of the American constitution.

III

INTEGRATION

There are two powerful drives operating in the new Asian states; one, reflected in the declarations of economic and social

policy referred to above, is the aspiration for improving the
conditions of life — the aim of rising out of poverty and
establishing a free and progressive society. There is another
drive, however, which is perhaps even more compulsive and
not always parallel, and that is the urge for integration — to
make the nation more of a unity. The nationalist movements
favoured centralization because in unity lay strength and because they reacted against what they believed to be a policy of
divide and rule on the part of the colonial powers. In some
cases the very idea of nationhood was the result of foreign rule,
and the nationalist movement sought to disseminate and keep
alive this concept as the basis for the new state. For this purpose
two institutional devices were adopted.

LANGUAGE

One was the attempt to create or institute a national language.
Some constitutions specified what the national language should
be (for example, Indonesia, Cambodia and Laos). Others
recognized that in the early stages of independence the national
language would have to be supplemented by another. So
Malay was made the national language of Malaya but the use
of English was allowed for an initial period of ten years after
independence. There was a similar provision in the constitutions
of Burma, India and Pakistan. In the Philippines steps were to
be taken towards the adoption of a common national language
but meanwhile English and Spanish were to continue as official
languages. There was no reference to this point in the Thai
constitution, probably because it was self-evident; but the
Vietnamese constitution was also silent where some provisions
for the use of French in the transitional phase might have been
expected. The omission conveniently allowed the continued use
of French without causing offence to national sentiment.

These exceptions were made in favour of the former imperial
language and not the language of an internal minority. In two
other cases the difficulty has been recognized as lying deeper.
Pakistan's constitution provided for two state languages, not
one; and in Ceylon the attempt to institute Sinhalese as the
state language, thereby relegating Tamil to an inferior position,

had tragic consequences. In general the trend is clearly towards the adoption of a single indigenous language as the national language with modifications to ease the transitional period, or in one case, acceptance of the fact that a single language would not fit the situation. It is arguable that the Indian attempt to institute Hindi as the sole state language has encountered just this obstacle.

There is a striking contrast in attitudes towards Western languages on the one hand and institutions on the other: the languages are to be superseded but the institutions are retained. The reason may be that there is always an indigenous alternative to the Western language even if it requires development, as in Indonesia or the Philippines; but there has not been a similar alternative to Western democratic institutions, at least on a national level. If there had been, the nationalist leaders would surely have preferred it. The introduction of 'guided democracy' and 'basic democracy' may be regarded as moves towards the development of such an alternative.

FEDERALISM

Another aspect of the drive towards integration is reflected in attitudes towards federalism. In some cases, particularly the Philippines and Indonesia, the constitution provides for a unitary state where a federal system might have seemed more appropriate. Indonesia, a country spread over 3,000 miles and composed of as many islands, with a multiplicity of languages and distinctive cultures, seemed very well suited to a federal constitution; but federalism was rejected, and indeed became a word of opprobrium, very largely because the Dutch had sponsored it. The attempt to impose a unitary system gave rise to dissatisfaction in the outer islands and largely contributed to the revolt of 1958-9. The Tamils' claims in Ceylon similarly looked for a federal solution.

The adoption of a unitary system may foster integration, but it may also have the reverse effect of making minorities dissatisfied and intransigent. The other method of approach has been to recognize the claims of minorities and to attempt to meet them by means of a federal system — as in Malaya,

x

Burma, India and for a time, in Pakistan. The problems with which these constitutions were designed to cope, however, differed widely. In Pakistan it was primarily the division between East and West, geographic, linguistic and cultural. The particular form adopted, that of parity of representation, itself became a bone of contention. In Burma the object was to provide assurances and safeguards for minorities against Burmese domination, and so a second chamber was instituted in which minorities were given the majority of seats and state governments were erected for them but not for the Burmese. In Malaya, on the other hand, it was not so much a matter of guaranteeing states' rights, although they were given parity in the Senate, but rather of assuring the position of the Malays, for which a Conference of Rulers was established to act as a kind of third chamber. In India where the constituent elements are comparable in size and there is not any single group which is potentially dominant the problem is one of relations between the states and the centre.

MINORITIES

There remains the problem of those minorities which are not recognized for separate treatment. They may be aspiring to separate recognition (as in the case of the Mons and Arakanese in Burma) where they are localized in a fairly clearly defined area and where they are considerable in numbers. Other minorities cannot hope to become constituent elements of a federation. They have to depend upon the influence and pressure that they can bring to bear — as in the agitation against separate electorates in East Pakistan or competitive fasting in the Punjab — or rely upon the general guarantees of rights embodied in the constitution. The catalogue of rights is usually comprehensive but the guarantees are not equally so.

IV

THE JUDICIARY

Essentially the guarantee of rights for minorities as for citizens generally rests upon the courts. Only if the courts are independent of the executive can citizens feel protected. It is small consolation to find in the constitution of South Vietnam that no one may be illegally arrested, while by Presidential Ordinance anybody may be sent to a 'Political Re-education Camp' for two years. In Siam summary proceedings leading to a death penalty have been conducted by Marshal Sarit. By contrast the Pakistan Supreme Court has on a number of occasions been able to thwart the designs of the executive, and the courts have shown themselves independent in Burma, Malaya, the Philippines, India and Ceylon. In the other countries the courts may perhaps protest but the executive can have its way. The independence of the judiciary and their ability to withstand arbitrary acts of the executive is still a useful criterion of a free society, and by that test less than half the countries of Asia qualify. The rest fall below the line into the category of authoritarianism in varying forms and degrees.

V

HEAD OF STATE

The simplest distinction to be made here is between monarchies and republics. In Southern Asia seven of the countries are republics and five are kingdoms (counting Malaya with an elected monarchy) and one, Ceylon, still recognizes the British crown but is determined to become a republic. It is not the case that the monarchies tend to attach greater political importance to the Head of State. In general the monarchs reign but do not rule. Even in Cambodia where all power emanates from the King, executive power is exercised in his name by the ministers. Prince Sihanouk's *Apple Cart* decision to abdicate in order to become Prime Minister showed clearly which of those offices had greater political power. On the other hand in Nepal the King is currently ruling as well as reigning. In Malaya there are certain obligations placed upon the Supreme Ruler for safeguarding the position of the Malays. In Laos the King has recently been exercising an important influence in politics; and in Thailand, where the monarchy is at present in the background, it might conceivably play an active part in the future.

THE GOVERNMENT

On the whole the monarchical systems favour some form of cabinet government. Under this system power is exercised by the government and only limited discretion rests with the Head of State, mainly in the choice of prime minister. The republics are more evenly divided between two categories: those which operate a similar system, in which the President is merely an elected constitutional monarch, and those in which he is the effective head of the executive.

In the former category come India, Pakistan (until 1958), and Burma. Pakistan is now to be placed in the latter category, and even earlier, when operating a cabinet system, there were frequent interventions on the part of the President under Article 37. President's rule has also been instituted in India under the similar Article 356, but there it has been an action of the central government rather than of the President.

In the latter category there are three countries — Vietnam, Indonesia and the Philippines. In Vietnam at the time when the presidential system was instituted there was need for strong government in the view of many besides Diem. The result was a system in which the powers of the President are even greater than in the USA. Indonesia has gone through a constitutional cycle. The critical situation at the time of the Japanese surrender and declaration of Indonesian independence demanded strong leadership, and the 1945 constitution put the President in the position to give it. Later developments tended towards reducing the powers of the President and increasing those of the people's representatives in Parliament. In 1959 Sukarno decided to dispense with Parliament and revert to the 1945 constitution which gives the President far-reaching authority. The House of Representatives is maintained but the President has an absolute veto on legislation. The supremacy of the President was envisaged by the framers of the constitution. One of them, Soepomo, commented:

> The idea of the (1945) Constitution originally was that the Ministers are just assistants to the President without any responsibility for Government policy.

In the Philippines also the powers attributed to the President have been considerably augmented by comparison with the USA, at the expense of the Congress. Congress may not increase the appropriations in the President's budget proposals, with minor exceptions, and the President has not only the right of veto as in the American constitution but also a selective veto.

VI

LEGISLATURE

Every country except Nepal, including even Thailand under the dictatorship of Sarit, has some kind of Parliament, but their power differs widely. In Thailand for example, the National Assembly appointed under the current interim constitution has minimal authority. Members of the Government are excluded from it and the Prime Minister has wide powers to act without it. In Indonesia the President has the power of veto and the House of Representatives has not even the power of the purse. If the House does not approve the budget proposed by the Government, then the budget of the previous year remains in force. Similarly, in Vietnam Parliament has very little authority in practice although rather more on paper. The President has a veto on legislation but can be overridden by the vote of three-quarters of the National Assembly. In practice, however, the powers granted to the Assembly depend on its composition and, so far, effective authority has been in the hands of the President. The position has been similar in Laos and Cambodia, i.e. it is the executive power which has dominated the legislative.

On the other hand there are countries where the authority of the legislature has been clearly demonstrated, at least to the extent of determining the character of the Government. This is true of Burma where the fall of U Nu's Government was the result of a split in his party reflected in the voting in Parliament. The immediate cause of his resignation was his inability to secure a majority for the budget, and his return to office was due to a victory in the general election. In Malaya too the position of the Tunku rests upon his command of a parliamentary majority which has not hitherto been shaken but quite clearly could be. The Government of India rests upon the continued support of a majority in the legislature. A change of government has followed the last three elections in Ceylon. In Pakistan the power of the legislature to overthrow the Government was exercised somewhat too enthusiastically.

BICAMERALISM

In such cases the power of the legislature lends importance to its composition and the method of its selection. Conversely those factors may help to determine the importance of a legislature. As regards composition there is the obvious distinction between two-chamber and single-chamber systems. The countries with federal constitutions have provision for representation of the constituent states in the second chamber. But bicameralism is not confined to the federal states. Ceylon, Cambodia, Laos and the Philippines also have two chambers. The Ceylon Senate has power to hold up ordinary legislation but can be overridden by the House of Representatives. The Cambodian *Conseil du Royaume* and the Laotian *Conseil du Roi* are subordinate in each case to the National Assembly, broadly on the lines of the French *Conseil de la République*, although the Laotian *Conseil* appears to have rather more power than the Cambodian. The Senate of the Philippines has a rather weaker position in relation to the House of Representatives than the American Senate, as might be expected in a unitary constitution. Its term of office is six years as in the USA; but the term of the Lower House is four years, not two years. The House of Representatives has priority in financial legislation and the concurrence of two-thirds of the Senate is required for treaties; but approval of appointments is vested, not in the Senate, but in a Commission on Appointments with equal membership from both Houses.

Unicameral systems have been adopted by Thailand, Vietnam and Indonesia. In Thailand after a post-war experiment with a bicameral system there was a return to the framework of the 1932 constitution which was superseded by the current dictatorship. In Indonesia the abolition of the Senate was part of the repudiation of the federalism of the 1949 constitution, and a reversion to the ideas of 1945. It is often argued that, theoretically, a unicameral system is more democratic, on the grounds summed up in the dictum of the Abbé Sieyès that a second chamber, if it agrees with the first, is superfluous; if it disagrees, objectionable. Few countries, however, have been willing to follow the dictates of theory: even the French, when faced with the choice in 1946, declined. It is perhaps worth noting that in Southern Asia two of the countries with unicameral legislatures — Thailand and Vietnam — are among those with the least democratic systems of government. Pakistan tried the novelty of a federal system with a single chamber and came to grief. Indonesia also has a unicameral system and is in a critical political condition. This may be no more than a coincidence, but it could be adduced as a practical argument in favour of bicameralism. In Thailand and Vietnam it may be a symptom rather than a cause: for if Parliament is not intended to have real power, there is little point in elaborating a bicameral system.

VII

ELECTORAL SYSTEMS

Most of the countries employ a single-member simple-majority system. In one case there is an element of cumulative voting; two use a distributive or 'block vote'; and one has, or had, an elaborate system of proportional representation.

PROPORTIONAL REPRESENTATION

The solitary example of proportional representation was provided by Indonesia. A list system was adopted with all the trimmings borrowed from the Netherlands. *Prima facie* there was a good deal to be said for a method of election which would avoid the possibility of one party, by a small plurality, taking all the seats. Voters were able to express their preference for a particular candidate although these opportunities were little used. Generally the votes were cast for the party lists. Nevertheless the apportionment of seats did ensure that even relatively small sections of the electorate might secure some representation. In the event the election produced an unexpected kind of result. It did indeed afford representation to

minorities and as many as twenty-eight parties were represented in the new House. But it also gave a long lead to four,
and only four, political parties which thenceforward dominated
the political scene. The effect, however, of the list system, in
Indonesia as elsewhere, was to place considerable power in the
hands of the party machine in the drawing up of the lists. For
this reason and because of the size of the multi-member constituencies it suffered from the drawback of remoteness from
the electorate. However, there is little question that the results
did represent more or less accurately the political inclinations of
the Indonesian electorate. The multi-party system which it
produced in the House of Representatives brought with it, as
often happens in Europe, the frustrations of assembling and
holding together government coalitions. On one interpretation,
this eventually drove President Sukarno beyond the point of
endurance and led him to revive the 1945 constitution. One
conclusion that might be drawn from the Indonesian experience
is that proportional representation, although providing some
satisfaction for minorities, may have that advantage outweighed
by its inability to sustain an effective government. But a more
plausible interpretation is that the 1950 constitution was unable
to reconcile cabinet government with President Sukarno. The
present House appointed by him is also multi-party although
the main Opposition has been excluded; the chief difference is
that the Government is not dependent upon it.

CUMULATIVE VOTE

Ceylon adopted a system of single-member constituencies
combined with a handful of plural-member constituencies with
cumulative voting designed to assist minority representation. In
a three-member constituency a minority could be sure of one
seat if it could muster 25 per cent of the voters, but this provision did not greatly affect the electoral pattern. The results
depended much more upon the geographical delimitation of the
constituencies. As devices to deal with a communal problem
neither of these expedients appears particularly successful.

THE 'BLOCK VOTE'

Under this system the constituencies have more than one seat and electors are entitled to cast as many votes as there are seats. The most familiar example of it is to be found in British borough council elections. If party discipline and allegiance are strong the effect of this system of election is similar to that of the single-member system, i.e. it tends to enhance the size of the majority in terms of seats. Indeed, theoretically, a party which can count upon 51 per cent of votes can sweep the board. The two countries which employ this system of election in Southern Asia are Thailand and Laos. Neither of them is a very good example of the system in operation.

In Thailand, the nature of political parties and the conduct of elections distort the electoral process and little can be deduced from the results. However, the system does afford some flexibility, always supposing that it is honestly operated. Even the last general election provided an illustration. In the constituency of Bangkok where there were nine seats, the Government party headed by Pibul Songgram did not sweep the board although the Prime Minister led in terms of votes. The second member elected was the leader of the opposition, Khuang Aphaiwongse, and another member of the Democratic Party also squeezed in for the sixth seat. But if it were not for the personal popularity of Khuang Aphaiwongse the Government would probably have arranged for its party, the Seri Managasila, to take all the seats.

Laos does not provide a good example of the system in operation either, as the election in December 1955 was limited to those areas which the Government controlled. The National Progressive Party won a narrow majority of the seats contested (21 out of 39), the remainder being divided between three other parties and independents. In the following election of May 1958 in which the Communist Party participated under the title of Neo Lao Hak Sat it won 9 out of the 21 seats in the two provinces which had not previously been represented and their allies won 4, so that they had a majority in that area and a considerable minority in the National Assembly. This is not enough evidence to base any conclusion upon except that in Laos as in

Thailand party discipline was not very effective in controlling voters.

The Indian system although primarily based on single-member constituencies also allotted some reserved seats to scheduled castes and tribes for which distributive voting was used. The effect of this in electoral terms was merely to create another set of single-member constituencies while at the same time guaranteeing some minority representation. As the electorate consisted of the same body of voters, communalism was less emphasized than in Pakistan where minorities were assigned to separate electorates and so prevented from exercising their electoral influence in the ordinary constituencies.

SINGLE-MEMBER SIMPLE-MAJORITY SYSTEM

All the other countries in the area employ the single-member system. This is partly due to familiarity, having inherited it from the former metropolitan powers, Britain or the USA, but it holds good for former French territories, Cambodia and Vietnam. Why this popularity of the single-member system?

The first point is its simplicity. It is readily intelligible and because the constituencies are relatively small there is closer contact between candidate and electorate. The process of voting is also easy, and so is the count.

The second motive is its integrating effect. In any constituency where only one candidate is to be elected there is a strong incentive to have no more than two contestants. Hence the tendency of the single-member system to produce the two-party system. This, it should be emphasized, is only a tendency and not necessarily a prevailing one. In fact it has not produced this effect yet in any country in Southern Asia. However, it can help to counteract the separatism of plural societies. In Malaya the single-member system tends to hold together the reigning Alliance, for if they do not hang together they are liable to hang separately. Similarly in Burma the system helped to cement the ruling coalition and consolidate the Opposition in the form of the NUF for the 1956 election; and in the last election also it has fostered a development towards a two-party system out of the division in the AFPFL. The disadvantage of the system is shown in the 1956 election in Burma when the Democratic Party which got third highest number of votes failed to win a single seat. It requires a good deal of political self-discipline to rise above this kind of electoral hazard. In the 1955 election in Malaya 7 parties contested 52 seats. The Alliance won 51 seats with 80 per cent of the votes. The Pan-Malayan Islamic Party won 1 seat with 4 per cent; the Party Negara won none with $7\frac{1}{2}$ per cent. There was an unhealthy elimination of opposition. But there are dangers and disadvantages in this situation. If for example the Alliance were to break up, the UMNO and other parties exploiting the anti-Chinese Malay vote could sweep the board; or if the Chinese population and registration increased to more than 50 per cent the MCA or the Communists might do likewise.

The third motive for adopting the single-member system is that it tends to produce a stable government by magnifying the majority in terms of seats, as in Malaya and still more in India where the Congress has repeatedly won a majority of seats in Parliament with a minority of the total votes. It has not produced stability in Cambodia but this is not for want of a nominal government majority. The personal ascendancy of Prince Norodom Sihanouk is such that the election result was a foregone conclusion and the politics of Cambodia have been conducted within the party of the Prince rather than between parties. The Prince alone can command a majority whenever he chooses. However, it is true in Cambodia also that the single-member system enhanced the Prince's majority, for the Sangkum captured every seat.

The case of the Philippines is different in that it has a presidential executive. This system, where the President is directly elected, tends towards the two-party confrontation since the whole country forms one constituency for the presidential election and there is an incentive to present no more than two candidates. Another effect of a directly elected presidential executive is to enhance the position of the national leader in relation to both Parliament and people. So far, however, this effect has had little time to show itself in Asia. The role of the leader is prominent in every country but less prominent in the country in which this system has been longest established. Sukarno dominates Indonesia but he has never been elected directly or otherwise and in the 1945 constitution there is provision only for indirect election. The constitution of Vietnam provided for direct election of the President. The result was made fairly certain by the elimination of the only serious alternative candidate. In the other countries it is the Prime Minister who has the foremost political role and there is no provision for direct election there as yet. Because of the influence of political leadership in Asia general elections tend to take on the aspect of a choice of the head of government, which is familiar enough in the West also. So in Malaya the vote is cast for or against the Tunku, in Burma for or against U Nu, in India for or against Nehru: in Cambodia a few eccentric voters may cast their vote against the Prince.

VIII

POLITICAL PARTIES

A common feature of political parties arising out of their earlier colonial background is their extra-parliamentary character. In some countries where the imperial power permitted a degree of parliamentary activity there is some tradition of parliamentary politics, notably in Ceylon. But for the most part the political parties currently dominant in Southern Asia began their careers outside Parliament and often before a Parliament was established. The result of this order of development was to place the political emphasis on the party rather than on Parliament and to attach more importance to party decisions than to parliamentary processes. Thus during the operation of the 1935 Government of India Act the provincial cabinets merely echoed decisions taken previously by the Congress organization. A similar relationship existed in Burma between the Parliament and the AFPFL. This feature has made it more difficult for parliamentary institutions to take root and function as they were intended. Political decisions were taken elsewhere.

OPPOSITION

This feature was particularly evident where the national front, having successfully achieved independence, took over the reins of power without any perceptible opposition surviving.

In that situation it was difficult for the idea of a constitutional Opposition to develop, partly because it was hard for it to gain a foothold and partly because of the stigma attaching to anybody who opposed the national movement. The difficulty was well illustrated in South Vietnam where, although all the members of the Assembly were supporters of the Government, some were designated as the official Opposition, much to their dissatisfaction. Yet when a genuine opposition made its appearance the Government took steps to refuse recognition to the party and excluded its leader from the election campaign. In Indonesia the development of Sukarno's 'guided democracy' was alleged to be in response to the factionalism of the party system and opposition for opposition's sake. The intention was to substitute *mufakat*, or the sense of the meeting, as a means of reaching decisions, facilitated by a ban imposed upon the major opposition party. In Burma on the other hand there has been a similar attempt on a voluntary basis, the parties having agreed upon a sixteen-year economic development programme to avoid the obstruction that political opposition might cause and to avoid auction bidding in election campaigns.

This trend is only partly due to the continuance after independence of the idea that opposition to the national government is traitorous. It stems also from the internal condition of a number of the countries where the line between constitutional opposition and subversion is hard to draw. Burma has attempted to sharpen the distinction by taking drastic military action against the insurgents on the one hand whilst encouraging their parliamentary front, the Burma Workers' Party, on the other. The spectacle in 1958 of the defeated leader of the 'stable' faction crossing the floor to shake hands with the victorious leader of the 'clean' faction was one which would have drawn forth cheers at the Palace of Westminster. The provision of a salary by the Government for the Leader of the Opposition is a step in the same direction.

ORGANIZATION

The nature of political parties was conditioned by the circumstances of their growth. Under imperial rule political activity was restricted or entirely prohibited and consequently political parties fell into two main categories. They were either clandestine organizations engaged in conspiratorial activity or open organizations functioning within the limits laid down by the imperial power.

Clandestine or closed organizations

Clandestine activity in itself imposes on a political organization a particular pattern, which is represented by the standard organization of a Communist Party. The basic unit is necessarily a small group personally known to their leader though not always to each other. The nature of their activity and the risks run demand strong discipline and a careful selection and training of any new recruits. The party is necessarily small in numbers and has to achieve its effect either by direct action which leads it into the paths of terrorism or by control of organizations with broader-based membership. So in Asia we find a number of parties, not only the Communist Party, organized on these lines, and because the Communist Party generally was one of the first in the field, other parties following suit tended to adopt Communist organization as their model, in some cases because they were themselves the products of that organization. This was notably the case in Burma where the Socialist and Communist parties were off-shoots of one parent organization. While the special features of 'cells' and 'cadres' are not to be found everywhere, many of the parties in the region are apt to distinguish between their activists or active members who correspond to 'cadres' and the rest of their membership.

Open organization

Élite parties: Some open organizations also distinguished between their active and passive membership, a distinction which is observed in the West as well although not usually formalized. One reason for this was the narrowness of the educated élite. On the whole political activity tended to be concentrated in their hands and since they were relatively few they tended to form a caucus within the party. Consequently, even where the requirements of clandestine activity did not exist or had ceased to operate, the narrowness of the élite from whom party activists could be drawn shaped the character of some political parties to something like that of a 'cadre' party.

Mass organizations: The colonial situation determined also the character of mass political organization. Granted that a common objective, if not the common objective, was the elimination of imperial rule, two possibilities were open. One was the *coup d'état* for which the clandestine organization was suitable. However, the imperial rulers disposed of such superiority of force that this possibility was remote, and the most that could be done in that direction was to make life uncomfortable for them by acts of terrorism. If imperial rule was to be overthrown, as distinct from the liquidation of particular rulers, the obvious recourse was to the support of the mass of the native population. Against the uniform hostility of the people of the territory colonial rule would not in the long run be able to stand. Consequently, in conjunction with the development of cadre and élite parties there were attempts to create mass organizations. The Communist Party of Indonesia has passed through all three phases (two of them after independence) beginning as a clandestine organization, developing into an open élite party (165,000 members in 1954) and then becoming a mass organization (1½ million members in 1959).

National front: The ultimate in mass organization was the national front. This type of organization was designed to rally the maximum support on the basis of the single common denominator — nationalism. To that end particular differences on other questions were subordinated, and narrower political organizations which differed fundamentally from each other joined in the national front, often with a view to capturing it or to prevent it from being captured by their rivals. By its nature the national front could not be a disciplined body and could only be described as an organization in a loose sense. In contrast to the cadre and élite organizations it was dependent rather on support than on membership, although it would seek to acquire members, as did the Indian National Congress, in order to attach them to the common cause. Its success was tested by its ability to call strikes, to hold demonstrations, and generally to show its command of the allegiance of the masses. The AFPFL in Burma was a successful example.

A more recent development has been the creation of national fronts after independence. In South Vietnam the MNR falls in this category, as does the national front established in Indonesia by Sukarno. In Thailand after the political parties were banned in 1958 the Government set up a Revolutionary Party. The urge to consolidate persists; but whereas in the colonial period it was directed against alien rule it is now aimed at dissent.

THE LEADER

The common factor essential to all three types of political organization is the leader. For the 'cadre' party centralization and discipline ('democratic centralism' in Communist jargon) is essential. For an élite organization the necessity of individual leadership is not so obvious, but in practice, given the circumstances of political parties in Asia, it was found necessary for them also. This was in no small measure because the leader was so necessary for mass organization. To be effective, the appeal to the masses had to be symbolized and personified in one man, and so throughout the area there is the common phenomenon of the charismatic leader: Nehru in India, Sukarno in Indonesia, Aung San and then U Nu in Burma, Tunku Abdul Rahman in Malaya, Prince Norodom Sihanouk in Cambodia. Their portraits have proved valuable electoral assets. In Cambodia voters had a choice between the Prince, an elephant and a plough — an unequal competition.

POLITICAL BASIS

Another factor emphasizing the position of the leader is the general relationship between master and pupil, leader and follower, which is found in Asia. One important foundation for political association is devotion to a particular person, and much of the political contest in the area is a competition between personal followings. The consequence of this is that political organizations are very apt to split. The rise of a new leader with ambition to get to the top cannot be contained within the original party structure, and the newcomer may well decamp and take his following with him. This pattern has often been repeated.

This is not to say that the following will simply cling to their leader wherever he chooses to take them. There is usually an element of doctrinal solidarity. The amount of doctrine and the degree of rigidity varies from the extreme dogma of the Communists on the one hand and the equally extreme dogma of some religious groups on the other to the vaguer slogans of some nationalist groups. It is probably true that the more doctrinaire parties are more liable to splits. Certainly deviations and breakaways have been a recurrent feature of Left-wing organizations.

A third basis of political organization is that of common interest. Religious groupings have been mentioned as examples of organizations built on doctrine: they could also be regarded as organizations based on interest. In addition there are parties founded on communal distinctions such as the components of the Alliance in Malaya, or the caste associations which can be seen at work in Indian politics. Regionalism provides the common interest for some parties. There are also some which are linked by economic interest. The class party is not, however, normal. The Malayan-Chinese Association may be described as a businessman's party but that is because of the economic role of the Chinese community. The Democratic Party in the Philippines is particularly associated with the sugar planters while the Democratic Alliance derived its main support from small rice-farmers. Generally such a simple relationship between party and economic interest is not common. The reason is probably the sudden transition to universal suffrage and the small size of the middle class. A party resting upon middle-class economic interests would generally have a bleak outlook confronted with a mass franchise. Wider bases and better prospects are offered by religion, race, nationalism, or, in terms of economic class, the peasantry. There have been some attempts to exploit the appeal of class interest, as in the Labour Party of Malaya or the Burma Workers' and Peasants' Party; but these titles represented in terms of party membership are aspirations rather than actuality.

Organization according to economic interest is more often to be found in what the Communists call 'transmission belts', that is, ancillary organizations attached to the national front. Organizations of this kind were usually incorporated in the

Y

independence movement as part of the process of rallying maxi
mum support from the population. They also assisted cadre an
élite parties to extend their influence to wider fields. Whereas i
the West trade unions have intervened in politics as pressur
groups, in Asia political parties have often created trade union
to increase their own resources. In consequence the trade unio
organizations have tended to be divided on political lines, a
have the other ancillary organizations. The four main attach
ments of the 'transmission belts' are to workers, peasants, wome
and youth, each having an organization designed for them. Th
importance of these bodies from the point of view of the politica
parties is not only that they afford a means of contact with th
masses but that they may also determine the parties' position i
the national movement as a whole.

IX

ADMINISTRATION

In the West public administration tends to be judged by it
impartiality and integrity. There are Asian countries in whic
these standards are accepted if not achieved; there are others i
which they are not accepted. In Burma and Malaya the Britis
tradition in this respect is continued, at least in intention, bu
even there the role of civil servants in politics may appear exces
sive. The smallness of the educated élite makes it difficult to de
bar a considerable section of it from political activity. In othe
countries, such as the Philippines where American tradition
are dominant, the political character of the civil service i
accepted; and in Vietnam this has been carried to the point c
having a National Revolutionary Civil Servants' League as on
of the parties supporting the Government with membershi
practically obligatory for any official. In Indonesia senior civ
servants have now been prohibited from membership c
political parties; but in 1956 a police association contested th
election.

The British administrative legacy in the Indian Empire ha
often been described as a 'steel frame', and some of the diff
culties which have beset government in Pakistan have bee
attributed to the disproportion between Muslim and Hindu i

the ICS. When partition came, India was better supplied with administrators. But the tradition of the service was carried on in Pakistan also, and the new régime, although headed by a soldier, is based upon the Deputy-Commissioners who are the 'mothers and fathers' of their districts as they were in the days of the British *Raj*. Even before this latest phase the civil service had been assuming a semi-political role with emphasis on cohesion and centralization offsetting the fissiparous tendencies of provincial politicians. In India a relatively high degree of political sophistication and some experience in government reduced the scope for intervention by the civil service. India's administrative structure, in comparison with most other Asian countries, may well be compared to a 'steel frame': it is tougher, more resilient and stable, and altogether more impressive; but it is not without patches of rust.

Similarly, the picture of the police force as an impartial and incorruptible executant of the law is not always applicable in the West, still less in Asia where such an armed and more or less disciplined body can hardly be omitted from political calculations. That the police have been regarded and used as an arm of the executive does not call for criticism; but it is another matter when, as in Burma, they gain the reputation of being the instrument of the party in power. In Thailand their corruption has been legendary, and for a time they were the main support of General Phao,[1] one of the triumvirate who were contending for supreme power. Phao lost: the army won.

THE MILITARY

The most striking development in the politics of South Asia in recent years has been the role of the military. Containing, as it must do, a considerable portion of the available educated élite, and based, as it must be, on a system of discipline, it has potentialities both as a stabilizing and as a revolutionary force. It has come to the fore in each case at a time of crisis in the political system. In Burma the army was called in, after the split in the ruling coalition had produced a deadlock, to take over

[1] Phao was simultaneously Secretary-General of the main Government party, the Seri Managasila.

the Government and to stage free elections. It answered the call somewhat reluctantly and then retired again into the background, having in the process cleaned up the administration of the country and the streets of Rangoon. It established and retains control of the National Solidarity Association designed to keep a check on corruption and maladministration. In Indonesia the army has emerged as the main prop of such political stability as exists and the main counterweight to the Communists. In Thailand there is a tradition of military *coups d'état*, and it was Marshal Sarit, the Commander-in-Chief, who established himself as dictator. In Laos the army has itself been divided by the political crisis. In Pakistan the army took charge with the intention not merely of stabilizing but also of renovating the country.

X

Some observers have seen in these developments the beginning of an Asian answer to the problems of government. In their view democracy on the Western model has been tried and found wanting. In the Asian environment it places too much emphasis on liberty and not enough on discipline; it is too much concerned with the protection of rights and not enough with the performance of obligations; it encourages diversity at the expense of cohesion. They are willing to accept both the title and the justification for 'basic democracy' or 'guided democracy' arguing from the alleged popularity of those régimes that dictatorship can be democratic if it represents the general will. This is different from the argument that dictatorship can get better results. The latter contention is sufficiently familiar to have a stock response: (*a*) that it is doubtful whether a dictatorship can in fact get better results in the long run and (*b*) even if it can, the price is not worth paying. If ability to produce the goods is the main criterion, then a Communist dictatorship has as much claim to consideration as any other — and more than most.

The case for an 'Asian solution' does not, however, rest upon this line of argument. The assertion is that Asian democracy is different in kind from Western democracy and cannot be cast in the traditional moulds. But on closer inspection the 'new look' appears suspiciously like old-fashioned autocracy with a different label. Both Hitler and Stalin could in their day claim the support of the overwhelming majority of the people; but even if those claims had been genuine their régimes would still not have been democratic. In Indonesia the principle of *mufakat*, or decision by the sense of the meeting instead of by majority, could conceivably inspire a new form of democracy, but not if dissenters are excluded. Nor, judging by the experience of the *bhoodan* movement in India, is it likely to prove a more effective way of getting results.

For the purpose of academic analysis it may be relevant to trace the derivation of Asian institutions from Western models, but this does not mean that those institutions remain 'Western' any more than that tea is an 'Asian' drink. The problem of the relationship between government and the governed is similar in both hemispheres, and the solutions propounded have much in common. The assessment of them depends rather on their content than on their provenance; and so far no peculiarly Asian democracy has emerged. Democracy is still a universal concept.

Richard Butwell

The assertion by Saul Rose at the end of his paper on political institutions in South and South-East Asia that democracy is 'a universal concept' recalls the remarks of Burmese Premier U Nu in 1960 before the Indian Council of World Affairs. Nu said:

... If we take a good look at the nations of the West, we find that barely half of them are practising democracies today, and that in only a handful of them has democracy been firmly established. In view of this state of affairs, it would be permissible for us to ask, 'Are Westerners fit for democracy?' But, of course, we do not ask it because we realize that it would not be a fair question. It would not be fair because we know that the democratic system of government, though the most desirable, is at the same time the most difficult ... to operate. No amount of academic study will by itself produce a democratic society. Democracy simply cannot be forced on a people, however enlightened the rulers may be. The basic principles of democracy have to be applied in each country in such a way as to suit local conditions, local beliefs and local customs. This means a slow process of gradual growth, and of education of the people. That is why, if we look into the record of those countries in which democracy has been firmly established, we will find that it has taken them hundreds of years to get where they are today. Most of the countries of Asia have been independent for just over a decade. This fact makes doubly unfair the question, 'Are Asians fit for democracy?' I suppose the correct answer to the question, even if it sounds a little facetious, is: 'Ask me in a few hundred years' time, and I will tell you not only whether the Asians but all the other peoples of the world are fit for democracy.'[1]

U Nu's Burma, like most of the recently colonial lands of Asia, began its renewed independence with political institutions inspired both by Western models in general and British parliamentary government in particular. In the late 1940's there was fairly general optimism concerning the ability of such institutions to take root in Asian soil; at the start of the 1960's — with conspicuous exceptions (such as India and the Philippines) — a marked air of pessimism is to be noted. Why? Burma's Nu may be quoted again in reply:

> In the final analysis, the success or failure of a democratic experiment depends on the human element. Good men are essential to the successful working of a democracy. . . . Having come to power by democratic means, many . . . leaders have fallen prey to . . . evils, and have thereby forfeited the confidence of their peoples. In a long established democracy, such a government would be thrown out by the electorate at the next election. . . . But in countries where a long tradition of democracy does not exist, these same corrupted leaders are only too often tempted to evade the democratic consequences of their conduct by adopting unfair means to perpetuate themselves in power. Every success in that direction spells danger to democracy, and if it continues long enough, the road is wide open to revolution and eventual dictatorship. In Burma we have a saying, 'Only a gold cup is good enough to hold a lion's fat.' Similarly, only good men can successfully operate a democratic system of government. . . .[2]

There is a large element of truth in this 'good men theory of democracy', as it may be called; it is neither unsophisticated nor unduly oversimplified. The political evolution of South and South-East Asia since independence is in fact the result, in large measure, of the

[1] 'Asians and Democracy', in *Burma Weekly Bulletin*, IX, 24 November, 1960, No. 30, p. 287.
[2] ibid.

kind of men who have governed the countries of this part of the world. This, in turn, is a reflection of the under-developed character of the political institutions, governmental and otherwise, in various of these nations as well as of such lands as political societies in a broader sense. Burma, for example, continues to attempt to practise democracy today mainly because of the efforts of one man: U Nu. Nu it was, and Nu alone, who held out against surrender to the Communist insurrectionists in 1949. Nu, too — and only Nu — spoke out vigorously against the excesses of the Ne Win military caretaker government in 1958–60. Nu also has led the way since his return to office in April 1960 to co-operative relations among previously bitterly opposed elements on the Burmese political scene (through 'tension-easing meals' and other means).

Likewise, President Sukarno has been the man who has mattered most of all in Indonesia. If Burma's political institutions today bear the strong imprint of Nu, those of the Indonesian republic are veritably the creation of Sukarno. Prime Minister Jawaharlal Nehru in India, Marshal Sarit Thannarat in Thailand, and President Ngo Dinh Diem in South Vietnam are some of the other men whose political ideas and behaviour have significantly shaped the form and method of operation of the main political institutions of their lands.

In his remarks on the necessity of 'good men' for the successful functioning of democratic political institutions, U Nu clearly had in mind 'good men' morally — but not only morally and certainly not morally wholly in terms of corruption and other self-seeking behaviour. He meant, too, effective and responsible leaders, and these have been only too few in number and too limited in impact in South and South-East Asia since independence. Elections, for example, are less important institutionally as a means of changing governments at the start of the 1960's than a decade earlier — and *coups d'état* more important (a fact for which leaders or would-be leaders are mainly immediately responsible). Parliamentary institutions are frequently by-passed not directly because the masses are not ready for democracy but as a result of the impatience of leaders or the desire of particular persons to perpetuate their hold on public office.

Democracy has survived — as an evolving system if not a full-grown product — in India and the Philippines in particular as a result of the political predispositions of governmental personnel at various levels of society as well as of the participants in the various other spheres of the total political process. Such factors as Communism in Indochina and illiteracy and geography in Pakistan have been important in shaping the character of the political institutions of these countries. But, even without these hurdles, the political institutions of these lands might not be particularly different today. President Ngo Dinh Diem of South Vietnam, for example, was not particularly more autocratic in the wake of the 1960–2 upsurge in Viet Cong attacks than after he had seemed to contain the Communist threat earlier. Democratic institutions in U Nu's Burma have survived rebellion, ethnic antagonisms, economic slump, and even military rule; Indonesia's — under Sukarno — have not fared so well. Probably few countries in recent history provide so many instances of the impact of individual leaders on the survival of particular political institutions as those of South and South-East Asia since independence.

The survival of institutions, however, is a different thing from their functioning as meaningful social organizations. The political party is a case in point. In Pakistan, experimenting with what is called 'basic democracy', parties are banned (raising the question of just how democratic 'basic democracy' is). Parties survive, on the other hand — or at least a few of them do — in the 'guided democracy' of Sukarno's Indonesia, but are they any more relevant politically just because they exist? It is questionable, indeed, whether particular political organizations should be regarded as parties in the traditional sense if they fail to fulfil certain functional or other criteria. Political parties, as they generally exist in the West (where they perform the function of representation), have been singled out by Indonesia's President Sukarno as major contributors to his country's not inconsiderable disunity and lack of movement. U Nu of Burma, on the other hand, has placed party above government in his speeches, likening government to a walking stick and party to its holder or manipulator. But Nu has taken a similar stand to Sukarno's in his approach to the satellite mass organizations that used to be the chief components of the once seemingly all-powerful (and ruling) united Anti-Fascist People's Freedom League (AFPFL). In his present Union Party, the former 'clean' faction of the split AFPFL, Nu has allowed only individual (as contrasted with group) membership — and opposed holding of leadership posts in both party and the formerly satellite mass organizations. In both cases the leaders — Sukarno and Nu — have moved against the political organizations that seemed most to threaten their survival as leaders; party evolution, or devolution, has been the result (in the main) of the response of chief political figures to threats to their paramountcy. Moreover, even in Burma, the ruling party as such was never as supreme as is sometimes suggested. Nu, for example, made various important decisions in the era of the united AFPFL in opposition to a majority of the party executive — such as his 1956 negotiations in China with Premier Chou En-lai on the border question despite specific instructions from the party executive committee not to negotiate on this issue.

Indonesia's political parties today bear certain similarities to the controlled mass organizations of the past in Burma. The would-be directing agent of the latter organizations, moreover, was not always what it appeared to be: the country's chief political decision-making body. Parties in the various lands of South and South-East Asia vary considerably, and they have also changed greatly through the years since independence. Some of them perform different functions today than they did a decade ago (as in Indonesia), and in some lands functions discharged by parties in other countries are the prerogative of a different type of political organization. These facts raise questions concerning the meaningfulness of comparisons of what may be called parties in South and South-East Asia.

That the hold of democracy on the political leadership should vary from country to country is not surprising, particularly in view of the limited attractiveness of this approach to government to many in South and South-East Asia both before and since the coming of independence. Even such a contemporary champion of democracy as Burma's Premier U Nu, for example, was once impressed with the institutions of dictatorial rule established by the Germans, Italians and Japanese. In his inaugural address as President of the Rangoon University Students' Union in the middle 1930's, Nu said:

> . . . I dislike democracy where much time is wasted in persuading the majority and in trying to get the consent of the majority. Democracy is good in name only. It cannot be used effectively. It cannot work in this period of dictatorship of Hitler and Mussolini. . . . I like dictatorship where things can be done quickly without any interference. . . .[1]

Dr Ba Maw presided over a pseudo-independent régime in wartime Burma that was not directly Western in origin — and certainly not democratic. Soepomo's description of the Indonesian presidency in the 1945 constitution, quoted by Rose, also seems neither Western nor democratic. Western-style institutions were adopted in part — in some lands — for the same reason that Communist institutions are attractive to some today: they seemed to explain the accomplishments of the nations apparently most effective in solving various problems. In the 1930's, however, the choice might have been

[1] U Thein Pe, *Student Boycotter*, Vol. I (Rangoon: Red Dragon Book Club, 1938), p. 143.

different, as Nu's remarks suggest. Communism today surely is a real alternative — as shown in Laos. Moreover, for the Communists at the time of the coming of independence, democratic political institutions were not the only possible approach; this the Burmese, Indonesian and other revolts (or attempted revolts) of 1948 indicate. Not only has Indonesia's President Sukarno in recent years seemed to find an alternative, quixotic though it may seem, to Western political institutions, but everywhere army rule — perhaps for reasons similar to those which occasioned its establishment in Thailand in the 1930's — is a very definite alternative at the present time. In short, perhaps democratic political institutions came to be inaugurated at the most auspicious possible time rather than too early, as some have suggested.

There is also the question of what various of the leaders of South and South-East Asia had in mind when they established democratic political institutions with the coming of freedom from colonial rule. U Nu, for example, has described democracy as the 'freedom to do as one pleases subject to the legitimate interests of others'. Is this what democracy is? Worse definitions surely have been offered by persons in equally high places in Southern Asia. The point is that democratic political institutions — indeed, democratic societies as a whole (of the West, that is) — were seen by Burmese and Indonesians and Vietnamese in the framework of their own frequently quite limited experiences. Many of the nationalist leaders of South and South-East Asia were more acquainted with democracy as a slogan than as a set of integrated political institutions when independence arrived — earlier than most of them had expected. Some of these leaders are today wiser and firmer in their democratic attachment; others, however, are disillusioned or seem so.

U Nu, in the remarks quoted at the outset of this discussion, emphasized the time necessary to establish effective democratic political institutions. His point was well made and is of obvious relevance to any consideration of the evolution of political institutions in South and South-East Asia. Given the limited time that has passed since independence, there probably have been a comparatively large number of institutional changes in Southern Asia. To take Burma again as an example: the government of U Nu advanced in the year following the latter's return to office in April 1960 the unique idea of two cabinets, one for national questions and the other for questions in which the states (of the Burmese union) were primarily involved (and comprising the premier and the various state ministers). The advisory commission of elder statesmen, headed by former President Ba U, represents an attempt to provide some kind of check on a government in a situation where the parliamentary opposition is limited in number. The National Solidarity Associations, set up by the army to keep the civilian politicians in line, is another innovation — despite the fact that it has largely fallen into disuse.

These institutional changes in Burma were born of experience — a lot of it sad experience. Probably there will be greater than lesser changes in institutional arrangements, governmentally and otherwise, in the second decade of independence in Burma and the various other countries of South and South-East Asia. This may be true even of such comparatively stable lands as India and the Philippines.

It will be interesting to see the degree to which institutions founded on theory and observation from a distance are influenced in the next decades by the experiences of the past decade and the fuller emergence of a post-revolutionary generation of politicians to positions of influence. The late J. S. Furnivall told me in early 1960: 'U Nu will be different after 18 months out of power.' In what ways will Congress be different when it ultimately falls from power in India? And what kind of institutions will Pakistan's military leaders finally leave their country, and how will these institutions be used after the withdrawal of President Ayub Khan from his present post of authority?

How far will Western-style institutions continue to be changed by the seemingly growing influence of traditional forces in some of the countries of South and South-East Asia? The role of the politically-oriented clergy in Buddhist Burma and Ceylon will be particularly interesting to watch. Sukarno is a secularist, and Indonesia's Communist Party is second in size in Asia only to China's — but Aung San of Burma was also a secularist and the Communists were the best organized component of the AFPFL a decade-and-a-half ago, and today Burma boasts a state religion and Buddhism is of growing political importance. Is a change in the political importance of religious institutions in Indonesia also possible? The fading impact of the colonial era — from district officers to conspiratorial political parties — will be interesting to observe, too. The political institutions of Southern Asia are varying mixtures of the old and the new, the experienced and the observed — resulting in more complex (and confused) political systems than those of the West. Watching, accordingly, may not be easy.

The essentials of a political system, embracing supporting as well as governing institutions, are political socialization, interest presentation, and policy formation and execution. These functions need not be carried out by the same institutions, however, or in the same way, in all societies; moreover, they need not be carried out by organs of the state. Policy can be formed even if government as such does nothing, if government abdicates what are regarded as its responsibilities in the West to others. Institutions, political but not governmental, may play key roles in this process. Too little is known of the role of such institutions in many of the countries of South and South-East Asia — for example, the monks in Burma.

Categories based on experience in dealing with particular institutions in the West, however, may not be sufficient for clear and meaningful analysis of multi-functional political organizations in the less-developed societies. Take the military, for example. What is it, or was it, in various recent important political situations? It is responsible for the governing of the state, and is regarded by the population as such, in Thailand and Pakistan; such also was the case formerly in Burma. In the latter land — and in Thailand and Indonesia — it is one of the most important economic groups, if not the most important economic group, today. As such it plays a major role in both the formulation and implementation of economic policy, sometimes at odds with the views of the civilian leadership of the state which may have set its sights on quite different ends and chosen other means to attain them — making the military a kind of government within the government. Almost everywhere the army is an important interest group seeking to influence public policy; sometimes even it is willing to take over the government itself to get what it wants, distinguishing it from most interest groups in the West. Military elements also have become weapons of competing political factions — as in Laos. In Burma in 1959 army officers campaigned — unsuccessfully — for independent candidates in order that the latter might hold the balance between what were expected to be 'Clean' and 'Stable' AFPFL political factions in Parliament as a result of the February 1960 elections. Some of the soldiers, in short, intended to play a role in legislative manoeuvring through influencing these independents.

All of this raises the question of what the army basically is in Southern Asia as a political institution. Similar questions could be raised with regard to the civil service, labour and other interest groups, students and even the universities, the press, and so on. This clearly suggests limitations in comparative institutional analysis and that there may be more helpful ways of finding out what the observer wants to know.

What has happened in South and South-East Asia is that institutions have been borrowed from the West, and these have either been used for different purposes in such lands — for example, the institution of the Opposition in Burma — or misused, such as Parliament in various countries. Burma's U Nu, as an example, clearly seems to see the Opposition at the present time — the former 'Stable' AFPFL faction of U Ba Swe and U Kyaw Nyein — as a political group whose support must be won in order that his major programme should not be compromised by a future government of a different political complexion. This makes a lot of sense in Burma, but it is a somewhat unusual notion of the function of the Opposition. Saul Rose has clearly indicated that legislatures exist in all the lands of South and South-East Asia, but he has also stated that they are quite different institutions from country to country. The Indonesian House of Representatives cannot realistically be said to be similar to its Ceylonese counterpart at the present time — in function, method of selection, or spirit (among other considerations). Other dissimilarities could also be suggested.

There is no question, in summary, that the political institutions of South and South-East Asia were borrowed from the West — but less inevitably than is generally thought and within the context of indigenous values and experiences. Such institutions were probably much shakier at the start of independence than we realized; their survival is somewhat surprising. That they should change, even become unrecognizable (as seems to be happening in Indonesia), is not startling.

Saul Rose ended his discussion with the statement that democracy is a 'universal concept', with which Nehru, Nu and some others in South and South-East Asia clearly agree. But it is as a concept — and not as a set of particular institutions — that it has this universal validity. American and British democratic political institutions differ greatly, and it is not surprising that the political institutions which are democratic in South and South-East Asia differ even more from those democratic parts of the Western world. Indeed, in some respects there may be more similarities between the approaches to political decision-making in would-be democratic Burma and non-democratic Indonesia, for example, than, say, Burma and Britain. The unanimity no-vote procedure of the powerful Executive Committee of the united pre-split AFPFL in Burma, as an illustration, bore a marked resemblance to *mufakat* — agreement by general consent — which President Sukarno has sought to institutionalize in Indonesia. Democracy can assume many forms, and all possible — let alone the most desirable — ones may in fact not already have been discovered by the West.

The character and significance of most of the institutions treated by Rose vary considerably from country to country, as has been noted — parliaments, parties, armies, and so on. Why? For reasons that are essentially unique to each land, the catch-all of many specialists on the Soviet Union for years, or are there general rules of political behaviour that may contribute to an understanding of the governments and politics of all of the developing areas (regardless of their geographical locale) and indeed to a fuller understanding even of Western political institutions and behaviour? Should we — can we — compare the performance of particular functions or the role of specific institutions across national lines, abstracting them from their broader political processes? Or should we compare total processes or systems? Whatever the answer of the individual observer, the evolution of the political institutions of South and South-East Asia provides challenging opportunities for learning more about the way he governs himself and solves his problems through political means.

George Kahin

I wonder whether we would have a clearer picture of these institutions if we recognize that perhaps there are basically two kinds of parties, quite different. In some of these countries obligations towards government are much more clearly perceived than rights. Where that is the case you are perhaps more likely to have the party system that has developed in Indonesia and Cambodia and South Vietnam, where there really is not a representative function as far as parties are concerned: impulses flow downward from government to people rather than the reverse. The parties are a channel, not for articulating public opinion, but for shaping it on the part of government, and more than that, the party is seen by government as a means of marshalling social forces in the country in order to serve the government. It does seem to me that there is this kind of party, and it perhaps has a substantial future in South-East Asia as well as the kind of party which is more to our own Western experience.

Percival Spear

It seems to me that one of the difficulties between the working of democratic institutions in the West and, so far, in the East, is that whereas in the West the drive for change comes from below, from groups which organize themselves into parties — whether it is a two-party system or a series of groups — in the East the drive has mainly come from above. It has been a drive in the first place of nationalists stirring up their people in order to get rid of the colonial power, and then it is in many cases a drive to organize the country along Western lines. There again the drive necessarily comes from the top because the people down below do not know which Western institutions to bring into the country. With leaders at the top putting their roots down into the popular soil and giving the people the feeling of participation, a feeling that the new government is their own government, as it were, the new, transformed society takes shape, and the drive begins to come from below. I would suggest that that is what is beginning to happen in India — that having had this digging down process going on for perhaps two generations and having pushed the introduction of Western institutions quite a long way, you begin to get the people themselves stirring in villages and beginning to demand things on their part. In Pakistan, on the other hand, the process is still very much from the top downwards, emphasized by the fact that the only effective régime has been the take-over by the military. I think you can trace in the different areas the degree to which the drive from above is being transformed into, first, participation from below, and then a drive from below.

Hugh Tinker

May I suggest that the classification many of us have adopted, of an élite and a mass, is now completely out of date in this area? The view we have taken of an active, middle-class, Westernized group and passive peasant mass needs to be modified, and this is probably one of the great changes of the last ten or fifteen years. Even in politically backward countries, like Burma, there is the growth of a real middle class in the sense that it links up with the villages and the peasants and links up with the towns. It is both urban and rural; it is both semi-educated, and in many ways educated — it has members who have gone to college — but it is not middle class at all in the old sense. It stems out of village society and forms the real basis of the parties now. These are the equivalents of people we see in our own countries; people who organize politics in the street and in the ward, people who distribute pamphlets, people who get up processions. These people, it may be argued, exist only to provide a background to the leaders; but I do not think this is entirely true. The leaders do have to take account of these people to a greater extent; and if we look at this element (which I think one can see increasingly in Burma, for example, or in the Philippines) one does have a much more optimistic view of democracy than a straightforward assessment of parties and leaders would indicate.

Raghavan Iyer

In discussing democracy in Asia we have no doubt to get away to some extent from the continual emphasis on the possibility of frequent changes of government which is so important to democracy in the West. However, if we feel that we need not bother very much about changing the power élite at the top who take all the crucial national decisions and that we should stress the need to decentralize decision-making on local problems on a very wide scale, we must face the fact that although this might contribute to the political education of large masses of people there would be no real chance of these people ever decisively changing policy at the top unless there are effective intermediate institutions at the district and state level. The Gandhians in India who have contemplated a pyramidal structure, and Vinoba Bhave who has advocated something like a committee of sages or philosopher-kings at the top, have been very concerned about the working of responsible government not merely at the local level but also at intermediate levels in the national polity.

The question arises whether people who are gaining political education and experience in taking decisions say, in the community development programme, are really going to keep quiet in the long run about the plans produced from the top. In India it is now the fashion even in government circles to talk about 'planning from below', but this is not really taken very seriously. If it were, quite olearly we would not only find a great variety of village plans but also ways in which people taking initial decisions about the kind of village plan they want would influence the shape of the regional and ultimately of the national plan, and this would require such a tremendous leap in democratic thinking that we can hardly begin to visualize it. Therefore it is very important to stress not merely the intermediate links in the transmission belt but also the need for non-governmental institutions which are genuinely independent and national in character. In the case of an authoritarian régime, although it could be argued that ultimately the fermentation of discussion will eventually make itself felt through the party structure by the cadres reaching up to the top, as long as there is tight control through police repression and the identification of the party with the state and the civil service there is simply no guarantee that this would automatically and always occur. In a developing democracy if effective non-governmental institutions do emerge which knit together people — maybe only community development officers in various parts of the country — into forms of political association other than the conventional political party, then there would be different ways in which new types of leadership could appear from below and become capable of affecting government policy.

The crux of the problem for a developing democracy is not so much the possibility of periodic replacement of the élite at the top but the extent to which effective and genuine non-governmental organizations are actually springing up at the local and national level. If a government is content with its claim that it is responsive to mass opinion and is seeking a national consensus, it is very easy for it to think as in India today that it could itself create through its community development programme a whole range of non-official leaders who would willingly co-operate with the government. Then of course real difficulties do arise, especially when some kind of party factionalism intervenes in the process. So the prospect of democracy in Asia does very much depend upon whether the government is willing to use its own main transmission belt while also allowing independent political groupings and associations, not of the orthodox form, to establish other transmission belts and create new classes of leaders at a national level who would eventually be able even to produce quite decisive changes at the top. It is not enough that the ruling élite in a developing democracy is open and neither closed nor self-perpetuating. It is also necessary that the ruling élite should be continuously responsive to pressures within the system and increasingly willing to share some of the burden of decision-making with those who are at the periphery and at intermediate levels of the system.

Chapter sixteen

OPERATIVE FORCES

by Maurice Zinkin

Not everybody in Southern Asia is interested in politics. Some people seek God, others only want to make a living, some love cricket and some are concerned mainly with marrying their daughters. Those who are interested in politics, however, and there are more of them than there have ever been before, are driven above all by the desire for equality.

This equality is of many sorts. Equality between men and women, equality between classes, equality between castes, equality between ex-colonial nations and their ex-rulers, equality between rich and poor, even — just beginning — equality between parents and children.

Not all of it takes a strictly political form. The fight between parents and children, for instance, takes place largely on the same ground as in Europe, over the clothes the children wish to wear, or the time they can come home, or with whom they may be seen in a coffee-house. Even some of the change in the relationships between classes is quite independent of politics. A plantation overseer will today not hit his coolies with the freedom he permitted himself before the war. This is the result of a change in the general atmosphere and in the attitude of the coolie quite as much as of a harsher attitude by the government to such behaviour.

Nevertheless, a surprisingly large amount of the drive to equality does take political form, and, in doing so, it dominates the politics of every South Asian country. The form is not the same in every one of these countries, for the nature of inequality in their societies is different. The women of Burma have always been very much the equals of their men. Thailand has never been a colony. Pakistan has no class system as we know it, Islamic society is very fluid. But in every one of these countries there is inequality of some sort, and enough of it to make its eradication the major objective of all the great political parties. All these countries have rich and poor, they all feel themselves poor as nations as against the rich nations of the West, they all have had a tradition of authoritarian government and they all have had considerable gulfs between the educated and the uneducated.

The form of the struggle for equality which is most obvious to Western minds is the way in which the countries of South Asia look at the world outside. Some, like Thailand and Pakistan, are Western allies, some, like India and Burma, are the high priests of non-alignment. But these differences are the result of different calculations of the national interest rather than of differences of general outlook. On most issues Pakistan and Thailand will urge on their allies exactly the same policies as India and Burma will urge on their friends. On most issues at the United Nations, India and Pakistan, to take the extreme example, will in fact be on the same side though they may express their views with differing degrees of vehemence according to the necessities and combinations of the moment.

Through all the attitudes to the outside world of Southern Asian countries runs a revolt against the old white nineteenth-century view that there are advanced nations and backward nations, and that the advanced nations have both a right and a duty to guide the progress of the backward nations and to provide leadership for the politics of the world.

This old view was expressed in many forms, sometimes creditable like the doctrine of trusteeship, sometimes discreditable like the straight assertion of racial superiority that one gets in South Africa. Creditable or discreditable, all of these forms are equally unacceptable to the nations of Southern Asia. They believe, with the men of the American Revolution, that all men are born equal, and all nations have an equal right to self-government. As time goes on, they may be willing to see some delay in the attainment of independence by colonial countries so that there may be a smooth transition and self-government may be adequately prepared for, but they never really depart from the view that self-government is everybody's right, that of Angolans and Mozambiques, just as much as their own. All Burma's unhappy experiences of the last thirteen years have not made the Burmese regret the old British days. In Algeria Asian sympathy is universally with the Algerian Moslems. In Rhodesia it is invariably with the blacks. In the Congo it is with the central Government because they feel Katanga lets whites occupy too many key places and make too much of its policy. It is sometimes said that behind these sympathies lies an anti-white colour prejudice. This is not so. The nations of South Asia are not against the French colonists in Algeria or the whites in Rhodesia because they are white, but because they are a minority; and it is the Asian view that the majority must be allowed to prevail. It is true that just as most Europeans tend to identify themselves in an African struggle with their fellow whites, most Asians, aware that to whites they are coloured, will tend to identify themselves with their fellow coloured. But even then it is probably true that the identification which comes from a common colour is less important than the identification which comes from an apparently common past experience. An Indian or a Pakistani was once a colonial struggling to be free. Naturally his sympathy in Kenya and Rhodesia is with Mr Kenyatta and Mr Kaunda, equally colonials struggling to be free.

It has perhaps not yet been fully realized in the West, or indeed in Russia, how upsetting to the present order of the world the Asian assertion of equality of men and of nations is likely to be.

Americans and Englishmen and Russians have taken for granted so far that their opinions are entitled to more respect in the councils of the world than the opinions of others who are less powerful. There are certain matters where Asians accept that this must be so. Mr Nehru has repeatedly pointed out that only the Russians and the Americans can in the end settle the cold war. What Asians are not prepared to accept is that the view of an Englishman or Russian or American on how the world should be ordered should be counted as any more important than the view of a Pakistani or an Indian or a Burmese.

This attitude that they are just as important as anyone else has not yet been asserted fully. Indians do not yet make it a great national grievance that India is not a permanent member of the Security Council; Pakistan and Indonesia do not yet say that they are bigger than England or France, and so must carry at least as much weight in everybody's calculations. But one only has to look back to 1945 when Southern Asia was almost totally unimportant in order to see how far the Asian countries have already come in achieving a position in the world commensurate with their numbers, and to realize that this is a continuing process. One day India *will* count for at least as much as the United States, one day Pakistan and Indonesia *will* count for at least as much as England or France. Certainly their foreign policy will be steadily directed towards this end, and their peoples will tend to judge what happens in the world by whether or not other countries do pay an increasing respect to their opinions. So far, they are not asserting themselves in any unpleasant way. They are on the winning side and they know it; colonialism, as Mr Nehru has recognized, is nearly dead, a Burmese is Acting Secretary-General of the United Nations, both sides in the cold war count the votes of the Afro-Asian bloc. The countries of Southern Asia can afford to go gently.

At home the drive to equality is conducted with equal delicacy. The countries of South Asia are countries in revolution but they are not countries of class war. They are being pushed towards equality from above and below at once. Indeed, more often than not over the last generation in South Asia the real pressure for equality has come not from the bottom but from the top. It is those who have the privileges who have insisted on taking them away from themselves. The men have insisted on equality for women. In Pakistan the army officers, themselves often of landed families, and not the tenants, have carried through land reforms. Brahmins from the cities, rather than untouchables from the villages, have made the most effective attack on untouchability.

This is not a historically unique phenomenon. There are very clear parallels with nineteenth-century England, where the radicals were more often members of the upper middle class with a conscience than members of the working class with a grievance. But it is particularly important that it should be so in Southern Asia in the 1950's and the 1960's because Southern Asia is an area and now is a moment where the educated professional classes have a historically quite unusual political importance.

The professional politicians are in general men who have at least matriculated; many are university graduates. In the countries where the army dominates, the army officers on the whole are of middle-class, often lower middle-class, background and of relatively high standards of education. The journalists, the editors, the business managers, the government servants, all the makers of opinion, are professional and educated. The aristocracies no longer matter. The industrial working classes are still very small, the peasants have translated their traditional respect for the man who could read and write into a willingness to vote for the man with a university degree.

What these men think therefore is politically of overwhelming importance. This may not last. As time goes on one can expect the peasantry and the industrial working class to vote increasingly for men from their own ranks. But this may not happen for another generation, and it is unlikely ever to be complete. In a world where government is getting constantly more complex, the politician to succeed must increasingly be educated. The uneducated may get in, but they normally stay on the back benches.

If it is important that what the educated think dominates politics, it is doubly important that the educated of Southern Asia, with the exception perhaps of Thailand, have been brought up in the liberal tradition. They believe, with more or less enthusiasm according to circumstance and temperament, in liberty, equality and fraternity. They believe, more rather than less, in the career open to talent; they believe, on the whole, in the equality of women. They believe almost always in the unimportance of birth. They are allergic to privilege in others and quite often ashamed of the privileges they have themselves. Therefore, even when they would like to protect their privileges they find themselves unable to do so; any resistance to equality they might like to make is undermined by a certain sense of guilt.

The paradoxical result is that in India and Pakistan and

Ceylon one finds governments of the middle-class educated imposing on the middle-class educated a higher rate of taxation than such people have to pay almost anywhere else in the world, and doing so in part specifically in order to bring their incomes down nearer to those of the mass of the population; and although all the media of communication are dominated by this same class of the educated, the governments are able to do this with an absolute minimum of resistance. The middle-class educated no more enjoy paying taxes than anyone else but at least they feel the taxes are right in principle. They may be tempted into evasion; they are rarely prepared to make a frontal attack on the principle that inequality of income is too great and should be diminished.

It is the same with land reform. In the 1880's when a quite moderate Bengal land tenancy bill was introduced into the Indian Legislative Council, the resistance from landowners was such that the Government had to give up its idea of restricting rents to one-fifth of the crop. Today landowners try to delay reform by actions in the courts, they try to evade it by collusive action with relations or tenants in the village; they are no longer able simply to resist it with the conviction and sense of outrage of the 1880's. Now they put up with rents limited to one-sixth of the crop and are happy that it is not worse.

The most extraordinary result of this attitude of the educated is the universal socialism of Southern Asia. It is everywhere considered proper for the state to dominate the economy. There are different views on how far the state should directly own industry or drill for oil. But there is very little opposition on principle to the idea that the state should own many of the economy's commanding heights, and almost none to the idea that the state has the right to control the economy in a detailed way whenever and however it feels necessary.

This acceptance of a primary role for the state in economic development derives from many sources. There is history. The state, because of irrigation, has always played a considerable part in Southern Asia. There is sociology. The professional classes, who dominate both opinion and the government, are very often more prepared to work as government servants than either to start new businesses of their own or to work for existing businessmen. Trade does not rank high in the hierarchy of professions and the existing indigenous businessmen are often rather despised. There is pure politics. The more the state does, the more the politicians can promise.

All these by themselves would not, however, be enough to give socialist ideas the hold they have. After all, one could find many parallels in France, and the French Government makes no claim to be socialist. Behind the socialism of Southern Asia, there is something more, there is the deep need for equality.

Partly this is perfectly straightforward. The peasant, the worker, the clerk, wish no longer to remain in the poverty of centuries. They wish to have the amenities of those better off than themselves, and the politician of the Left can offer results, even if he may afterwards have to welsh on his offer, where the politician of the Right can only either suggest that they raise themselves by their own efforts, or preach contentment with the status to which they were born. This straightforward appeal to envy, or simply to the desire to be better off than one is, is important in explaining the constant push towards socialism in South Asian politics. But it is not as important as one might think. Much of the population still accepts hierarchy and privilege as right, and can see their advantages. One reason why Indian land reforms intended to give the land to the tiller have sometimes been ineffective is that the tenant himself quite often thinks it is wrong to take somebody else's land away from him, and is therefore perfectly willing to join with his landlord in a collusive surrender.

More important is the terrible shame of the educated at the poverty and backwardness they see around them. This feeling is much stronger in India and Pakistan than in Thailand or Burma, but it exists everywhere. As communications have improved and the world has grown smaller, the educated have come more and more to realize that their countries have fallen behind. Since they know that this is not through some inherent inferiority in themselves or their fellow-citizens, they naturally feel it is a position not to be tolerated. The discovery that England has of late been near the bottom of the league table for economic growth has, in a minor way, recently had exactly the same effect on the educated of Great Britain. Part of the answer in Britain recently has been a dose of planning.

The problems of Southern Asia are worse; so their answer is to demand more planning than in Britain, even though they may know that the plans will not benefit themselves personally. In most countries the people who are eager for development have some reasonably immediate personal interest. Their profits will go up or their wages will go up or they will make money dealing in land. In Southern Asia it is not as simple as that, though all these motives do apply. Many of the people who control government and opinion do not get any very direct benefit from development, unless of course they are corrupt. Their children and their grandchildren will have more jobs open to them and these will perhaps be better jobs than they could have had in an undeveloped society. But they themselves are very liable to suffer. Development in Southern Asia nearly always involves either higher taxation or inflation or both, and the people who hold power are very largely men on fixed or relatively fixed incomes. Almost all the key officials who have made the Indian five-year plans find their own real incomes reduced. The army officers of Pakistan no longer have the real incomes of 1947. Mr Bandaranaike came from one of Ceylon's richest families; the high taxes of his party have made the Bandaranaike family poorer, not richer.

The driving force behind South Asian planning is not the personal benefit of the planners but the desire to develop the country. This desire has behind it the immense sense of shame that the great mass of the population are so much poorer than the planners and that their country itself is so much poorer than so many of the other countries of the world. The planner is trying to make both the poor and his own country more equal.

This emphasis on equality explains many of the oddities of planning. If, for example, one was considering only economic efficiency one would put one's factories in the places where costs are lowest and one would choose for one's priorities those developments which would give the maximum increase in the national income for the minimum use of resources. The planners often do neither. They spread their factories about so as to ensure that there is some equality between regions. They choose as projects not only those which are profitable but also those which will give their country greater independence or greater position in the world. They want to make their own tanks even before they make their own cosmetics; they like to make their own steel or their own locomotives even when it would be more profitable to import. Nor are these priorities confined to the planners. The public supports them because the public shares the planners' eagerness to enable their country to hold up its head in the councils of the nations, and the public shares the planners' belief, which is indeed probably correct, that the comity of nations somehow ranks higher people who make their own locomotives and steel than people who do not.

There is more resistance to equality amongst the educated when one comes to private matters. If one is trying to get rid of *purdah* one comes up against some very severe opposition, and when India increased the inheritance rights of daughters there were many who were very unhappy. Nevertheless the educated on the whole accept even these very intimate changes. They do generally feel that in a modern state wives and daughters must be properly treated. It is amongst the uneducated that the resistance can be paralysing. There is many an Indian village where the daughter simply does not get the inheritance to which the law entitles her and perhaps even herself thinks she ought not to get it. Nor has the movement out of *purdah* spread very far amongst Pakistan's more uneducated people.

When one goes from family equality to other forms of equality, however, the feelings of the poor and the uneducated are giving increasing support to the demands of their better-off and more educated brothers. The idea of equality, whether social or economic, began in Southern Asia at the top. It is now being taken up with more and more enthusiasm at the bottom. At first it was the upper-class man who said that the untouchable must be given rights. The provision in the Indian constitution forbidding the practice of untouchability was passed by a predominantly upper-caste Constituent Assembly. Now it is beginning to be the untouchable who demands his rights, who votes for the party who will give him his rights, and who is prepared to go to the police at considerable personal risk in order to assert his rights. Equally, factory legislation was originally passed to protect workers who were fundamentally helpless. So was a great deal of the legislation for compulsory arbitration. Now the worker is getting himself organized into increasingly effective trade unions and is asserting more and more his rights to a fair share of the profits of the business, to protection from arbitrary redundancy, even sometimes to a share in making the business's policy. Indeed, he is now so successful in asserting his rights that the entrenched privileges of existing workers are very often a major obstacle to efficiency, and particularly to rationalization.

The desire for equality permeates the whole of South Asian life. Most of the ideals inspiring it have been taken from the Western liberal tradition. It will, however, end in an equality greater than any Western society knows, for in Asia this movement admits neither the traditional class distinctions of England, nor the class distinctions based on education of the European continent, nor the respect for wealth of the United States. Asia has still a very long way to go. Privilege is still very much more obvious in Bombay or Karachi or Colombo than it is in Leeds or Lille or Chicago; but whereas in every Western country there is some clear conservative tradition behind differentiation, it is not clear where in Asia the better-off, the better-educated, and the better-born will be able to find similar defences. In practice they ought to be able to put off the day of total equality for a long time, but it will continue to advance on them relentlessly unless they can find some better theoretical justification for inequality than they have up to now even tried to devise.

Closely linked with the desire for equality is the need to become modern.

Everywhere in South and South-East Asia one finds this desire. Old orthodoxies are under attack, new industries are being created, the educational system is being given an ever more scientific orientation, the educated young live more and more like their contemporaries in London or Paris or New York, and armed forces demand jet aircraft and the newest tanks. At first sight this seems to the average Westerner to require no explanation. South and South-East Asia wants to live as he does. What could be more reasonable?

In fact there are very considerable oddities about this phenomenon of Asian modernization.

First of all, this enthusiastic acceptance of modernity is, on the whole, new. Some people, especially amongst the governing classes of Asian society, have always been eager to Westernize, as it significantly used to be called. But they used to be a minority; and in the old days, even they had doubts. It took a

long time before Ram Mohan Roy's doctrines became acceptable even to the educated. All through the second half of the
nineteenth century only the very exceptional parent desired
university education for his son, and hardly anybody desired it
for his daughter. A degree in engineering or a science has only
finally become fashionable in the last generation. In the inter-
war years the Indian Congress preached a return to the self-
sufficient village; Pakistan might not have been born without
Islamic orthodoxy and the *mullahs;* the Buddhism of the
Burmese or the Thais is just beginning to be disturbed. In 1938
there were many in South Asia who believed that the West
might obtain great material advantage from its particular form
of civilization, but that it sacrificed in return a certain spiritual
grace that was the peculiar possession of the East.

This lack of enthusiasm for modernity was perfectly reasonable. Many people were deeply attached to the old beliefs and
the old social structure and they shrank from the shock modernization would necessarily involve. Modernization is not just a
series of end-products, steel works or educated young women or
an impartial judiciary; it is also a whole set of habits and beliefs
and ways of doing things, whose reconciliation with Asia's older
habits and beliefs and ways of doing things can be daunting and
unpleasant.

However reasonable, the doubts now seem to have disappeared. The Government of Pakistan has its *mullahs* under very
good control. India has almost forgotten Gandhian economics;
nothing would alarm the Government of India more than the
idea of its villages suddenly becoming self-sufficient. When
Burma declares itself a Buddhist state, the fear of the minorities
is the modern one, that they will be discriminated against in
government jobs, not the old-fashioned one, that their faiths
may be persecuted. Even the equality of women is no longer
theoretically denied, however often practice may cling to a past
of male dominance. It causes much less comment in India or
Pakistan when a woman becomes an ambassador than it would
in England if one were to become a consul; and in South Asia an
educational institution which discriminated against women in
the way Oxford and Cambridge and the British medical schools
do would be quickly brought to heel by government action.

Accompanying South Asia's desire for equality is the dropping of its own claims to superiority. So far as my experience goes, Indians, say, are much more certain than they were in 1938 that they can command a division or split an atom just as well as anybody else. But they are much less sure than they were in 1938 that they are less materialistic or more non-violent than others. Pakistanis are now perfectly sure they can govern themselves, as not everybody in the Punjab was in 1938; but they no longer give one the lectures I got from some of my college contemporaries on how *purdah* produces a much purer sexual morality than dancing or mixed bathing.

This is the odder in that, in those matters in which South Asians claimed superiority before the war, the rest of the world has not improved. There has been one war, and there is the threat of another, to show that the rest of us have not lost our belief in violence; and few who were shocked by Western sexual morals in 1938 would be less shocked by those of today. Nor has there been in Asia itself in the intervening years some great revolution of mind, a Havelock Ellis to argue for greater sexual freedom or a Mussolini to talk of the joys of war. The old doubts, the old assertions of their own superiority, seem simply to have died off, like old people who have reached their allotted time. The new generation seems to have grown up innocent of them, knowing nothing but one world of which they intend to be citizens, one set of global ideas in which they too believe.

Modernization as such, therefore, is now for the first time the accepted doctrine of every political party. The Hindu communal parties, for instance, attack untouchability; Ceylon toys with the idea of a steel industry. This gives politics a certain relaxation. Everybody believes in so many of the same things. Moreover, since in South Asia one is so often starting from scratch, there are fewer obstacles to their acting on their beliefs than there are in the West. It is always easier to get everybody to agree on a socialist solution if the industry to be created is a totally new one, not an old one which has first to be nationalized. It is always easier to let women into all men's jobs, if there was no preceding division by which women secretaries were all right but women salesmen were very odd.

There is, however, one sort of modernity on which everybody is agreed but which is nevertheless not always easy fully to achieve: that is the creation of nation states.

Nobody in South Asia suggests that the area should be organized on any other basis. There is no proposal for federation comparable with the attempts to get political unity in Western Europe. Whispers about world government are of the faintest. There is not even as much surrender of sovereignty as one gets in NATO or in the European Economic Community. In South and South-East Asia devotion to the Austinian sovereign state is still general.

That this state has the undivided right to the loyalty of its subjects is unquestioned. There is no organization which can provide the state with the sort of competition that church and party and class have all at different times provided in Europe. Such competition could, it is true, be created quite easily; religion or linguistic group, for instance, could very quickly provide an alternative focus of loyalty, as one saw when India was partitioned, and as one is seeing again in the troubles between Tamils and Sinhalese in Ceylon. The state has to be careful all the time not to make these loyalties political, not to permit them to take form in opposition to itself; or so the educated, who so far govern and make opinion, feel.

This does not mean that loyalty to the nation state is weak. On the contrary, it is one of the main operative forces of politics. To some extent everybody accepts himself as a Ceylonese, a Pakistani, a Burmese, an Indian, and so on. The boundaries they have are, on the whole, the boundaries they want. Except for the Kashmir Valley, there are no *irredentas*. There are no great bodies of people who wish to split away from the state in which they find themselves. South Asia is much more stable than pre-war Europe.

The difficulties and arguments arise within the state, over who should control it and how. They are the direct result of twin drives, to equality and to modernity. If modernity is to be achieved, a great deal of the initiative in achieving it must be taken by the state; therefore, if equality is to be achieved, everybody must have the same chance of having his view on which way the so important state should go accepted. This requires more than universal suffrage. It requires that no definable group should be in a permanent majority or a permanent minority.

In Southern Asia this is not a class problem, and it is less and less a religious problem. On most of the policies the states of Southern Asia are trying to pursue the religions do not offer obviously different answers. One may have two views on priorities for heavy industry, but they will not depend on whether one is a Christian or a Hindu or a Buddhist. Religious differences may be immensely important when it comes to jobs; they are not important for policy. The Pakistani and Indian governments follow very similar policies quite surprisingly often; and when they do not, it has usually very little to do with Hinduism or Islam.

The grouping which matters in South Asia, and which gives the governments their greatest cause for anxiety is the linguistic. In Indochina the state has already broken up into its linguistic components; elsewhere only Thailand is a one-language state, and even it has a large Chinese minority.

Even the danger from linguism, except when the government courts trouble as in Ceylon, is, however, quite limited. The language groups do not want to break away. They do not even have different ideas about such central subjects as defence or foreign policy or national insurance or planning. There is no Tamil form of non-alignment, or Pushtu view on the value of aircraft carriers. There is an argument about loaves and fishes — everybody wants his share of central jobs and central industrial plants — but this is not difficult to settle. The argument which matters is cultural. People want to be at home with their government, so they want their local administration to be conducted in the mother tongue. They do not want to find themselves speaking a lesser language (equality again!) so they are reluctant to see one local language out of several replace the old imperial language as the vehicle of university teaching or central administration. They want to be able to run education and agricultural reform and such-like social matters in the way that suits them best, so they want such subjects to be state and not federal. But given this much play, they are then perfectly willing to give their loyalty to the centre for the rest, even if, as in the new Federation of Malaysia if it comes into being, the centre is very new. Everybody realizes that unity, not division, is the way to achieve the equality and modernity which are so dear to South Asia's heart.

George Kahin

We are being invited to go beyond political ideas and ideologies to a squarer confrontation of what it is that motivates people in political activity in South and South-East Asia. It would seem to me that if we are to come to grips with this matter effectively we are obliged to cross over into an area where many of us, and certainly myself, will feel insecure and rather inadequate; but parenthetically I would observe that a substantial part of the Western-educated leadership of these countries might have good reason to feel the same. For we are not of course dealing with homogeneous societies, but with societies which incorporate several often rather loosely integrated levels in which the paramount values and their relative importance are not necessarily congruent. Given the increasing interaction between these levels, it should, I believe, be all the more necessary for us to understand the values and motivations operative in the lower social strata as well as those held by the political leaders at the national level.

If we seek to understand what motivates politically active elements in this part of the world, I should think that we must give considerable attention to the often impressive residua of traditional social values, values which I feel still impinge, often quite heavily, on the course of political conduct. If we can accomplish this, perhaps we can better appreciate the nature of some of the new values which interact with these older ones. Although we may discover that this interaction will sometimes result in synthesis, I think we would do well to keep in mind Mr Carnell's caveat that this interaction can also result in a situation where seemingly incompatible values will exist autonomously, side by side, in what might in chemical terms be described as a state of suspension. And as for new values, we shall want to remember that they are of course only in part a selective borrowing from abroad and that they also derive in substantial measure from the recent intensive and turbulent historical experiences of these countries, particularly during the last two decades.

The major thrust of Mr Zinkin's argument is that a distinguishing quality of political activity in South and South-East Asia is the strong and all-pervasive motivation for equality among those who are interested in politics, and I would assume that it is because he believes this quality to be so prominent that he has singled it out as the operative force deserving his major attention. He tells us that those interested in politics are driven above all by the desire for equality and that this concern dominates the politics of every country in this area of the world. Indeed, he suggests that their societies will end in an equality greater than that known in any Western country.

Now if one is to follow the Oxford English Dictionary, *equality* is described as the condition of having equal dignity, rank or privileges with others, the fact of being on an equal footing. There is one element in this definition that I would like to reiterate and stress, namely the fact of being on an equal footing. Equality does not mean, then, merely heightened status and position as such for an individual within his country or for a nation within the international community. And within a society it is not a mere escalation upwards by which everyone rises in similar degree with roughly the same relative difference in their levels persisting.

Let me say at the outset that I do heartily hope that Mr Zinkin is right in his evaluation and in his prediction, but frankly I find myself unable to be so sanguine. It seems to me that among a great many of those who are interested in politics in South and South-East Asia there are a number of powerful values and motivations which militate rather significantly against the urge for domestic social and economic equality. It is probable, I think, that taken together these factors so blunt this urge as to ensure that even in the long run the character of most of these societies is unlikely to be more egalitarian than what one might describe as the average in Western Europe or North America. There is, I think, reason to believe that the desire for equality is at least as pervasive among politically conscious individuals in contemporary Britain or the United States as it is in South and South-East Asia and, indeed, permeates much broader strata of their populations; and I can see no very convincing reason for not being persuaded that ten, fifty or a hundred years from now these Western societies will not know a greater measure of equality than those of South and South-East Asia. Actually it strikes me that in this part of Asia the record since independence gives some reason for arguing that the trend has slackened and that in some of the countries the egalitarian *élan* appeared more marked fifteen years ago than it is today.

I have no doubt that in South and South-East Asia a goodly number of those interested in politics are sincerely dedicated to working towards egalitarian goals, but I am not sure whether they are a majority. And I am even less sure whether those who will soon supersede them — and who will have come from a generation less powerfully affected by nationalist movements and the struggle for independence — will have a similar dedication. Are there not a considerable number of political leaders in this part of the world who, like their counterparts elsewhere, feel obliged to make gestures in the direction of equality so as to make their leadership more acceptable to the domestic or international community but who in practice put other values higher? Or if they do have a substantial commitment to egalitarian goals, are they not often so absorbed by their efforts to maintain their power (and sometimes to enhance it) as to be left with insufficient means, or energy, to press effectively for these goals? And I wonder how many of these leaders are appreciably more disposed than are their counterparts in the West to surrender any significant portion of their prerogatives and perquisites in favour of any egalitarian levelling process?

Germane to this, I think, is Mr Zinkin's point that since in the countries of South and South-East Asia one is so often starting from scratch there are many fewer obstacles to their leaders acting on their beliefs than has been the case in the West. (He notes that it is always easier to get everybody to agree on a socialist solution if the industry to be created is a totally new one, not an old one which has to be nationalized.) I feel that this raises an important question: for how long can you continue to say that these new states are starting from scratch? How long does it take before there is so substantial a reshaping of society, at least at the top, as to create new vested interests in terms of prestige, status, as well as access to material benefits? And is not the propensity for power-holders to try to be self-perpetuating just as strong in South and South-East Asia as it is elsewhere in the world? To stay in power, may not a political leadership in South or South-East Asia be inclined in a degree roughly similar to that of its counterparts in many other areas to deal gently with relatively powerful anti-egalitarian interests in the country and in so doing be prevented from carrying through policies designed to achieve socio-economic equality?

I know, for instance, that political leaders in Indonesia in the early and middle 1950's, who themselves had little or no vested interest in capitalism and who regarded themselves as proponents of socialism, frequently found it more to their interests to wed themselves to and nurture a new national commercial élite, which in turn nourished their political parties financially, than to press effectively for socialist measures. I wonder whether the Congress Party, in facing the coming elections, and even more after Mr Nehru leaves the scene, will not be tempted to compromise rather severely with some of its egalitarian goals in order to secure sufficient financial backing for the party and to ensure the active support of many local party leaders.

Now if the word *socialism* is used to convey some sort of socio-economic equality, then I would ask whether the primary role of the state in economic development in so much of South and South-East

Asia should so generally be translated as dedication to socialism? Is not the emphasis just as often on building national strength and perhaps on the development of new and suitable opportunities for those who are politically dominant (and for the politically articulate but often economically insecure educated minority with which the dominant element must come to terms) as it is on achieving a general nation-wide social and economic equality? Perhaps the frequent lip-service given to socialism by the leaders of some of these countries tends to obscure the reality, and perhaps one should be more alive to the necessity of differentiating between socialism and what one might term a paternalistic benevolent statism.

It may well be, it seems to me, that the latter describes more accurately than socialism the point of view of most of the politically active people in many of these countries, and that frequently this is a better clue for understanding the current and potential direction of their political and economic development. One might well find that, consciously or unconsciously, the term socialism is to a large extent being used as something of a stylish cloak for a statism which, although benevolent, is hardly egalitarian. This matter is, I think, sometimes further confused because of the propensity of some Western observers (and some Westernized Asians) to view certain persisting traditional values of Asian cultures as incorporating a particular ideal, which they themselves happen to cherish, prominent in some branch of Western culture. An example of this tendency might be the ascription of an egalitarian emphasis to the traditional Hindu virtue of charity.[1]

Francis Carnell has noted in his paper that in economically backward countries the pursuit of political freedom is in the long run very likely to be incompatible with the pursuit of economic growth. Could one perhaps also say that in the case of such countries there is a basic incompatibility between rapid economic development and socio-economic equality? Is this not perhaps a built-in problem, varying to some extent from country to country and from culture to culture but in general unavoidable? Can one in economically backward societies effect the rationalization of activity and resources necessary to an effective programme of rapid economic development without at the same time developing and strengthening socio-economic differentiation?

Although state control of the process of economic development will

[1] For what I believe is an enlightening discussion of the operation of this value in the modern Indian political milieu, see the April, 1962 article by Phyllis J. Rolnick, 'Charity, Trusteeship, and Social Change in India: A Study of a Political Ideology', in *World Politics*.

undoubtedly result in considerably less inequality than under unrestricted capitalism, will it not in the countries of South and South-East Asia, for at least a considerable period of time, unavoidably lead to an increased rather than a diminished degree of socio-economic differentiation? What for instance of the egalitarian drive in Soviet Russia? Has not one of the important consequences of rapid economic development there been the emergence of a powerful new managerial group, in a relative sense highly privileged, a development which is really inconsistent with economic equality? Even in Indonesia, a country which is not well known for rapid economic development, merely to maintain certain sectors of the economy it has recently been necessary to build up a privileged group of managers and equip them with incentives for working harder and more efficiently, a process which inevitably militates against economic equality. Indeed, can it not perhaps be postulated for countries such as Indonesia and Burma, where colonial rule left virtually no indigenous entrepreneurial, commercial or industrial middle class, that governments undertaking any considerable degree of economic development must inevitably create greater economic differentiation, introducing a new and vitally important managerial class which must in significant measure be privileged in order to ensure its dedication to working effectively for the state? Can one argue plausibly that such men can be so schooled in altruism and dedication to social service that they will be content to live at the same economic level as the urban workers and the peasantry whose energies they are undertaking to organize and direct?

These last observations would seem to me to emphasize the need for more attention to other motivating factors, some of which are surely universal and not peculiar to these areas. Undoubtedly in some cases an altruistic concern for social and economic equality has gone far towards crowding out other values and motivations, but I wonder whether in the minds of most politically active people in the area the egalitarian concern is really dominant. Do not calculations of power, status, prestige, loyalty and partiality to family and friends, not to mention interest in material wealth — in one combination or another — command a greater authority in the minds of most of these people? I wonder whether Mr Zinkin attaches sufficient weight to the often lively persistence of more culturally bound religious and other traditional values which would seem to me in many cases to stand in the way of equality. I would ask whether perhaps those Asian leaders who are genuinely dedicated to the idea of social and economic equality have not discovered in the last ten or fifteen years that among other powerful individuals in their societies, men with whom they must deal politically, there is a much greater regard for traditional values, for maintenance and increase of wealth, status, power, prestige, than these leaders had originally expected to encounter? And, among such individuals, do not these concerns often quite decisively outweigh any dedication to the goals of social and economic equality towards which these leaders would like to bring them? May not these factors be of equal importance with what Mr Zinkin terms the twin drive to equality and modernity in creating the difficulties and arguments which arise within the state over 'who should control it and how'? And have not these leaders perhaps discovered that among the educated elements the fear engendered by the prospect of economic insecurity and inability to secure a position commensurate with educational achievement — so often a consequence of the rate of economic development lagging well behind the output of colleges and secondary schools — can sometimes work quite powerfully against efforts calculated to raise the level of those whose economic status is already well below that of the more politically articulate groups which harbour these concerns?

Mr Zinkin also includes within his concept of equality the desire for progress and modernization and the urge to approximate more closely the status of economically advanced and more powerful states. It seems to me that these drives are often quite independent of any egalitarian urge and that by subsuming them under egalitarianism we are likely to be hindered in our efforts to understand the nature of current and potential political developments in South and South-East Asia. And I would add that the striving for increased national strength often works powerfully against equality within these countries. Whether the urge is generated in response to the threat of a minatory neighbour or results simply from a desire for respect or prestige in the international community (or from what perhaps appears to be an irrational compulsion for national self-assertion), it may well work against prospects for the kinds of political and economic development best calculated to achieve equality within the country.

Moreover, I do not believe that the dynamics of contemporary nationalism in most countries of South and South-East Asia can be most accurately described as primarily a desire for equality in the international community. At least, there would seem to be few of these countries willing to settle for equal status with their immediate South and South-East Asian neighbours.

My remarks have given primary emphasis to factors militating against egalitarianism as an operative force. This arises not only because of my conviction as to the potency of modifying and counteracting forces but also, of course, because in commenting on Mr Zinkin's paper I have felt an obligation to encourage as lively a discussion as possible. On balance I am not as pessimistic as my emphasis might suggest, although, as I mentioned earlier, I must own to being a good bit less hopeful than Mr Zinkin.

Certainly in attempting to understand the processes of political change in Asia it is important to identify the basic operative forces, and undoubtedly the urge for equality is in many of these countries a very important one. But surely it is only one of several major forces, and I would think that seldom, if ever, is it the most important. In any case, I believe our approach ought to be more pluralistic, encompassing a much wider range of operative forces, traditional as well as modern, and alive to the ways in which they interact — blunting, modifying, cancelling or reinforcing one another — and to the tensions, dislocations and adjustments which result from such interaction.

Percival Spear

Thinking of this question of equality, or lack of it, the case of Pakistan was mentioned and I quite agree that until the last year or two it might be said to be a condition of almost dedicated inequality. But there is a distinct change perceptible under the new régime. It was the, as it were, unequal people, a lot of them, who have been moved out by the army and there are a number of measures tending in the direction of equality — for example the land reform — and so one could be a little hopeful that the extreme inequality is tending to be decreased in Pakistan at the present moment.

It is an interesting point that this tendency towards equality is linked up with the desire to create a modern state — or develop the state along modern lines. The more glaring inequalities seen as an obstacle to this have been attacked. In the case of India I quite agree that there are probably very strong forces, perhaps reasserting themselves, in favour of traditional inequality, but there are the other forces which one should take note of, in particular the upsurge of the lesser castes, especially in the rural areas. Now that upsurge is certainly going to tend towards equality in the whole social structure and I think that in the case of Ceylon you could see this sort of process going on in the movements occurring there.

Equality was a theoretical idea which needed some drive behind it and I would suggest that the effective drive behind the urge to equality is in fact the need to become modern. In any of these countries of the region with which I have any experience I have always been very much impressed by the intense desire, on the part of the new generations, to be level with the West, both internationally and in their internal organization, not in a spirit of vindictiveness but simply in a spirit of emulation and as a matter of self-respect. That motive is something which will induce numbers of people in these regions to agree to changes and reforms which they do not at all like in themselves, because they will give them, they think, this feeling of being on a level with the West whether in its Atlantic form or its Russian form.

The need to become modern involves various big operations — usually a big education programme, the introduction of modern industry, technology and so on, which also means the introduction of a good many modern Western technicians for teaching and instructional purposes. All those new enterprises are outside the traditional range of social values and they therefore tend to have a levelling effect in the country concerned. They are not subject to the restrictions of, for example, caste or class, and in consequence it is possible for people of all classes to get into the new groups. Since the new groups give a new status, the effect is towards equality. That urge to become modern may be said to be the driving force behind the movement for equality, and it is likely to go on indefinitely into the future. Though the drive for equality in itself may slacken and some of the older forces may try to obstruct it, I think it will continue as an accessory of the drive to modernity.

Wang Gung-wu

My feeling that the urge for equality is an operative force, a major operative force, does not mean that I approve of it, or that I think it is necessarily a good thing, or even that it is an integrating force in society. Once we accept the fact that it is not necessarily good or bad, then we can observe, in Malaya for instance, that there are group urges for equality in plural societies in Asia. One of the binding forces for the Malay people is the need to be economically equal to the Chinese. This is a drive which is real even in the most remote Malay villages throughout the country. It may not take exactly that form. It may have religious and other ways of expressing this need to be powerful, this need to keep the Chinese down; but one of the most important expressions of this need is to be economically equal, and I think the Government in Malaya has taken important steps in this direction and has always appealed to the Malay population on this theme — that essential equality is lacking and that only by gaining that equality can they hope to retain the privileged positions that they have at the moment. Similarly with the Chinese, the question is that of political equality. One of the few things that unite the Chinese community in Malaya is the common feeling of being discriminated against in the political field — that they have difficulties in obtaining citizenship, that there is discrimination in the civil service and that there are a number of other discriminations in scholarships and so on for their children. Although they admit their economic superiority, they are at the same time constantly forced to fight for political equality. Because the urge for equality is so well understood now, not necessarily in the same way that it is understood in Europe, but nevertheless so well understood in each man's mind, the Chinese are prepared to be sympathetic with the Malay urge for equality — economic equality. This may seem unreal to an outsider, but within Malaya I am prepared to say that there are more Chinese than could be expected a few years ago who are sympathetic with the Malay urge to be economically equal.

In other words, on both sides of this communal barrier there is an acceptance of the common group urge to be equal. They feel, you may say, that perhaps it is only a bargaining point at the moment — that I would bargain your economic equality against my political equality — perhaps it is as crude as that; but I think that it goes deeper than that. The sense of equality has been grasped even in areas where there is a plural society. The urge for equality might now be described not in terms of individual urges for equality, but group urges, which may be a disintegrating force perhaps in a national unit for the time being. But in the long run the common urge on both sides, or three or four sides, to be equal, should help and not hinder the integrating forces — the forces of national unity — which many people pay lip-service to in Malaya. I am perhaps a little optimistic in believing that this urge will create a consciousness of class which will break through the barriers. We do not have the kind of class which cuts across communities; but once the urge for equality brings about the feeling that there is no need to discriminate against another community because we are now equal, this would create other common ties on a horizontal division of society.

Hugh Tinker

I would wish to question the theme of equality as the linking theme for South and South-East Asia. Clearly a difficulty we all find is to produce a worthwhile generalization. This probably is what we are all trying to do but as soon as we evolve one which we think is any good we immediately find ourselves saying, except Thailand, except the Philippines, and so on. I really doubt whether this generalization does operate very far. I can see the search for equality as between the South Asian countries and the West as a theme of great importance, but otherwise it would be necessary to go from country to country in order to check how far this theme is working out. Starting in the West, in Pakistan, I suggest that the search for equality really does not exist there, that there is really much more a search for inequality. The whole ethos and dynamic of lads going through college is not to serve the people but to separate themselves from the people. In India there is a very mixed kind of situation in which one must admit the Gandhian ideal still survives but, as Frank Moraes stresses in his book, there are strong forces working against the Gandhian spirit.[1] When we go to Burma I think there one finds a situation of equality. Malaya, to a surprising extent, is becoming a kind of middle-class country in which the man raising rubber really is not so far separated from the official or the trader. Thailand, however, is a country in which status and inequality are almost institutionalized.

I suggest two ways of looking at this. One way that may be meaningful is to look at the administration and see how far people's attitudes to the administration are at the back of this search for equality. It is very significant that Dr Spear in his attempt to find some kind of political future for Pakistan could only find it in the theme of a revived administrative élite — a leadership group. Administration in India includes, to a considerable extent, the survival of the old *hakeem* type of dominance; and yet when one goes to look at community development one finds, for example, that at training centres everybody from high officials down to village-level workers has to go through the same process of deliberately getting his hands dirty and doing menial jobs. This surely must reflect upon administration and attitudes of people to it.

There is one other aspect of equality — that is the attitude of the peoples of South-East Asia to the immigrants in their midst. Here there is complete absence of any concept of equality as it seems to me. The foreigner — the immigrant foreigner — still remains an inferior being in South-East Asia.

The governments of this area have to face feeling amongst their people that development really must produce results quite quickly and have to face comparison with other countries. But at the same

[1] Frank Moraes, *India Today* (New York, Macmillan, 1960), pp. 86–92.

time they are dedicated to the idea of government by persuasion which can be more effective than the old form of government by dictation. But when government passes on from law and order to development, and becomes involved in economic and social change of a very considerable kind, it is going to find itself in a dilemma. On the one hand to persuade; on the other hand to produce results. So often persuasion and participation just do not happen quickly enough, and then the official is in the old difficulty that he has to produce some form of result. If he does not produce results then the scheme is judged a failure. You may have interested the people, you may have involved the people, but at the same time you may not have got the physical results that you need. Therefore, so often in the community development schemes in India and elsewhere, the official falls back on the old technique of giving orders, from the village-level worker up to the district officer.

This has a distinct bearing on the whole development of democracy because there is, the whole time, this unspoken comparison between the results achieved by democracy in Southern Asia and the results that might be achieved by methods of compulsion. Here, modernity may serve the purposes of compulsion, because in many people's eyes the armies of South and South-East Asia represent modernity. Not the politicians nor the civil servants even, but the armies seem to have discovered the way of doing things. Even in India the army has been called upon in many crises to carry through a project that the civil power has not been considered adequate to get through. The army and efficiency are being equated and they are being equated with modernity.

This adds up to the question: what are national expectations? Do people set their sights exclusively on economic ends? The Burmese experience is illuminating because the Burmese have gone through these phases and, at any rate temporarily, seem to have given a negative answer to modernity. When the army took over in Burma things really did move. For the first time you had to pay fares on the trains, for the first time you were not allowed to spit in the street. The army really produced results, and the people at first quite liked this: they were pleased because, instead of all the foreigners coming and saying how filthy Rangoon was, foreigners came and said what a clean place it had become. But after a bit they got fed up with being pushed around, they got fed up with corporals making them scrub the street when they spat, and, as everybody knows, the military government was replaced by U Nu's Government which was much more in the traditional stream. There is quite an important qualification here, as to how democracy develops; what are the expectations of the people? Are these expectations always economic as we tend to think?

Professor Somjee

I would like to give a couple of illustrations from the village where I worked. In this village the *panchayat* or the village council has existed for the past fifty years and its members were nominated by government officials from among the dominant caste families. In 1956 the first *panchayat* election was held and there was a great desire on the part of the middle castes and the poor castes to get into the *panchayat* largely for reasons of social prestige. They were told that the *panchayat* was to be given a certain amount of power, it would be able to spend some money and submit schemes for constructing roads and schools and running a dispensary and so on. The dominant caste was equally keen on retaining its membership. So far it had not been very conscious or very concerned about its seats in the *panchayat* but after 1956 it suddenly woke up and realized that here was an instrument of power that should not be allowed to slip out of its hands. The elders in some of the families of the dominant caste used to be in the *panchayat* but when the election took place they found the rough and tumble of democratic politics a little unpleasant for them, and in the following election they passed on this responsibility of holding on to political leadership to their younger brothers or to their sons-in-law or to their cousins and so on who could face this rough crowd of the middle castes and the lower castes. Some of these leaders still get into the *panchayat* by mobilizing the labour force in the village because they still have the land divided among various members of the family. They give employment to people of lower castes and dictate at the time of the election. Sometimes they bribe them or give them a bottle of liquor in a prohibited area and make them vote for them. But it is very clear what their purpose is in staying in the *panchayat*. It is nothing but a form of social prestige. People of other villages would say, 'Now look at your village, a person from a lower caste is controlling the village *panchayat*, what a shameful state of affairs!' Some of the leaders of the rising castes are extremely shrewd and perhaps as skilful in politics and in dividing their opponents as the leaders of the upper caste. But they also have some sort of constructive approach over and above political skill.

The village is now moving towards not the idea of majority rule, but majority community rule. It is not easy to wipe out the caste factor which has been there for centuries and has now developed some sort of political ambition and perhaps acts as a substitute for political parties which do not exist in most of the Indian villages. Some of the leaders of the lower castes also appear to be fully conscious of what is happening in the village and quite often they talk through the idiom of class rather than caste. But while the leaders of the *harijans* talk through the idiom of class, their followers do not think in these terms. They would rather be governed by the people of higher castes who have been traditional exploiters and have a bad name in the village. It is again a matter of prestige to an average *harijan*. How could he be ruled by people who are held in low esteem by the people of higher caste?

There is another question, the drive towards equality through modernity. Over a few years the lower caste groups in some of these villages, particularly the *harijans*, have got some education, and have improved their income by going to factories, and the next question for them is how to raise their social status. Economically they have become independent because of the factories in the nearby towns. They have become independent of the village economy but they still continue to be part of the village social structure and remain at the bottom. Consequently they have started looking to the town. They would like to migrate to the towns, and have started thinking in terms of towns where they can walk into a restaurant and go to a cinema and get lost in a huge crowd without being questioned as to who they are or which particular caste they come from. Along with this desire to have social equality largely by losing one's identity in towns, there is a very interesting move on the part of these people to adopt classic Rajput surnames. Quite often one gets confused as to whether they are Rajputs or pseudo-Rajputs. In areas where Rajputs live, this trick does not work because they say that these are '*harijan*' Rajputs.

Maurice Zinkin

I do not place the weight on the idealism of those with privilege, but on the demands of those without the privilege. The importance of the idealism is only that the privileged have just enough guilty conscience to make their resistance rather ineffective. It does not mean to say that they do not often try to resist.

Most of these countries have universal suffrage and in some of them like India, Ceylon and, I understand, Burma this universal suffrage is effective in the sense that people really do vote. It is I think the general experience of the last hundred years that where you have universal suffrage the voter finds it difficult to understand why any-body else should be better off than he is. You can give him all sorts of temporary explanations: for the moment it is necessary for the economy, or necessary for the educational system, or some such reason, that other people should be better off — but he always tends to come back to challenging this. This is now a permanent part of the situation, certainly in those countries where the electorate really does vote. They will always be demanding better terms for them-selves.

If you go and look at any of these countries at a photographic moment of time, the thing that strikes you is that these are countries of great inequality. Burma may perhaps be an exception, but it is certainly true of India, Pakistan and Ceylon, and I imagine it is true of Indonesia. But if you live there over a long period what you are conscious of is the fact that every year your original privileged position is being eroded, and this is a consciousness which you share with virtually the whole of the rest of the privileged classes from your clerks upwards. If I may give some concrete and quite simple illustrations. I had twenty years in India of, I flatter myself, reason-ably steady promotion. I finished up at the end with almost exactly the same real income as I had in the beginning. I consider that quite a levelling down. I began in India as a bachelor with eleven servants; I ended as a married man with, I think, four and a half. When I first went out to India, if an official of my relatively junior status stood in a queue at a booking office this was a deliberate and rather flamboyant assertion of a refusal to make use of his proper privileges. By the time we left India if I had refused to stand in a queue at a booking office there would have been a major row. If when I first went to India you went up in the office lift you would often find that other people would leave the lift to you. At the end of my time in India your messenger boy came up in the lift with you quite auto-matically. Now some of these differences, like the messenger boy coming up in the lift, I would regard as improvements. Others, like the erosion of one's real income, I have more doubts about. But my point is that this went on all the time and that it did not only affect me. What is much more important is that the gap between, say, the clerk and the messenger had greatly diminished over these twenty years — the gap in income and still more the gap in status.

When I first went out, my senior subordinates considered it their duty to treat me with profound respect. To have failed to say *huzoor*, to have actually argued, although I knew much less than they did, and they knew perfectly well that I knew much less than they did and so did I, would have been rude — something that would not have crossed their minds. Now this is no longer so at all sorts of managerial and official levels because the modern theory is that if you wish to work effectively you must get the participation of your subordinates, you must get them to join you in the process of decision-making. The decision that is made must be one that they will carry out with reasonable enthusiasm.

This change in theory is backed up by a change in function. When your primary function is to ensure law and order, or when you are acting as a magistrate, the important thing is that you should get obedience. If you say 'shoot' in a riot, you must be obeyed, and if you say 'This fellow goes to jail for a year', he must go to jail. But if your primary function is to persuade villagers, for instance, to use more fertilizers, to pay half the cost of a school, to take to improved seed, to assist in building a road, then the whole situation changes. You must have agreement: they must know what it is about. You must have participation, or the thing does not operate effectively. In other words, not merely does the theory say you should have all these things, but if you are out for promotion and you understand which side your bread is buttered, you make quite a considerable effort to get these things. I do not want to be romantic about this. Plenty of officials kick around plenty of subordinates today as they used to; but the whole pressure of the job they are doing is pushing them to change the way they act towards their subordinates. Exactly the same process is happening in the Indian administration as is, for instance, happening in business in this country. If you wish to operate effectively you must treat your subordinates much more as equals than you used to have to do.

The process of development tends to give an inbuilt push towards equality in two quite different ways. One is that development tends to be accompanied by inflation and very few Chancellors of the Exchequer change the tax rates because there has been inflation. What they say is 'Thank God we got an increase in taxation without having to say so'. The result is that countries like India, Pakistan and Ceylon that already have, except at quite limited ranges of income, just about the highest tax rates in the world, have their tax rates get higher each year, so that on anybody that is in any sense rich, they are now — provided that they pay — absolutely crushing and they get more crushing with time. The other is that as you develop you create a great middle class; and because you are creating this middle class you fill in the great interstices of society. When you have one great landlord or one collector of a district and a lot of peasants, the big man treats the little man in what it is fashionable to call a feudal way; in other words he treats him as a chap who does as he is told, is kicked about and in the extreme case can reasonably be asked to produce his daughter for the night. Now as soon as you get all sorts of gradations the gap becomes less visible. People begin to be more careful about how they behave. Instead of there being a small class of the big and a large class of the small, so that any of the big recognize any of the small and kick them around when they feel like it, you have more people in the middle to whom it may be dangerous to behave like this; and once you have learnt to behave in a reasonable way to all the people in the middle it tends to spill over to your behaviour to the people lower down, so that you get a great improvement in the level of behaviour.

At the same time, in all these countries, the top has been knocked off. They have got rid of the Indian princes and of the landlords, not only the big landlords, but also to a very large extent the little landlords — the man in the village who owned thirty acres and let it out to ten people all of whom became his clients. He has not necessarily lost all the land: in some cases he has simply resumed it and cultivated it himself. But the power relation when you and the family cultivate is quite different from the power relation when you have ten tenants any of whom you can evict with three months' notice. This has happened even in West Pakistan, where the landlords are still very considerable persons but are no longer the great chiefs that the Gurmanis and the rest used to be in the old days; and in East Bengal where the *Zamindar* class was largely Hindu, it has simply gone altogether.

Finally, and this is very important in the whole process, there is a very rapidly expanding educational system. There are now I think in India about 60 per cent of those between six and eleven going to school. This affects the relation between the sexes. A great deal of the advantage of the men over the women in Asia has been that the men were better educated; and as you get girls going to college, secondary school and so on, this relationship is changing. It also affects the position of those at the bottom. Of this we are only just seeing the beginning, but there is an immense change coming. Indeed, this is really one of the major reasons why I do not think the drive to equality will slow down. The biggest change that education makes is when the illiterate become literate. The gap between the illiterate and the literate is much bigger than between the literate and the university professor. Once you are literate, everything else is open to you. When you are illiterate you are totally dependent on other people. You cannot read your land revenue receipt: you do not know what you sign for the moneylender: you cannot read a leaflet about a new fertilizer: all change slows down. You are going to have in Asia, in say fifteen years' time, societies where everybody over the age of thirty, perhaps, can read and write. This means that new ideas will penetrate much more quickly. Their demand for equality will therefore increase very rapidly. It also, of course, means that people will be economically much more efficient. The small peasant who can read and write understands the use of fertilizers, improved seed, contour binding and all the rest of it much more quickly than the man who cannot read and write. His willingness to accept change progresses not merely because he is more able to learn about change but because he loses a certain fear. The illiterate clings to the old ways because he knows them and he has a deep suspicion that the rest of the world only wants to cheat him. Ignorance always leads to suspicion. If you clear the ignorance you also clear some of the suspicion, because the man becomes better able to judge for himself which changes are reasonable and which are not.

The old societies were statically, hierarchically organized. If you have an unchanging society, if you have a hierarchy, it is best to base it on an unchanging way: you are born into a caste, you are born into a chiefly family, you are born into an aristocratic family, and so on. The hierarchy was something that did not change very much and certainly not quickly, except perhaps for a few individuals. Now it is quite true that in the modern world you still create hierarchies. The engineer is better off than the fitter, the fitter is better off than the unskilled labourer; these are new categories of inequality that development creates. But the new hierarchies of Asia are immensely more unstable than the old were. This of course is something we see in Europe. So much of these new hierarchies depends upon education. The man who gets a doctorate is ahead of the man who gets a B.A., who is ahead of the man who gets an Intermediate, who is ahead of the man who gets Matriculation, who is ahead of the man who only finished primary school. In any society where the way of advance is through your profession this must obviously be so; but because it is so, it is immensely unstable. It is unstable even within a man's own lifetime. You get half-way up your professional ladder and then you find that the young men coming along behind you are better educated and they go over you. This happens in British business today quite often. Your expectations therefore are uncertain; and although your children start with an obvious advantage — they have a more educated home, the money to go to better schools and so on — the fact remains that they may fail their matriculation, they may fail their B.A., they may fail whatever it is. If they do fail in these more backward societies than ours with fewer general job opportunities, down they go and up comes the other fellow; so that such inequality as you may attain is an inequality that is much harder to keep for your children than the inequality of a tribal chief with a large landholding which goes on and on.

With the expansion of the educational system goes a constant increase in the number of scholarships. The number provided in India, for example, for tribals and untouchables, now quite often goes beyond the capacity of the tribals and untouchables to fill the vacancies, to provide people with enough education to reach the minimum level. Societies in which you now have thousands of people who were traditionally fixed at the bottom of society going up through the universities are obviously societies where social relations are in a state of revolution.

Leadership is passing into the hands of the modern educated. You no longer get as your great leaders traditional landowners, the people who used for instance to lead Muslim society; you no longer get the traditionally educated, the Sanskrit scholar; you get the lower middle class led, quite often, or at any rate inspired, by the upper middle class, simply because these are the only people capable of doing for the society what it wants done. If you want an efficient army, then you must have properly trained officers. If you want an efficient civil service, and they would all like efficient civil services, then you must have properly trained administrators, and if you want to have politicians capable of carrying out a development plan they must be competent. The leadership of India in the area is due to the fact that she has a large number of competent politicians, men like the late Vallabhbhai Patel, men like S. K. Patel who is a party boss of no small quality, men like Morarji Desai, Chavan, B. C. Roy, names that you do not necessarily even hear in the West. Without them Nehru would be nothing though Nehru himself, of course, is a politician of the highest competence with the highest responsiveness to public opinion and the highest capacity for party management. I think probably compared with those abilities the high ideals that so often impress people in London or Washington are relatively unimportant. It is nice that he should have them, but that is not what has kept him Prime Minister for fifteen years. If you are to have this sort of political competence in the modern world, if you are to have men who can be in charge of great departments, who can at the very least, if not work out, approach sensibly five-year plans, who can use an army to go into Goa, who can enforce the social reforms that they put through — not merely pass tenancy legislation but actually see that it happens — then they have to be trained in the modern way, they have to come from the same sort of class, though not necessarily from the same section of it, and they have to have the same sort of education,

2B

though not always to quite the same extent, as the engineers and the doctors and the administrators and the soldiers. This means that the traditional upper class either loses its leadership or only keeps its leadership by changing its own nature and accepting as equals a large number of people whom twenty years ago they would not have dreamt of accepting as equals. When I had amongst my managers the son of one of India's oldest Rajput families, he was doing something his father would never have dreamt of doing and, in the doing of it, he had to accept as equals promoted salesmen, sons of clerks, all sorts of people whom his father would never have dreamt of talking to, let alone working with, on terms of equality. In other words, when these people change so as to keep their governing role, they change class; they do not only change their type of education. They have to accept a much wider range of people as equals, they have to govern in a quite different way.

The leaders, in turn, are dependent on another lot of people. This is true in India and in Ceylon; if you get an effectively functioning political system it will be true in the other countries, though I imagine it is only very partially true in those countries so far. You become dependent on the people who make village opinion, and these are a mixed class. They may be the dominant caste, they may be the educated of the village, they may be the local professional men like the ayurvedic physician or even some junior official. Whoever they are, they are very important and they are people who are beginning to demand for people like themselves, for the first time, positions on a national instead of a local scale. They do not merely want to be people in their village, which was previously the height of their ambition. They want to be the makers of MPs. Because they want to be the makers of MPs and because they are dealing with a universal suffrage society, they themselves have in turn to behave more equally. Nowadays, the local leaders have to say to themselves, 'These people are 50 per cent of the population. If we want to win the *panchayat* elections, if we want to get our man in as MLA, we've got to see that these people are on our side'; and this revolutionizes the way they behave to the other people in the village. The village is — much more than the town — a place of power relations, where what matters is the power relation of me to you and my group to your group, because it is much more a place where what matters is status and respect, because you cannot get away from each other. In the town if you think you are not being given enough respect in place 'A' you move to place 'B' and pretend to be somebody else. You cannot do this in the village. Let me give a quite simple example. The original reason why the British Government in India introduced nominated seats for the great landholders was that the great landholders said 'We cannot be expected to canvass our tenants' and in the 1880's this was accepted as a perfectly valid reason. Now they have to canvass their tenants, or rather, since tenancy has largely been abolished, they have to canvass the people lower down in the village. If you want to be on the *panchayat*, if you want to become the MLA, you have to canvass; and if you do not canvass, the consequence is that the control of political power passes to a caste layer or a class layer or an economic layer lower down. The immediate result of that, of course, is that they use the power that they get to improve their own position. Then, as they make their bargains with the people still lower down, with the untouchable and so on, what do they have to do? They have to see that he has a seat on the *panchayat*; they have to see that he gets his scholarships. Now you cannot give people seats on *panchayats* without consequences. At first it may be that not much happens; the unfortunate *harijan* member of the *panchayat* continues to stand outside the door. But this does not last. He comes in the door, he begins to take part in making decisions. This makes much more difficult the old village way of treating him, and if on top of that you get a *harijan* in a government post reserved for *harijans* coming to the village as revenue accountant, or you get a local *harijan* going off from the village on a special scholarship, all your relations change, all your assumptions that 'A' must necessarily be above 'B' are challenged.

There is also one binding force that one needs to mention, one civil religion, and that is the desire for economic development. This is partly a matter of desire for modernity, partly, I think, of shame that so many of your fellow countrymen should be so poor, a feeling that something must be done to stop this terrible poverty around you, and partly it is just a challenge that people wish to meet. I do not believe that Asian politics work all that differently from our own. The reasons and the ways in which they go for equality are not that much different from ours, and I think it is the same with economic growth.

O. D. Corpuz

It seems that there is tension between the forces at work in the two sectors of a transitional society, between the forces of traditionalism that support the essentially indigenous and non-modernized sector, and the forces of dynamic change that give shape to the modernizing sector of the society. The process of modernization gives rise to new social values, which soon establish themselves beside the traditional values. Here you have a crucial feature of the transitional society: two value-systems existing side by side, because, for as long as the transition is not completed, the new values are not completely adopted, and the old are not completely abandoned. These two sets of values appear to the people as alternatives, and often are competitive with each other. And since values serve as social norms or standards for deciding whether actions and decisions are right or wrong, the existence of alternative value-systems often makes it possible to justify almost any behaviour in terms of one or the other set of values. In the Philippines, the multi-norm character of the value system is responsible for a great deal of the recent corruption in politics and in the civil service, because the persons involved could always justify their conduct by invoking socially acceptable kinship or local values as against national values. From an overall viewpoint, the politics of transitional societies often seem to be unpredictable or analytically difficult because of this incomplete transition or unresolved tension.

INDEX

PRINTED IN GREAT BRITAIN
BY ROBERT MACLEHOSE AND CO. LTD
THE UNIVERSITY PRESS, GLASGOW

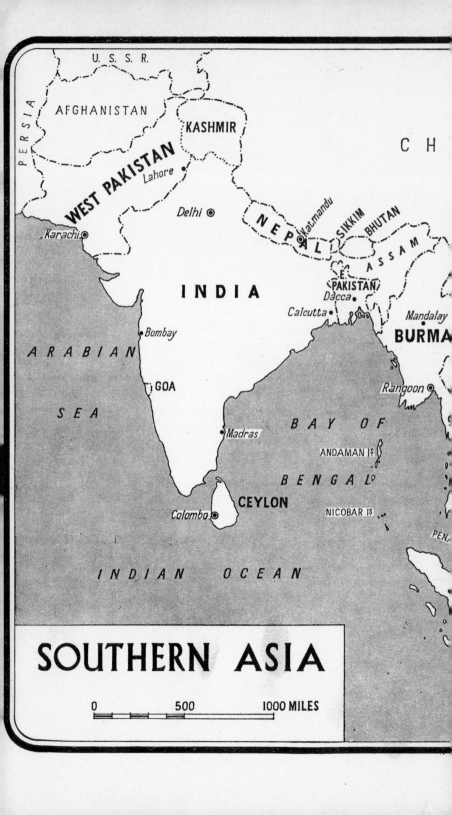

SOUTHERN ASIA

U.S.S.R.

PERSIA

AFGHANISTAN

KASHMIR

WEST PAKISTAN

Lahore

Karachi

Delhi

NEPAL

Katmandu

SIKKIM

BHUTAN

ASSAM

CH

INDIA

E. PAKISTAN

Dacca

Calcutta

Mandalay

BURMA

Bombay

ARABIAN

SEA

GOA

Madras

BAY OF

Rangoon

ANDAMAN IS

BENGAL

CEYLON

NICOBAR IS

Colombo

PEN

INDIAN OCEAN

0   500   1000 MILES